STARTING A
BUSINESS IN
IRELAND

A Comprehensive Guide and Directory

5th edition

Brian O'Kane

www.oaktreepress.com

OAK TREE PRESS
19 Rutland Street, Cork, Ireland
www.oaktreepress.com
www.startingabusinessinireland.com

© 2004 Brian O'Kane
Cover and Text illustrations © Chris Reid

A catalogue record of this book is
available from the British Library.

ISBN 1-86076-267-0

First edition published 1993; Second edition 1995;
Third edition 1998; Fourth edition 2001.

Printed in Ireland by Colour Books.

CONTENTS

PREFACE

For the first time in 10 years, in this the fifth edition of *Starting a Business in Ireland,* I am writing the Preface in a period of relative stability in the enterprise support scene in Ireland.

Previous editions of the book coincided with the introduction of the **City/County Enterprise Boards**[1] (first edition, 1993), the formation of Forbairt (second edition, 1995), later to become **Enterprise Ireland** (third edition, 1997), and most recently with the shift towards "soft supports" in lieu of cash grants as the focus of State support for start-ups and small businesses (fourth edition, 2001).

But the two years since the last edition have not been quiet – far from it. However, the activity took place mainly north of the Border, where an entire new support landscape – the centrepieces of which are **Invest Northern Ireland** and **Enterprise Northern Ireland** – has developed. One of the key features of this is the new emphasis on cross-border activity, led by **InterTradeIreland**.

Much has changed in the past 10 years, most of all public attitude towards enterprise, small business and start-ups. Where previously the "proper job", one with a pension after a lifetime of service, was the be-all-and-end-all, there's a genuine interest across Irish society in entrepreneurship. And our neighbours in Europe, and further afield, appear entranced by

---

[1] The bold text indicates that more information on the organisation and its activities in support of start-ups is available in the *Directory of Sources of Assistance* at the back of this book.

what we in Ireland have achieved in such a short time and are eager for information on how to replicate our success.

With all due modesty, *Starting a Business in Ireland* can lay claim to credit for some of Ireland's entrepreneurial success and for the more positive view in Irish society towards enterprise. It struck a chord with the Irish public right from its launch in 1993. It sells consistently well, month in month out, mainly by word-of-mouth and recommendation – the most effective form of marketing! And its two-year-old companion website, **www.startingabusinessinireland.com**, attracts annual traffic of about 100,000 unique visitors. Of course, I cannot (and would not) claim all the credit – the many people whose job (in some cases, their mission) it is to assist start-ups and small businesses deserve recognition, too.

But the real heroes in Irish enterprise are Irish entrepreneurs – the men and women who have taken the plunge and built successful businesses where none existed before. As I speak on courses, at conferences, or at exhibitions, I am always dumbstruck by the sheer inventiveness, innovation and enthusiasm of people whom I meet at these events, who have shared their dreams and ambitions with me (good luck to you all), and who have done me the honour of asking for my advice and opinion. To them belongs the lion's share of the credit.

OAK TREE PRESS

In the past two years, Oak Tree Press too has changed – refocusing its activities on micro and small businesses, internationally. Earlier this year, Virgin Books published my *Starting a Business in Britain*, based closely on this book's successful formula. Other titles are in use by enterprise support organisations in the UK and across Europe and we are represented on European networks and working groups – from setting standards for business support services to enterprise education.

Again, the clear message we consistently receive is that Ireland is well-regarded for its approach to, and support, of small business.

THE BOOK

Starting a business in Ireland is frustrating, time-consuming and difficult – I know, because I have done it – but it can also be highly satisfying and enjoyable.

The first edition of this book was born out of the frustration of dealing with the bureaucracy and information dead-ends that surrounded starting a business at that time – and, sadly, still do to some extent today. This fifth edition of *Starting a Business in Ireland* continues the formula of earlier editions by:

- Taking you step-by-step through the stages in going into business for yourself
- Helping you to identify, from the many organisations that provide assistance to entrepreneurs, those that are likely to be appropriate to your needs.

The chapters are arranged to take you through the stages:

- Deciding whether you have what it takes
- Researching your idea
- Writing a business plan
- Raising money to set up your business
- Getting help from State and other agencies
- Getting your business up and running.

Chapter 9, Implementation outlines some of the steps you need to complete in order to get your new business up and running. **Chapter 10, Moving to Ireland to Start a Business**, provides information especially applicable to the increasing number of people who are returning to Ireland, or relocating here, to start a business.

The **Directory of Sources of Assistance** provides information (including contact details) for many organisations that may be of use to you as you go through the stages of starting your own business. Expanded, and now with nearly 700 separate entries for organisations North and South, this Directory is beyond doubt the most comprehensive directory of support available to start-ups and small businesses available in Ireland today. It is kept up-to-date on **www.startingabusinessinireland.com**.

THANK YOU

A book such as this can never be the work of one person alone.

My idea lay fallow for several years, until David Givens (Oak Tree Press' first general manager, now managing director of his own business, The Liffey Press) pushed me to complete what I had begun – and so the first edition of *Starting a Business in Ireland* was written. David's encouragement is appreciated more than he realises.

Ron Immink, who researched and co-wrote the *Starting Your Own Business* workbook with me in 1997 for the **Department of Enterprise, Trade & Employment** (updated in 2002), and more recently, *TENBizPlan*, the *Steps to Entrepreneurship* series and the *Growing Your Own Business* workbook, deserves special thanks for his constant encouragement and unstoppable flow of ideas.

Despite my reluctance to delegate, someone always gets stuck with the job of checking the many entries in the Directory to ensure that they are all correct. This time, my daughter, Niamh, rose to the challenge.

I am also grateful to the staff of the many organisations listed in this book for their helpfulness, patience and support in preparing and checking this and previous editions and in recommending the book to so many people. I'd also like to thank the organisations that have advertised in this edition – please support them.

I am pleased and somewhat surprised to find *Starting a Business in Ireland* now in its fifth edition and past its 10th birthday! The reaction to its publication has far exceeded all my expectations.

I have enjoyed writing and updating this book. I hope it is of help to you, the reader, as you take your first steps on your journey. May the road always rise to meet you!

Brian O'Kane
Cork
September 2003

DEDICATION

This book is dedicated especially to my wife, Rita, without whose constant support and encouragement none of this would have been possible, and to my children, Niamh, Conall, Kevin and Deirdre.

1: Getting Started

For some people, starting their own business is as obvious as the nose on their face. For others, it is a risk not to be contemplated.

For you, it is an idea in the back of your mind, one you cannot get rid of. You may already know what kind of business you want to be in. What you want from this book are a few short cuts to help you get there faster and with fewer problems.

On the other hand, you may simply be toying with the idea of starting a business of some kind, unsure of which direction to take. You are hoping that this book will present you with a ready-formed solution. In fact, you must provide your own solution but this book can help by providing a structure for your thinking.

The Stages in a Start-up

The stages involved in starting a business include:

- Deciding whether you have the right temperament to start (and persevere with) your own business – a critical first step, often overlooked in the rush to get started

- Finding an idea – it's worth taking time on this stage to explore all the options; sometimes your first idea is not always the best

- Doing the market research – this involves finding out about your customers, your competition, how you will make your product or deliver your service, what price to charge, where your business will be located, how to market your product or service, what staff you require and with what skills, and so on
- Writing a business plan – this draws together all the work you have done in the research stage and presents it in a form that is readily understandable
- Finding the necessary money – since it's likely you won't have enough of your own capital to start, you'll have to raise money elsewhere
- Identifying and accessing sources of assistance – as the Directory shows, there are hundreds of organisations dedicated to helping small businesses get started
- Implementing your plan – this is where you put your plan into action.

Sometimes, in practice, these stages will not follow in the order set out above; in other cases, you will have to double back, perhaps even several times, to adjust the results of a stage because of new information you find out later.

For instance, your idea might be to sell to the local community a product that you make yourself. After doing your market research, you write your business plan and look for money on this basis but, as you proceed, you find that there is a national demand for the product. To supply it, you need to plan on a larger scale and need more money – so you revise your plans and finances accordingly.

Most of these stages in starting a business will be covered in this book. Some are dealt with in greater detail in other books published by **Oak Tree Press** and available from our website at **www.oaktreepress.com**. Other stages, like finding an idea, lie with you alone.

STAGES IN STARTING A BUSINESS

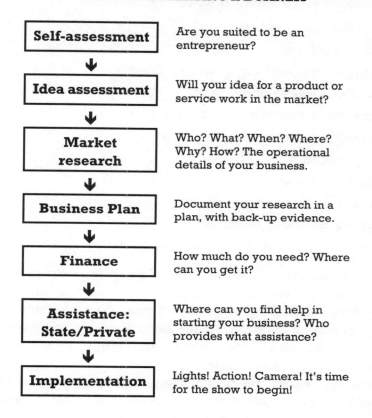

Self-assessment	Are you suited to be an entrepreneur?
Idea assessment	Will your idea for a product or service work in the market?
Market research	Who? What? When? Where? Why? How? The operational details of your business.
Business Plan	Document your research in a plan, with back-up evidence.
Finance	How much do you need? Where can you get it?
Assistance: State/Private	Where can you find help in starting your business? Who provides what assistance?
Implementation	Lights! Action! Camera! It's time for the show to begin!

ARE YOU SUITED TO LIFE AS AN ENTREPRENEUR?

Sadly, there is no fail-safe method of becoming a successful entrepreneur. Research, quoted in *You Can Do It* by Joyce O'Connor and Helen Ruddle (Gill & Macmillan, 1989 – currently out of print), shows that successful entrepreneurs have:

- Strong needs for control and independence
- Drive and energy
- Self-confidence
- A point of view of money as a measure of performance

- A tolerance of ambiguity and uncertainty
- A sense of social responsibility

and that they are good at:

- Problem-solving
- Setting (and achieving) goals and targets
- Calculated risk-taking
- Committing themselves for the long term
- Dealing with failure
- Using feedback
- Taking the initiative
- Seeking personal responsibility
- Tapping and using resources
- Competing against self-imposed standards.

How do *you* measure on these criteria? Be honest with yourself.

Very few entrepreneurs can lay claim to all of these characteristics. Making the most of your best characteristics and using ingenuity (including the skills of others) to bridge the gaps is perhaps the most frequently encountered entrepreneurial characteristic of all!

However, despite the great variety of people who end up as business-owners, probably the most important personal characteristic for an entrepreneur is determination.

It's easy to start a business; it's more difficult to keep it going. When you are faced with long hours, with working through nights and weekends, with extended periods away from your family, and with the horrors of financial worries, the thought of a secure permanent pensionable job is tempting. Determination is what will see you through these lows until you break through to success!

You should also consider your general state of health. Both the physical and mental stresses of running your own business can be very great. If you are driven to a state of collapse by the experience, you may leave your spouse and family much more exposed financially than would be the case if you were in a secure job with benefits attached.

YOUR SUITABILITY AS AN ENTREPRENEUR

Where are you on each of the following, on a score from 1 (weak) to 10 (strong)?

	1	2	3	4	5	6	7	8	9	10
Need for control/independence										
Drive and energy										
Self-confidence										
Money to measure performance										
Tolerate ambiguity/uncertainty										
Sense of social responsibility										
Problem-solving										
Setting (and achieving) goals										
Calculated risk-taking										
Committing for the long term										
Dealing with failure										
Using feedback										
Taking the initiative										
Seeking personal responsibility										
Tapping and using resources										
Self-imposed standards										

There are no correct answers to the exercise above but, obviously, the higher your scores the more likely you are to be suited to being an entrepreneur.

You should be aware of the part your spouse and family will play in achieving your ambition of becoming an entrepreneur. Are they as committed as you are? Are they as willing to accept the lows as the highs? Without their support, you will find it difficult to start and develop your business. If they are actively pulling against you, quit now! Read *"My Family Doesn't Understand Me!"* (Yanky Fachler, Oak Tree Press) for an insight into the part that family can play in the success of your business and the strategies you need to use to make sure that they are on board.

Part of the experience of running your own business is learning to apply the appropriate personal resource at the right time. For example, deciding to become an exporter at a time when your resources – foreign language skills, contacts, finances – are not adequate is to misuse an opportunity that might lead to success in other circumstances. A touch of realism instead would have revealed the impracticality of your plan.

So the first thing you should do when thinking about starting a business is to conduct a rigorous self-assessment:

- What skills and experience do you have?
- What training do you need?
- What characteristics do you have that will help (or hinder) you?
- Why do you want to start a business?

Write down the answers – it's not as easy to fudge uncomfortable answers in writing.

Then write your own application for the position of managing director and general factotum of your proposed business. Give your application to a friend not noted for tact and wait for the laughs. You need to be able to see yourself as others see you.

Are your keyboard and literary skills really up to sending out customer letters and writing marketing blurbs? Perhaps you excel in production and technical innovation? Maybe you need to acquire other skills? If so, can you get by with a little training for yourself or should you buy in these skills on a freelance basis as and when required?

Will you need a management team, or are there family members who are sufficiently committed to help (and capable of doing so)? What will hiring all these people do to your costs?

Salaries usually represent a high percentage of costs in a small business. You need to be realistic about how many people you need, and how many you can afford – and what you do about the difference.

In terms of your business skills, you should consider, in addition to management experience, actual contacts and sales leads, as these are the concrete beginnings of your trading. If you plan to supply other retailers or manufacturers, you will be hoping to establish several guaranteed sales contracts before you finally start trading. If you are leaving employment to set up this kind of business, check that your employment contract allows you to canvass business on your own account (and time) while still an employee.

You should read this chapter again in a year's time. Why? Because you will only begin to discover the extent of your personal resources as you go along. Starting your own business will not only lead you to find hidden resources within yourself, but will build up existing strengths. It may also, of course, identify unsuspected weaknesses, but recognising them is the first step towards correcting them.

A useful guide in the early stage of deciding whether you have what it takes is Yanky Fachler's classic, *Fire in the Belly: An Exploration of the Entrepreneurial Spirit* (Oak Tree Press, 2001).

START YOUR OWN BUSINESS COURSES

This book is designed to help you through the early stages of starting a business. Together with other books published by Oak Tree Press, it gives you an edge.

For further guidance, or for the comfort of meeting like-minded people who are about to embark on the same adventure as yourself, consider a Start Your Own Business course. These courses can be useful because they draw together all the aspects of running a business – it is often easy to ignore those tasks that bore you or for which you feel ill-equipped.

Another advantage of attending a course is that you get to know advisers who may be useful to contact later with queries. Many of the courses run by State or State-related organisations are particularly useful for steering participants towards further support.

Organisations that offer start-up training to would-be entrepreneurs are identified in the Directory and include:

- **Action Clondalkin Enterprise**
- **Ardee Business Park**
- **Area Partnership Companies** (some, not all)
- **Ballyhoo Entrepreneurial Consulting**
- **Base Centre**
- **Belfast First Stop Business Shop Ltd**
- **Business Innovation Centres** (some, not all)
- **Céim Enterprise Development Programme**
- **Centre for Entrepreneurial Studies**
- **City / County Enterprise Boards**
- **City of Dublin Vocational Education Committee**
- **City of Dublin YMCA**
- **Coca-Cola National Enterprise Awards**
- **Community Groups** (some, not all)
- **Dun Laoire Institute of Art, Design and Technology**
- **Enter Enterprise**
- **Enterprise Agencies / Centres in Northern Ireland** (some not all)
- **Enterprise Northern Ireland**
- **Enterprise Programmes**
- **FÁS**
- **First Point Business Development Consultancy Ltd**
- **Inner City Enterprise**
- **InnovationWorks**
- **Institutes of Technology** (most)
- **Invent**
- **LEADER+ groups** (some, not all)
- **Liffey Trust**
- **Loughry Campus, College of Agriculture, Food & Rural Enterprise, Dept. of Agriculture & Rural Development**

- **Michael Smurfit Graduate School of Business Hatchery**
- **Moran & Associates**
- **Northern Ireland Business Start Programme**
- **Northern Ireland Centre for Entrepreneurship**
- **Oak Tree Press**
- **Optimum Results ltd**
- **Partas**
- **PDC**
- **Regional Development Centre**
- **Shannon Development**
- **Údarás na Gaeltachta**
- **Universities** (some as part of degree programmes, some separately)
- **University of Limerick Alumni Association Entrepreneurship Programme.**

How Do You Choose the Right Course?

Before you book a place on a course, meet the organisers. Ask about the backgrounds of the presenters. Those who run their own business or who, like many accountants and other professionals, make their living from advising entrepreneurs are the best bet.

Ask about the success rate of the course in establishing new businesses. Ask about the success rate of those businesses after two or three years. Remember that the average failure rate of new businesses is very high. Although a success rate of between 15 and 30 per cent may seem low, it is not exceptional – and need not apply to you, if you plan your start-up carefully.

Make an effort to find people who have completed any courses you are seriously considering, and talk to them. They are in the best position to know whether what they learnt on the course actually was of use in practice. Their answers will tell you whether you should take a place on the course.

If You Can't Attend a Course

If you cannot participate in a Start Your Own Business course, try to attend some of the seminars on specific aspects of enterprise development and small business management presented from time to time by the banks and other organisations. These are aimed at reducing the fall-out rate of business start-ups and are usually open to the public (sometimes for a fee). Watch the newspapers for details.

Otherwise, read as widely as you can in the area of enterprise and business start-ups. There are plenty of good books and newspapers and magazines (for example, **Business Plus**, **Initiative**, **Irish Entrepreneur** and **Running Your Business**) regularly publish special features that give useful advice.

INCUBATORS

Perhaps, instead of merely a training programme, what you need is a push-start. Here an "incubator" can help.

An incubator is a programme/facility, usually focused on technology businesses, that encourages the faster development of a new business by providing a range of supports from workspace to finance to administrative assistance (and training, where necessary) in order to free up the entrepreneur to concentrate on the business alone. Note the overlap of organisations between this category and "Start-up Training".

Because of their success in reducing the failure rate of start-ups, dozens of these have sprung all over the country – **Enterprise Ireland** is active in funding the development of incubators in all the **Institutes of Technology**, for example.

Sometimes, the term is used loosely to cover mere provision of workspace – if you're offered "incubation workspace", check what is included.

Incubators include:

- **Area Partnership Companies** (some, not all)
- **Bolton Trust / Docklands Innovation Park**
- **Brookfield Business Centre Ltd**

- **Business Innovation Centres**
- **Cavan Innovation & Technology Centre**
- **Céim Enterprise Development Programme**
- **City / County Enterprise Boards** (some, not all)
- **Community Enterprise Development Society Ltd**
- **Community Groups** (some, not all)
- **Crosbie Business Centre**
- **Dun Laoire Enterprise Centre**
- **Dun Laoire Institute of Art, Design and Technology**
- **Enterprise Agencies / Centres in Northern Ireland** (most)
- **Enterprise Programmes**
- **Flax Trust**
- **Food Innovation Centre**
- **Galway Technology Centre**
- **Gorann Ltd**
- **Growcorp Group Ltd**
- **Guinness Enterprise Centre**
- **HotOrigin**
- **InnovationWorks**
- **Institutes of Technology** (most)
- **Invent**
- **IRD Duhallow**
- **IRD Kiltimagh**
- **Kerry Technology Park**
- **Kilkenny Industrial Development Company**
- **Killarney Technology Innovation Ltd**
- **Letterkenny Business Development Centre**
- **Liffey Trust**
- **Limerick Enterprise Development Partnership**
- **Loughry Campus, College of Agriculture, Food & Rural Enterprise, Dept. of Agriculture & Rural Development**
- **Loughry College Food Business Innovation Centre**

- **Michael Smurfit Graduate School of Business Hatchery**
- **National Software Centre**
- **National Technology Park Limerick**
- **Northern Ireland Science Park**
- **NovaUCD**
- **Partas**
- **PDC**
- **Prince's Trust Northern Ireland**
- **Regional Development Centre**
- **Richmond Business Campus**
- **Shannon Development / Shannon Development Knowledge Network**
- **SPADE Enterprise Centre**
- **Synergy eBusiness Incubator**
- **TCD Enterprise Centre**
- **Technology West**
- **Údarás na Gaeltachta**
- **Universities** (most)
- **University of Limerick Alumni Association Entrepreneurship Programme**
- **UUSRP**
- **UUTech**
- **Wexford Enterprise Centre.**

START EARLY!

You're never too young to start thinking about enterprise and running your own business. Even if you're still in school or at college, there are programmes designed to attract you towards the notion of self-employment and to help you begin to gain the necessary skills. They include:

- **Choose Enterprise.com**
- **Junior Achievement / Young Enterprise Ireland**

- **Shell LiveWire**
- Student Enterprise Awards (**Enterprise Ireland**)
- **Young Enterprise Northern Ireland**
- **Young Entrepreneurs Scheme.**

START-UP ALTERNATIVES

Of course, it's not always necessary to start a business from scratch. Brokers exist who will help you to identify and buy a suitable business, whose owner lacks the capital or enthusiasm to develop it further. Such brokers include:

- **Boylan & Dodd Corporate Services Ltd**
- **Company Broking Consultants**
- **Franchise Direct.com**
- **Irish Business Sales**
- **IrishBusinessesforSale.com.**

If you do go down this route, make sure that you take professional advice before making any financial or legal commitment. And continue to read the rest of this book, since you will still need to plan for the development of your business.

2: RESEARCHING YOUR IDEA

After considering your own capacity to run a business, you need to ask yourself whether a market exists for your product or service. The market may be incredibly tough to break into but, as long as it exists, you can fight for your share of it. If there is no market at all for your product, it is clearly a non-starter.

You are not yet attempting to measure the size or location of the market, nor to distinguish its characteristics. What you want are the answers to the following questions:

- Do others already offer the same product or service as I intend to offer?

- Is my product/service an improvement on what already exists?

- What evidence is there that customers want to buy my improvement?

If your product/service is new to the market, you need to ask:

- What evidence is there that the market wants to buy this product/service?

- What evidence is there that the market is aware of its need for my product/service?

You may be able to find answers to these questions quite easily. For example, the market for ready-mixed concrete is quite visible but is dominated by a few big companies. So the question here quickly changes from whether a market exists to whether it is feasible to enter that market when there are already strong competitors in place.

On the other hand, the inventor of a solar-powered bicycle might have more difficulty assessing the existence of a market. All the Irish cyclists he talks to may tell him that they only cycle for the exercise value, since they cannot depend on sufficient sun to make any difference to the energy they must expend in cycling. They might have no interest in any source of power beyond their own muscles. Yet, in environmentally conscious (and sunnier) countries that encourage the use of a bicycle and/or solar power, the product could be greeted with cries of delight and massive demand. However, if the inventor does not know where to look, he or she may never get their business off the ground.

This quick feasibility review will tell you whether it's worth progressing to more formal market research, or whether you should go back to the drawing board to think of a new product or service.

MARKET RESEARCH

Once you have provided yourself with proof – not just a gut feeling – of the existence of the market (see below, *Sources of Information*), you can move on to more detailed research. Analysing the nature of the market, competition and customer base will tell you whether your idea is feasible. The information you compile will allow you to develop your business plan in more detail.

Although a professional market research company will conduct research for you, at a price, you can often do your own research without too much difficulty, time or cost.

In collecting information during this research stage, remember that, as well as satisfying yourself, you may have to prove to outside investors that your figures and findings are valid. For this reason, independent proof is worth collecting wherever you can find it. Sources include:

- Talking to potential customers and even competitors
- Questionnaires and surveys
- Official government statistics or statistics compiled by trade associations and consumer bodies.

You need to sift carefully through the information you collect:

- To understand the business you are in
- To work out the size and location of the market for your product/service
- To build up a profile of your customers and their needs
- To understand how competition operates in your market
- To establish a reasonable price for your product/service – one at which your customers will buy
- To forecast sales – both volume and value
- To establish the cost of making your product or delivering your service – and how it will be done – the profit margins you can expect
- To establish the investment needed to start your business
- To decide what form your business must take.

What Is Your Business?

This may seem an obvious question, one not worth asking, but setting it down in writing may provide a useful reference exercise.

For example, Waterford Crystal is not in the market of providing everyday glassware. Despite the fact that it produces glasses, bowls and vases, it does not compete with the producer of the everyday glass tumbler that you find in the supermarket or department store. Rather, it is in the international market for luxury goods and special occasion gifts. It will look to growth trends in these luxury markets, mainly overseas, rather than to growth in glassware sales generally.

MARKET RESEARCH

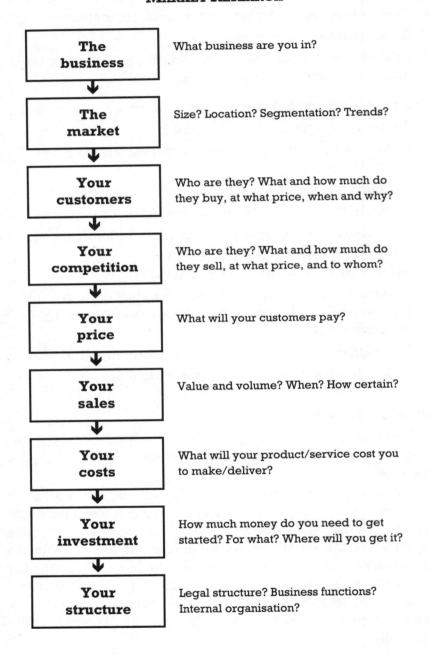

The business	What business are you in?
The market	Size? Location? Segmentation? Trends?
Your customers	Who are they? What and how much do they buy, at what price, when and why?
Your competition	Who are they? What and how much do they sell, at what price, and to whom?
Your price	What will your customers pay?
Your sales	Value and volume? When? How certain?
Your costs	What will your product/service cost you to make/deliver?
Your investment	How much money do you need to get started? For what? Where will you get it?
Your structure	Legal structure? Business functions? Internal organisation?

In contrast, a contract carpet-cleaning business in Dublin is providing a very specific service in the city, or possibly even only in one area of the city.

Be aware that if you are a manufacturer, you are a manufacturer, not a retailer. You may sell your product to or through a dealer, but you are not a dealer, nor are you selling direct to the public. To try to be more than you are can spell doom for a small business, because your business may not have the resources and you may not have the necessary skills to take on your new ideas.

For example, a manufacturer of trailers in Mayo might wish to sell them to the end-customer himself (perhaps, in order to avoid losing a large share of the retail price to middlemen). But manufacturing and retailing are essentially two separate businesses. People in Cork are unlikely to travel to Mayo to buy a trailer, when there is probably a supplier of a range of comparable trailers already based in their own county. Even if the Mayo manufacturer sets up a shop in Cork, people may still be inclined to visit other retailers who offer a wider range of choice, or have local contacts. More sales will be achieved by sticking firmly to the core activity of manufacturing, and developing a distribution network through dealers around the country.

In time, your business may have the resources to expand its operation and become something else, but, initially, if you try to start two businesses, you will have to generate the cash flow and return for two businesses, which is (at least) twice as difficult as generating them for one.

Where Is Your Market?

Starting out, you are unlikely to be able to tackle the whole market for your product or service. You will instead look for a suitable segment of that market. That might be defined geographically – Cork, the North West counties, even a particular housing estate.

Alternatively, your segment might be defined as a product niche. For example, specialised stop-watches for use in sports, but not all sorts of watches or clocks.

However, even though you may decide only to tackle a small part of a market, you cannot afford to ignore what is happening in the whole market. For example, if you are opening the first small corner shop on a new housing estate, you should foresee that any one of several chains of supermarkets might open a shop nearby and become your main competition. Perhaps you could overcome this by becoming a franchisee of one of the chains yourself.

On the other hand, if your product will be manufactured and sold locally, for instance, in Dublin, but must compete against products from big international suppliers, you have to monitor what is going on in the international field as well as in the national market.

You need to look beyond your immediate market to see what the longer-term trends are:

- Is the size of your market growing or declining?
- Is it characterised by rapid innovation or evolution of products?
- Is it expanding geographically (as might be the case with an innovative product/service)?
- Is the number of competitors expanding or declining?
- Are prices rising or falling?

You need to end up with figures that show the size and growth potential of the total market – but these must be made relevant to your business proposal, in terms of the part of the market (the market segment) that you are targeting.

These concepts will help you to define your market:

- Wholesale or retail?
- One product or a range of products?
- A service?
- The luxury market?
- Necessities?

If your idea is very innovative and no market yet exists for it, it may be difficult to define what your market is likely to be. Obtaining hard information about the size and value of your market may be daunting. However, you must be able to provide this information in your business plan because it is a key element in establishing the existence of a market for your product and the cost structure that your business must attain in order to be competitive.

If you get this information wrong, other assumptions are likely to be invalid and your project may fail, perhaps at considerable loss to yourself. Equally, if bankers and other investors cannot find independent verification for the figures in your proposal, they will certainly have doubts regarding its overall viability, and are likely to refuse to finance you.

Who Are Your Customers?

You must build as accurate a profile of your customers as you can. This depends on the type of business that you plan to start.

For a corner shop, the customers will be diverse in age, gender and requirements: everyone from children wanting sweets for a few pennies to adults wanting newspapers, grocery items and perhaps small gift items. On the other hand, an information technology company producing a single product, say an automated accounting package for bookmakers, has a very narrowly defined customer base.

Some useful questions to ask about your customers are:

- General public or business, or both?
- Public sector or private?
- Where do they live/operate?
- What and how much do they buy, at what price, when and why?
- What age are they?
- What gender?
- Are they spending for a necessity or a luxury; in other words, do they buy out of surplus income?
- Are they rich or poor?

For your product/service, are there criteria that define your customers, such as:

- A particular interest (for example, travel or sport)?
- Need for a particular service (for example, training to use accounting software)?

In terms of business customers, there may be other criteria to consider:

- Size of customer – will you only supply customers taking more than (or less than) a certain volume?
- Quality levels for the product (these may be imposed by certain wholesale purchasers, department/chain stores, etc.)
- Type of packaging preferred.

In considering who your customers are, you may also need to consider how easy it will be to deal with them. Larger organisations will have more decision-makers than small ones, and it may take longer to negotiate contracts and persuade them to take your product – although the resulting orders are likely to be bigger. To deal with the public sector, it is necessary to understand how it is structured, how decisions are made and who makes them.

Will your business deal only with one segment of the market, such as the public sector, or will you be tackling several segments? How much experience do you have in dealing with each segment? Do you have the resources to service more than one segment? Will you deal with them on the same terms? And, if not, how will you prevent sales "leaking" to the segment that gets the most favourable terms?

Who Is Your Competition?

Look hard at your own product/service. How does it differ from competing products/services? Very few businesses are genuinely innovative; most compete with existing businesses.

Why should a customer prefer your product/service?

- Better quality?
- Lower price?
- Higher profile?

What do your sales depend on?

- Price?
- Design?
- Advertising?
- Quality?
- Volume?
- After-sales service?
- Speed of delivery?
- Accessibility?

An important question is whether your product/service's differentiating feature is the one that makes the customer prefer it. Take the example of a Hermès scarf or a Rolls Royce car. It would be pointless to sell cheaper versions of either, since buyers value the image that the high price gives. Exclusive products are characterised by low-volume/high-margin sales. Their success depends on high marketing expenditure and careful selection and monitoring of distribution outlets.

If, on the other hand, your product/service's sale is characterised by high volumes and low margins, such as margarine or flour or fast food, your business needs to be structured very differently, with more emphasis on volume production, warehousing, constancy of supply and a good distribution network.

When looking at your competition, you may need to consider products/services that compete indirectly with yours, as well as those that compete directly. For example, if you produce frozen hamburgers, you compete not only against other frozen hamburger manufacturers, but against a variety of other cheap frozen food products, including fish fingers, vegetable burgers, pies and so on.

You need to find out:

- How many other companies supply products/services similar to yours?
- How will they react to your entry to the market place?
- Are all the companies in the market place the same size?

- Are they very much bigger than you?
- Have you the resources to equal their power in the market?
- Do new entrants normally start small and grow, or will you have to make a major commitment from the start?

Price

The next piece of market information that you should research is the price that the market will pay for your product/service. How much will customers pay? Under what circumstances will they pay more?

You will generally be constrained by the market. You cannot charge more for your product/service than the going price for similar products/services unless it has something special to recommend it. Even then, a large number of customers may still choose the lower-priced option.

Forecasting Sales

If you thought the earlier elements of your market research were hard, forecasting sales makes them look like child's play.

You need to have a good idea of likely sales (with some evidence to underpin your figures) in order to:

- Build your financial projections
- Estimate the production capacity you require
- Arrange for supply of materials
- Hire staff.

Your requirements on each of these will vary depending on the sales volumes and values that you expect.

One way to do this is to start with a clean sheet of paper. Draw columns for each month and deep rows for each product or service (or variant thereof) that you expect to sell. Within each row, list the promotional and other activity that you plan to use to generate sales. (If you haven't planned any yet, it's time to start – products don't just sell on their own, they usually have to be sold).

Then, make some estimates month by month of the sales that will result from this activity. You may find it easier to forecast unit sales first and then to estimate sales value.

For example, if you intend to design and sell St Patrick's Day greetings cards, it's likely that most of your sales will happen in February and March – with perhaps a few early orders in January – but none after that, until the next year. So, in this case, your sales forecast exercise should naturally lead you into new product development – Easter cards, or cards for Mother's Day or Halloween and so on.

It's important to break down sales to the lowest level of product/service that you can manage without overwhelming yourself in detail. For example, if you were designing and selling greeting cards generally, it would be easy to overlook the potential for niche opportunities during the year, unless you specifically identified St Patrick's Day cards or the like.

Where you can, get forward orders or "letters of comfort" from customers. These are better evidence in support of your forecasts than any market research – although your market research is still essential.

Calculating Costs and Profit Margins

As part of your business planning (see **Chapter 4**), you will prepare financial projections for inclusion in your business plan.

However, at this stage, it is a good idea to estimate (even crudely) the minimum size or capacity at which you will make a profit – the break-even point – as well as the maximum operating capacity that you can afford to establish. To do this, you will need to work out what your costs of production will be – you already know the price the market will pay for your product, and how many units you expect to be able to sell.

You also need to identify the current market profit margins – how much your competitors are making. You may be prepared to accept a slimmer margin, but this may reduce your flexibility to deal with unexpected demands. It may also shorten the length of time your business can afford to wait to reach the break-even point. If you look for larger than average profit margins, without either reducing costs or convincing customers that your product is worth paying more for, you will quickly find yourself in difficulty.

Will your entry to the market place reduce profit margins generally? If you increase the total supply of product available, it may have the effect of reducing the price for which it sells. It may even trigger a price war, as existing suppliers try to kill off your business before it gets going by cutting their prices below the price you must get to stay in business.

You will most likely get a part of the market, not the whole. Yet, if you cannot meet the average costs achieved by your direct competitors, you may fail, even though your product/ service may be better than theirs.

The income generated by sales must provide sufficient cash flow to enable your business to cover all costs. If money comes in too slowly, your business can choke to death while demand booms. Cash flow – collecting money from customers as quickly as possible and getting the longest possible credit period from your suppliers – is often more important in the short term for a small business than profit. But, overall, you must make a profit to stay in business.

Estimating Your Initial Investment

At this stage, you should draw up a list of what premises and equipment you absolutely must have (not what it would be nice to have).

You need to answer these questions:

- Will it be possible to keep overheads low by working from your garage or a spare room?
- Do you need retail premises in a good location?
- What about warehouse space?
- Do you need specialised equipment? How big is it?
- Will you have to make a large capital investment in equipment? Can you lease equipment instead? Can you buy it second-hand?

From this information, and your other market research, you will be able to estimate your initial investment – what you need to get started.

Finding the Best Business Structure

Lastly, you need to decide what form your business organisation should take. When starting in business, you have a choice of five main types of business entity through which to conduct your enterprise:

- Sole trader
- Partnership (Ltd partnership in Northern Ireland)
- Unlimited company
- Ltd company
- Co-operative.

Four things will decide which you choose:

- The kind of business you are starting. Some professional firms, for instance, can only be formed as sole traders or partnerships.
- The expectations of those with whom you plan to do business. Many business people expect to deal with limited companies and are wary of other forms of business entities as trading partners.
- Your attitude to risk – in particular, to risking those of your assets that you are not planning to commit to the business. A limited liability company limits the risk of losing your capital if your enterprise is not successful.
- How you wish to organise your taxation affairs. Certain kinds of favourable tax treatment are only available to limited liability companies.

You are taking a risk in starting an enterprise. You are risking your money, time and reputation. You are entitled to protect those of your assets that you do not wish to commit to your enterprise. For this reason, and for your family's sake, you are strongly advised to form a limited liability company. Nonetheless, you should take professional advice for your accountant or solicitor in making your decision. If you do not yet have an accountant or solicitor, read the appropriate sections in **Chapter 9**.

Next, consider how your business will be organised. The main functional areas in any business are:

- Administration
- Production
- Marketing
- Sales
- Distribution.

What should be the balance between these functions within your company? Among the questions you need to ask yourself are:

- How will you get your product to the purchaser?
- Will you need large amounts of warehouse space?
- What are your costs of production?
- What are the overheads involved?

SOURCES OF INFORMATION

There is no shortage of information available to help you in your market research – most entrepreneurs find their main problem is too much information!

Consider all of these sources:

- Yourself
- Professional advisers
- Trade and professional associations
- Libraries
- Telephone directories
- Other people
- State and private sector enterprise support agencies
- Professional researchers
- The Internet.

Yourself

Most people will have started to research their idea long before they come to the formal planning stage. Often, the idea has grown out of a long period of personal interest and the "research" is based on:

- Personal experience
- Talking to friends
- Talking to suppliers.

If you have an idea for a new type of light fitting, it is probably because over the years you have been driven mad by the failings of the many light fittings that you have used. So, immediately, you know what advantage your potential product offers above others in the market.

You may have to find out about the costs of making it, how it is distributed and who the competitors are before you can make an estimate of the size of the market and, most importantly, whether it is financially feasible to be a small manufacturer of light fittings only. You might discover that the machinery required is so expensive that you would have to make and sell a huge number of fittings in order to pay for it.

Many good business ideas provide an answer to a problem with existing products.

Professional Advisers

Bank managers and accountants often have a good idea of how different types of businesses are faring, and what differentiates the successes from those that cannot pay the bills. Also, talking to your bank manager like this is a gentle introduction for him/her to your idea of starting your own business.

Banks and investment businesses often have specialists in a variety of industry sectors, who can be useful sources of market information and statistics. Approach your bank manager or the small business lending unit of your bank as a first step. They may be able to find the information for you, or direct you to someone in the corporate lending or investment divisions.

Trade and Professional Associations

If a trade or professional association exists for the market sector in which you are interested, it may be an excellent source of information about the total size and value of your market. It may even have statistics broken down by region.

Some associations may only make this information available to members – and, if you are not yet in business, you may find it difficult to gain access to it. Other associations will make the information publicly available, though there is usually a charge involved as the organisation tries to recover some of its own costs.

Many associations have links to sister bodies internationally and thus can be a source of international statistics and information.

Associations that may be able to help you in your research include:

- **Association for Purchasing and Supply**
- **Association of Advertisers in Ireland**
- **Chambers of Commerce of Ireland**
- **Chartered Institute of Logistics & Transport**
- **Chartered Institute of Personnel & Development**
- **Crafts Council of Ireland**
- **IBEC**
- **Institute of Directors in Ireland**
- **Institute of Industrial Engineers**
- **Institute of Leisure & Amenity Management**
- **Institute of Management Consultants in Ireland**
- **Institution of Engineers of Ireland**
- **Inventors Association of Ireland**
- **Irish Computer Society**
- **Irish Countrywomen's Association**
- **Irish Direct Marketing Association**
- **Irish Exporters Association**
- **Irish Farmers' Association**

- **Irish Franchise Association**
- **Irish Hotels Federation**
- **Irish Institute for Training & Development**
- **Irish Institute of Credit Management**
- **Irish Institute of Purchasing and Materials Management**
- **Irish Internet Association**
- **Irish League of Credit Unions**
- **Irish Management Institute**
- **Irish Management Institute (Northern Ireland) Ltd**
- **Irish Organic Farmers and Growers Association**
- **Irish Research Scientists' Association**
- **Irish Retail Newsagents Association**
- **Irish Road Haulage Association**
- **Irish Small and Medium Enterprises Association**
- **Irish Software Association**
- **Irish Travel Agents Association**
- **Irish Wind Energy Association**
- **Marketing Institute of Ireland**
- **Momentum, the Northern Ireland ICT Federation**
- **National Guild of Master Craftsmen**
- **National Safety Council**
- **Network Ireland**
- **Northern Ireland Chamber of Commerce and Industry**
- **Northern Ireland Food and Drink Association**
- **Public Relations Consultants Association**
- **Public Relations Institute of Ireland**
- **Register of Electrical Contractors of Ireland**
- **Restaurants Association of Ireland**
- **Sales Institute of Ireland**
- **Small Firms Association**
- **Sustainable Energy Ireland**
- **Telework Ireland.**

Most of these organisations provide training, networking and other services to their members so, if an association is relevant to your business, it's worth considering joining at the earliest possible opportunity.

Libraries

Often overlooked, local libraries have a wealth of information available – either on the spot or available through inter-library loans. Make a friend of your local librarian – he or she has valuable research skills that you will spend a great deal of time to acquire yourself.

And, increasingly, libraries provide access to the Internet (see below) for a modest charge.

Three excellent libraries are:

- **Belfast Business Library** at the Central Library, Royal Avenue
- **Business Information Centre** at the ILAC Centre library
- **Enterprise Ireland** library, Merrion Hall, Strand Road, Dublin 4 (call first to make an appointment).

Telephone Directories

The **Golden Pages** – the classified part of the telephone directory – is a useful guide to the number of people doing what you want to do and their location.

You want to be a carpenter? Look up carpenters in the phone book. If there are 15 in your locality, either it is a great place for carpenters or they are all very poor!

Other useful directories are:

- *MAPS*, published by the **Association of Advertisers in Ireland**
- *Administration Yearbook & Diary*, published by the **Institute of Public Administration**.

Other People in the Business

Talk to people already involved in the industry. Make use of their experience.

Trade and professional associations may be able to put you in contact with some of their members who may be willing to share their experience and expertise.

If yours is (or will be) a technology business, identify a "Centre of Excellence" in your field. The **Institutes of Technology** and **Universities** have a wealth of information and experience at their disposal, much of which is available – usually, for a fee. Use **TecNet** as a starting point.

State and Private Sector Enterprise Support Agencies

There is a vast range of support available to entrepreneurs and those thinking of starting a business – much expanded even in the few years since the last edition of this book. Much of it is provided by State or State-funded agencies; some of it is provided by the private sector.

Chapters 5, 6 and **7** give details of State, private sector and European support for entrepreneurs and small business. **Chapter 8** provides this information for Northern Ireland. In addition, the comprehensive **Directory of Sources of Assistance** provides contact details for all organisations mentioned and this book's companion website, **www.startingabusinessinireland.com**, will keep you up-to-date.

Professional Researchers

If the market for your product is geographically extensive, or highly competitive, you might consider getting professional market researchers to prepare a report for you. Look in the *Golden Pages* classified telephone directory for contact details of market researchers in your area.

The Internet

Another source of information – particularly on international trends – is the Internet. If you are not already connected to the Internet, ask a friend to show you or visit your local library or one of the "cybercafés" where you can rent access by the hour.

Use one of the search engines – Yahoo, Lycos, Alta Vista, etc. – to help narrow your enquiries. Contact the companies whose websites you visit for more information.

Useful websites include:

- **AIB Bank**
- **Amárach Consulting**
- **Aquaculture.ie**
- **Ask-Ireland.com**
- **BASIS.ie**
- **BioNorthernIreland.com**
- **BioTechInfo.ie**
- **BioTechnologyIreland.com**
- **BorderBizLaw.com**
- **BPlans.org.uk**
- **Business Plus**
- **BusinessInformationPoint.com**
- **Central Statistics Office**
- **CreativeIreland.com**
- **DoingBusinessinDunlaoghaireRathdown.com**
- **EBusinesslex.net**
- **EBusinessLex.net**
- **Economic Statistics Northern Ireland**
- **Entreworld.org**
- **ETradeBusinessIreland.com**
- **Europa**
- **Excellerator**
- **Expertiseireland.com**
- **FarmOptions.ie**
- **FranchiseDirect.com**
- **Galway City and County Enterprise Board**
- **Government Direct for Business**
- **GreenEntrepreneurs.net**

- **Infrastructure.ie**
- **Irish Internet Association** – for its "IIA Internet resources"
- **Irlgov.ie**
- **Liveandlearn.ie**
- **LouthCraftmark.com**
- **ManagementDirect.com**
- **MovetoIreland.com**
- **NDP.ie**
- **Oak Tree Press**
- **Revenue Commissioners**
- **Ruraldev-learningonline.ie**
- **Ruralsupport.org.uk**
- **South Dublin County Enterprise Board**
- **Startup.ie**
- **TradeNetIreland Ltd**
- **Wanbo.org.**

INTERPRETING RESEARCH RESULTS

Researching your proposed business is not just a matter of asking the right questions. Interpreting the results is equally important. You may be too close to your idea to see problems (or, less often, to see opportunities). Bringing in outsiders may be helpful. Consider friends whose business skills you respect. Ask your accountant, banker or other professional adviser – even if you have to pay for their opinion. It is important to arrive at an independently objective point of view, and it will be worth paying for if it saves you from disaster.

In addition to giving an independent view of your plans, a good accountant can help you draw up financial projections. In any case, you will probably need an accountant once you have begun trading. An accountant who is introduced at the planning stage will have a greater insight into the objectives of the business as well as the systems by which it functions. Your planning will benefit from the experience of your accountant, who, in turn, will be better placed to give you good service in future years.

THE FINAL QUESTION

Now you are in a position to answer the question at the start of this chapter: Does a market for your product or service exist? Your answer will tell you whether to proceed to the next stage.

If not, don't despair. It's better to have found out that your idea won't work before you have invested much time and effort into it – and, if you're serious about starting your own business, there'll be plenty of other opportunities.

3: WRITING A BUSINESS PLAN

Once you have thoroughly done the necessary market research for your project and decided to go ahead and start your own business, your next step is to write a business plan that summarises the following points about your business:

- Where it has come from
- Where it is now
- Where it is going in the future
- How it intends to get there
- How much money it needs to fulfil its plans
- What makes it likely to succeed
- What threats or disadvantages must be overcome on the way.

The document can range in length from a few typed sheets of paper to several hundred pages. However, since professional readers of business plans – bankers, venture capitalists and enterprise officers – are offered more business plans than they can intelligently digest, the more concise your business plan, the more likely it is to be read.

THE PURPOSE OF A BUSINESS PLAN

A business plan can have several purposes. The main ones usually are:

- To establish the fundamental viability of your project
- To document your plan for the business
- To act as a yardstick for measuring progress against plans
- To communicate your plans for your business to outsiders, particularly those you want to invest in your business.

Although the business plan is most often used as a marketing document for raising finance, even if you do not need to raise finance you should still prepare one since it will:

- Focus your thoughts
- Check your numbers
- Provide a basis for monitoring results
- Enable communication of your ideas.

Each of these purposes places its own demands on the format and contents of the business plan.

The focus of your business plan will vary, depending on the relative priorities that you assign to these purposes. Let's look at each in turn.

Establishing the Viability of Your Project

There are many ways of researching whether your project will succeed. All, however, finally require an act of faith from the entrepreneur when the time comes to commit to the business. Before this point is reached, a great deal of planning and careful thought should have been completed.

A well-prepared business plan will assist immeasurably with that process, simply through the discipline it imposes. Too often, entrepreneurs are carried away with their own enthusiasm. They neglect the most cursory checks on the viability of their brainchild. Broad, and sometimes rash, assumptions are made about the market for the product, its cost of manufacture, distribution channels, acceptability to customers etc. But when a reasoned, written case must be made – even if only to oneself – it is less easy to overlook the unpalatable. At least, it is difficult to do so without being aware of it.

Documenting the Plan

"The plan doesn't matter, it's the planning that counts," said Dwight D. Eisenhower, former US President. He was right. The quality of the planning you do for your business is critical to its success; how you document that planning process is less so. Nonetheless, a good business plan document actively aids the planning process by providing a structure. It forces you:

- To cover ground that you might otherwise, in your enthusiasm, skip over
- To clarify your thinking – it is almost impossible to get your plan onto paper until you have formulated it clearly
- To justify your arguments, since they will be written down for all to see
- To focus on the risks and potential for loss in your plans as well as on the potential for profit and success.

Avoid unnecessary pessimism. Be realistic, but don't carry caution to extremes. If your proposal is realistic, have confidence in it.

A Yardstick for Measuring Progress

Preparing any plan demands an objective. An objective assumes that you are going to make some effort to achieve it. Some objectives are quantifiable: if your aim is to sell 500 gadgets, sales of 480 is below target, while 510 units sold gives you reason to feel pleased with your performance. Other objectives cannot be quantified; all the more reason then to document them so that you can clearly establish whether or not you have achieved them.

Your business plan should contain the objectives, quantifiable and otherwise, that you have set for your business. Reading through your plan at regular intervals and comparing your performance to date with the objectives you set yourself one month, six months or two years earlier can help to focus your attention on the important things that need to be done if targets are to be achieved.

Communicating Plans to Third Parties

Though they would readily acknowledge the importance of good planning, many businesses would not prepare a formal business plan document if it were not for the need to present their plans for the business to outsiders – usually to raise finance. Too often, the urgent pushes aside the important. But, if you wish to raise finance for your business to develop, you will have to prepare a business plan.

Financiers, whether bankers, venture capitalists or private investors, need:

- A document they can study in their own time, and which makes its case independently of the promoters of the business
- Evidence that the future of the business has been properly thought through and that all risks have been taken into account
- Information about the business.

In addition, others may have reason to read your business plan – key employees or suppliers, for example. So it must communicate your message clearly.

No matter how good a writer you consider yourself to be, if you can't put your business proposition clearly and persuasively in writing, it suggests that you have more thinking to do. It doesn't mean that your project won't work. On the contrary, your business may be a resounding success – but you need to be able to communicate it!

WHO SHOULD WRITE YOUR BUSINESS PLAN?

Very simply, you. No one else. You may receive offers from consultants, many of them highly reputable and professional in their work, to write your business plan for you. They will quote their extensive experience of business, of raising finance for start-up businesses, of presenting financial information – all valid points and, in many cases, true.

However, whatever experience consultants may have of business in general, and drafting business plans in particular, they lack one essential ingredient: your intimate relationship with your business. You are the one who has spent your waking hours – and many of your sleeping ones, too, probably – dreaming, planning and guiding your tender and frail creation to this point. You know what makes you tick; what makes your team tick; what will and will not work for you. Only you can assemble these thoughts.

Therefore, the first draft of the business plan is your responsibility. Do it yourself. Refine and redraft it – again, and again, if necessary – until it's finished.

Then, and only then, should you entrust it to someone who can put the right gloss on it. But let them do only that. Don't let them put *their* words on your pages.

How Long Should Your Business Plan Be?

How long is a piece of string? Your business plan should be as long as it needs to be – no longer and no shorter.

How long is that? No one can decide that except yourself. It depends on the purpose for which you are preparing the plan, the level of knowledge that likely readers will have of your business, and the complexity of your business.

Few businesses can be done justice to in less than, say, 10 A4 pages; equally, it will be a dedicated reader (or one who has spotted an outstandingly good business proposition) who will continue past the first hundred pages or so.

If a reader wants more information, they will ask for it. But make sure that they don't have to ask for information they should have had from the start – or, worse still (and sometimes fatal to your hopes of raising finance), that the absence of the information doesn't lead them to discard your plan altogether.

FIGURES

Too many figures and your plan may become off-putting, but too few and your plans will simply be treated as ambitions without any underlying substance. Quantify as much as you can. Your plan is likely to be read by people whose currency is numbers. You help your cause by talking their language.

Make sure figures add up correctly. Nothing is more worrying to an investor than the suspicion that:

- You can't handle figures
- There's a figure wrong or missing – or worse still, hidden.

You need to be able to show the existence of a market for your product, and some indication of its size, in a way that can be verified independently. You will also have to prove to the satisfaction of the bank manager or investor that adequate margins can be achieved to cover cash flow needs and meet repayment of debt or growth objectives.

Don't clog up the body of the business plan with detailed statistical analysis, although it must contain all the information a reader needs. For example, quote the proposed sales target, but show how you will achieve it at the back in an Appendix, and explain the underlying assumptions there also. The same applies to the CVs of key employees – mention crucial information where appropriate in the plan, but place the details in an Appendix.

Business Models and Projected Figures

A financial model of the business is effectively a set of accounts, represented on computer spreadsheets or in a dedicated modelling package for ease of manipulation – for example, *Business Plan Pro* from **Palo Alto Software**.

While a financial model is useful for businesses of all sizes, for a business of any complexity it is essential. Your model should enable you to change certain variables, such as the number of units of product sold, or the price at which you sell them, or the cost of supplies, and discover what the effect will be on the business.

Your financial model should consist of:

- Balance sheet
- Profit and loss account
- Cash flow statement.

You may also create some management accounts that look in more detail at production and overhead costs and allow you to manipulate certain of those variables.

It is crucial that the figures you use in your model are as close to reality as can be. Your model must show what your breakeven point is likely to be in different circumstances, and allow you to estimate how long it will take to reach it. This calculation is very important when it comes to raising finance. If you will be able to repay borrowings in three to six months, you may be willing to risk a bigger initial loan than if your earliest estimated repayment date is a year away.

The rule is to be cautious and prudent, but realistic. If your figures are too optimistic, you could find that you cannot meet your repayment schedule, and the additional cost of borrowing over a longer time frame damages your business' growth prospects, if not its viability – and your credibility with your bank manager. Equally, if you are unnecessarily pessimistic about the length of time it will take to repay the loan, your calculations may indicate that the entire project should be dropped – which is exactly what your bank manager will do!

Some of the main reasons for using a financial model are to estimate:

- A breakeven point under different market conditions
- How long it will take to reach a desired level of operation
- The consequences of price changes
- The consequences of undertaking expansion, R&D, and other special projects.

If you have no experience of financial modelling, you should seek help from your bank, **City / County Enterprise Board**, your accountant or one of the other organisations listed in the "Business Plans" section of the *Directory*.

Again, the details of the assumptions on which the model is based should go into an Appendix to the business plan, as should any detailed statistical analysis. Quote the important final figures in the body of the plan.

A STANDARD BUSINESS PLAN FORMAT

Each business plan is unique. However, those whom you seek to convince to invest in your project have come to expect certain information in a broadly standard format that presents information in an easily-digested logical sequence.

For a very small or simple business, the following intuitive format (adapted from *Applying the Rules of Business, Steps to Entrepreneurship* series, Ron Immink & Brian O'Kane, Oak Tree Press) may be sufficient.

It sets out 10 key questions, the answers to which:

- Cover all the information that a reader of a business plan is likely to want to know in order to come to a decision on the plan
- Ensure that you have fully thought through all aspects of your business.

For larger businesses, the second format shown on **page 44**, adapted from *Planning for Success, Steps to Entrepreneurship* series (Ron Immink & Brian O'Kane, Oak Tree Press) may be more appropriate.

This format is also closer to conventional business planning formats expected by banks and other financial institutions, a version of which (based on the template in *Starting Your Own Business: A Workbook*, Ron Immink & Brian O'Kane, Oak Tree Press) is available on **www.startingabusinessinireland.com**.

SIMPLE BUSINESS PLAN OUTLINE

I am ...	Explain who you are, your education/work experience etc, especially insofar as it applies to your proposed business.
My product is ...	Explain your product: What it is, what is does, how it works, how it is made, what makes it different/unique, etc.
My customers are ...	Explain who your customers will be and what evidence you have to support this.
My customers will buy my product because ...	Explain why your customers will buy your product and what evidence you have to support this.
My customers will pay ...	Explain how much your customers will pay for each unit of your product and what evidence you have to support this.
At this price, my customers will buy ...	Explain how many units of your product your customers will buy at the price set and what evidence you have to support this.
I can make ...	Explain how many units of your product you can make in a given time period and what evidence you have to support this.
To make each unit of product costs ...	Explain how much each unit of product costs you to make and what evidence you have to support this.
The start-up investment I require is ...	Explain the start-up investment you need, what it will be used for and what evidence you have to support this.
I have a viable business because ...	Explain why you believe you have a viable business and what evidence you have to support this.
In summary ...	On a single page, list the main points of your plan, in bullet point form. This is the part of the business plan that will make the biggest impression on your reader – make sure it's easy to read and understand. Then put it at the front of your plan, where it will be seen!

PLANNING FOR SUCCESS BUSINESS PLAN OUTLINE

1: Summary/Overview

- **Founder(s)**
- **Business name**
- **Contact details:** Address, Telephone/Fax, E-mail, Website
- **Status:** Sole trader, partnership or limited company
- **Registered for:** VAT, PAYE, Corporation Tax
- **Formed as:** Purchase of existing business/purchase of franchise/start-up/other
- **Business Objective**
- **External Accountant:** Address, telephone/fax number, contact name
- **Product/Service Range:** Include descriptions and prices
- **Staff:** Numbers employed in production, sales/promotion, administration, other duties
- **Competitors:** Include estimates of competitors' turnover
- **Investment and Financing:** Details of fixed assets, personal assets, current assets, long/medium-term assets, liquid assets, short-term finance, start-up costs, subsidies/grants, allowance for contingencies, total investment, total available finance
- **Budgets:** Forecasts for turnover, gross profit, gross profit percentage, net profit, cash flow and personal expenses over first three years
- **Other Information**.

2: The Entrepreneur
(If there is more than one founder, each must complete this section.)

- **Personal details:** Name, address, date of birth, etc.
- **Income**: Details of present income, source of income, benefits, income of spouse/partner, etc.
- **Education**: Details of post-primary education, including any courses that you are currently attending.

- **Practical Experience**: Details of your working history and experience and any other significant experience that could be useful for your business.

- **Motivation, Objectives and Goals**: Why do you want to start a business? What do you want to achieve with your business?

- **Personal Qualities**: What special qualities of yours are important for your business? List both your strong and your weak points. What are you going to do about your weak points?

3: Formal Requirements

- **Overall Description**: Give a general description of your proposed business.

- **Research**: List the organisations you have contacted to discuss your plans and summarise the outcome of these discussions.

- **Legal Status**: What legal status will your business take? What considerations led you to this choice?

- **Name and Location**: What is the name of the business? Have you checked that this name is available? Describe your location. How can customers reach your location? Is access for supply and removal of goods available? Is there enough parking for your customers' cars and for your own cars? How big are your office premises? Are there expansion possibilities at these premises? Are the premises leased or purchased? Give details of cost of lease/mortgage. Have the premises been professionally valued? Has a lease or purchase contract been prepared by a solicitor? (If so, give the name of the solicitor.) Is there any pollution in the ground at your premises?

- **Licences**: Do you fulfil all of the licensing and permit requirements for the field you will be working in? If so, which and on what grounds? If not, why not and what are you doing about it? Is your business registered at the Companies Registration Office? What other licences do you need? Are there any other legal applications required (for example, environmental concerns). If so, which?

- **Employer and Employees**: Initially, how will your staffing be organised? Have you drawn up clear job descriptions for your future employees? Do you plan to expand your employee numbers quickly? Who will replace you during any required absences?

- **Administration**: Who will do your accounting? Who will do your bookkeeping? Give names, addresses and contact numbers.

- **Insurance**: Are you insured against the normal risks? If so, what is insured and for how much?

- **Terms of Trade**: How is responsibility for product delivery arranged? Are product deliveries insured? If so, for how much? Summarise your terms of trade.

- **VAT**: Is your business registered for VAT? What is your VAT number? What rates of VAT apply to your business?

- **Start Date**: On what date do you want to start the business, or when did you start?

4: Marketing

- **Market**: Who are your target groups? What do you have to offer? What is your business objective in seven words?

- **Market Research**: Describe your market, future developments and your potential customers (local, county, national, and international). Describe the level of competition you face. What are the leading indicators in your market sector? Estimate the size of the Irish market for your product. What part of this market do you intend to service? Have you contacted future customers? What was their reaction? Have you obtained any forward orders? What comments did you receive with these orders?

- **Image**: What image will your business present? Formulate the core of your marketing plan based on your target groups, product assortment, price level, etc.

- **Product (Range)**: Describe briefly the product(s) you want to launch. Describe the primary and secondary functions of your product(s). What choices do you offer your customers? What extras do you offer compared to the competition?

- **Price**: What are customers prepared to pay? What are customers accustomed to paying? What are your competitors' prices? What is your price? How is your price made up? Will you offer discounts? If so, what will they be? Will you make special offers? If so, what will they be? Will cost calculations be monitored during operation? If so, how?

- **Place**: Explain your choice of location. Are there future developments that will change the attractiveness of your location? How did you allocate space for the various necessary functions?

- **Personnel**: Profile yourself as a business person. How many people will be involved in production, sales/promotion, administration, other duties? How are you going to make sure that your staff uphold the image of your business?

- **Presentation**: How are you going to present your business (layout, colours, music, atmosphere, correspondence, brochures, business cards, van signs)?

- **Promotion**: Rate those areas your customers are most interested in, and your relative strengths in those areas. How are you going to approach your customers and what buying motives are you going to emphasise? What marketing and promotion resources will you emphasise? Explain your promotion methods (how, where, frequency, etc.)

- **Competitors**: List your main competitors. Assess their strengths compared to your own. In what ways do your products/services differ from those of your competitors? Can you estimate the total turnover of your competitors? What are your strong points compared to those of your direct competitors? What are your weak points compared to those of your direct competitors?

- **Purchasing**: Have you contacted your future suppliers? If so, what are their terms of trade? Are there alternative suppliers? What advantages do these alternative suppliers offer you?

- **Production Process**: Are you involved with (or will you be using) new techniques or new products in your production processes? If so, are you receiving assistance from experts? If so, who are they and how are they involved? Describe your production process. What experience do you have with this process? What equipment do you use in the production process? List the equipment you intend to lease, buy new, or buy used. What guarantees/back-up do you have for this equipment in case of malfunction? Have you enough capacity to achieve the revenue for which you have budgeted? Have you checked your products and production processes for environmental considerations? If so, are there any environmental objections? If so, what are you planning to do about them?

5: Investment and Financing

- **Investment**: Describe the investment you will have to make to start your business, and to run it over the first three years (amounts exclusive of VAT).

- **Personal Assets**: What assets can you (and your business partner(s)) put up yourselves? How did you value your personal assets?

- **Other (Bank) Finance**: Details of long/medium-term finance, short-term finance, subsidies/grants; shortfall, surplus etc.

- **Credit Assessment**: Can you support the required investment in fixed assets with quotations from suppliers? If not, how did you calculate your investment? Is your investment cost-effective? In your estimates, did you take seasonal business influences into account, and calculate based on your maximum requirements? How did you estimate your stock and work-in-progress levels? How did you estimate the value of your debtors? Do you have sufficient liquid assets to cope with disappointments and unexpected expenses? Did you approach a bank(s) about the financing of your plans? If yes, which bank(s), and who was your contact person? Did those contacts lead to any agreements? Did you approach other finance companies about your plans? If yes, with whom did you speak? Were any decisions reached, or arrangements made?

6: The Operating Budget

- **Turnover Forecast**: List your revenue sources, and project the amounts you expect from each in the first three years.

- **Costs**: Give details of costs for staff, production, premises, transport, sales and promotion, general expenses, finance and depreciation in each of the first three years.
- **Profits and Cash Flow**: Give detailed cash-flow projections for the first three years.
- **Comments on the Budget**: Describe how you calculated and estimated your revenue (number of customers, average order per customer, turnaround). What expansion do you expect over the next few years? How did you calculate your purchase costs? How did you estimate salaries? What effect will any shortfall in turnover have on your business and how do you plan to handle it? What is your minimum required turnover?

7: Personal Expenses

- **Personal Expenses**: Fixed expenses; rent/interest and repayment gas, water, electricity; taxes/charges; insurance; study expenses; membership expenses/contributions; TV licence; private use of car; repayments (enclose loan details); household expenses, etc.
- **Home Equity**: Do you own your own home? If so, have you had it valued? What is its market value? How much equity do you have in your house?
- **Additional Debts**: What other debts do you have (personal/ private loan or credit, car financing, study costs, etc.)?
- **Minimum Required Turnover**: What is the minimum required turnover for your business, including your personal expenses?

8: Cash Flow

- Detailed cash-flow projections for each month of each quarter, outlining all income and expenditure, together with the opening and closing bank balances each quarter over the first three years.

Sometimes the Summary/Overview is expanded with a narrative Executive Summary, a concise one- or two-page summary of the entire plan.

This Executive Summary is the last thing to be written, and the first to be read. It must persuade the reader that the idea is good, otherwise he or she may not read on. It summarises the company, its objectives, why it will be successful. It describes the products, the market, critical financial information and, finally, outlines what form of finance is required, how much, and when. It assumes that its reader is not expert in your industry and knows nothing about your business. And it does all this in as few words as possible!

You should avoid giving detailed personal reasons for wanting to be your own boss. It is very easy to confuse your personal ambitions with your objectives for the business. Bankers and other investors are primarily considering your prospects for success (getting them a good return), not your prospects for personal satisfaction. It is quite important to keep your focus, like theirs, on the business. Nonetheless, your character and skills will be of importance to them; these are the things to mention.

How a Financier Reads a Business Plan

How a financier reads a business plan depends on what kind of financier he, or increasingly she, is. There are two types of financier – the lender and the investor.

The lender is typically your bank manager. Lenders will invest money in your business, if they think it worth doing so by their criteria, in return for interest on the capital. The professional investor, on the other hand, will invest equity in your business and share in your risk as owner of the business. Professional investors will postpone their return for a period – typically, three to five years – but will look for an above-average return for the risk involved in doing so.

The Lender

The average bank manager will be looking to see how you have handled, or propose to handle, the risks, particularly the financial risks, that your business is likely to encounter. Bank managers are concerned about the security of the bank's money – or more properly, the depositors' money – which you are seeking and for which they are responsible.

That is not to say that a bank manager will not back you. Most bank managers have discretion in the amounts they lend to businesses and will sometimes back their own hunches or gut feelings against the apparent odds. But do not bet on it. Turn the odds in your favour by writing your business plan and framing your request for finance in the best possible light.

Arnold S. Goldstein, American author of *Starting on a Shoestring* (John Wiley & Sons), suggests the following likely line of questioning from a bank manager:

- Why do you need the amount requested?
- What will you do with it?
- How do you know it's enough?
- How much less can you live with?
- Who else will you borrow from?
- How do you propose to repay it?
- How can you prove that you can?
- What collateral can you offer?

Unless you can answer these questions to your bank manager's satisfaction, it is unlikely that you will get the money you are looking for.

And don't wait for the interview with the manager for an opportunity to give the answers to these questions – that is far too late. The bank manager's mind will already be made up, more or less, before your meeting. Your plan will have been read thoroughly. The interview is intended to firm up the manager's decision. If you have not answered the relevant questions in the plan, you are not likely to have much chance to do so later.

You don't need to write your business plan in a style that asks the questions in the form above and then gives the answers. What you need to do is to ensure that the information that answers the questions is:

- Contained within the plan
- Visible within the plan
- Capable of being extracted by a reader from the plan.

Putting all this in another way, a bank manager will look for three things:

- Character
- Collateral
- Cash flow.

Character means you. A bank manager who has any reason to distrust or disbelieve you – from previous dealings or because of your reputation or because of errors or inconsistencies in your business plan – will not invest money with you.

Collateral means the backing that you can give as security for the loan. In some cases, collateral is not needed. But to the banker, who is responsible to the bank's depositors for their money, security is all. If you can offer collateral, it will certainly help your case.

Cash flow means your ability to repay the loan on time, out of the proceeds of the investment. The bank manager will prefer to see the loan repaid at regular monthly or quarterly intervals with interest paid on the due dates – anything else upsets the system. Unless you can show that the business will generate enough cash to make the payments the bank manager requires – or you have explained clearly in your business plan why this will not be possible for an initial period – you will not get the money that you ask for.

Professional Investors

Professional investors – venture capitalists, for example – have a different viewpoint. They accept risk, though, like any prudent investor, they will avoid undue risk and seek to limit their exposure to unavoidable risk. David Silver, another American venture capitalist and author on enterprise, suggests that their questions will be along the lines of:

- How much can I make?
- How much can I lose?
- How do I get my money out?
- Who says this is any good?
- Who else is in it?

How much can I make? decides whether the project fits the profile of 30 to 50 per cent annual compound growth (well in excess of bank interest) usually required by such investors.

How much can I lose? identifies the downside risk. Although venture capitalists are used to investing in 10 projects for every one that succeeds, they cannot invest in projects that would jeopardise their own business of investment in the event of their failure.

How do I get my money out? is important since few venture capitalists invest for the long term. Most are happy to turn over their investments every three to five years. None will invest in a project unless they can see clearly an exit mechanism. There is no point in holding a 25 per cent share in a company valued at several millions if you cannot realise the shareholding when you want to.

Who says this is any good? Professional investors maintain networks of advisers, often on an informal basis. Venture capitalists will check out all that you say or include in your business plan. This is part of the "due diligence" process. If you can supply a venture capitalist with evidence that those who ought to know support your plans, you will strengthen your case.

Who else is in this? panders to the investor's residual need for security. Even if investors know that they are going to take a risk, to place their faith and money in your hands, they like to know that others have come to the same conclusion. There is nothing like unanimity to convince people that they are right.

One should not mock – particularly if you're trying to persuade someone to invest. Some venture capitalists have such a reputation for being right, for picking winners, that others try to follow their lead whenever they can.

Above all, in assessing the project itself, a professional investor will look at three key areas:

- The market – Is it large and growing rapidly?
- The product – Does it solve an important problem in the market, one that customers are prepared to pay for?
- Management – Are all the key functional areas on board and up to strength?

WRITING THE BUSINESS PLAN

There are three stages in writing a business plan:

- Thinking
- Writing
- Editing.

Each is important but the most important is the first – thinking. Be prepared to spend at least 75 per cent of the time you have allocated to preparing your business plan in thinking. Time spent here will not be wasted. Use this time to talk through your business with anyone who will listen; read widely, especially about others in your area of business; and avoid finding reasons why things cannot be done.

Writing can be done fastest of all. Use a word processor to give yourself the flexibility you will need to edit the document later.

If you find it difficult to start writing on a blank page or computer screen, talk instead. Buy, or borrow, a hand-held dictating machine. Talk to yourself about your business. Explain it to someone who knows nothing about it. Get the tape transcribed and your business plan will be on the way.

Editing is the last task. Editing is an art. Some people are better at it than others, but everyone can learn the basics. Essentially, it's about clear communication. Read through your draft business plan – aloud, if you find that helps. Does what you have written say what you want? Start deleting. You will find that quite a lot can come out without doing damage. When you are happy with your draft, put it aside for a day or two. Come back to it fresh and see whether it still makes sense. Edit again where it does not. And when it is right, leave it alone!

4: Financing Your Start-up

The "Golden Rule" for financing a new business is: As little as possible, as cheaply as possible. Do not put money into the unnecessary. It is better to start off running your business from the attic without a loan than in a glossy, but unnecessary, high-street office with heavy bank borrowings.

On the other hand, do adopt a realistic position on the amount of money that you need to get going. Your financing will have to be sufficient to carry the business for a reasonable period before it reaches some kind of balance, where money coming in equals money going out. In addition to capital investment in plant, equipment and premises, your financing may have to supply most of the working capital until sales begin to generate sufficient income to give you an adequate cash flow.

You have two options in raising finance:

- Equity – capital invested in the business, usually not repayable
- Debt – capital lent to the business, usually repayable at a specified date.

EQUITY

For equity, the alternatives are:

- Your own equity – which leads to two questions: How much do you have? How much do you need?
- Other people's equity – which also leads to two questions: Are you prepared to allow other people to own part of your business? Can your business offer the sort of return that will attract outside investors?

Because equity means giving away part of your business, it's in your interest to minimise the amount held by outside investors. However, be sensible – it's better to own 70% of a thriving profitable business than 100% of a business going nowhere because it's starved for funds.

Owners' Equity

In terms of the equity that you are able to put into the business, you must establish what assets you must retain as a fall-back position, and remove these from the equation. For example, you may not want to mortgage your house to raise finance for your business. Then consider what assets remain in the following terms:

- How easily can they be sold and how much will their sale raise?
- Are they mortgagable assets?
- Will they be acceptable as collateral?

Typical assets include:

- Cash
- Shares
- Car
- Land
- House
- Boats, second/holiday homes, antiques, jewellery, paintings.

If you are considering mortgaging your family home for the sake of the business, you should be aware that this is a very serious step and professional advice should be obtained. The issues to be considered include:

- Ownership of the property
- What would happen to the family home and your family should the business fail
- The approach that the banks and the courts take in such circumstances.

Note that if you mortgage your home, or borrow personally, in order to invest equity into your business and the business fails, you still remain liable to repay the loan. There's a big difference between this and the situation where the bank lends directly to the business.

Other Equity

For many small businesses, the option of raising equity capital is not a reality. Either the sums they need are too small to interest an investor, or the level of return, while adequate to pay a standard bank loan, is not sufficient to tempt the investor who is exposed to a greater risk. Most equity investors look to invest at least €500,000 in a company, arguing that amounts below this do not justify the amount of checking they need to do before making an investment. Thus, perversely perhaps, it is easier to raise €5,000,000 than it is to raise €50,000.

Fuelled by the "Celtic Tiger" economy, the recent spectacular successes of some Irish technology companies and a growing awareness of the importance of private equity for business development, the number of venture capital funds in Ireland has increased significantly in the past few years. Some of these will consider investing seed capital (less than €100,000), although most prefer to invest venture (€100,000 to €500,000, for businesses at an early stage of development) or development (€500,000+) capital. Note that these amounts are arbitrary; some funds will invest in more than one category.

Sources of Equity

Sources of equity in Ireland include:

- **3i Group plc**
- **4th Level Ventures University Seed Fund**
- **ACT Venture Capital**
- **AIB Bank / AIB Equity / AIB Equity Fund 2002**
- **Alchemy Partners**
- **Alliance Investment Capital**
- **AWG Investment Fund**
- **Bank of Ireland Kernel Capital Partners Private Equity Fund**
- **BOI Venture Capital**
- **Business Expansion Scheme**
- **Business Innovation Centres**
- **Campus Companies Venture Capital Fund**
- **City / County Enterprise Boards**
- **Corporate Finance Ireland**
- **Crescent Capital**
- **Cross Atlantic Capital Partners**
- **Crucible Corporation**
- **Delta Partners / Delta Equity Fund II Ltd Partnership**
- **Dublin Seed Capital Fund**
- **Enterprise 2000 Fund**
- **Enterprise Equity / Enterprise Equity Investment Fund / Enterprise Equity Seed capital Investment Fund**
- **Enterprise Ireland**
- **European BioScience Fund 1**
- **Executive Venture Partners / EVP Early Stage Technology Fund**
- **First Step**
- **Gorann**
- **Growcorp Group Ltd**

- **Guinness Ireland Ulster Bank Equity Fund**
- **Hibernia Capital Partners**
- **HotOrigin / HotOrigin Fund**
- **ICC Venture Capital / ICC Regional Venture Capital Fund**
- **International Fund for Ireland**
- **Ion Equity**
- **Irish BICs Seed Capital Fund**
- **Irish BioScience Venture Capital Fund**
- **Irish Film Board**
- **Mazars**
- **Mentor Capital Partners**
- **Millennium Entrepreneur Fund**
- **NCB Ventures**
- **Powerscourt Capital Partners**
- **Qubis**
- **Seed Capital Scheme**
- **Seroba BioVentures**
- **Shannon Development**
- **Small Enterprise Seed Fund**
- **Synergy 2000**
- **Trinity Venture Capital / Trinity Venture Fund**
- **University of Limerick Alumni Association Entrepreneurship Programme**
- **Viridian Growth Fund**
- **Western Development Commission / Western Investment Fund.**

Sources of information on equity and equity sources include:
- **BDO Simpson Xavier**
- **Bolton Trust**
- **CFM Capital**
- **EquityNetwork**

- **Irish Venture Capital Association**
- **PDC.**

In most cases – certainly where you require seed capital – you can approach the fund manager directly. A check on the fund's website to make sure that you meet the fund's criteria, a phone call to check the name of the person to whom you should send your business plan – then go for it!

Larger, technology-based projects requiring greater and more complex financing can choose whether to go directly to an appropriate fund or to work through a corporate finance house, which has specialist skills in fund-raising.

Whatever your route, remember that it's not just about money, as the growth of incubators shows. Depending on the strengths of your new business, supports may be as important as cash.

Family equity

But, despite all the new funds, the best source of small-scale seed capital for most start-ups continues to be family or friends. If you do decide to involve family and friends as investors in your business, make sure both sides know – and agree on – the ground rules:

- Their investment is "risk capital" – it may be lost and is not repayable (unless you agree otherwise)
- Equity investment does not automatically give a right to management involvement – even if it's clear that you cannot cope
- Their investment may be diluted by other later investors, whose money is needed to continue the development of the business.

Put everything in writing – in a formal shareholders' agreement, if appropriate, or a simple letter of understanding signed by all parties.

Business Angels

"Business Angels", a term adapted from the world of theatre where private investors ("angels") are often the source of finance for a new show on New York's Broadway or in London's West End, are private investors who take (usually) a minority stake in a business – sometimes with an active management role, too. They're hard to find and, since they're usually experienced businesspeople, often hard to convince.

Sources of business angels include:

- **Binary Partners**
- Business Angel Network run by **Shannon Development**
- Dublin Investor Register Service run by the **Dublin Business Innovation Centre**
- **Enterprise Ireland**
- **EquityNetwork**
- **FirstTuesday.ie / Investnet**
- **Mentor Network**
- **Synergy 2000.**

Tax-based equity

While the **Revenue Commissioners** will not invest directly in your business, they provide a source of equity capital through the **Business Expansion Scheme** and the **Seed Capital Scheme**.

DEBT

When considering financing your business with debt, you must consider:

- Fixed or floating
- Long term or short term.

Fixed debt is a loan that is secured on a specific asset, for example, on premises. Floating debt is secured on assets that change regularly, for example, debtors. "Secured" means that, in the event that the loan is not repaid, the lender can appoint a receiver to sell the asset on which the loan is secured in order to recover the amount due. Thus, giving security for a loan is not something to be done lightly.

Long term for most lenders means five to seven years; short term means one year or less.

Because you have to pay interest on debt, you should try to manage with as little as possible. However, few businesses get off the ground without putting some form of debt on the balance sheet. The issues are usually:

- What is the cheapest form of debt?

- What is the correct balance between debt and equity?

- How can you sensibly reduce the amount of borrowing required?

- To what extent must borrowing be backed by personal assets?

Matching Loans and Assets

It is a good idea to try to match the term of the loan to the type of asset that you are acquiring:

- To avoid constant renewing or restructuring problems

- To ensure that each loan is covered by the break-up value of the assets in case of disaster.

For example, a loan to buy premises should be a long-term loan, unless you can see clearly that you will have enough money within a short period to repay the loan. Taking out a short-term loan or overdraft to buy premises is a recipe for disaster. You may have to renegotiate it time and again – and, if your business runs into temporary difficulties, you run the risk of losing everything.

Short-term loans, or even overdrafts, are more suited to funding stock or debtors because you should be able to repay the loan once you have sold the goods or got the money in.

Short-term finance is also used to fund other forms of working capital and cash flow. It should always be repaid within the year – even if at the end of the period you still need to borrow more to fund future cash flow. In other words, your overdraft or short-term loan should be periodically cleared (or substantially reduced) by money coming in before you need to increase it again. If you have to borrow the same sum of money against the same asset for longer than a year at a time, you should be considering longer-term finance.

If disaster strikes and you have to repay the loan, it will be much easier to do so if the value of the assets is roughly equivalent to the outstanding value of the loan. Thus, for instance, you will hope to sell your premises for at least as much as you borrowed to buy them. Machinery may be more difficult, as the resale price is rarely comparable with the purchase price. For this reason, you may consider purchasing second-hand equipment for your start-up.

If you can, you should arrange your loans so that un-realisable assets are purchased out of your own equity, using borrowing only for realisable assets. If an asset is easily realisable, the bank is much more likely to accept it as security.

The main sources of loan finance (overdrafts, term loans and commercial mortgages) for start-ups are the banks:

- **ACC Bank plc**
- **AIB Bank / AIB Bank Enterprise Development Bureau / AIB Equity**
- **Anglo Irish Bank Corporation plc**
- **Bank of Ireland / Bank of Ireland Enterprise Support Unit**
- **Bank of Ireland Northern Ireland**
- **Bank of Scotland (Ireland) Ltd**
- **First Trust Bank**
- **Lombard & Ulster Banking Ltd.**
- **National Irish Bank**
- **Northern Bank**
- **Permanent TSB**
- **Ulster Bank.**

Other Sources

Don't look only to banks for debt. Credit unions may consider a small loan to get your business off the ground, particularly if you have been a regular saver. Check the **Irish League of Credit Unions** website to find a credit union near you.

As well as dealing with banks, you may also find yourself dealing with finance companies. Finance companies exist to lend money and make a return on it. They sometimes are more willing to lend than a bank, as long as they can secure the loan with assets or personal guarantees. They are not often cheaper than banks, but may sometimes be prepared to lend when banks refuse. This is not always a good thing. While it may shore up your own confidence in your project, it does not of itself increase the chances of success.

If you are having trouble getting finance, it may be an indication that you should reappraise the project. Talk to those who have refused you finance about their reasons before proceeding to other financiers. You may end up increasing your chances of success, both in raising finance second time around and in the business itself.

Some finance companies (and foreign banks) specialise in certain types of finance, or special industry sectors. Because of their greater expertise and knowledge, they may be able to give you a better deal than the main retail banks because they understand your situation better.

When looking for finance, beware of "specialists" who claim that they can find you money at favourable rates of interest if you pay an up-front fee. Don't pay anything until you have the money.

And don't forget the following as sources of loan finance – often as part of a support package (see *Chapter 5*):

- **Area Partnership Companies** (some, not all)
- **Aspire Microloans for Business**
- **Charity Bank**
- **City / County Enterprise Boards**
- **Clann Credo**
- **Emerging Business Trust**

- **Enterprise 2000 Fund**
- **Enterprise Agencies / Centres in Northern Ireland** (most)
- **Enterprise Ireland**
- **Enterprise North West**
- **First Step**
- **Guinness Workers' Employment Fund Ltd**
- **International Fund for Ireland**
- **Irish Film Board**
- **Limerick Enterprise Network**
- **Louth County Enterprise Fund**
- **Prince's Trust Northern Ireland**
- **Sligo County Enterprise Fund Company**
- **Small Firms Loan Guarantee Scheme** (Northern Ireland)
- **Social Economy Agency**
- **Society of St Vincent de Paul**
- State agencies, for example, **Bord Iascaigh Mhara** (see **Chapter 5** for details)
- **Tallaght Trust Fund**
- **Triodos Bank**
- **Ulster Community Investment Trust**
- **Viridian Growth Fund**
- **Western Development Commission / Western Investment Fund.**

Expanding Your Credit Line

When (or, preferably, before) you have exhausted the borrowing facilities that your bank is prepared to provide (your credit line), you should consider two other forms of financing: leasing and factoring.

Leasing is particularly attractive as a way of acquiring the use of fixed assets – for example, plant and machinery, cars, office equipment – with the minimum up-front cost. Instead, you pay a regular monthly or quarterly payment, which is usually allowable for tax purposes. At the end of the lease, depending on the terms of the particular lease, you may have the option to continue using the asset for a modest continuing payment or to buy it outright from the lessor.

Sources of leasing include:

- **AIB Bank**
- **BNP Paribas Finance**
- **GE Capital Woodchester.**

Factoring, or invoice discounting, is a means of raising working capital, by "selling" your debtors. The factoring company (usually a division or subsidiary of a bank) will pay you, say, 80 per cent of the face value of an invoice when it is issued. The balance, less charges, will be paid to you when the debt is settled. This form of financing is especially useful for the company that is rapidly expanding and in danger of being choked for lack of cash flow.

Sources of factoring/invoice discounting include:

- **Celtic Invoice Discounting plc**
- **Clancy Business Finance**
- **Ulster Factors.**

In addition, the major banks all offer invoice discounting, sometimes through specialist subsidiaries. Check with their small business unit.

Who to Approach?

Who you approach for funds will depend on:

- How much finance you need
- What you need finance for
- Your company's risk profile.

Often, if you only need a small amount of money, the best way to raise it is still to approach a bank or credit union with which you have already built up some relationship, whether on a personal basis or in a business capacity. The larger borrower may feel it worthwhile to seek professional help to put together a more sophisticated finance package. Your accountant is the best person to give you advice in this area and may have contacts that will ease your path.

DEALING WITH BANKS

Whatever the means of finance you adopt, you will almost certainly have to deal with a bank for your daily needs, if not for your whole financial package.

Banks are conservative institutions with fixed procedures. You will hopefully have laid a good foundation for your business relationship with the bank by the way in which you have handled your personal finances. In smaller towns, you may already be well-known to the bank manager.

However, the relationship that your business will have with the bank is likely to be different from any personal relationship that you had with them before. You probably had a regular, guaranteed income going into your personal account. You may have had an overdraft, a mortgage, or perhaps a personal loan, but unless you were careless with your finances, the risk of getting into serious financial difficulty was slight.

In dealing with you as a business, some of the personal element disappears from the relationship and is replaced by an "unknown risk" factor.

This risk factor stems from the following facts:

- The business is (usually) a separate legal entity from yourself and has no previous relationship with them

- The business has no guaranteed income (to the extent that your previous employment was secure, your personal income was "guaranteed" – it no longer is, and don't be surprised if that changes your bank manager's attitude towards your own personal account)

- A high proportion of new businesses fail or experience financial difficulty for a variety of reasons that are difficult to predict

- The amount you have borrowed from the bank – for which the bank manager is ultimately responsible to shareholders

– is likely to be much larger than any personal loan you have
had in the past.

The more of the unknown risk that you are able to eliminate for
the bank manager, the more the bank manager will be able to
do for you, both in terms of providing the money you want and,
in many cases, by giving you the benefit of their experience in
commenting on your plans.

The sort of information you can supply includes:

- A business plan, and updates when necessary
- Regular reports on the financial state of your business
- Information on a timely basis about any emerging problems
  that are going to result in late repayments, choked cash flow
  or a need for additional funding. A problem many bankers
  mention is that clients do not tell the bank what is wrong until
  the situation has grown so terrible that it is too late to correct
- Encouraging your banker to visit on-site to see for
  themselves.

It is also true that too many bankers put a lot of effort into the
initial analysis of a start-up loan, but fail to keep a close enough
eye on their investment thereafter – hence, at least some of the
losses on their small business lending the banks have
experienced in recent years.

You can gain the maximum amount of assistance from your
bank, not only by keeping the manager informed, but by
asking occasionally for an opinion of the financial outcome of a
certain course of action. You should certainly have a face-to-
face chat with your banker at least twice a year, and once a
quarter if you can arrange it.

Other Points

If your business plan is approved and you are awarded your
loan, overdraft etc.:

- Don't be afraid to negotiate for the best possible terms. Most
  entrepreneurs will haggle over the price of a computer but
  will accept a bank's terms like lambs

- It may be a good idea to have an accountant or solicitor look at any loan agreement before you sign it. They may spot gaps, or unnecessary clauses, and their professional backing will give you added confidence in arguing your case

- Make all payments on time and in the agreed manner. If, for some reason, you will be late with a repayment, at least warn the bank in advance and, if possible, discuss the reasons with your bank manager.

Security

Providing security – pledging assets against a loan in case you are unable to repay it – is an ongoing issue (and a most vexatious one) between the small business community and the banks. Small business owners often feel it unjust that a large corporation can borrow a huge amount of money often without providing security, while they have to produce security for small loans.

Ideally, bankers will look for security in the business itself – premises, equipment or stock – but often small businesses rent their premises, lease their equipment and hold limited quantities of stock. Business machinery is not always suitable as security because it may have a low resale value, or may be built into the building where it is housed, making it difficult for the bank to sell it, if necessary, without incurring substantial additional costs. For this reason, the bank will often seek personal guarantees, that is, the pledge of personal assets against business loans.

Beware of personal guarantees. The bank may ask for them, although the major banks have repeatedly told the **Small Firms Association** and **ISME** that they do not ask for guarantees "as a matter of course".

A personal guarantee is exactly that. You are guaranteeing that, if the company cannot pay back the loan to the bank, you will do so. *How?* Think about it before you sign.

Try to avoid giving a personal guarantee. It is probably better to borrow less, or pay a higher rate of interest, or use leasing as a means of financing specific fixed assets, than to be saddled with a personal guarantee.

As a condition of a loan, you may be asked by the bank not to pay any dividends or repay any other loans (especially ones you have made personally to the company) until the bank has been repaid. Though this is less onerous than a personal guarantee, only agree if these conditions are reasonable.

Check that whatever legal document you sign agrees with what you agreed with your bank manager. And, if the condition is for a limited period of time or until the loan is repaid, don't be shy about asking to be released from it when you have done your part and repaid the bank.

NON-EQUITY, NON-DEBT FINANCE

Although equity and debt represent the classic academic forms of financing, entrepreneurs are less concerned about such distinctions and are perfectly happy to consider sources of finance not listed in textbooks, for example:

- **Seed Capital Scheme** operated by the **Revenue Commissioners**, which can give you back some of your past five years' tax if you leave employment to start a new business
- Enterprise competition prizes, for example, **Coca-Cola National Enterprise Awards**, **Enterprise Ireland Student Enterprise Awards**, **Shell LiveWire** and **O2 Business & Professional Woman** awards.
- Grants from the organisations in *Chapters 5*, *6* and *7* (*Chapter 8* for Northern Ireland).

5: STATE SUPPORT FOR START-UPS

There is no shortage of State support in Ireland at present for start-ups and small businesses. Instead, the very number of agencies, nationally and locally, that co-exist (and, on occasion, appear to compete for the entrepreneur pool) gives rise to confusion. This chapter aims to help you through the maze to find the agency that can help your fledgling business to get off the ground.

But, first, a note about the changing nature of State support. When *Starting a Business in Ireland* was first published, the expressed priority of Irish enterprise support agencies was the creation of sustainable jobs. "How many jobs?" was the benchmark used to assess projects. To be sure, other criteria were used too, but jobs over-rode everything else.

Today, despite significant numbers still on the welfare rolls, the wheel has turned and employers now face difficulty in attracting and retaining staff. The growth (to quoted company status, in some cases) of several dozen major job recruitment agencies and hundreds of smaller agencies is testimony to the changed employment market. So, jobs can no longer act as the focus of State support.

Instead, competitiveness and capability are the watchwords, as we will see as we explore further into the maze. But, nonetheless, jobs are an important defining criterion.

Let's start with the basic geography of the landscape, as shown in the diagrams.

STATE SUPPORT FOR START-UPS (1)

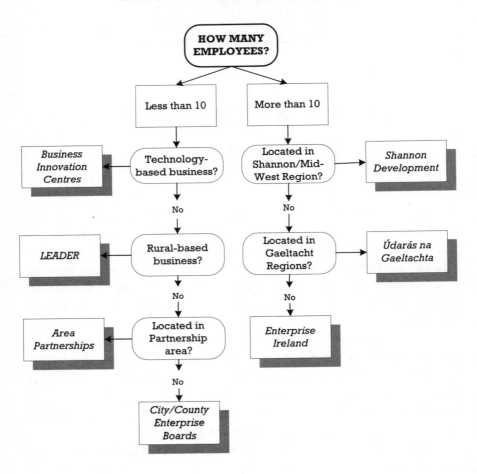

STATE SUPPORT FOR START-UPS (2)

Is the support/assistance you require related to . . .

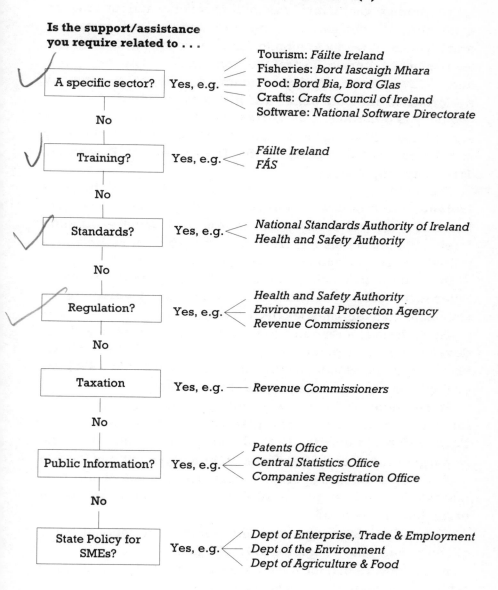

A specific sector? — Yes, e.g.
Tourism: *Fáilte Ireland*
Fisheries: *Bord Iascaigh Mhara*
Food: *Bord Bia, Bord Glas*
Crafts: *Crafts Council of Ireland*
Software: *National Software Directorate*

No

Training? — Yes, e.g.
Fáilte Ireland
FÁS

No

Standards? — Yes, e.g.
National Standards Authority of Ireland
Health and Safety Authority

No

Regulation? — Yes, e.g.
Health and Safety Authority
Environmental Protection Agency
Revenue Commissioners

No

Taxation — Yes, e.g. — *Revenue Commissioners*

No

Public Information? — Yes, e.g.
Patents Office
Central Statistics Office
Companies Registration Office

No

State Policy for SMEs? — Yes, e.g.
Dept of Enterprise, Trade & Employment
Dept of the Environment
Dept of Agriculture & Food

Overall responsibility for enterprise lies with the **Department of Enterprise, Trade and Employment**, which is responsible for promoting competitiveness in the economy and for creating a favourable climate for the creation of self-sustaining employment. It works to monitor and improve the environment for business by ensuring that the framework of law, regulation and Government policy promotes effective company performance and both public and business confidence.

Policy is determined by **Forfás**, which is the national Policy and Advisory Board for Enterprise, Trade, Science, Technology and Innovation. It reports to the Department of Enterprise, Trade and Employment.

The next layer consists of **IDA Ireland** and **Enterprise Ireland**, which both report to Forfás and implement policy set by it. IDA Ireland focuses on inwards investment – bringing foreign multinationals into Ireland – while Enterprise Ireland is tasked with supporting indigenous (local) businesses.

In the Mid-West, **Shannon Development** replaces Enterprise Ireland – likewise, **Údarás na Gaeltachta** in Gaeltacht (native Irish-speaking) areas.

Then, there is a range of specialist agencies, tasked with the development of a particular industry sector – **Fáilte Ireland**, for example, in relation to tourism – or specialist area – **FÁS**, for example, in relation to employment and training.

Some agencies have a regulatory role or monitoring role – for example, the **Environmental Protection Agency** or the **Food Safety Authority**. Not all the agencies report to the Department for Enterprise, Trade and Employment, but instead to the Government Department most closely associated with their work – for example, **Bord Bia** reports to the **Department of Agriculture & Food.**

The various State agencies all operate at a national level, although many have regional or local offices.

But, to ensure that local needs are met at local level, another range of agencies also exists. These include:

- **Area Partnerships**
- **Business Innovation Centres**
- **City / County Enterprise Boards**

- **Community Groups**
- **IRD (Integrated Rural Development) Companies**
- **LEADER + groups.**

And **County Development Boards** have been established in each county, and in the five cities, to ensure co-ordination of local resources towards enterprise development.

So, where should the potential entrepreneur begin to look for help? Indeed, what sort of help is available, and from whom?

Although there has been a huge shift away from a jobs focus among the enterprise support agencies, ironically the first question that you must answer to decide where you should look for help still relates to the employment potential of your new business (see diagram: *State support for Start-ups (1)*).

If, within three years or so of start-up, you are likely still to employ under 10 people, you should make your way to the **City /County Enterprise Boards** and/or the other local support agencies.

Once you can show that you are likely to employ more than 10 people within three years or so of start-up (and meet some other criteria, including demonstrating export potential), **Enterprise Ireland** (or **Shannon Development / Údarás na Gaeltachta,** as appropriate, depending on your location) will classify your business as a "high potential start-up" and take you under its wing.

So, let's start with Enterprise Ireland.

ENTERPRISE IRELAND

The best source for information on Enterprise Ireland and how it helps small businesses is its own excellent website, www.enterprise-ireland.com.

Enterprise Ireland helps manufacturing and internationally-traded services businesses that employ more than 10 people to grow internationally. The agency is primarily focused on providing advice and support to companies in three areas: technology innovation, business development and internationalisation. Its aim is to work in partnership with these businesses to develop a sustainable competitive advantage that leads to a significant increase in profitable sales, exports and employment.

Further, as the *Directory* shows, Enterprise Ireland is focused on commercialising research and working with clients to invest in R&D. It works to help companies build their capabilities in business strategy, productivity, human resource development and export marketing. Through its network of international offices, it aims to build awareness of market opportunities, access international buyers, and build overseas presence . It is also active in other areas that contribute towards an enterprise culture, for example, the Student Enterprise Awards, joint financing of venture capital funds, joint projects with other agencies (for example, its involvement with **Shannon Development** in the National Microelectronics Application Centre), development of enterprise centres and incubator units and projects such as the **National Software Directorate**.

Financial support is delivered across five main categories of support (for more information, see Enterprise Ireland's brochure on financial support):

- Exploring new opportunities: Preliminary funding to exploit new ideas for businesses with 10 to 250 staff or high potential start-ups (HPSUs)

- High potential start- ups: Such start-ups should have a technologically-innovative product, be export-oriented, expect rapid sales growth within 3 years exceeding € 1.3 m and have an experienced management team

- Existing company expansion, where more than 10 people are already employed

- Building international competitiveness: A new Competitiveness Fund for SMEs offers assistance to businesses with 10 to 250 staff, that have not received more than €200,000 in support over the past three years

- Research and development: Support under the Research technology and Innovation (RTI) Competitiveness Scheme for significant R&D projects.

Key considerations in evaluating a project application include:

- Need for financial assistance
- Value for money
- Commercial considerations
- Technical considerations
- Financial track record.

Accordingly, a strong well-thought-through business plan is essential (see **Chapter 3**).

Enterprise Ireland's financial support is now usually a mix of non-repayable grants and equity investment (in the form of preference and ordinary shares), seeking to optimise the level of repayability. The argument behind this move is that, since Enterprise Ireland's resources are limited, they must be wisely invested in businesses that give the best return. In addition, a measure of repayability provides resources that can be recycled into other companies later on.

Once a financial package has been agreed between a business and its Enterprise Ireland Development Adviser, the adviser sends out a letter of offer, after which legal documentation is prepared for signature by both parties.

In addition to financial support from its own resources, Enterprise Ireland can provide access to:

- Its register of "Business Angels" – private investors who usually take an active part in the business as well as an equity stake in return for their investment
- Venture capital funds, often in conjunction with other organisations.

SHANNON DEVELOPMENT

As noted earlier, in the Shannon Region, Shannon Development carries out many of the functions handled by **Enterprise Ireland** elsewhere. But don't make the mistake of dismissing Shannon Development as a regional clone of Enterprise Ireland – far from it! Shannon Development was promoting the Shannon Region, developing its infrastructure and sowing the seeds for the high-tech boom before enterprise development became fashionable. In partnership with the **University of Limerick**, it pioneered the **National Technology Park** as far back as 1980.

Shannon Development's technology locations now include the **National Technology Park Limerick**, Tipperary Technology Park, Birr Technology Centre and Information Age Park Ennis, each location also having an InnovationWorks facility for technology start-ups. These locations collectively form the **Shannon Development Knowledge Network**.

Shannon Development has developed its own range of venture capital funds, the **Limerick Food Centre** and other facilities that make the Shannon Region a prime technological base.

ÚDARÁS NA GAELTACHTA

As noted earlier, in the Gaeltacht areas, Údarás na Gaeltachta carries out the functions handled by **Enterprise Ireland** elsewhere. Again, Údarás is far from an Enterprise Ireland clone.

In addition to its enterprise development role, Údarás has a mission to preserve and promote the Irish language. Its remit spreads across a wide geographical area – from Macroom in Co Cork through Connemara and into Donegal – which adds to the complexity of its task.

If your new business does not qualify for Enterprise Ireland support, you should look to the **City / County Enterprise Boards** – and other local agencies – instead.

CITY/COUNTY ENTERPRISE BOARDS

City/County Enterprise Boards (CEBs) are arguably the most important source of assistance for a start-up business.

The 35 City and County Enterprise Boards (a list appears in the *Directory*) aim to encourage local initiative. Each is a company limited by guarantee, and has an executive staff, headed by a Chief Executive Officer. The 12 or 14 Board members are drawn from elected members of the local authority, the social partners, State agencies, ICTU, **IBEC**, the farming organisations, the county manager and community and other representatives.

The CEBs are responsible for enterprise development in areas not already covered by other State agencies – specifically, enterprises employing (or likely to employ) fewer than 10 persons and service businesses. Where CEBs receive applications for funding and advice that are more appropriate to the remit of other agencies (**Enterprise Ireland**, for example), they will re-direct them to the appropriate agency.

Each CEB has access to an Enterprise Fund, which assists small projects by way of revolving loans. However, note that CEBs do not normally consider proposals involving grant support in excess of €63,500 or projects with investment costs in excess of €127,000.

Project promoters must demonstrate that:

- There is a market for the proposed product/service
- Adequate overall finance will be available to fund the project
- They possess the management and technical capacity to implement the proposed project
- The projects will add value so as to generate income or supplement income for those involved, and will have the capacity to create new direct employment whether full-time, part-time or seasonal, or will, as a minimum, contribute directly to maintaining employment in existing small enterprises
- They will comply with State policies on tax clearance, the certification of subcontractors, and related matters.

The CEBs do not fund projects that are contrary to public policy, nor do they duplicate support for projects that would be eligible for assistance from any existing sectoral or grant structure, or which involve primary agricultural production.

The following grants are available:

- A maximum of 50% of the cost of capital and other investment, or €63,500 – whichever is the lesser

- A maximum of 50% (€5,100) (60%, €6,350 in BMW areas) of the cost of preparing a feasibility study/business plan.

Assistance is not confined to grants, since the CEBs have authority to provide loans and loan guarantees and to take equity stakes in businesses. In addition, the CEBs act as a source of advice and information. Many provide training and mentoring services.

In the period 2000-2006, under the National Development Plan, the focus of the CEBs has moved away from direct financial support towards a broader range of "soft" supports – training (in particular, management development), mentoring and other forms of assistance – designed to increase the survival rates of start-ups and small businesses.

Since the activities of each CEB are tailored to the needs of its local community, you should check with your local CEB for the full range of assistance available.

You should contact your local CEB before taking your project much beyond an initial stage. An initial informal discussion will quickly determine whether:

- The CEB can support your project
- A feasibility study grant may be available
- You should make changes to your project to make it acceptable to the CEB for assistance.

Your application should be on an official application form, obtainable from your local CEB (in some cases, from the CEB's website). Read the notes with the application form carefully before completing.

Almost always, except in cases where very small amounts of money are involved, CEBs will require a Business Plan with your application. A Feasibility Study Grant may help you to prepare one.

The CEBs also deliver the **Empower.ie** e-initiative, aimed at providing e-business services and incentives to micro-businesses.

CITY/COUNTY ENTERPRISE BOARDS – THE GRANT APPLICATION PROCESS*

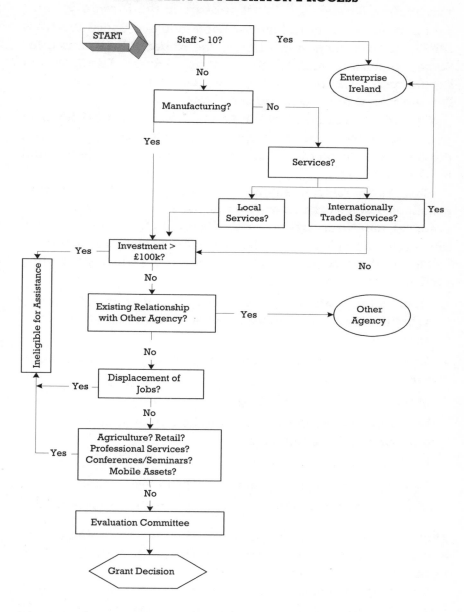

---

*   *Reproduced with permission from* Starting Your Own Business, *Oak Tree Press for the Department of Enterprise, Trade and Employment under Measure 4 of the Operational Programme for Small Business.*

AREA PARTNERSHIPS

The 38 *Area Partnerships* (a list appears in the **Directory**) were set up under the Programme for Economic and Social Progress (PESP) in 1993. Most now operate the National Programme for Social Inclusion and/or the National Rural Development Programme. Their funding is co-ordinated by **Area Development Management Ltd.**

One of the Partnerships' aims is to work at local level to generate more jobs through sustainable enterprises and through the promotion of local economic projects and initiatives.

Each Partnership is autonomous and agrees different work practices. Each works on an Area Action Plan for its own region. Practical measures are taken to discriminate in favour of the long-term unemployed and those who are socially excluded.

Partnerships provide support for unemployed people setting up their own business, through:

- Financial support, including non-repayable grants, interest subsidies, loan guarantees, small-scale investment and joint ventures
- Support for the development of business plans and business ideas
- Mentoring system, including sources of advice
- Provision of workspace, including help in obtaining enterprise incubation units
- Rent subsidies
- Marketing, including identifying gaps in the market
- Training and education in enterprise, with the support of **FÁS.**

There is variety in what each Partnership offers, and entrepreneurs should contact the Partnership in their area for further details.

The Area Allowance (Enterprise) is payable to people who live in a Partnership area, have been unemployed for 12 months or more and have been signing the Live Register, and who have a suitable enterprise/business project within a

Partnership area. The project must be one that does not displace existing enterprises/businesses, and must be approved by the Partnership. When approved, applicants will receive an allowance equivalent to their full unemployment payment, and will receive any secondary benefits to which they were entitled while in receipt of the unemployment payment. This will continue for 12 months, after which the applicant may be entitled for a further three years to the Back to Work Allowance operated by the **Department of Social and Family Affairs**. Apply directly to your local Partnership.

Note that some of the Partnerships also operate the **LEADER+** programme in their areas, or provide support for other enterprise activities of local benefit – for example, **South Kerry Development Partnership** hosts **Carréfour Cahirciveen**.

COMMUNITY GROUPS

A third strand of local enterprise support are the 35 Community Groups (a list appears in the *Directory*), established by **Area Development Management Ltd**, as part of its Local Development Programme. Their remit is more broadly focused on community development, although some have significant enterprise development activity.

As each Community Group identifies and responds to needs within its own communities, its activities are unique to its own situation. Entrepreneurs seeking assistance should make contact with their local Community Group to see whether and what help is available.

LEADER+

LEADER+ is an EU initiative for rural development (part-funded by the Irish Government) that enables groups in rural areas to implement their own multi-sectoral integrated plans for the development of their areas.

There are 35 LEADER+ groups and two collective bodies (a list appears in the *Directory*).

Typical LEADER activities include:

- Technical support to rural development including group administration
- Training and recruitment assistance
- Rural tourism
- Small firms, craft enterprises and local services
- Local exploitation and marketing of agricultural, horticultural, forest and fishery products
- Preservation and improvement of the environment and living conditions.

LEADER+ aims at encouraging and supporting high quality and ambitious integrated strategies for local rural development, putting a strong emphasis on co-operation and networking between rural areas.

Again, as each LEADER Group identifies and responds to needs within its own communities, its activities are unique to its own situation. Because of this, entrepreneurs seeking assistance should make contact with their local LEADER Group to see whether and what help is available.

BUSINESS INNOVATION CENTRES

The six Business Innovation Centres (a list appears in the *Directory*) are primarily targeted at technology-based businesses. They encourage and foster innovation in new or existing businesses, through services directed at the development of new ideas and their conversion into real business projects. As BIC support services may vary between centres, entrepreneurs seeking assistance should make contact with their local BIC to see whether and what help is available.

STATE AND SEMI-STATE AGENCIES

As mentioned earlier, there are a wide range of these agencies, covering a variety of roles and responsibilities and reporting to appropriate Government Departments.

Industry or sector-related bodies include:

- **Arts Council**
- **Bord Bia**
- **Bord Fáilte**
- **Bord Glas**
- **Bord Iascaigh Mhara**
- **CERT**
- **Coillte**
- **Crafts Council of Ireland**
- **ENFO**
- **FÁS**
- **Marine Institute**
- **Teagasc.**

Bodies that collect and disseminate information include:

- **Central Statistics Office**
- **Companies Registration Office**
- **Patents Office**
- **Registry of Business Names**
- **Registry of Friendly Societies.**

Bodies with a regulatory or monitoring role include:

- **Director of Consumer Affairs**
- **Environmental Protection Agency**
- **Food Safety Authority of Ireland**
- **Health & Safety Authority**
- **National Standards Authority of Ireland**
- **Revenue Commissioners.**

Bodies with a more general remit include:

- **Comhar**
- **Dublin Docklands Development Authority**
- **Government Publications.**

Details of all these bodies, their activities and links with other organisations are included in the Directory.

GOVERNMENT DEPARTMENTS

Not all the State agencies that have a role in enterprise development or support report to the **Department of Enterprise, Trade and Employment**.

Other Departments that support start-ups include:

- **Department of Agriculture & Food and Rural Development**
- **Department of Justice, Equality and Law Reform**
- **Department of Social and Family Affairs**
- **Department of the Environment & Local Government.**

Useful websites for information on Government Departments and their activities are:

- **www.ask-ireland.com**
- **www.irlgov.ie.**

In addition, **BASIS.ie** provides information on State support for business.

UNIVERSITIES & INSTITUTES OF TECHNOLOGY

A final source of State support for enterprise are the **Universities** and **Institutes of Technology**. All have Industrial Liaison Officers or Heads of External Services or Development whose task it is to build links between the college and the business world. In many cases, this results in the college carrying our technical research for a local business or commercialising through a local business the fruits of their own research. **TecNet** co-ordinates and manages this process for the ITs.

The Universities and Institutes of Technology also operate "Centres of Excellence" in a variety of disciplines. Some of these have grown into organisations of significant size, with profiles of their own, including:

- **Aquaculture Development Centre (University College Cork)**
- **BioResearch Ireland**
- **Bolton Trust (Dublin Institute of Technology)**
- **Centre for Entrepreneurial Studies (University of Limerick)**
- **Food Product Development Centre (DIT)**
- **Michael Smurfit Graduate School of Business Hatchery (UCD)**
- **National Institute of Transport and Logistics (DIT)**
- **National Microelectronics Research Centre (UCC)**
- **Project Development Centre (DIT)**
- **Regional Development Centre (Dundalk Institute of Technology)**
- **Small Business Institute (UL)**
- **Tower TCD Enterprise Centre (University of Dublin, Trinity College).**

ENTERPRISE LINK

And last, but definitely not least, **Enterprise Ireland** runs, on behalf of the Department for Enterprise, Trade and Employment, a service called **Enterprise Link** – a one-stop shop for information and direction.

If you're not sure where to look for information on what you want to do, if you want information on the availability of grants or just general guidance on starting a business, Enterprise Link – **1850 35 33 33** – is where you should begin.

SUPPORT BY CATEGORIES

The *Directory of Sources of Assistance* is organised by categories. To make it easy to find the appropriate source of State assistance, this section lists State organisations by the type of support they offer. See *Chapter 6* for explanations of the categories.

Business Angels

- See *Chapter 4*.

Business Plans

- **Area Partnership Companies** (some, not all)
- **Community Groups** (some, not all)
- **Crafts Council of Ireland**
- **Finglas Business Initiative**
- **PDC.**

Community & Rural Development

- **Area Partnership Companies**
- **Community Groups**
- **Department of Community, Rural & Gaeltacht Affairs**
- **FarmOptions.ie**
- **FÁS**
- **IRD Duhallow**
- **IRD Kiltimagh**
- **LEADER+**
- **National University of Ireland, Galway**
- **Rural Economy Research Centre**
- **Ruraldev-learningonline.ie**
- **Tipperary Institute**
- **Western Development Commission.**

Consulting

- **Aquaculture Development Centre**
- **Centre for Co-operative Studies**
- **Centre for Entrepreneurial Studies**
- **Coillte**
- **Dairy Products Research Centre**
- **Food Product Development Centre**
- **Institutes of Technology**
- **Irish Productivity Centre**
- **Limerick Food Centre**
- **Marketing Centre for Small Business**
- **National Food Centre**
- **National Institute for Transport and Logistics**
- **National Microelectronics Application Centre (MAC)**
- **National Microelectronics Research Centre**
- **Regional Development Centre**
- **Small Business Institute**
- **Teagasc**
- **TecNet**
- **Universities.**

Co-operatives

- **Centre for Co-operative Studies**
- **Registry of Friendly Societies.**

Cross-Border

- **Area Partnership Companies** (some, not all)
- **Centre for Cross-Border Studies**
- **City / County Enterprise Boards** (some, not all)
- **Community Groups** (some, not all)
- **LEADER+ Groups** (some, not all)

- **North East Enterprise Programme**
- **TradeNetIreland Ltd**

Debt

- **See** *Chapter 4.*

E-Business

- **City / County Enterprise Boards**
- **Empower.ie**
- **National Microelectronics Application Centre**
- **TradeNetIreland Ltd.**

Enterprise Support

- **Area Development Management.**

Equity

- **See** *Chapter 4.*

EU Information

- **National University of Ireland Galway.**

Grants

- **Area Partnership Companies** (some, not all)
- **Arts Council**
- **Bord Bia**
- **Bord Iascaigh Mhara**
- **Céim Enterprise Development Programme**
- **City / County Enterprise Boards**
- **Community Groups** (some, not all)
- **Department of Justice, Equality and Law Reform Equal Opportunities Childcare Section**

- **Department of Social and Family Affairs**
- **Empower.ie**
- **Enterprise Ireland**
- **Enterprise Programmes**
- **Fáilte Ireland**
- **FÁS**
- **Finglas Business Initiative**
- **IRD Duhallow**
- **LEADER+ Groups** (some, not all)
- **Michael Smurfit Graduate School of Business Hatchery**
- **Science Foundation Ireland**
- **Shannon Development**
- **Údarás na Gaeltachta.**

Incubator

- **See** *Chapter 1.*

Information (see also Chapter 2)

- **Bord Bia**
- **Bord Glas**
- **Bord Iascaigh Mhara**
- **Centre for Co-operative Studies**
- **Centre for Cross-Border Studies**
- **Centre for Entrepreneurial Studies**
- **Coford**
- **Coillte**
- **Companies Registration Office**
- **Department of Social and Family Affairs**
- **Director of Consumer Affairs**
- **ENFO**
- **Enterprise Ireland**

- Enterprise Link
- Environmental Protection Agency
- Excellence Ireland
- Fáilte Ireland
- Finglas Business Initiative
- Food Safety Authority of Ireland
- Government Publications
- Health & Safety Authority
- Institutes of Technology
- Limerick Food Centre
- Marine Institute
- National College of Ireland
- National Software Directorate
- National Standards Authority of Ireland
- Patents Office
- Regional Development Centre
- Registry of Business Names
- Rural Economy Research Centre
- Shannon Development
- Technology Transfer Initiative
- Údarás na Gaeltachta
- Universities.

Intellectual Property

- NovaUCD
- Patents Office.

Inwards Investment

- IDA Ireland.

Marketing

- **Bord Bia**
- **Bord Glas**
- **Bord Iascaigh Mhara**
- **Community Groups** (some, not all)
- **Crafts Council of Ireland**
- **Fáilte Ireland**
- **Limerick Food Centre**
- **Marketing Centre for Small Business**
- **TradeNetIreland Ltd**
- **University of Limerick.**

Mentoring

- **Area Partnership Companies**
- **Céim Enterprise Development Programme**
- **City / County Enterprise Boards**
- **Community Groups** (some, not all)
- **Crafts Council of Ireland**
- **Dun Laoire Institute of Art, Design and Technology**
- **Empower.ie**
- **Enterprise Ireland**
- **Enterprise Programmes**
- **Finglas Business Initiative**
- **InnovationWorks**
- **LEADER+ Groups** (some, not all)
- **Mentor Network**
- **Shannon Development**
- **Technology Transfer Initiative**
- **Tipperary Institute**
- **Údarás na Gaeltachta.**

Networking

- **Area Partnership Companies**
- **Dun Laoire Institute of Art, Design and Technology**
- **National Software Directorate.**

Policy

- **Borders Midlands and Western Regional Assembly**
- **Centre for Cross-Border Studies**
- **Comhar**
- **County Development Boards**
- **Department of Agriculture and Food**
- **Department of Community, Rural & Gaeltacht Affairs**
- **Department of Enterprise, Trade and Employment**
- **Department of Justice, Equality and Law Reform**
- **Department of the Environment and Local Government**
- **Dublin Docklands Development Authority**
- **Forfás**
- **Irish Council for Science, Technology & Innovation**
- **Western Development Commission.**

Publications

- **Central Statistics Office**
- **City / County Enterprise Boards** (some, not all)
- **Crafts Council of Ireland**
- **Government Publications**
- **Health & Safety Authority**
- **Institute of Public Administration**
- **Revenue Commissioners.**

R & D

- **Aquaculture Development Centre**

- **BioResearch Ireland**
- **Dairy Products Research Centre**
- **Food Product Development Centre**
- **InnovationWorks**
- **Institutes of Technology**
- **Limerick Food Centre**
- **Marine Institute**
- **National Food Centre**
- **National Microelectronics Application Centre**
- **National Microelectronics Research Centre**
- **Regional Development Centre**
- **Technology Transfer Initiative**
- **TecNet**
- **Universities.**

Regulator & Standards

- **Bord Bia**
- **Bord Glas**
- **Bord Iascaigh Mhara**
- **Companies Registration Office**
- **Data Protection Commissioner**
- **Director of Consumer Affairs**
- **Environmental Protection Agency**
- **Excellence Ireland**
- **Food Safety Authority of Ireland**
- **Health & Safety Authority**
- **National Standards Authority of Ireland**
- **Registry of Business Names**
- **Registry of Friendly Societies**
- **Revenue Commissioners**

Social Economy

- **Area Partnership Companies** (some, not all)
- **Community Groups** (some, not all)
- **FÁS.**

Start-up Training

- See *Chapter 1.*

Training

- **Aquaculture Development Centre**
- **Area Partnership Companies** (some, not all)
- **Bord Iascaigh Mhara**
- **Centre for Co-operative Studies**
- **Centre for Entrepreneurial Studies**
- **City / County Enterprise Boards**
- **City of Dublin Vocational Education Committee**
- **Community Groups** (some, not all)
- **Crafts Council of Ireland**
- **Dun Laoire Institute of Art, Design and Technology**
- **Empower.ie**
- **Fáilte Ireland**
- **FÁS**
- **Food Product Development Centre**
- **Health & Safety Authority**
- **InnovationWorks**
- **Institutes of Technology**
- **IRD Duhallow**
- **LEADER+ Groups** (some, not all)
- **Limerick Food Centre**
- **Liveandlearn.ie**
- **LiveandLearn.ie**

- **LouthCraftmark.com**
- **National College of Ireland**
- **National Food Centre**
- **National Institute for Transport and Logistics**
- **National Microelectronics Research Centre**
- **National Safety Council**
- **Regional Development Centre**
- **Ruraldev-learningonline.ie**
- **Shannon Development**
- **Sustainable Energy Ireland**
- **Teagasc**
- **Tipperary Institute**
- **Údarás na Gaeltachta**
- **World Class Rural Cluster**
- **Universities.**

Tourism Development

- **Area Partnership Companies** (some, not all)
- **Community Groups** (some, not all)
- **Fáilte Ireland**
- **LEADER+ Groups** (some, not all).

Website

- **See Chapter 2.**

Women

- **Area Partnership Companies** (some, not all)
- **City / County Enterprise Boards** (some, not all).

Workspace

- **Area Partnership Companies** (some, not all)

- **Community Groups** (some, not all)
- **Digital Hub**
- **Innovation Works**
- **Institutes of Technology** (some, not all)
- **Shannon Development / Shannon Development Knowledge Network.**

6: PRIVATE SECTOR SUPPORT FOR START-UPS

If confusion exists in the State sector due to the number of organisations that provide support for enterprise, it's nothing compared to the private sector, where the range of organisations – and the breadth of their activities – is even greater and lacks any form of co-ordination.

The simplest way through this maze is to identify the main private sector enterprise support organisations by the type of support they provide (clearly, some fit into more than one category).

The *Directory of Sources of Assistance* provides details on each of the organisations included. This chapter explains what the organisations within each category do in broad terms.

The chapter should be read with the other chapters for a full understanding of the sources of assistance available.

ACCOUNTANTS

Accountants provide a variety of services to start-ups. They can assist and advise you on:

- The legal structure, taxation and accounting systems suitable for your business
- Business planning (though you should not let your accountant write your business plan – after all, it's your plan, not theirs!)
- Fund-raising and/or funding applications to banks, venture capitalists and grant-giving organisations.

Accountants are usually members of one or other of a small number of professional bodies, which include:

- **Association of Chartered Certified Accountants**
- **Chartered Institute of Management Accountants**
- **Institute of Certified Public Accountants in Ireland**
- **Institute of Chartered Accountants in Ireland.**

These bodies will help you find a suitable accountant from among their members.

Accounting firms with particular expertise in small business issues include:

- **BDO Simpson Xavier**
- **Big Red Book**
- **Crowleys DFK**
- **Deloitte & Touche**
- **Ernst & Young**
- **FGS**
- **Gahan & Co**
- **JPA Brenson Lawlor**
- **KPMG**
- **Mazars**
- **O'Connor, Leddy & Holmes**
- **OSK Accountants & Business Consultants**

- **PricewaterhouseCoopers.**
- **Sage Ireland**

BUSINESS ANGELS

"Business Angels" take their name from the world of theatre, where private investors who back shows in the early stages when success is less than certain are known as "angels". Business angels are usually experienced businesspeople, willing to invest both money and time in a start-up with potential. Note that they are rarely passive investors.

See *Chapter 4*.

BUSINESS PLANS

As *Chapter 3* makes clear, a business plan is essential for every start-up, regardless of its size, potential or the background of the promoters.

The *Directory* lists organisations that assist entrepreneurs, directly or indirectly, with developing a business plan or an application (to themselves or a third party) for finance. (The *caveats* already expressed about doing it yourself apply.) These organisations include:

- **Action Tallaght**
- **Ascend**
- **Bplans.org.uk**
- **Community Enterprise Society Ltd**
- **Innovation Partners**
- **Invest-Tech**
- **Liffey Trust**
- **Madden Consultants**
- **O'Connor, Leddy & Holmes**
- **Palo Alto Software UK**
- **PricewaterhouseCoopers**

Many of the enterprise support agencies provide grants or other support for feasibility studies – a good test-bed for a business plan.

BUSINESS SALES/PURCHASES

As explained earlier, it's not necessary to start a business from scratch yourself – sometimes there are opportunities to buy an existing business or to buy into a management role in one.

The Directory lists organisations that provide a service to buyer or seller – if they're not of interest to you now at start-up, they may be when you're looking for an exit strategy!

See *Chapter 1*.

COMMUNITY & RURAL DEVELOPMENT

A sizeable element of the support for enterprise in Ireland comes from efforts towards community development, particularly where these are aimed at replacing industries that have closed down or relocated (or reducing dependence on them in advance).

The Directory lists organisations active in this area, as well as those active more generally in rural development, including:

- **Ardee Community Development Company Ltd**
- **Business in the Community Ireland**
- **Clann Credo**
- **Community Enterprise Society Ltd**
- **Community Exchange**
- **Connemara West plc**
- **Co-operation Ireland**
- **Doonbeg Community Development Ltd**
- **East Mayo Forestry Co-operative**
- **Foundation for Investing in Communities**
- **International Fund for Ireland**
- **Limerick Enterprise Network**

- **Macra na Feirme**
- **Partas**
- **Society of Saint Vincent de Paul**
- **Tyrone Donegal Partnership.**

Guidance in business planning in this increasingly important area is provided in *Community Enterprise: A Business Planning Workbook for the Social Economy* (Ron Immink & Pat Kearney, Oak Tree Press).

COMPETITIONS

In addition to the student-focused enterprise competitions identified in **Chapter 1**, which are aimed at introducing participants to the world of business, the **Directory** identifies a number of competitions and awards aimed at real-world entrepreneurs, including:

- **Coca-Cola National Enterprise Awards**
- **Entrepreneur of the Year Awards**
- **Global Technology, Entrepreneurship and Commercialisation Business Plan Competition**
- **Mallinn / Invent Start-up Awards**
- **O2 Business & Professional Woman 2003**
- **Rolex Awards for Enterprise**
- **Shell LiveWire**
- **Young Entrepreneurs Scheme.**

If you're eligible, it's often worth applying. Even if you don't win (and not everyone can, obviously), you often have to go through a useful screening/review process that can help you to identify ways in which you can improve aspects of your business. You also can make useful contacts among the other participants or the judges. And, if you do win, there's usually good publicity to be gained from an award, if you're ready to capitalise on it – and the prize money never goes astray either!

CONSULTING

As the ***Directory*** shows, there are dozens – even hundreds – of consultants with a bewildering array of expertise, available to help you to develop your start-up business and help it grow.

Use consultants carefully. Know what you want them to do, when, and at what cost to you. Make sure they deliver before you sign off and pay their fees. Look for the consultant who thinks long-term – and is prepared to invest in you and your future success. But recognise that consultants must eat too – if you want work done, you must be prepared to pay for it. Free advice will not take you far!

Consultants with experience of value to start-ups include:

- **Action Tallaght**
- **Amárach Consulting**
- **Ascend**
- **Aspire! Marketing Consultants**
- **Ballyhoo Entrepreneurial Consulting**
- **Binary Partners**
- **Century Management Ltd**
- **Chartered Institute of Logistics and Transport**
- **Chartered Institute of Management Accountants**
- **Comerford Technology Management Ltd**
- **Competitive Business Intelligence**
- **Crowleys DFK**
- **Darlington Consulting**
- **Deloitte & Touche**
- **Envision Marketing Consultants**
- **Ernst & Young**
- **FGS**
- **First Point Business Development Consultancy Ltd**
- **Gorann Ltd**
- **HotOrigin**
- **Innovation Partners**

- **Institute of Business Advisers**
- **Invest-tech**
- **KPMG**
- **Liffey Trust**
- **Madden Consultants**
- **Mazars**
- **Moorepark Technology Ltd**
- **OSK Accountants & Business Consultants**
- **Partas**
- **PricewaterhouseCoopers**
- **Profiles Ireland**
- **TIU Technology Investment & Underwriting**
- **TSA Consultancy**
- **Unique Perspectives Ltd**
- **Xanthal Ltd.**

CO-OPERATIVES

As Chapter 9 explains, there are a variety of legal structures that you can choose when establishing your new business. One of these is the co-operative, for a democratically controlled business.

The Directory identifies organisations that promote the co-operative concept and/or assist in their formation, including:

- **Co-operative Development Society Ltd**
- **Irish Co-operative Organisation Society Ltd**
- **National Association of Building Co-operatives Ltd**
- **Tallaght Trust Fund.**

CROSS-BORDER

A growing number of organisations are active in this area – good news for entrepreneurs and for the Border regions generally. If you live in the Border regions, or are willing to relocate there, check with these organisations about the support they offer:

- **Tyrone Donegal Partnership.**

DEBT

See *Chapter 4*.

E-BUSINESSS

The bloom has definitely faded from the e-business "gold rush" that marked the end of the millennium. A sad, but harsh truth was learnt by the early e-entrepreneurs (and their investors) – that you have to make a profit to stay in business and that profits require a business model that works (back to planning!).

Nonetheless, technology is changing the way we live and do business. The *Directory* lists initiatives and sources of advice or assistance in this area. Many of these are aimed at providing small businesses with the tools and techniques to succeed in this new age, including:

- **EBusinessLex.net**
- **First Tuesday**
- **IE Domain Registry Ltd**
- **Investnet Ltd**
- **Irish Internet Association**
- **Telework Ireland.**

ENTERPRISE SUPPORT

A "catch-all" category for organisations whose activities cannot be captured elsewhere, including:

- **Bolton Trust.**

EQUITY

See **Chapter 4**.

FRANCHISES

Organisations active in the franchise area include:

- **FranchiseDirect.com**
- **Irish Franchise Association**
- **Ulster Bank.**

GRANTS

Once the focus of would-be entrepreneurs' attention, now there is a realisation by both entrepreneurs and support organisations that "soft supports" can be more valuable even than cash.

Sources of grants include:

- **Co-operation Ireland**
- **Fingal Employees Youth Business Fund.**

See also **Chapter 5**.

INCUBATOR

See **Chapter 1**.

INFORMATION

Information is critical to a good business plan and a well-planned and managed start-up. Many potential sources of market research information were identified in **Chapters 2** and **5**. The **Directory** expands on these, giving you a headstart in finding out what you need to know. The other organisations listed include:

- **Action Tallaght**
- **Ardee Business Park**
- **Ardee Community Development Company Ltd**
- **Balbriggan Enterprise Development Group**
- **Boardroom Centre**
- **Community Enterprise Society Ltd**
- **Company Formations International Ltd**
- **Competitive Business Intelligence**
- **Co-operative Development Society Ltd**
- **EBusinesslex.net**
- **EquityNetwork**
- **IBEC**
- **Inner City Enterprise**
- **Invest-Tech**
- **Irish Co-operative Organisation Society Ltd**
- **Kompass Ireland**
- **Legal-Island**
- **MovetoIreland.com**
- **Society of Saint Vincent de Paul**
- **Telework Ireland.**

Recognise that some of these organisations are member-based and restrict their services to members only, or charge fees to non-members. Most of the organisations listed are key players in their own industries, with a good finger on what's happening – it may be well worth your while paying for their specialist insight.

INTELLECTUAL PROPERTY

Intellectual property is a catch-all phrase used to describe the various rights conferred by patents, trade marks, copyright, etc. Under Irish, UK and EU law, you can protect your "rights" in inventions and so on (but not in ideas alone).

You can then exploit these rights yourself or license or sell them to others – this is called "technology transfer". Often technology transfer works on an inwards basis, with Irish businesses acquiring rights to use technologies developed elsewhere.

It's a specialist area in which you should take advice and proceed with caution.

Organisations that can assist you here include:

- **Cruickshank & Co**
- **FR Kelly & Co**
- **Inventors Garage**
- **MacLachlan & Donaldson**
- **Tomkins.**

INWARDS INVESTMENT

This is primarily a State responsibility. However, a number of organisations provide information of general use, including:

- **MovetoIreland.com.**

LEGAL

Legal advice can be critical for a start-up. Sources include:

- **Action Tallaght**
- **BorderBizLaw.com**
- **EbusinessLex.net**
- **Law Society of Ireland**
- **Legal-Island.**

MARKETING

A consistent failing of Irish business has been – and still is – its lack of emphasis on, and commitment to, marketing.

This is changing as is shown by the number of organisations committed to helping small businesses succeed at marketing. Here the *Directory* lists both consultants and support agencies with programmes to support small businesses' own marketing efforts, including:

- **Action Tallaght**
- **Aspire! Marketing Consultants**
- **Century Management Ltd**
- **Company Formations International Ltd**
- **Envision Marketing Consultants**
- **Guaranteed Irish**
- **Irish Direct Marketing Association**
- **Kompass Ireland**
- **Liffey Trust**
- **Madden Consultants**
- **Marketing Institute of Ireland**
- **Sales Institute of Ireland**
- **Unique Perspectives Ltd**
- **Xanthal Ltd.**

MENTORING

A key support offered by most agencies now is mentoring – the provision of an experienced businessperson with skills, be they specialist or general, appropriate to the needs of the mentored business/entrepreneur at the time.

Mentors are neither consultants nor executives. They do not carry the burden of responsibility involved in running a business, nor are they paid to do a specific task or job in it. Their role is to share their experience – all mentors are experienced businesspeople – to assist the entrepreneur in coming to their own decisions.

The Directory lists agencies that provide mentoring, often a part of a broader package of supports, including:

- **Chartered Institute of Management Accountants**

- **Coca-Cola National Enterprise Awards**
- **Institute of Business Advisers**
- **ManagementDirect.com**
- **Mentor Capital Partners Limited Partnership**
- **Partas.**

How mentoring works – both from the perspective of the mentor and the mentoree – is explained in *Mentoring Entrepreneurs: Shared Wisdom through Experience* (Brian Doyle & N Vincent O Neill, Oak Tree Press), which is based on the experience of the **Mentor Network**.

NETWORKING

The Directory identifies a large number of organisations that provide networking opportunities or facilitate them – sometimes for members only, since many of these are the same key industry player organisations that were a source of market research and other information earlier.

If you're not out and about meeting people for some part of your time, you're probably missing opportunities to meet potential customers, to find out what competitors are up to, or to spot new business leads.

Networking opportunities include:

- **Chambers of Commerce of Ireland**
- **Community Exchange**
- **CreativeIreland.com**
- **First Tuesday**
- **Institute of Directors in Ireland**
- **Institute of Industrial Engineers**
- **Institute of Leisure & Amenity Management**
- **Institution of Engineers in Ireland**
- **Inventors Association of Ireland**
- **Investnet Ltd**
- **Irish Computer Society**

- **Irish Countrywomen's Association**
- **Irish Direct Marketing Association**
- **Irish Exporters Association**
- **Irish Farmers Association**
- **Irish Institute for Purchasing & Materials Management**
- **Irish Institute for Training & Development**
- **Irish Internet Association**
- **Irish Management Institute**
- **Irish Research Scientists' Association**
- **Irish Retail Newsagents Association**
- **Irish Road Haulage Association**
- **Irish Small & Medium Enterprises Association**
- **Irish Software Association**
- **Irish Wind Energy Association**
- **Macra na Feirme**
- **National Federation of Business & Professional Women's Clubs, Ireland**
- **Network Ireland**
- **PLATO**
- **Restaurants Association of Ireland**
- **Sales Institute of Ireland**
- **Small Firms Association**
- **Technology West**
- **Telework Ireland**
- **Women in Technology & Science.**

PUBLICATIONS

As a writer and publisher (and more recently, a computer devotee), publications are always of interest to me personally. But they should be of interest to you too – as a source of information, a replacement for training (some, not all), and as a means of developing yourself.

I have identified in the *Directory* those I think of especial interest to the Irish enterprise situation, including:

- **AIB Bank Enterprise Development Bureau**
- **Amárach Consulting**
- **Association of Advertisers in Ireland**
- **Century Management Ltd**
- **Firsthand Publishing Ltd**
- **Golden Pages**
- **Initiative**
- **Irish Entrepreneur**
- **Irish Small & Medium Enterprises Association**
- **Kompass Ireland**
- **Oak Tree Press**
- **PricewaterhouseCoopers**
- **Small Firms Association**
- **Sunday Business Post**
- **Telework Ireland**
- **Ulster Bank.**

Even allowing for a natural bias here, it's fair to say that **Oak Tree Press** has a special focus on publications and resources of value and interest to the owner/managers of micro and small businesses – all available from **www.oaktreepress.com**.

R & D

Critical to the development of most small businesses, even if not always identified as such. Support is available from a range of organisations, including:

- **Comerford Technology Management Ltd**
- **Innovation Partners**
- **Innovator**
- **Inventors Association of Ireland**
- **Inventors Garage**

- **MediaLab Europe**
- **Moorepark Technology Ltd.**

REGULATORS & STANDARDS

Neither is the most popular of subjects, but both are equally necessary. In Ireland, by and large, both regulators and standards-setters are approachable and informative – even the Revenue Commissioners provide early assistance and encouragement towards developing the habit of compliance rather than merely enforcing it by rule of law subsequently. The Directory identifies key regulatory and standards-setting bodies of interest and relevance to start-ups and small businesses, including:

- **Guaranteed Irish Ltd**
- **IE Domain Registry Ltd**
- **National Guild of Master Craftsmen**
- **Register of Electrical Contractors of Ireland.**

SOCIAL ECONOMY

The Directory identifies organisations that support "social economy" or "third economy" approaches to enterprise, including:

- **Ardee Community Development Company Ltd**
- **Clann Credo**
- **Community Exchange**
- **TSA Consultancy.**

START-UP TRAINING

See *Chapter 1*.

TOURISM DEVELOPMENT

A number of organisations are active in this area, including:
- **Irish Hotels Federation**
- **Irish Travel Agents Association.**

TRAINING

It's not enough to start a business – in some ways, that's the easy bit! – you have to keep it going. And as you do, you will discover that you need new skills or to develop existing skills further – you need training on an on-going basis.

Most professional bodies have long since identified this requirement and have made some quantum of continuing training a condition of membership. You could do worse than adopt the same high standards for your new profession of entrepreneur. And the *Directory* will help with some useful sources, depending on your own specific needs and circumstances.

Training organisations include:
- **Action Clondalkin Enterprise**
- **Ardee Business Park**
- **Boardroom Centre**
- **Century Management Ltd**
- **Chartered Institute of Logistics & Transport**
- **Chartered Institute of Personnel & Development**
- **Competitive Business Intelligence**
- **Darlington Consulting**
- **Excellerator**
- **First Point Business Development Consultancy Ltd**
- **Gahan & Co**
- **Innovation Partners**
- **Institute of Business Advisers**
- **Institute of Directors in Ireland**

- **Institute of Leisure & Amenity Management**
- **Institute of Project Management**
- **Irish Countrywomen's Association**
- **Irish Direct Marketing Association**
- **Irish Exporters Association**
- **Irish Institute for Purchasing & Materials Management**
- **Irish Institute for Training & Development**
- **Irish Institute of Credit Management**
- **Irish Management Institute**
- **Irish Small & Medium Enterprises Association**
- **Madden Consultants**
- **Marketing Institute of Ireland**
- **Moran & Associates**
- **Network Ireland**
- **Oak Tree Press**
- **Optimum Results ltd**
- **Organic College**
- **Partas**
- **PLATO**
- **Sales Institute of Ireland**
- **Small Firms Association**
- **TSA Consultancy**
- **Western Management Centre.**

WEBSITES

- **See *Chapter 2.***

WOMEN

Surprisingly, or perhaps not depending on your point of view, the research identified relatively few organisations that specifically catered for the needs of women entrepreneurs. Those that were identified are listed in the Directory, including:

- **Irish Countrywomen's Association**
- **National Federation of Business & Professional Women's Clubs, Ireland**
- **Network Ireland**
- **O2 Business & Professional Woman 2003**
- **Women in Technology & Science.**

WORKSPACE

A number of organisations provide (often as part of a support package) workspace tailored to the needs of a start-up. These include:

- **Action Clondalkin Enterprise**
- **Base Centre**
- **Brookfield Enterprise Centre**
- **Crosbie Business Centre**
- **Docklands Innovation Park**
- **Dun Laoire Enterprise Centre**
- **Partas**
- **Premier Business Centres**
- **Richmond Business Campus**
- **SPADE Enterprise Centre**

YOUNG ENTERPRISE

See *Chapter 1*.

7: EU SUPPORT FOR START-UPS

Support from the European Union for start-ups and small businesses in Ireland comes in three forms:

- EU Institutions
- Direct
- Indirect.

EU INSTITUTIONS

Some EU institutions provide assistance direct to Irish start-up entrepreneurs – mainly in the form of information or policy. These institutions include:

- **Enterprise DG**
- **Europa**
- **European Commission.**

DIRECT ASSISTANCE

This is usually in the form of information and guidance through EU-funded agencies such as:

- **Business Innovation Centres**
- **Carréfours**

- **European Info Centres**
- **Info Point Europe**
- **Innovation Relay Centres.**

INDIRECT ASSISTANCE

This is delivered indirectly through State and other agencies, for example:

- The Global Loan Facility for SMEs from the **European Investment Bank,** which cannot be accessed by businesses directly but is made available through the major banks
- The **European Investment Fund**, which has invested in a number of Irish venture capital funds
- **EU Structural Funds**, which support Government spending.

Full information on the European Union and its support for enterprise is available on the **Europa** website.

SUPPORT BY CATEGORY

EU support by category for start-ups and small businesses in Ireland includes:

Business Plans

- **Business Innovation Centres.**

Community & Rural Development

- **Carréfours.**

EU Information

- **Carréfours**
- **Enterprise DG**
- **Euro Info Centres**
- **Europa**

- **European Commission**
- **European Investment Bank**
- **European Investment Fund**
- **Info Point Europe.**

Information

- **Business Innovation Centres.**

Marketing

- **Business Innovation Centres.**

Policy

- **Enterprise DG.**

R & D

- **Innovation Relay Centre for Ireland**
- **Innovation Relay Centre for Northern Ireland**

Training

- **Business Innovation Centres.**

Workspace

- **Business Innovation Centres.**

8: SUPPORTS FOR START-UPS IN NORTHERN IRELAND

This chapter identifies the organisations and agencies responsible involved in supporting start-ups and small businesses in Northern Ireland. You should read *Chapter 6* for information on the various categories and earlier chapters, as indicated, for additional entries in some categories.

GOVERNMENT SUPPORT

The Government Department responsible for enterprise in Northern Ireland is the **Department of Enterprise, Trade & Investment**. As with the **Department of Enterprise, Trade and Employment** in the Republic, much of DETI's work is in creating an environment in which enterprise can flourish.

Implementation is handled primarily by **Invest Northern Ireland**.

OTHER STATE SUPPORT

Other State support in Northern Ireland is provided by:
- **Companies Registry**

- Department of Agriculture & Rural Development
- Government Direct for Business
- Health & Safety Executive for Northern Ireland
- HM Customs & Excise
- Inland Revenue
- Northern Ireland Statistics and Research Agency
- Northern Ireland Tourist Board
- Rural Development Council
- Social Economy Agency.

ACCOUNTANTS

- Management Training & Finance Group.

BUSINESS ANGELS

- See *Chapter 4*.

BUSINESS PLANS

- Bplans.org.uk
- Noribic (Business Innovation Centre, Derry)
- Ormeau Business Park
- Palo Alto Software UK
- Social Economy Agency.

COMMUNITY & RURAL DEVELOPMENT

- Business Results Ltd
- Co-operation Ireland
- Creggan Enterprises Ltd
- Department of Agriculture & Rural Development

- **Enniskillen Campus, College of Agriculture, Food & Rural Development, Dept. of Agriculture & Rural Development**
- **Enterprise Agencies / Centres** (some, not all)
- **Flax Trust**
- **Greenmount Campus, College of Agriculture, Food & Rural Development, Dept. of Agriculture & Rural Development**
- **LEADER+ Northern Ireland**
- **Rural Community Network**
- **Rural Development Council**
- **RuralSupport.org.uk**
- **Social Economy Agency**
- **Triodos Bank**
- **Tyrone Donegal Partnership**
- **Ulster Community Investment Trust**
- **University of Ulster**
- **University of Ulster, Regional Development Services.**

COMPETITIONS

- **Global Technology, Entrepreneurship & Commercialisation Business Plan Competition**
- **Rolex Awards for Enterprise.**

CONSULTING

- **Business Results Ltd**
- **Enterprise Agencies / Centres** (some, not all)
- **First Point Business Development Consultancy Ltd**
- **Manufacturing Technology Partnership**
- **University of Ulster**
- **University of Ulster, Office of Innovation & Enterprise.**

CO-OPERATIVES

- Social Economy Agency.

CROSS-BORDER

- Centre for Cross-Border Studies
- InterTradeIreland Acumen
- Newry & Mourne Enterprise Agency
- TradeNetIreland Ltd
- Tyrone Donegal Partnership.

DEBT

- See *Chapter 4*.

E-BUSINESS

- Synergy eBusiness Incubator.

EQUITY

- See *Chapter 4*.

EU INFORMATION

- Carréfour Ulster
- Euro Info Centre Belfast
- Northern Ireland Centre in Europe.

FRANCHISES

- Ulster Bank.

GRANTS

- Arts Council of Northern Ireland
- Business Innovation Link
- Co-operation Ireland
- Creativity Seed Fund
- InterTradeIreland Acumen
- Invest Northern Ireland
- Noribic (Business Innovation Centre, Derry)
- Northern Ireland Tourist Board
- Prince's Trust Northern Ireland.

INCUBATOR

- See *Chapter 1*.

INFORMATION

- Belfast Business Library
- Belfast First Stop Business Shop Ltd
- Centre for Cross-Border Studies
- ChooseEnterprise.com
- Companies Registry
- Enniskillen Campus, College of Agriculture, Food & Rural Development, Dept. of Agriculture & Rural Development
- Enterprise Agencies / Centres
- Greenmount Campus, College of Agriculture, Food & Rural Development, Dept. of Agriculture & Rural Development
- Health & Safety Executive for Northern Ireland
- InterTradeIreland
- Invest Northern Ireland

- Legal-Island
- Loughry Campus, College of Agriculture, Food & Rural Development, Dept. of Agriculture & Rural Development
- Noribic (Business Innovation Centre, Derry)
- Northern Ireland Centre for Entrepreneurship
- Northern Ireland Statistics & Research Agency
- Northern Ireland Tourist Board
- Rural Community Network
- Social Economy Agency
- Trading Standards Service Northern Ireland
- University of Ulster, Regional Development Services.

INWARDS INVESTMENT

- Invest Northern Ireland
- Newry & Mourne Enterprise Agency.

LEGAL

- BorderBizLaw.com
- Law Society of Northern Ireland
- Legal-Island.

MARKETING

- Enterprise Agencies / Centres (some, not all)
- Management Training & Finance Group
- Noribic (Business Innovation Centre, Derry)
- Northern Ireland Food & Drink Association
- Northern Ireland Tourist Board.

MENTORING

- **Institute of Business Advisers**
- **Ormeau Business Park**
- **Prince's Trust Northern Ireland**
- **Workspace (Draperstown) Ltd.**

NETWORKING

- **Irish Management Institute (Northern Ireland) Ltd**
- **Momentum, the Northern Ireland ICT Federation**
- **Northern Ireland Chamber of Commerce & Industry**
- **Northern Ireland Food & Drink Association**
- **Rural Community Network.**

POLICY

- **Centre for Cross-Border Studies**
- **Department for Employment & Learning**
- **Department of Agriculture & Rural Development**
- **Department of Enterprise, Trade & Investment**
- **InterTradeIreland.**

PUBLICATIONS

- **Health & Safety Executive for Northern Ireland**
- **Inland Revenue**
- **Ulster Bank.**

R & D

- **Business Innovation Link.**

- Loughry Campus, College of Agriculture, Food & Rural Development, Dept. of Agriculture & Rural Development
- Manufacturing Technology Partnership
- University of Ulster
- University of Ulster, Office of Innovation & Enterprise
- UUTech Ltd.

REGULATOR & STANDARDS

- Companies Registry
- General Consumer Council for Northern Ireland
- Health & Safety Executive for Northern Ireland
- HM Customs & Excise
- Inland Revenue
- Investors in People
- Trading Standards Service Northern Ireland.

SOCIAL ECONOMY

- Creggan Enterprises Ltd
- Glenwood Enterprises Ltd
- Social Economy Agency
- Ulster Community Investment Trust.

START-UP TRAINING

- See *Chapter 1*.

TOURISM DEVELOPMENT

- Northern Ireland Tourism Board.

TRAINING

- **Department of Employment & Learning**
- **Enniskillen Campus, College of Agriculture, Food & Rural Development, Dept. of Agriculture & Rural Development**
- **Enterprise Agencies / Centres** (most)
- **Enterprise Northern Ireland**
- **Greenmount Campus, College of Agriculture, Food & Rural Development, Dept. of Agriculture & Rural Development**
- **Health & Safety Executive for Northern Ireland**
- **Institute of Business Advisers**
- **Irish Management Institute (Northern Ireland) Ltd**
- **Loughry Campus, College of Agriculture, Food & Rural Development, Dept. of Agriculture & Rural Development**
- **Management Training & Finance Group**
- **Northern Ireland Centre for Entrepreneurship**
- **Prince's Trust for Northern Ireland**
- **Social Economy Agency**
- **University of Ulster**
- **University of Ulster, Office of Innovation & Enterprise**
- **UUTech Ltd**
- **Your People Manager.**

WEBSITE

- See *Chapter 2.*

WOMEN

- **Glenwood Enterprises Ltd**
- **ORTUS, the West Belfast Development Trust.**

WORKSPACE

- **Brookfield Business Centre**
- **Enterprise Agencies / Centres (most)**
- **Enterprise Northern Ireland**
- **Flax Trust.**

YOUNG ENTERPRISE

- **ChooseEnterprise.com**
- **Young Enterprise Northern Ireland.**

9: IMPLEMENTATION

OK! So you're ready to go – market research done, business plan drafted, finance and supports in place. But there are a few small hurdles that could still trip you.

You ought to consider each of the following and build them into your business plan:

- Bank account
- Legal structure
- Tax registration
- Advisers
- Accountants
- Solicitors
- Company administration
- Accounting systems
- Quality certification
- Premises.

BANK ACCOUNT

At least one bank account is an essential for any business, however small. Don't be tempted to run your business through your own personal bank account "until it gets off the ground". That is a recipe for disaster. Open a separate bank account for your business as soon as (or before) you begin to trade.

A limited company needs to pass a resolution of the Board of Directors to open a bank account. The steps are:

- Ask your bank manager for a copy of the form of resolution that they require. This is called a Bank Mandate because it mandates (that is, authorises) the bank to carry out the instructions of the directors regarding the operation of the account

- Hold a meeting of the directors of the company

- Decide what instructions you want to give the bank regarding who is authorised to sign cheques on behalf of the company, and how often you want to receive statements

- Propose the resolution in the form required by the bank – see the mandate form for the wording – and have it adopted by the directors at a formal Board meeting

- Complete the mandate form. Usually this is in the format of a request to the bank to open an account, and certifies that the resolution, in the prescribed wording, was passed at a meeting of the directors held on the date noted

- Get sample signatures from each of the people authorised to sign cheques on behalf of the company

- Return the mandate form and sample signatures to your bank manager

- Give the bank manager a copy of your company's Memorandum of Association and Articles of Association. These will be kept for the manager's files

- Show the original of the company's Certificate of Incorporation to your bank manager. A copy of this will be taken for the manager's files and on the copy will be marked the fact that the original has been seen by the manager. You will not be asked for, and you should not give the bank manager, the original Certificate of Incorporation. (The only exception to this is in the larger city branches where the documents needed to open your bank account go to the Securities department for checking. In this case, your bank manager should give you a receipt for the certificate and give you a date when you can return to collect it.)

- Have available some money to lodge to the new account
- Decide the name in which you want the account to be opened. You can use only the registered name of the company, unless you are trading under a registered business name – that is, trading as *West Cork Forest Advisory Services* even though the company is registered in your own name as *Frank Kelly Ltd*. In this case, you will also need to show the bank manager the Certificate of Registration of Business Name for the company (note that it is no longer possible or necessary to register "business names" in Northern Ireland).

Depending on the bank and branch, it may take a few days or a few weeks to clear all the paperwork associated with opening your company's bank account. Allow for this in your planning.

If you need immediate access to the funds you are lodging, your bank manager can usually arrange for temporary cheques to be made available while a chequebook is being printed.

LEGAL STRUCTURE

You have most likely already made a choice as to your legal structure (see *Chapter 2*). Now you need to implement it.

Setting Up as a Sole Trader

You automatically become a sole trader by starting up a business. Setting up as a sole trader needs almost nothing by way of legal formality. A further advantage of being a sole trader is that apart from normal tax returns, which every business must make, a sole trader is not required to make public any information on the business.

However, if you plan to run your business under a name other than your own, you must register with the *Registry of Business Names* (except in Northern Ireland, where registration of business name is not possible).

Setting Up as a Partnership

A partnership, essentially, is an agreement between two or more people to go into business together. It may be no more formal than a handshake or may run to a multi-page legal document. Whichever route you take, build the following points into your planning:

- In a partnership, each partner is liable for all the liabilities of the business. If the business fails, and your partner(s) abandon(s) you, you could be left to pay for everything out of your own pocket. Before entering a partnership, decide whether you trust your partner(s)-to-be with everything you own – because that's what you will be doing.

- If you write down nothing else, write down and have all the partners sign a document setting out how the business is to be financed, how profits and losses are to be shared, and what will happen if one of the partners decides to leave. These are important points. Failure to agree on them at an early stage can lead to difficulty later.

In Northern Ireland, it is possible to form a "limited partnership". Full details of the procedures involved, and implications of this, are available on the **Companies Registry Northern Ireland** website.

Forming an Unlimited Company

An unlimited company is formed in much the same way as a limited liability company. The principal difference is that the company's Memorandum of Association (part of the company's constitution) states that the liability of members is unlimited. Again, like sole traders and partnerships, this exposes your total assets in the event of the failure of the company. There seems little advantage in going through the formation requirements without benefiting from limited liability.

Forming a Ltd Company

A limited company is a legal entity separate from its share-holders. The shareholders are only liable, in the event of the business becoming unable to pay its debts, for any amount out-standing on their subscribed shareholdings.

The steps involved in forming a limited company are:

- Decide on a name for your company
- Define the purpose for which the company is being formed. This will make up the company's Objects clause
- Prepare the Memorandum of Association, which states what the company has been set up to do, who the initial share-holders are and how much they have subscribed
- Prepare the Articles of Association, which details the rules governing internal procedures of the company
- Submit the appropriate forms, together with the Memorandum and Articles of Association and a cheque or draft for the formation fees, to the **Companies Registration Office** or **Companies Registry Northern Ireland**.

The cost of forming a limited company depends on whether you do the work yourself or ask an accountant, solicitor, or company formation agent to do it for you. Typically, using a professional adds considerably to the cost.

If your application to form a company is accepted, the Registrar will issue a Certificate of Incorporation. Only after its issue, and the first meeting of the Board of Directors of the company, may the company begin to trade.

Forming a Co-operative

A worker co-operative is where a team comes together to form and run a business according to a set of values that includes self-help, self-responsibility, democracy, equality and solidarity. The business is jointly owned and democratically controlled. Co-operative members believe in the ethical values of honesty, openness, social responsibility and caring for others. The Co-operative Principles provide guidelines on how the business should conduct itself.

Co-operatives can be registered as an Industrial and Provident Society, a company limited by guarantee or a company limited by shares.

TAX REGISTRATION (REPUBLIC)

The **Revenue Commissioners** now use a single form to register a business for the many taxes to which it is liable. Form TR1 applies to individuals and Form TR2 to companies.

Your business's PAYE/PRSI registration number, its VAT registration number and its Corporation Tax number should be the same, though it has nothing to do with the company's Registered Number, which is issued by the **Companies Registration Office** when the company is formed.

As a first step, download the Revenue's *Starting in Business* guide (reference IT 48) and *VAT for Small Businesses* (IT 49) from its website.

Employers

Employers must register for PAYE when they pay remuneration exceeding a rate of €8 a week (€36 a month) to a full-time employee or €2 a week (€9 a month) to an individual with other employment – in other words, **all** employees.

When you take on an employee, you should first obtain from them a form P45 or tax-free allowance certificate. Then you must notify the tax office in respect of the new employee's former employment that you have employed them.

If neither a P45 nor a current year's tax-free allowance certificate is available (for example, in the case of an employee in first-time employment), you must complete form P46 (ring the tax office for a copy) and send it to the tax office. In those circumstances, PAYE/PRSI should be operated on the "emergency basis" until a tax-free allowance certificate is received. Details on how to do this are available from the tax office.

An employer must:

• Maintain PAYE/PRSI records

- Deduct tax and the employee's share of PRSI and keep records of the amount.
- Submit a monthly return on form P30 between the 5th and 14th of the month, detailing the tax payable and PRSI (including employer's share)
- Submit a cheque for the total amount due with each monthly return
- Submit yearly returns on forms P35 and P35L to the Collector General after the end of the tax year
- Give to each employee working on 31 December each year a completed form P60 showing details of earnings and deductions for the income tax year ended on that date.
- Advise the Inspector of Taxes of any employee commencing or ceasing employment.

The main forms involved in the PAYE process are:
- P30: Monthly return
- P35: Yearly return
- P35LT: For employees for whom you do not know the PPS number
- P45: Form given to employee on termination of employment, detailing earnings, tax and PRSI paid while in employment during current tax year
- P60: For the employee who (a) might be claiming a tax repayment for the above year, (b) might be claiming PRSI contributions on the amount of pay in excess of the pay ceiling for contribution purposes.

You should consider using the Revenue Online Service to submit your returns electronically.

Your Own Position as an Employee

If you are a director of a limited company, then you must send in a P45 or P46 to the tax office in order to become a registered employee. Thereafter, with the exception of PRSI rates, which are lower for owner-directors, you will be treated on a day-to-day basis like any other PAYE employee.

However, directors are now subject to self-assessment, even though their income from the company may already be subject to PAYE. Directors will be liable to a surcharge where they fail to make a return of income by the appropriate date. You should discuss your own situation with your accountant.

If you are self-employed, write to your local tax office explaining your situation. You are not liable for tax payments until after the first year of trading. Two months before the first year of trading ends, you will be sent a preliminary tax notice that informs you when your first tax payment is due.

Registering for VAT

You must register your business for Value Added Tax as soon as its taxable supplies (that is, your business transactions that are liable to VAT) exceed or become likely to exceed the limits for registration. The current limits are:

- €51,000, where the supplies are of goods
- €25,500, where the supplies are of services.

Your registration for VAT is notified to you on Form VAT 2. This will tell you:

- The date from which your business is registered for VAT. From this date onwards, you will have to charge VAT to all your customers and account to the Revenue Commissioners for it
- Your VAT number, which you will have to quote on all invoices, statements, credit notes etc.

In certain circumstances, you may register for VAT before you begin to trade or while your turnover is below the limits for registration. Doing so allows you to reclaim VAT paid on purchases of goods and may be of advantage to you. However, voluntary registration for VAT should not be done without professional advice. Consult your accountant and/or local tax office for further information.

Registering for Corporation Tax

Once your new company has been registered, and you have submitted Form TR2, it will be registered for Corporation Profits tax, which is payable in two instalments following the end of your accounting year. Consult your accountant and/or local tax office for further information.

Tax Registration (Northern Ireland)

Businesses in the Northern Ireland, which is part of the UK, are subject to:

- **Income Tax** – Sole traders and partnerships on their profits
- **Corporation Tax** – Limited companies on their profits
- **Value Added Tax (VAT)** – All businesses with turnover over £55,000
- **National Insurance Contributions (NIC)** – All businesses with employees (including owner/directors).

Two agencies are involved:

- **Inland Revenue** – for Income Tax, Corporation Tax and National Insurance Contributions
- **HM Customs & Excise** – for VAT.

Registration for tax

It is your obligation to notify the Inland Revenue / HM Customs & Excise through your local tax office of the establishment of your business and to provide them with the information required to register your business for the relevant taxes.

Your starting point is to get a copy of the Inland Revenue/HM Customs & Excise *Starting Up in Business* pack by telephoning **08457 646 646**, contacting your local tax office (check the telephone directory), or through **www.inlandrevenue.gov.uk**.

You should also consider attending a Business Advice Open Day – telephone **0121 697 4065** for more information.

Corporation Tax

Limited liability companies pay Corporation Tax on the company's total profits, including any capital gains, for an accounting period – normally the period for which the company's accounts are prepared, though an accounting period cannot exceed 12 months.

A self-assessment system applies to companies. The company assesses its own liability to tax and pays it no later than nine months after the end of the accounting period. Payments can be made by cheque, GIRO, or electronically through the BACS or CHAPS systems. Interest will be charged if payments are made after their due date.

The company will also complete a Company Tax Return (CT600) and send it to the Inland Revenue with its accounts for the period.

The company's self-assessment is then complete, unless changes are made to the return by the company or the Inland Revenue query it. Inland Revenue queries some returns to check that they are correct or to understand better the figures in them.

The rates of Corporation Tax are:

- **Main Rate** – 30%, on profits over £1,500,000
- **Small Companies' Rate** – 19% on profits between £50,001 and £300,000
- **Starting Rate** – Nil on profits up to £10,000.

Marginal relief, which applies less than the full rate of the next tax band, applies to profits between £10,001 and £50,000 and between £300,001 and £1,500,000.

You should read *A general guide to Corporation Tax Self-Assessment* (CTSA/BK4), available from your local tax office or from the Inland Revenue web-site.

Income Tax

Income tax is payable by self-employed individuals on income earned in the tax year – that is, on annual profits or gains from an individual's trade, profession or vocation and on other income, such as investment income, rental income etc.

As soon as you start business as a self-employed person, you must complete Form CWF1, *Notification of Self-employment* and send it to the Inland Revenue National Insurance Contributions Office. This office will then tell:

- Your local tax office
- HM Customs & Excise (if your turnover is more than £55,000 in a 12-month period, you must register for VAT – see below)
- Your Job Centre, if you are registered with one.

Your tax office requires a return of your business income and expenses in a standard format. You do not need to prepare separate accounts, although you may find that your bank wants to see formal accounts anyway.

Income tax is calculated on a 12-month basis, for a year running from 6 April to the following 5 April.

In April, you will receive a tax return, asking you for the information needed to calculate your tax bill for the year. If you can calculate the bill yourself (the return explains how), you must send back the return by 31 January following. Alternatively, you can ask the Inland Revenue to calculate the tax bill, based on the information on your return. In this case, you must send back your return before 30 September.

In your second and later years in business, you must make two payments on account against your tax bill each year. These payments are due on 31 January (during the relevant tax year to 5 April) and 31 July (just after its end). The final payment of your tax bill must be made by 31 January following the end of the tax year.

Calculating taxable profits

Taxable profits are calculated by deducting allowable business expenses from turnover. Turnover is the gross amount of income earned by a business before deducting any business expenses – the total amounts from sale of goods or provision of services. If a business is registered for VAT, the turnover figure should exclude VAT.

Business expenses are normally referred to as revenue expenditure, which covers day-to-day running costs (exclusive of VAT, if the business is registered for VAT), including:

- Purchase of goods for resale
- Wages, rent, rates, repairs, lighting, heating etc
- Running costs of vehicles or machinery used in the business
- Accountancy and audit fees
- Interest paid on any monies borrowed to finance business expenses/items
- Lease payments on vehicles or machinery used in the business.

Some expenses cannot be claimed as revenue expenditure, including:

- Any expense, not wholly and exclusively paid for the purposes of the trade or profession
- Any private or domestic expenditure
- Business entertainment expenditure – the provision of accommodation, food, drink or any other form of hospitality
- Expenditure of a capital nature.

For expenditure relating to both business and private use, only that part relating to the business will be allowed.

Expenditure is regarded as 'capital' if it has been spent on acquiring or altering assets that are of lasting use in the business – for example, buying or altering business premises. Capital expenditure cannot be deducted in arriving at the taxable profit. However, capital allowances may be claimed on capital expenditure incurred on items such as office equipment, business plant and machinery, to take account of wear and tear on these items.

To arrive at the correct taxable income, the net profit should be calculated and any allowances and relief entitlements deducted.

Self-employed National Insurance Contributions

Self-employed people pay National Insurance Contributions in two classes: Class 2 and Class 4 (on profits above a certain level).

PAYE & National Insurance Contributions

When you employ someone in your business, you should immediately tell your local tax office. They will send you a *New Employer's Starter Pack* and tell the local Business Support Team, which provides payroll support to employers in their area.

The Pay As You Earn (PAYE) system operates on the basis that an employer deducts tax at a specified rate from an employee's pay. The system is designed so that, as far as is possible, the correct amount of tax is deducted from an employee's pay to meet his/her tax liability for the year. To achieve this, PAYE is normally computed on a cumulative basis, from the beginning of the tax year to the date on which a payment is being made.

In addition to deducting PAYE, employers are also obliged to deduct National Insurance Contributions (NIC) from employees.

You must:

- Work out employees' PAYE and NIC each pay day
- Pay this amount to the Inland Revenue monthly
- Tell your local tax office at the end of each tax year how much each employee has earned and what PAYE and NIC you have deducted.

Your local Inland Revenue Business Support Team will advise you on the details.

Value Added Tax

Value Added Tax (VAT) is a consumer tax collected by VAT-registered traders on their supplies of taxable goods and services in the course of business and by Customs & Excise on imports from outside the EU.

Each trader pays VAT on goods and services acquired for the business and charges VAT on goods and services supplied by the business. The amount by which VAT charged exceeds VAT paid must be paid to HM Customs & Excise.

If the amount of VAT paid exceeds the VAT charged, you will get a refund. This ensures that VAT is paid by the ultimate customer and not by the business.

You must register for VAT if your turnover for a 12-month period exceeds £55,000 (this amount is reviewed annually). Traders whose turnover is below this limit are not obliged to register for VAT but may do so if they wish. You should only do so on your accountant's advice.

The current rate of VAT is 17.5%, though some goods and services are zero rated or taxed at a reduced rate of 5%.

The Annual Accounting Scheme allows you to pay monthly direct debits and send in a single VAT return at the end of the year. The Cash Accounting Scheme lets you account for VAT on the basis of cash paid and received, rather than invoices issued and received. You should take advice from your accountant before registering for either of these schemes. Both schemes are subject to maximum turnover limits, currently £600,000.

Record-keeping

The Inland Revenue requires all businesses to keep 'sufficient' records of transactions to allow the correct tax to be calculated. You must keep:

- Details of all receipts and expenses incurred in the course of your business and of what they relate to
- Details of all sales and purchases made in the course of the trade, if you deal in goods
- All other supporting documents.

The Inland Revenue publishes a number of guides (available on its web-site) that provide guidance in this area. Most businesses set up as a limited liability company will be required by law to keep certain records in order to prepare accounts. In most cases, the Companies Acts requirements are the same as the Inland Revenue's – except that the Inland

Revenue requires records to be kept for six years, while the Companies Acts only requires private limited companies to keep records for three years. Note that alternatives to the original documents – for example, optical images, etc - are usually acceptable.

Returns

For each of the taxes, you are required to supply the Revenue Commissioners with specific information on or by specific dates. These are called 'returns' and there are severe penalties for late submission or not submitting returns at all.

Information and assistance

Comprehensive guides to all aspects of business taxation, including a 'Starting Your Own Business?' guide, may be obtained from any tax office or the Inland Revenue's web-site (**www.inlandrevenue.gov.uk**). Your accountant will also provide advice.

Taxpayers' Charter

It's not all one way, however. The Inland Revenue has issued a *Taxpayers' Charter*, which sets out your rights as a taxpayer. Ask at your local tax office for a copy.

On-line Services

The Inland Revenue is increasingly moving on-line. Not only are all forms and publications available on their web-site but increasingly taxpayers can make returns and payments on-line too.

Talk to an accountant

Because tax regulations are becoming increasingly complicated, it is worth talking to an accountant about your specific situation and needs.

ADVISERS

As you start in business, you need two key advisers: an accountant and a solicitor. In the pressures of setting up your new business, there will be a temptation to avoid finding either of these two. Not doing so saves you time and possibly money, both of which are important in a start-up situation. But it could cost you dearly later on.

The reasons for choosing a financial and a legal adviser at the start are:

- Their experience and expertise in dealing with other start-ups may save you hours of time and hundreds, or even thousands, of pounds. If they are the right advisers for you, they will be prepared to assist your enterprise with timely and constructive advice – take it and use it!

- With luck, you will never find yourself in a situation where you need to be bailed out of a difficult situation, but if you do, it's better to have your advisers on your team already than have to start looking for them with the millstone of your problem around your neck.

In choosing advisers, look for:

- Membership of the appropriate professional body. This is your guarantee of quality of work and source of redress, should the need ever arise

- Experience in the type of business or at least in the business area in which you intend to operate. You want to learn from your advisers' experience, not spend your time teaching them about your business

- Adequate resources to meet your needs. What is adequate will depend on you, but don't choose a one-man band if you expect a limitless range of expertise. There is only so much one person can be expert in. Ask about the advisers' hours of business (actual hours, not published hours). Can you telephone them at seven o'clock on a Sunday night? What happens when they go on holidays?

- People you can trust and work easily with. If you can't trust your advisers with your most confidential information, you shouldn't have them on your team. Find someone else.

Choosing an Accountant

If your business is set up as a limited company, your accountant will have one primary task: To carry out the annual audit (note that an audit is not required where the company's turnover is below €317,000 – £1 million in Northern Ireland – and certain other conditions are met). This is a statutory inspection of the company's accounting records, which results in a formal set of accounts and an audit report. This report is to the members (that is, the shareholders) of the company and gives the auditor's (the accountant's) opinion on:

- Whether the accounts give a true and fair view
- Whether proper books of account have been kept
- Whether a meeting as specified under the Companies (Amendment) Act, 1986 needs to be called (this would arise where the share capital of the company amounts to less than half the net assets of the company)
- Whether all the explanations and information considered necessary for the purposes of the audit were received

and, as a matter of fact:

- Whether the accounts agree with the books
- Whether proper returns were received from branches (if any) not visited by the auditor.

If you do not know a suitable accountant, check the **Golden Pages** or contact one of the following:

- **Association of Chartered Certified Accountants**
- **Institute of Certified Public Accountants in Ireland**
- **Institute of Chartered Accountants in Ireland.**

Many accountants provide advice and assistance in taking a business concept from viability assessment through to the production stage and also in obtaining assistance from State and other support organisations. An initial meeting between a potential entrepreneur and the accountant is usually free and is used to gather information about the promoter and the business proposal. Based on the information available, appropriate action to advance the project will be agreed. Where further information is required, a structured feasibility study is carried out, embracing key aspects such as products, markets, competitors, technology, funding etc. A fee should be agreed before work starts. If the proposal is viable, the accountant will assist in the preparation of a comprehensive business plan, at a further agreed cost. They will make application for grants appropriate to the project and assist in raising finance from banks or private investors. They may also help to obtain commercial partners.

Choosing a Solicitor

Unlike an accountant, a solicitor has no statutory duties in relation to a company. You will, however, need a solicitor for the following:

- To sign a statutory declaration when you are forming your company
- To check out the lease of any premises you decide to buy or rent
- To prepare employment contracts for you and your staff
- To draft or review contracts that you enter into with customers or suppliers.

In addition, from time to time, you may require advice on legal issues.

If you do not know a suitable solicitor, look in the **Golden Pages** or contact the **Law Society of Ireland** or **Law Society of Northern Ireland**.

ACCOUNTING SYSTEMS

Accounts systems provide a record of all the income and outgoings of a business and produce the basic information for the end-of-year accounts and for management information.

In a manual system, you may need some or all of the following (in varying levels of detail, depending on the size and complexity of your business – your accountant will advise):

- Cash book
- Petty-cash book
- Purchase day book
- Purchase ledger
- Sales day book
- Sales ledger
- Control accounts
- Wages book/deduction sheets
- Register of fixed assets
- Nominal ledger
- System for ordering goods/dealing with purchase invoices
- System for dealing with customers' orders, sales invoices
- Credit control procedures
- Control of workforce and hours worked
- Stock control procedures
- System for regular management information
- Adequate control procedures by management over employees.

You can also use a computerised accounting system – for example, **Big Red Book** (again, your accountant will advise).

Your accountant will also advise you on a system for filing and retrieving documents. You also need to consider the flow of documents and information around the business – for example, how a customer order is processed so that the goods are sent out, an invoice generated and payment received.

Whether manual or computerised, there are three simple aids that you should use to help you in the financial control of your business. These are:

- Bank balance book
- Still-to-be-received file
- Still-to-be-paid file.

The bank balance book does exactly what its name suggests – it tells you what your bank balance is. You need five columns – for the date, for the transaction detail (cheque or lodgement will do), for lodgements, for cheques and other withdrawals, and for the balance. If every transaction with your bank is written into this book *when it happens,* you will always know your correct bank balance. The little effort that it takes to keep this book up-to-date will be more than repaid as it keeps you out of trouble.

Cash flow is important for any business. If you sell goods on credit, you will probably find that you spend a great deal of time chasing debtors, trying to collect money. A "still-to-be-received" file helps you by providing all the information you need on outstanding debts. Just put a copy of every invoice into the file when you issue it, and take the copy out when it is paid – then every invoice in the file represents an unpaid debt, money due to you. You can list them out, total them up, cry over them – whatever takes your fancy – but you have accurate information on which to do so.

The "still-to-be-paid" file works in the opposite way – it reminds you of money you owe. Put a copy of every invoice you receive into it and take it out when you pay it (send the copy with your cheque so that your creditor knows which invoice you are paying!) – and what's left is what you owe. So, when you get a telephone call saying that such and such an invoice is due for payment or overdue, you can check it out immediately.

QUALITY CERTIFICATION

For some businesses in particular, and increasingly for all businesses, some form of quality certification is becoming essential. Schemes such as ISO 9000 are the norm among high-tech companies and are a minimum requirement to supply many of the foreign-owned multinationals operating in Ireland. ISO 9000 is the best known of such schemes, though the Q-Mark, awarded by **Excellence Ireland** is important in some sectors.

ISO 9000 is a standard for quality management systems, covering every stage of the production process – procurement, incoming materials, production performance, final inspection, and delivery. To implement ISO 9000 (or any quality standard):

- Management has to define clearly what is needed.
- The message must reach staff so that everybody knows what they have to do and how to do it.
- The right equipment, processes and tools must be there to do the job.
- The right information must reach the appropriate people at the right time.
- There must be a system of management and control.

For further information, read *ISO 9000*, by Brian Rothery (2nd edition, Gower).

Even if your business's involvement in quality certification stems purely from a supplier-imposed requirement, keep two things firmly in mind:

- Quality is an attitude of mind, a way of working, not just mindless compliance with written procedures. Most quality schemes involve the recording of operational procedures, together with systems to audit compliance. Beware that compliance with the system does not become the end, rather than quality itself
- Quality involves a cost and any investment in quality systems must be justified like any other business expense. Investing

in quality for its own sake may be very noble, but it's not good business.

PREMISES

In the property business, they say that only three things matter: Location, location, location. For certain kinds of business – shops, hotels, restaurants – location can make or break the business. But in all cases, the right working environment is important.

For workshops and factories, you need to check lay-out, logistics, transport, weight of machinery, health and safety regulations, environmental issues, availability of three-phase electricity, etc. Draw out your ideal space before starting to look for accommodation.

If you are looking for offices, and you expect to be working on your own for a while, consider somewhere like **Premier Business Centres** that offers secretarial support (for example, telephone answering, message-taking, fax, photocopying, reception, etc.) It will save you hiring a secretary until the workload justifies it. And you save the capital cost of little-used but essential equipment and meeting facilities – instead, you pay only as you need them.

A "Virtual Office", where you only pay for the facilities as you use them, can be the ideal way to combine working from home with having top-class facilities when you need to meet visitors – or just to provide yourself with flexibility while you assess your needs.

Wherever you locate, you need to consider insurance premiums, compliance with food hygiene and health and safety regulations, planning permission, lighting, heating, alarms, signs, locks, insurance, toilets, interior decor, fittings. And get a solicitor (see earlier) to check any lease before you sign.

10: MOVING TO IRELAND TO START A BUSINESS

Traditionally, Ireland has been associated with emigration. Images from the mid-19th century of half-starved people on coffin-ships escaping the famine back home are part and parcel of the Irish-American heritage. Many Irish men and women of that time first saw Australia from a prison-ship, courtesy of the British Government. In the 20th century, the Irish found jobs as labourers on the building sites of Britain and further afield in the United States. In the 1970s and 1980s, it was the educated young people, fresh from college with degrees, who "took the boat" or increasingly the plane, in search of jobs that were not available at home.

But, in the past five years, the tide has turned. Emigration has been replaced by net immigration – now, over 1,000 people come to Ireland each week. And, while many of the new immigrants come to fill jobs created by skills shortages, a significant number come to start their own businesses. Why?

First, put aside any preconceptions you may have of Ireland as a rural haven, populated by handsome lads and comely maidens, with dancing at crossroads and leprechauns at every turn of the winding lane. That may be what **Fáilte Ireland**, the Irish Tourist Board, will sell you, though it exists only in brochures and a few select tourist enclaves. The "real" Ireland is a modern, dynamic, European economy that is powering ahead, fuelled by export demand (exports account for 76% of GDP), deregulation and a flexible and well-educated workforce.

For the last 30 years, successive governments have pursued economic policies designed to make Ireland an attractive location for overseas investment. Their success can be seen, not just in the numbers of foreign businesses now operating in Ireland, but also in Ireland's ranking in the *World Competitiveness Yearbook* and *Global Entrepreneurship Monitor.*

Recognising that Ireland lacks the natural resources required to support large-scale industrial development, the government has encouraged inwards investment by industries that make use of the assets available: for example, chemicals and pharmaceuticals (clustered in Cork, around the deep-water harbour), electronics and software (Ireland is now the world's largest exporter of software) and internationally traded services (in particular, financial services from the International Financial Services Centre in Dublin's revitalised Docklands).

A relative newcomer on the scene – and still growing, despite the burst of the dot-com bubble – is e-commerce. The government, in partnership with the private sector, has sought to develop Ireland's communications infrastructure to world-class standards, with bureaucrats making decisions at distinctly non-bureaucratic speeds.

But the newest kid on the block is biotechnology – the **Directory** lists a number of organisations – both information-providers and VC funds – active in supporting this emerging area.

Ireland is ideally situated for exporting to Europe. With the United Kingdom declining to join the Euro-zone, Ireland is the only English-speaking member of this group. Whatever your view on the future strength of the Euro as a currency, there is no escaping the fact that the Euro-zone is the world's second largest economy, home to some 375 million people.

Almost half of Irish exports already go to Europe, showing how important Ireland is as a gateway to the EU for many companies, especially the 1,200 or so foreign multinationals with operations in Ireland.

ATTRACTIONS FOR BUSINESSES

One of the key attractions of Ireland for businesses is the relatively low (though rising) cost of labour. Add to this a young work-force, with almost half the population aged between 15 and 44, 60% of whom have a college or university degree.

But the key attraction for many businesses is the tax regime. All profits (except those from non-trading income – rental and investment income) are taxed at 12.5% (compared with US and UK rates of 35% and 30% respectively).

Although a withholding tax of 22% applies on dividends and other distributions of profit, this does not apply to payments to EU tax resident shareholders or those resident in the 40 or so countries with which Ireland has a tax treaty.

BUSINESS INCENTIVES

Incentives include grants towards capital and revenue costs (employment, training and R&D are the main categories) offered by government agencies. For larger companies, moving all or a significant part of their operations to Ireland, such grants (and other assistance) are offered by **IDA Ireland**, which has offices in 15 locations worldwide, including six in the United States, from which more information can be obtained. These grants are non-taxable and sometimes (but not always) non-repayable.

For smaller businesses, the source of government support depends on the employment potential of the business to be established. Businesses that are likely to employ 10 or more staff and generate turnover of €1.3 million within three years will be taken under the wing of **Enterprise Ireland** (or, in certain parts of the country, **Shannon Development** or **Údarás na Gaeltachta**).

Micro-businesses (under 10 employees – this category accounts for almost 90% of indigenous Irish businesses) are supported by the **City / County Enterprise Boards**, a network of 35 local organisations. Increasingly, both Enterprise Ireland and the Enterprise Boards are moving away from straight cash grants towards "soft" supports, in the form of training and other assistance, designed to bring the business to commercial viability.

Another key determinant of government support is the location of the proposed business. Because Dublin's infrastructure is groaning at the seams, government agencies are more generous in the financial assistance they offer to businesses locating outside Dublin. Indeed, it's now exceptional to be offered significant financial assistance for Dublin-based start-ups. And regional bodies are working to develop clusters of excellence in specific industries, for example, pharmaceuticals and electronics in Cork.

BUSINESS FORMS AND ACCOUNTING

Most trading in Ireland is carried out through private limited liability companies. Formation of such companies is straightforward, requiring the completion of a simple form and payment of a small fee. A company need only have one shareholder, though it must have at least two directors, one of whom must be resident in Ireland. Where a company does not have a resident director, it must provide a bond to the value of approximately €25,000. No individual may hold more than 25 directorships.

With the exception of the smallest companies, all Irish companies must have their financial statements audited annually by a chartered or certified accountant and must file these statements with the Registrar of Companies for public inspection. No exceptions are made for foreign-owned entities.

Further information is available from the agencies mentioned, from the Irish Government's website (**www.irlgov.ie**) or from **ask-ireland.com**.

REQUIREMENTS FOR RESIDENCY AND CITIZENSHIP

Residency is an important question for anyone planning to move to Ireland to set up a business. According to the **Department of Justice, Equality and Law Reform**, a non-Irish national who plans to establish a business in Ireland must provide:

- Evidence to satisfy the Department that he or she has at least €300,000 available

- A business plan

- Details of professional or trade qualifications, where these are relevant to the proposed business

- A "certificate of character" from the police authority in their home state, to confirm that they do not have a criminal record, etc.

In addition, the proposed business must employ at least two non-family members, who must be Irish or EU nationals.

Work permits are not required for non-nationals who establish a business, though they may be required for any staff who move with the business. Work permits are only available where suitable Irish or EU nationals cannot be recruited for the position, although in some sectors – nursing and electronics, for example – this requirement has recently been waived.

Citizenship in Ireland can be acquired through ancestry or by naturalisation. A parent or grandparent who was Irish entitles one to Irish citizenship, though the link must be proved through documentation. A foreign national resident in Ireland may apply for naturalised citizenship after seven years of residence. Where residency arises because of marriage to an Irish citizen, the waiting period for naturalisation is reduced to three years.

PERSONAL TAXATION

Personal taxation in Ireland is steadily being reduced, after years when it was among the highest in Europe. Foreign nationals resident in Ireland pay Irish tax on income earned by them in Ireland or the United Kingdom or income remitted to them from abroad. Income accumulated offshore, but not remitted to Ireland, is not subject to tax.

Currently, a tax credit system applies, under which an initial tranche of income is not subject to tax, with income above this figure being subject to tax at progressive rates. Each taxpayer receives an annual "tax credit", which reduces his/her tax liability. Details of tax rates, credits and thresholds are available on the Revenue Commissioners' website.

Special allowances for mortgage interest payments, health insurance, etc reduce further the amount of tax payable.

In addition, all employees in Ireland are covered by social insurance, which is pay-related. Social insurance must be paid by all foreign employees working in Ireland for more than a year, even if they are being paid from abroad, unless they are an EU national paying social insurance in another EU member-state.

DIRECTORY OF
SOURCES OF ASSISTANCE

The aims of this directory are:

- To highlight the many sources of assistance available to start-up and small/medium-sized enterprises in Ireland
- To direct readers to sources appropriate to their needs.

The directory is arranged alphabetically by organisation, with full contact details (address, telephone, fax, e-mail, website and contact name) for each, where possible. Note that STD codes are those applicable locally – readers may need to amend the code when making cross-border calls or faxes.

Each entry summarises the assistance provided by the organisation. Where an organisation has links with other organisations listed in the directory, these are shown in the text thus: **Other Organisation**. Only where a category applies to all organisations within a group (for example, City / County Enterprise Boards) is it shown against the group as a whole – where the category applies to individual organisations within the group, it is of course against that organisation.

All the information has been checked before publication but, of course, it is subject to change. See this book's companion website, **www.startingabusinessinireland.com**, or contact the organisations directly for the most up-to-date position.

3i GROUP PLC
91 Waterloo Road, London SE1 8XP
T: (0207) 928 3131 F: (0207) 928 0058
E: london@3i.com (London Head Office) W: www.3i.com

CATEGORIES: EQUITY

London-based, 3i provides venture capital and private equity for start-ups with high growth potential and strong management.

4th LEVEL VENTURES UNIVERSITY SEED FUND
4th Level Ventures Ltd, Dolmen House, 4 Earlsfort Terrace, Dublin 2
T: (01) 633 3843 F: (01) 672 5423
E: ronan.reid@4thlevelventures.ie or louise.sloan@4thlevelventures.ie
W: www.4thlevelventures.ie
Contact: Ronan Reid, Louise Sloan

CATEGORIES: EQUITY

This €20 million fund was established to commercialise the business opportunities arising from university research. It invests €75K to €500k in life sciences, materials sciences, technology and information, communications and technology (ICT) companies.

ACCBANK PLC
Business Banking Unit, Charlemont Place, Dublin 2
T: (01) 418 4000
E: info@accbank.ie W: www.accbank.ie
Contact: Willie Dollard, Stephen Murphy, Gerry Fahy

CATEGORIES: DEBT

ACCBank was purchased by Rabobank, one of the world's top 30 banks, in 2002. Rabobank has helped reinforce ACCBank's commitment to becoming market leader in delivering customer value to its agribusiness and SME customers.

ACORN, THE BUSINESS CENTRE
2 Riada Avenue, Garryduff Road, Ballymoney, Co Antrim BT53 7LH
T: (028) 2766 6133 F: (028) 2766 5019
E: enquiries@acornbusiness.co.uk W: www.acornbusiness.co.uk
Contact: Sarah Reilly, Business Development Consultant

CATEGORIES: INCUBATOR; INFORMATION; START-UP TRAINING; TRAINING

Acorn the Business Centre is an **Enterprise Agency** and a member of **Enterprise Northern Ireland**. It offers workspace, as well as start-up and ongoing training. Acorn, the Business Centre is committed to the creation of employment, business opportunity and training, primarily in the Ballymoney council area, and offers a wide range of programmes designed to help entrepreneurs start and grow their own business. Practical advice on all aspects of business start-up and expansion including access to support, assistance, training, premises and consultancy is available.

ACT VENTURE CAPITAL LTD

Jefferson House, Eglinton Road, Dublin 4
T: (01) 260 0966 F: (01) 260 0538
E: info@actvc.ie W: www.actventure.com
Contact: Niall Carroll, Owen Murphy, Aidan Byrnes, Walter Hobbs
Also at: Windsor Business Centre, 58 Howard Street, Belfast BT1 6PJ
T: (028) 9024 7266 F: (028) 9024 7372

CATEGORIES: EQUITY

ACT Venture Capital provides capital to growth-oriented private companies in the range of €750K to €15 million. Larger sums can be provided in syndication with institutional investors.

ACTION CLONDALKIN ENTERPRISE

Clondalkin Enterprise Centre, Neilstown Road, Clondalkin, Dublin 22
T: (01) 457 8115 F: (01) 457 8121
E: dbyrne@aceenterprise.ie W: www.enterpriseaction.ie
Contact: David Byrne

CATEGORIES: START-UP TRAINING; TRAINING; WORKSPACE

Action Clondalkin Enterprise provides support to people starting businesses, including training and workspace in the Bawnogue Enterprise Centre, which was jointly funded by South Dublin County Council, **South Dublin County Enterprise Board**, **Enterprise Ireland**, **FÁS** and **Clondalkin Partnership**.

ACTION SOUTH KILDARE LTD

Main Street, Kilcullen, Co Kildare
T: (045) 481 999 F: (045) 481 965
E: pkeenan@actionsouthkildare.ie W: www.actionsouthkildare.ie
Contact: Patricia Keenan, Enterprise Development Officer

CATEGORIES: COMMUNITY & RURAL DEVELOPMENT; GRANTS; TRAINING

Action South Kildare is one of the **Community Groups** funded by **Area Development Management,** as part of its Local Development programme.
It responds to long-term unemployment and social disadvantage in the South Kildare area by bringing together the efforts and resources of State bodies, the local authority, voluntary agencies, local communities and entrepreneurs.
It provides support for enterprise, as well as training, childcare, education and community development, through financial grant aid, leadership and technical assistance.

ACTION TALLAGHT

Bruckfield Enterprise Centre, Bruckfield, Tallaght, Dublin 24
T: (01) 462 3222
Contact: Olive Whellan

CATEGORIES: BUSINESS PLANS; CONSULTING; INFORMATION; LEGAL; MARKETING

Action Tallaght was formed in 1992 as the umbrella body for five community enterprise groups in Tallaght. It provides integrated support — sales and marketing advice, business consultancy, accountancy and legal advice, financial management and feasibility studies, business plans and funding applications — to people from Tallaght who intend to establish a business. Its Enterprise programme is supported by the **Society of Saint Vincent de Paul,** which provides seed capital and a professional business consultant.

AIB BANK
Bankcentre, Ballsbridge, Dublin 4
T: (01) 660 0311
W: www.aib.ie
CATEGORIES: DEBT; EQUITY; INFORMATION; WEBSITE

AIB Bank is Ireland's largest bank. It provides a full range of banking services to business customers. Within AIB Group are: **AIB Enterprise Development Bureau** and **AIB Equity**. It also operates an excellent business portal (click on "Business" from the homepage), where startingabusinessinireland.com is AIB's content partner in the "Starting a Business" section. AIB is one of the banks that administers the **European Investment Bank** Global Loan facility for SMEs. AIB operates in Northern Ireland as **First Trust Bank**. Its Inwards Investment Dept operates the website, www.locateinireland.com, aimed at businesses moving to Ireland.

AIB BANK ENTERPRISE DEVELOPMENT BUREAU
Bankcentre, Ballsbridge, Dublin 4
T: (01) 641 3090 F: (01) 641 3045
E: business.banking@aib.ie W: www.aib.ie
Contact: John Kelly; Caroline Tully
CATEGORIES: DEBT; PUBLICATIONS

The Enterprise Development Bureau is **AIB**'s focal point for start-up and expanding businesses, both in manufacturing and service industries. It provides access to AIB's range of banking facilities, including overdrafts, loans, leasing, hire purchase, invoice discounting, business insurance, credit cards and electronic banking and administers a number of spector-specific loan schemes. It publishes a useful Starting Your Own Business Work Pack.

AIB EQUITY
AIB International Centre, IFSC, Dublin 1
T: (01) 641 7993   F: (01) 829 0269
E: laurence.c.endersen@aib.ie W: www.aibequity.ie
Contact: Laurence Endersen
CATEGORIES: DEBT; EQUITY

AIB Equity provides funding for high-growth technology companies. Unusually, AIB Equity offers a "Venture Loan" - funding to allow a company time to negotiate terms with a new investor or complete a financing round. It manages the **AIB Equity Fund 2002.**

Going it alone in business...

thoughts

dreams

nightmares

start-up plans

sleepless nights

cut-throat competition

late night pizza at your desk

never ringing in sick again:

the only way to be.

Business life is full of possibilities.

Your nearest AIB branch or www.aib.ie/business

can help you with the practicalities.

Be with AIB.

AIB EQUITY FUND 2002

AIB Equity, AIB International Centre, IFSC, Dublin 1
T: (01) 641 7993 F: (01) 829 0269
E: laurence.c.endersen@aib.ie W: www.aibequity.ie
Contact: Laurence Endersen

CATEGORIES: EQUITY

A €12.7 million fund, investing primarily in the technology sector, managed by **AIB Equity**. Half its investments will be made in companies based outside Dublin.

ALCHEMY PARTNERS

10 Fitzwilliam Square, Dublin 2
T: (01) 661 2671 F: (01) 661 3057
E: bstephens@alchemypartners.com W: www.alchemypartners.com
Contact: Brian Stephens

CATEGORIES: EQUITY

Specialising in buy-outs, buy-ins and the provision of later stage development capital, Alchemy is a London-based private equity advisory business that operates in Ireland.

ALLIANCE INVESTMENT CAPITAL

Corporate Finance Ireland, CFI House, Clonskeagh Square, Dublin 14
T: (01) 283 7656 F: (01) 283 7256
E: frank.traynor@allinv.com W: www.allinv.com
Contact: Frank Traynor

CATEGORIES: EQUITY

Alliance Investment Capital operates a €9.5 million fund (NOW CLOSED), managed by **Corporate Finance Ireland**, which invests between €317,000 and €1.27 million in established Irish companies across a wide spectrum of manufacturing, distribution and services businesses with an emphasis on technology-based firms. The fund's investors are Royal Bank Development Capital (a Royal Bank of Scotland subsidiary) and **Enterprise Ireland** (under the EU Seed & Venture Capital Measure 1994-1999).

AMARACH CONSULTING

37 Northumberland Road, Dublin 4
T: (01) 660 5506 F: (01) 660 5508
E: info@amarach.com W: www.amarach.com
Contact: Gerard O'Neill

CATEGORIES: CONSULTING; INFORMATION; PUBLICATIONS; WEBSITE

Amárach (Irish for "tomorrow") specialises in predictive market research and business forecasting. It focuses on understanding the changes taking place in Irish markets and on linking these insights to effective business strategies designed to profit from anticipated change, using a multi-disciplinary approach that draws on economics, demographics, social psychology and technological forecasting. Many of Amárach's reports are published on its website.

ANGLO IRISH BANK CORPORATION
18-21 St. Stephens Green, Dublin 2
T: (01) 616 2000 F: (01) 616 2488
E: marynolan@angloirishbank.ie W: www.angloirishbank.ie
Contact: Mary Nolan, Group Marketing Manager
CATEGORIES: DEBT

Anglo Irish Bank offers banking, treasury, invoice discounting and leasing facilities through offices in Dublin, Belfast, Cork, Galway, Limerick and Waterford.

ANTRIM ENTERPRISE AGENCY LTD
58 Greystone Road, Antrim BT41 1JZ
T: (028) 9446 7774 F: (028) 9446 7292
E: admin@antrimenterprise.com W: www.antrimenterprise.com
Contact: Jennifer McWilliams
CATEGORIES: DEBT; INFORMATION; START-UP TRAINING; TRAINING; WORKSPACE

Antrim Enterprise Agency is an **Enterprise Agency** and a member of **Enterprise Northern Ireland**. It offers workspace, start-up and ongoing training and loans.

AQUACULTURE DEVELOPMENT CENTRE
Department of Zoology & Animal Ecology, University College Cork, Cork
T: (021) 490 4590 F: (021) 427 7922
E: aquaculture@ucc.ie W: www.ucc.ie/ucc/research/adc
Contact: Dr Gerry Mouzakitis, General Manager
CATEGORIES: CONSULTING; R & D; TRAINING .

The Aquaculture Development Centre at University College Cork supports, stimulates and promotes the development of aquaculture in all its forms, through research, training and consultancy. It provides consultancy and training services for public and private sector clients, nationally and internationally. It maintains the gateway, **Aquaculture.ie**.

AQUACULTURE.ie
W: www.aquaculture.ie
CATEGORIES: INFORMATION; WEBSITE

This gateway to aquaculture in Ireland is manitained by the **Aquaculture Development Centre** at **University College Cork**.

ARDEE BUSINESS PARK
Hale Street, Ardee, Co Louth
T: (041) 685 7680 F: (041) 685 7681
E: ardbuspark@eircom.net W: www.ardeebusinesspark.ie
CATEGORIES: INFORMATION; START-UP TRAINING; TRAINING; WORKSPACE

Established by **Ardee Community Development Ltd**, this community-owned project offers training, workspace and consultancy (through **First Point Business Development Consultancy**).

ARDEE COMMUNITY DEVELOPMENT COMPANY LTD

Ardee Business Park, Hale Street, Ardee, Co Louth
T: (041) 685 7680 F: (041) 685 7681
E: ardbuspark@eircom.net W: www.ardeebusinesspark.ie
CATEGORIES: COMMUNITY & RURAL DEVELOPMENT; INFORMATION; SOCIAL
ECONOMY

The primary objective of Ardee Community Development Co Ltd is to assist local enterpreneurs and businesses to boost employment in the region. It operates the **Ardee Business Park**.

ARDS BUSINESS CENTRE LTD

Jubilee Road, Newtownards, Co Down BT23 4YH
T: (028) 9181 9787 F: (028) 9182 0625
E: postbox@ardsbusiness.com W: www.ardsbusiness.com
Contact: Margaret Patterson, Chief Executive
CATEGORIES: DEBT; INFORMATION; START-UP TRAINING; TRAINING; WORKSPACE

Ards Business Centre is an **Enterprise Agency** and a member of **Enterprise Northern Ireland.** It offers workspace, start-up and ongoing training and loans. Ards Business Centre is one of the enterprise agencies that offers the **Enter Enterprise** programme for intending entrepreneurs.

AREA DEVELOPMENT MANAGEMENT LTD

Holbrook House, Holles Street, Dublin 2
T: (01) 240 0700 F: (01) 661 0411
E: enquiries@adm.ie W: www.adm.ie
Contact: Dr Tony Crooks, CEO
CATEGORIES: ENTERPRISE SUPPORT

ADM delivers its programmes, which support integrated local economic and social development through managing programmes targeted at countering disadvantage and exclusion, and promoting reconciliation and equality, through 38 **Area Partnership Companies** in the most disadvantaged areas of Ireland and a further 35 **Community Groups** in non-disadvantaged areas. It administers the Local Development Social Inclusion Programme, through these Partnerships and Community Groups, on behalf of the **Department of Community, Rural & Gaeltacht Affairs**.

AREA PARTNERSHIPS
See individual entries for:

- Ballyfermot Partnership
- Ballymun Partnership
- Blanchardstown Area Partnership
- Bray Partnership
- Canal Communities Partnership
- Clondalkin Partnership
- Comhair Chathair Chorcaí
- County Cavan Partnership
- County Leitrim Partnership Board
- County Wexford Partnership
- Donegal Local Development Co
- Drogheda Partnership Company
- Dublin Inner City Partnership
- Dundalk Employment Partnership Ltd
- Finglas/Cabra Partnership
- Galway City Partnership
- Galway Rural Development Company
- Inishowen Partnership Board
- Kimmage/Walkinstown/Crumlin /Drimnagh Partnership
- Longford Community Resources Ltd
- Meitheal Mhaigh Eo
- Monaghan Partnership Board
- North West Kildare/North Offaly Partnership (OAK)
- Northside Partnership
- Páirtíocht Chonamara
- Páirtíocht Gaeltacht Thír Chonaill
- Partnership Trá Lí
- PAUL Partnership Limerick
- Roscommon Partnership Company
- Sligo LEADER Partnership Company Ltd
- South Kerry Development Partnership
- Southside Partnership
- Tallaght Partnership
- Waterford Area Partnership
- Waterford LEADER Partnership Ltd
- West Limerick Resources Ltd
- Westmeath Community Development Ltd
- Wexford Area Partnership.

CATEGORIES: COMMUNITY & RURAL DEVELOPMENT; GRANTS; INCUBATOR; INFORMATION; MENTORING; NETWORKING; START-UP TRAINING; TRAINING; WORKSPACE

Area Partnerships are now supported under the Local Development Social Inclusion Programme in achieving local development through the promotion of sustainable enterprise. Although Partnerships vary, among the supports that Partnerships provide are: Business, financial and legal advice; Bookkeeping and financial training; Mentoring and enterprise networks; Pre-enterprise training and training in sales and marketing; Secretarial support services; Start-up finance, through grants or revolving loans; Incubation units for start-up businesses. The activities of the Area Partnerships are co-ordinated by **Area Development Management Ltd**

ARGYLE BUSINESS CENTRE LTD
39 North Howard Street, Belfast BT13 2AP
T: (028) 9181 9787 F: (028) 9182 0625
E: frank.hamill@abc-ni.co.uk W: www.abc-ni.co.uk
Contact: Frank Hamill

CATEGORIES: INFORMATION; WORKSPACE

One of several **Enterprise Agencies/Centres** in Belfast.

ARIGNA CATCHMENT AREA COMMUNITY COMPANY

Enterprise Centre, Arigna, Carrick-on-Shannon, Co Roscommon
T: (078) 46186 F: (078) 46188
E: arigna1@iol.ie W: www.arignaleader.org
Contact: Pat Daly, Manager

CATEGORIES: COMMUNITY & RURAL DEVELOPMENT; GRANTS

A **LEADER+** company serving North Roscommon and County Leitrim, Arigna
Catchment Area Community Company offers capital equipment grants to
innovative, small enterprises in manufacturing, crafts or local services at start-
up or development stage, within its operational area.

ARKLOW COMMUNITY ENTERPRISE LTD

8 St. Mary's Terrace, Arklow, Co Wicklow
T: (0402) 91092 F: (0402) 91091
E: arklowace@eircom.net W: www.arklow.ie/chamber/aceContact.asp

CATEGORIES: BUSINESS PLANS; COMMUNITY & RURAL DEVELOPMENT;
GRANTS; MARKETING; TRAINING

Arklow Community Enterprise is one of the **Community Groups** funded by
Area Development Management, as part of its Local Development
programme. ACE offers new and small businesses in the Arklow area: Advice
on creating a business plan; Advertising and marketing; Customer service;
Grants (subject to conditions); Training.

ARMAGH BUSINESS CENTRE LTD

2 Loughgall Road, Armagh BT61 7NH
T: (028) 3752 5050 F: (028) 3752 6717
E: info@abcarmagh.com W: www.abcarmagh.com
Contact: Anna Logan, Manager

CATEGORIES: DEBT; INFORMATION; START-UP TRAINING; TRAINING; WORKSPACE

Armagh Business Centre is an **Enterprise Agency** and a member of
Enterprise Northern Ireland. It encourages the formation, development and
subsequent growth of small and medium enterprises through extensive
business and technical expertise. It also operates the Markethill Business
Centre in Armagh.

ARTS COUNCIL (AN CHOMHAIRLE EALAÍON)

70 Merrion Square, Dublin 2
T: (01) 618 0200 CallSave: 1850 392 492 F: (01) 676 1302
E: paul@artscouncil.ie / sian@artscouncil.ie W: www.artscouncil.ie
Contact: Paul Johnson, Artists Services Manager

CATEGORIES: GRANTS

The Arts Council is the development agency for the arts in Ireland and the
primary source of support for the individual creative and interpretative artist.
Its role is to provide advice to government and non-governmental bodies,
individuals and arts organisations on artistic matters, and support and
financial assistance for artistic purposes to individuals and organisations.

It annually funds over 500 arts and non-arts organisations and makes awards to over 500 individuals across all art forms.

ARTS COUNCIL OF NORTHERN IRELAND
MacNeice House, 77 Malone Road, Belfast BT9 6AQ
T: (028) 9038 5200 F: (028) 9066 1715
E: reception@artscouncil-ni.org W: www.artscouncil-ni.org
CATEGORIES: GRANTS

The Arts Council of Northern Ireland is the prime distributor of public support for the arts in Northern Ireland. Its website gives details of the awards available - and information on application procedures.

ASCEND
44 Northumberland Road, Dublin 4
T: (01) 668 8244 F: (01) 668 6613
E: info@ascend.ie W: www.ascend.ie
Contact: Paul O'Dea
CATEGORIES: BUSINESS PLANS; CONSULTING

Ascend help entrepreneurs in early stage hi-tech companies develop and implement international growth strategies. The initial focus is on preparing a strategic plan, covering agreed objectives, opportunity/capability assessment, strategy to create competitive advantage, sales/marketing strategy, product planning, defensible financial model and funding requirements. The next step is to implement that plan. Its website has a useful article on "Thoughts before writing a high-tech business plan".

ASK-IRELAND.com
W: www.ask-ireland.com
CATEGORIES: INFORMATION; WEBSITE

A site sponsored by the Irish Government, to provide information and answer queries on Ireland and Irish-related matters.

ASPIRE MICRO LOANS FOR BUSINESS LTD
5 Union Street, Belfast BT1 2JF
T: (028) 9024 6245 F: (028) 9024 6255
E: mail@aspire-loans.com W: www.aspire-loans.com
CATEGORIES: DEBT

Aspire is the first dedicated micro-finance company in the UK. It provides fast, flexible and short-term loans to the self-employed all across Belfast, Newtownabbey, Mallusk, Lisburn, Derry/ Londonderry. Aspire provides first loans between stg£200 and stg£5,000 and repeat loans up to stg£15,000 for customers with a good repayment history. These loans are short-term - over 3-9 months for first loans. Repeat borrowers can go up to 18 months. The interest rate is 1.5% per month (APR 19.5%), reduced for repeat customers.

ASPIRE! MARKETING CONSULTANTS

28 South Mall, Cork, and also at Schull, Co Cork
T: (028) 22300 F: (01) 633 5149
E: simon.okeeffe@aspire.ie W: www.aspire.ie
Contact: Simon O'Keeffe

CATEGORIES: CONSULTING; MARKETING

aspire! helps businesses to develop new products and to open up new markets, work that Simon O'Keefe previously did for Nike, Nobel and RJ Reynolds Tobacco. It provides marketing strategy and branding expertise and works with clients to support them in the execution of the strategies and plans it develops with them.

ASSOCIATION FOR PURCHASING AND SUPPLY

Devoy House, 141 Clonliffe Road, Dublin 9
T: (01) 836 9685 F: (01) 836 9642
E: info@irishpurchasing.com W: www.irishpurchasing.com
Contact: Owen O'Neill, Managing Director

CATEGORIES: INFORMATION

The Association is the membership organisation for purchasing and supply professionals. Its website includes a Supplier Directory.

ASSOCIATION OF ADVERTISERS IN IRELAND

Rock House, Main Street, Blackrock, Co Dublin
T: (01) 278 0499 F: (01) 278 0488
E: info@aai.ie W: www.aai.ie
Contact: Aidan Burns

CATEGORIES: INFORMATION; PUBLICATIONS

The Association of Advertisers in Ireland is the voice of advertisers on national and international issues that impact on commercial communications. AAI publishes *MAPS*, a directory of the media and communications industry and an excellent reference source.

ASSOCIATION OF CHARTERED CERTIFIED ACCOUNTANTS

9 Leeson Park, Dublin 6
T: (01) 498 8900 F: (01) 496 3615
E: recruit.dublin@ie.accaglobal.com W: http://ireland.accaglobal.com/
Contact: Roger Acton

CATEGORIES: ACCOUNTANTS

ACCA is one of the accountancy bodies whose members are permitted to audit company accounts. It has nearly 10,000 members and students throughout the island of Ireland. If you're looking for an accountant, ACCA can direct you to one of its members.

You've bought the book, now visit the website

www.startingabusinessinireland.com
information, advice & resources for entrepreneurs

THE website for Irish start-ups, with the most comprehensive directory of sources of assistance available, North & South – over 700 entries! Plus templates for download

... and take the course ....

START-UP BOOT CAMP

An intensive one-day learning experience, designed to accelerate your progress towards start-up by providing you with the skills and information you need, plus one month's follow-up email support.

Growing places... ?

Use SPOTcheck, Oak Tree Press' online tool to rate your business' growth potential.

SPOTcheck is a web-based business assessment tool for:

- Entrepreneurs to 'rate' the growth potential of their businesses on a self-assessment basis
- Business advisers to structure a growth analysis of a client company
- Enterprise support organisations to measure their added value.

SPOTcheck:

- Provides an analytical framework against which owner/managers and business advisers can make a structured assessment of a business' potential for growth
- Provides a basis for prescribing the appropriate business development interventions for the business
- Tracks progress made between two or more SPOTcheck assessments at different times
- Compares the assessment against the averages for similar types of business (benchmarking).

SPOTcheck is suitable for both start-ups and growing businesses.

SPOTcheck®

Try SPOTcheck at www.spotcheckonline.com.

ATHLONE COMMUNITY TASKFORCE

Business Development Centre, Ball Alley Lane, Parnell Square,
Athlone, Co Westmeath
T: (0902) 94555 F: (0902) 93311
E: athlonecommunitytaskforce@eircom.net W: www.a-c-t.org
Contact: Ray Teskey, CEO

CATEGORIES: COMMUNITY & RURAL DEVELOPMENT; GRANTS; MENTORING;
TRAINING; WORKSPACE

Athlone Community Taskforce is one of the **Community Groups** supported by **Area Development Management**, as part of its Local Development programme. ACT has developed a strategic plan for the delivery of the Local Development Social Inclusion programme, and provides enterprise training, childcare development, and community development through direct service provision, leadership, financial grant aid and technical assistance in partnership with State bodies, the local authority, voluntary agencies, local communities and entrepreneurs.

ATHLONE INSTITUTE OF TECHNOLOGY

Dublin Road, Athlone, Co Westmeath
T: (090) 647 1805 F: (090) 642 4417
E: hfitzsimons@ait.ie W: www.ait.ie
Contact: External Services Manager

CATEGORIES: CONSULTING; INCUBATOR; INFORMATION; R & D; START-UP
TRAINING; TRAINING

AIT's External Services Unit acts as a central contact point for companies and community organisations to the Institute's range of industrial services, including: consultancy/business expertise, customised training programmes and opportunities for the development of collaborative research projects in the manufacturing, services, life sciences, physical sciences and information technology sectors. AIT also offers the **Midlands Enterprise Platform Programme** and is in the process of building an Incubation Centre.

AVONDHU DEVELOPMENT GROUP

5–6 Park West, Mallow, Co Cork
T: (022) 43553 F: (022) 43681
E: avondhu@indigo.ie
Contact: Jim Sheehan

CATEGORIES: COMMUNITY & RURAL DEVELOPMENT

Avondhu Development Group is one of the **Community Groups** funded by **Area Development Management**, as part of its Local Development programme.

AWG INVESTMENT FUND

Deal Management Ltd, 74 Pembroke Road, Ballsbridge, Dublin 4
T: (01) 660 9313 F: (01) 668 7904
E: dealman@eircom.net Contact: Joe Doddy

CATEGORIES: EQUITY

The AWG Investment Fund was established in 1998 by the Avonmore Waterford Group (now Glanbia) and is managed by Deal Management Ltd. It invests between €317,000 and €653,000 in early-stage and expanding businesses.

BALBRIGGAN ENTERPRISE DEVELOPMENT GROUP
Enterprise House, 13 Drogheda Street, Balbriggan, Co Dublin
T: (01) 841 5141 F: (01) 841 1010
E: info@balbrigganenterprise.ie W: www.balbrigganenterprise.ie
CATEGORIES: INFORMATION

Balbriggan Enterprise Development Group (BEDG) operates the Balbriggan Enterprise Office, a local one-stop-shop for information and advice on market research, feasibility studies, grant applications and employment supports for new and existing businesses.

BALLON–RATHOE DEVELOPMENT ASSOCIATION LTD
Rathloe Hall, Rathloe, Co Carlow
T: (0503) 48016 F: (0503) 59337
E: managerballon@eircom.net W: www.ballonvillage.com/BRDA.htm
Contact: Kathleen Fitzgerald, Manager
CATEGORIES: COMMUNITY & RURAL DEVELOPMENT

Ballon-Rathoe Development Association is one of the **Community Groups** funded by **Area Development Management**, as part of its Local Development programme.

BALLYFERMOT PARTNERSHIP
290 Ballyfermot Road, Dublin 10
T: (01) 620 7165 F: (01) 626 3416
E: info@ballyfermotpartnership.ie W: www.planet.ie
Contact: Mark Magee, Manager
CATEGORIES: COMMUNITY & RURAL DEVELOPMENT

One of the **Area Partnerships** established by **Area Development Management**, as part of its Local Development programme.

BALLYHOO ENTREPENEURIAL CONSULTING
10 Kilgar, Jocelyn Street, Dundalk, Co Louth
T: (042) 935 1099 F: (042) 935 1129
E: yanky@yankyfachler.com W: www.yankyfachler.com
Contact: Yanky Fachler
CATEGORIES: CONSULTING; START-UP TRAINING

Yanky's focuses on the emotional aspect of entrepreneurship – the "Why?" of starting your own business – often overlooked by other trainers. Before moving into the field of motivational speaking and entrepreneurial training, Yanky's career spanned management consultancy, freelance copywriting, acting, running drama festivals, event management, tourism marketing and communal affairs. Yanky Fachler is the author of: *Fire in the Belly: An*

Exploration of the Entrepreneurial Spirit and *"My Family Doesn't Understand Me!" Coping Strategies for Entrepreneurs*, both published by Oak Tree Press.

BALLYHOURA DEVELOPMENT LTD
Kilfinane, Co Limerick
T: (063) 91300 F: (063) 91330
E: localdev@ballyhoura.org W: www.ballyhouracountry.com
Contact: Carmel Fox, Chief Executive
CATEGORIES: COMMUNITY & RURAL DEVELOPMENT; GRANTS

One of the **Community Groups** funded by **Area Development Management**, as part of its Local Development programme and a **LEADER+** company serving parts of Counties Limerick & Cork. It operates the Galtee Valley Enterprise Park in Ballylanders, Co Limerick. It offers capital equipment grants to innovative, small enterprises in manufacturing, crafts or local services at start-up or development stage, within its operational area.

BALLYMENA BUSINESS DEVELOPMENT CENTRE LTD
62 Fenaghy Road, Galgorm Industrial Estate, Ballymena BT42 1FL
T: (028) 2565 8616 F: (028) 2563 0830
E: bb.dc@virgin.net W: www.bbdc.co.uk
Contact: Melanie Christie, Centre Manager
CATEGORIES: DEBT; INFORMATION; START-UP TRAINING; TRAINING; WORKSPACE

Ballymena BDC is an **Enterprise Agency** and a member of **Enterprise Northern Ireland**. It provides a range of Business support services primarily aimed at Ballymena-based businesses.

BALLYMUN PARTNERSHIP LTD
North Mall, Ballymun Town Centre, Dublin 11
T: (01) 842 3612 F: (01) 842 7004
E: info@ballymun.org W: www.ballymun.org
Contact: Terence Kavanagh, Business Advisor
CATEGORIES: COMMUNITY & RURAL DEVELOPMENT; INCUBATOR

One of the **Area Partnerships** established by **Area Development Management**, as part of its Local Development programme. The Partnership also operates an Incubator Centre.

BANBRIDGE DISTRICT ENTERPRISES LTD
Scarva Road Industrial Estate, Scarva Road, Banbridge, Co Down BT32 3QD
T: (028) 4066 2260 F: (028) 4066 2325
E: info@bdelonline.com W: www.bdelonline.com
Contact: Ciaran Cunningham
CATEGORIES: DEBT; INFORMATION; START-UP TRAINING; TRAINING; WORKSPACE

Banbridge District Enterprises is an **Enterprise Agency** and a member of **Enterprise Northern Ireland**. It offers workspace, start-up and ongoing training and loans. It is one of the enterprise agencies that offers the **Enter Enterprise** programme for intending entrepreneurs.

BANK OF IRELAND
Head Office, Lower Baggot Street, Dublin 2
T: (01) 661 5933
W: www.boi.ie
CATEGORIES: DEBT

Bank of Ireland is the second largest bank in Ireland, providing a range of banking services to business customers. Within the Bank of Ireland group are: **Bank of Ireland Enterprise Support Unit** and **Bank of Ireland Venture Capital**. Bank of Ireland is one of the banks that administers the **European Investment Bank** Global Loan facility for SMEs. It also has invested in the **Bank of Ireland Kernel Private Equity Fund**. It operates in Northern Ireland as **Bank of Ireland Northern Ireland**.

BANK OF IRELAND ENTERPRISE SUPPORT UNIT
Haddington Centre, Percy Place, Dublin 4
T: (01) 665 3300 F: (01) 665 3755
E: michael.gannon@boimail.com W: www.bankofireland.ie/sbb
Contact: Michael Gannon, Manager
CATEGORIES: DEBT

The Enterprise Support Unit is a specialist unit committed to the start-up and developing SME sector. It provides short and medium-term working capital, normally lending from €60,000 to €200,000. It works closely with businesses in providing the right financial package to allow the company grow. The ESU also provides hands-on support and offers a full range of lending products at AA lending rates. It provides access to the full range of **Bank of Ireland** facilities, including invoice discounting (Bank of Ireland Commercial Finance) and leasing/hire purchase. Bank of Ireland also has a nationwide network of Enterprise Advisors.

BANK OF IRELAND KERNEL CAPITAL PARTNERS PRIVATE EQUITY FUND
NSC Campus, Mahon, Cork
T: (021) 230 7164 F: (021) 230 7178
E: niall.olden@kernelcapital.ie W: www.kernelcapital.ie
Contact: Niall Olden
CATEGORIES: EQUITY

This €19 million fund targets early-stage companies in the technology and life sciences sectors. Typical investments are in the €300k to €1.5 million range. The fund was established with assistance from **Enterprise Ireland**, under the Seed & Venture Capital Measure of the Operational Programme 2001-2006. **Bank of Ireland** is a lead investor.

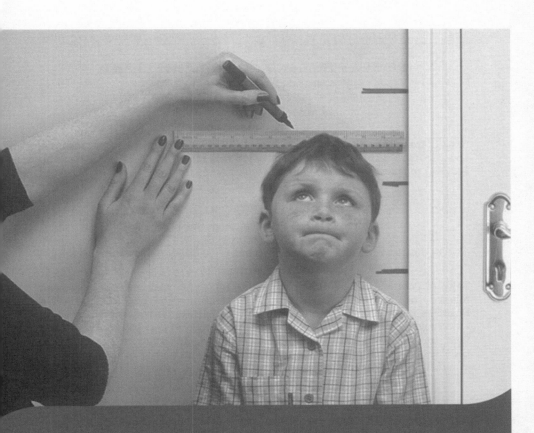

starting a business?

It may just be a baby now. But with the right care and nurturing, your new business can grow into something you can be really proud of. To help give it the best possible start, we have developed a highly competitive package that takes a lot of the financial pressure off.

So if you are thinking about starting your own business, you may wish to know more about our services to early stage companies through our Enterprise Support Unit, contactable directly at **01-6653300/6653466** or through your local branch. You can also call us for a free Business Start-up information pack at 1850 753 357.

www.bankofireland.ie/business

Bank of Ireland

Business Banking

BANK OF IRELAND NORTHERN IRELAND
54 Donegall Place, Belfast BT1 5BX
T: (028) 9023 4334 F: (028) 9023 4388
W: www.bankofireland.co.uk
CATEGORIES: DEBT

Bank of Ireland in Northern Ireland employs 1,100 staff across its various units and Province-wide retail branch network and offers a full range of banking services to start-ups and small businesses.

BANK OF SCOTLAND (IRELAND) LTD
Pinebrook House, 72-74 Harcourt Street, Dublin 2
T: (01) 415 5555 F: (01) 671 7797
E: business.banking@bankofscotland.ie W: www.bankofscotland.ie
CATEGORIES: DEBT

Bank of Scotland (Ireland) Ltd is part of HBOS plc. Services include asset finance, business banking and treasury and investments. BOSI offers a business current account, with an interest-bearing current account and an electronic overdraft facility. It also offers free banking to customers who keep their transactions within agreed limits. BOSI has branches in Belfast, Cork, Galway, Limerick and Waterford. Bank of Scotland is one of the banks that administers the **European Investment Bank** Global Loan facility for SMEs.

BANTRY INTEGRATED DEVELOPMENT GROUP
Unit 13, Enterprise Centre, Ropewalk, Bantry, Co Cork
T: (027) 52266 F: (027) 52251
E: info@bidg.org W: www.bidg.org
Contact: Fergal Conlon, Manager
CATEGORIES: BUSINESS PLANS; COMMUNITY & RURAL DEVELOPMENT;
MENTORING; TRAINING

BIDG is one of the **Community Groups** funded by **Area Development Management**, as part of its Local Development programme. For small businesses, BIDG offers: Step-by-step planning on developing your business idea; Financial Planning; Mentoring; Additional training; Advice on grant aid and interest free loans for your business, market research and setting up a farm enterprise; Use of computer equipment.

BARROW-NORE-SUIR RURAL DEVELOPMENT LTD
42 Parliament Street, Kilkenny
T: (056) 52111 F: (056) 52333
E: info@bnsrd.com W: www.bnsrd.com
Contact: Bernie Phelan
CATEGORIES: COMMUNITY & RURAL DEVELOPMENT; GRANTS

A **LEADER+** company serving Counties Carlow, Kilkenny & part of County Tipperary, BNS offers capital equipment grants to innovative, small enterprises in manufacturing, crafts or local services at start-up or development stage, within its operational area.

Making it easier for Business to deal with Government

- One-Stop-Shop for Government information and services
- Easier for business to deal with Government
- 24 hours a day, 7 days a week service
- Designed around the everyday needs of the business user
- An eGovernment initiative managed by the Department of Enterprise, Trade & Employment

www.basis.ie

BASE CENTRE
Patrickstown House, Ladyswell Road, Mulhuddart, Dublin 15
T: (01) 820 3020 F: (01) 820 9469
E: info@base-centre.com W: www.base-centre.com
CATEGORIES: START-UP TRAINING; WORKSPACE

The BASE (Blanchardstown Area Small Enterprises) Centre is an Enterprise Centre that serves the Dublin 15 area. It provides nurturing services and one-day intensive workshops particularly for new businesses.

BASIS.ie
BASIS Project, Department of Enterprise, Trade & Employment, 4th Floor, Earlsfort Centre, Lower Hatch Street, Dublin 2
T: (01) 631 2787 / (01) 631 2788 F: (01) 631 2563
E: basis@enemp.ie W: www.basis.ie
CATEGORIES: INFORMATION; WEBSITE

BASIS stands for "Business Access to State Information Services". It aims to provide information about State services and regulations to all businesses with Web access.

BDO SIMPSON XAVIER
Beaux Lane House, Mercer Street Lower, Dublin 2
T: (01) 470 0000 F: (01) 477 0000
E: info@bdosx.ie W: www.bdosx.ie
Contact: Colm Nagle
CATEGORIES: ACCOUNTANTS; EQUITY

Accountants and advisers to entrepreneurial and growing owner-managed businesses, BDO Simpson Xavier provides a useful online checklist for start-ups on its website. The firm also assists in raising **Business Expansion Scheme** funding for small businesses.

BELCOO ENTERPRISE CENTRE
Railway Road, Belcoo, Co Fermanagh BT93 5FG
T: (028) 6638 6377 F: (028) 6638 6377
Contact: John Tracey, Manager
CATEGORIES: INFORMATION; START-UP TRAINING; WORKSPACE

One of several **Enterprise Centres** in Fermanagh.

BELFAST BUSINESS LIBRARY
Central Library, Royal Avenue, Belfast BT1 1EA
T: (028) 9050 9150 F: (028) 9033 2819
E: info@libraries.belfast-elb.gov.uk
Contact: Stephen McFarlane, Librarian
CATEGORIES: INFORMATION

The Library provides a reference, lending and information service: Books on accountancy, computing, human resource management, legislation and management; Over 250 current periodicals and market research reports; Company financial and background information; General and specialised trade directories; HMSO and selected non-governmental statistics; UK & Northern Ireland legislation.

BELFAST FIRST STOP BUSINESS SHOP LTD
14 Wellington Place, Belfast BT1 6GE
T: (028) 9027 8399 F: (028) 9027 8398
E: info@firststopshop.co.uk W: www.firststopshop.co.uk
Contact: Michelle Harding/Brian Stratford, Information Officers
CATEGORIES: INFORMATION; START-UP TRAINING

Belfast First Stop Business Shop offers an information, advisory and signposting service for potential and existing businesses. Assistance is principally for those based in the Belfast City Council area, but anyone with a new business idea is encouraged to visit the shop to avail of its services. The First Stop Shop is an independent organisation with established links to both public and private sector agencies involved in enterprise development in Belfast. It has an extensive information library and a highly experienced, qualified team of people who can provide advice and counselling as well as signposting to other business development agencies. The First Stop Shop is one of the agencies that delivers the **Business Start** programme.

BIG RED BOOK
Rathdown Hall, Upper Glenageary Road, Glenageary, Co Dublin
T: (01) 204 8300 F: (01) 204 8324
E: info@bigredbook.com W: www.bigredbook.com
CATEGORIES: ACCOUNTANTS

Designed by professional accountants, Big Red Book is a computerised but easy-to-use bookkeeping package ideal for small businesses.

BINARY PARTNERS
17 Ashton, Blessington, Co Wicklow
T: (045) 891400 / (087) 243 2798 F: (045) 891400
E: blawlor@binary.ie W: www.binary.ie
Contact: Brendan Lawlor
CATEGORIES: BUSINESS ANGELS; CONSULTING

Binary Partners is a private network of business angels, active primarily (though not exclusively) in the technology sector. Binary also offers consultancy for businesses that need asistance but are not ready for funding.

For updates to this directory, go to
www.startingabusinessinireland.com
information, advice & resources for entrepreneurs

BIONORTHERNIRELAND.com

Life and Health Technologies Partnership, University of Ulster, Cromore Road,
Coleraine, Co Londonderry
T: (028) 7032 4654 F: (028) 7032 4965
E: info@bionorthernireland.com W: www.bionorthernireland.com
Contact: Aileen Moore, Development Officer

CATEGORIES: INFORMATION; WEBSITE

BioNorthernIreland.com is the online centre for news, information, contacts,
and jobs in the biotechnology sector in Northern Ireland, maintained and
promoted by the Life and Health Technologies Partnership at the Centre for
Innovation in Biotechnology, **University of Ulster**.

BIORESEARCH IRELAND

Technology House, Glasnevin, Dublin 9
T: (01) 837 0177 F: (01) 837 0176
E: info@biores-irl.ie W: www.biores-irl.ie
Contact: Dr Ena Prosser, Director

CATEGORIES: R&D

BioResearch Ireland (BRI) is an **Enterprise Ireland** initiative, in partnership
with the **Universities**, that commercialises opportunities arising from Irish
biotechnology research. It operates the Advanced Technology Research
Programme and Research Innovation Fund, as well as providing access to
Enterprise Ireland's new Commercialisation Fund. It set up and maintains the
portal website, **BiotechnologyIreland.com**.

BIOTECHINFO.ie

Forfás, Wilton Park House, Wilton Place, Dublin 2
T: (01) 607 3000 F: (01) 607 3030
E: info@biotechinfo.ie W: www.forfas.ie
Contact: Paula McKillen, Secretary to the IDG Modern Biotechnology

CATEGORIES: INFORMATION; WEBSITE

A Government-sponsored website, managed by **Forfás**, www.biotechinfo.ie
aims to increase public knowledge and awareness of the application and
impact of biotechnology in Ireland through the provision of information,
resources, contacts and bulletin boards for online discussion.

BIOTECHNOLOGYIRELAND.com

W: www.biotechnologyireland.com

CATEGORIES: INFORMATION; WEBSITE

BiotechnologyIreland.com is a portal website, set up and manintained by
BioResearch Ireland.

BLACKWATER RESOURCE DEVELOPMENT
68 Patrick Street, Fermoy, Co Cork
T: (025) 33411 F: (025) 33422
W: www.blackwater-resources.com
Contact: Niamh Kenny, Chief Executive Officer

CATEGORIES: COMMUNITY & RURAL DEVELOPMENT; GRANTS

Blackwater Resource Development is a partnership committed to a model of social justice, self-help, inclusion and respect, and to the sustainable social and economic development of the area. It delivers a range of programmes, including: **LEADER+;** National Agri/Tourism programme; EQUAL. It is the designated lead partner in the "Rural Options" North Cork/South East Limerick Development Partnership, which is made up of organisations with similar goals in tackling inequality in relation to the workforce in the region.

BLANCHARDSTOWN AREA PARTNERSHIP
Deanstown House, Main Street, Blanchardstown, Dublin 15
T: (01) 820 9550 F: (01) 820 9551
E: info@bap.ie W: www.bap.ie
Contact: Derek Hanway, Manager

CATEGORIES: COMMUNITY & RURAL DEVELOPMENT; GRANTS; INFORMATION; START-UP TRAINING

One of the **Area Partnerships** established by **Area Development Management,** as part of its Local Development programme. BAP initiatives in the area of economic development include enterprise supports for people wishing to become self-employed and the development of local community enterprises, which both employ local people and provide valuable services to the local community.

BNP PARIBAS FINANCE
Merchants Court, Merchants Quay, Dublin 8
T: (01) 612 5200 F: (01) 612 52500
W: http://bnpparibas.ie/en/nossites/Ireland.asp
Contact: Sean O'Flanagan, Commercial Manager

CATEGORIES: DEBT

BNP Finance provides leasing and hire purchase finance for industrial plant and equipment and vehicles.

BOARDROOM CENTRE
Institute of Directors in Ireland, 89 James's Street, Dublin 8
T: (01) 408 4549 F: (01) 408 4550
E: boardroom@iodireland.ie W: www.iodireland.ie
Contact: Rosemary Wilson

CATEGORIES: INFORMATION; TRAINING

The Boardroom Centre is a resource for companies looking for non-executive directors to strengthen their board, operated by the **Institute of Directors in Ireland**.

BOI VENTURE CAPITAL LTD
43 Pearse Street, Dublin 2
T: (01) 604 1752 F: (01) 677 5588
E: margaret.broderick@boimail.com
Contact: Margaret Broderick

CATEGORIES: EQUITY

A €19 million fund, targeting high growth manufacturing and information, communication and technology (ICT) businesses throughout Ireland, with typical investments ranging between €350k and €2 million. The fund was established with assistance from **Enterprise Ireland**, under the Seed & Venture Capital Measure of the Operational Programme 2001-2006.

BOLTON TRUST
Docklands Innovation Park, 128-130 East Wall Road, Dublin 3
T: (01) 240 1300 F: (01) 240 1310
E: info@boltontrust.com W: www.boltontrust.com
Contact: Michael Drennan, Estate Manager

CATEGORIES: ENTERPRISE SUPPORT; EQUITY; INCUBATOR

The Bolton Trust encourages and promotes new business enterprise in Ireland. It is an independent voluntary trust, actively committed to assisting people create sustainable business. Established in 1986 by staff of the **Dublin Institute of Technology,** the trust currently has over 200 members. The Bolton Trust's centre-piece is the **Docklands Innovation Park**. It also manages the **Small Enterprise Seed Fund**.

BORD BIA : THE IRISH FOOD BOARD
Clanwilliam Court, Lower Mount Street, Dublin 2
T: (01) 668 5155 F: (01) 668 7521
E: info@bordbia.ie W: www.bordbia.ie

CATEGORIES: GRANTS; INFORMATION; MARKETING; REGULATOR & STANDARDS

Bord Bia develops export markets for Irish food and drink companies. It provides information on exports, production, quality standards, health regulations and controls, and new developments in the industry. Its services include programmes to foster contact between international buyers and Irish companies, to protect and defend the quality and integrity of Irish food and drink, and to provide up-to-date market information. It operates the Marketing Participation Programme and the Marketing Improvement Assistance Programme, offering grants aimed at assisting SMEs improve their marketing techniques and capabilities.

BORD FÁILTE
See **Fáilte Ireland**.

BORD GLAS : THE HORTICULTURAL DEVELOPMENT BOARD

Commercial House, West End Commercial Village, Blanchardstown,
Dublin 15
T: (01) 803 0398 F: (01) 803 0399
E: info@bordglas.ie W: www.bordglas.ie

CATEGORIES: INFORMATION; MARKETING; REGULATOR & STANDARDS

Bord Glas is responsible for the development of the horticultural industry in Ireland - both the amenity sector (trees, shrubs, flowers and bulbs) and the food sector (fruit and vegetables, including mushrooms, potatoes and glasshouse crops). Its programmes assist the production, marketing and consumption of horticultural produce, and help existing and new enterprises to improve standards, develop new products and markets, and plan for the future.

BORD IASCAIGH MHARA : THE IRISH SEA FISHERIES BOARD

PO Box 12, Crofton Road, Dunlaoire, Co Dublin
T: (01) 214 4100 F: (01) 284 1123
E: info@bim.ie W: www.bim.ie
Contact: Imelda Bradley

CATEGORIES: GRANTS; INFORMATION; MARKETING; REGULATOR &
STANDARDS; TRAINING

BIM is responsible for the sustainable development of the Irish sea-food industry and stimulates investment, technological innovation, enterprise and growth. A primary objective is to expand the volume, quality and value of output from the seafish and aquaculture sectors within the context of the Common Fisheries Policy, thereby generating employment and income.
BIM provides integrated development programmes providing advisory, financial, technical, marketing and training support.

BORDERBIZLAW.com

Morgan McManus Solicitors, The Diamond, Clones, Co Monaghan
T: (047) 51011 F: (047) 51679
E: info@morganmcmanus.ie W: www.borderbizlaw.com

CATEGORIES: INFORMATION; LEGAL; WEBSITE

Provided by Morgan McManus Solicitors, this website offers legal advice to businesses on either side of the Border, or which want to do business across the Border.

BORDERS MIDLANDS & WESTERN REGIONAL ASSEMBLY

The Square, Ballaghaderreen, Co Roscommon
T: (0907) 62970 F: (0907) 62973
E: info@bmwassembly.ie W: www.bmwassembly.ie

CATEGORIES: POLICY

The Border, Midland & Western Regional Assembly was established in 1999 and consists of 29 elected members from the constituent local authorities. The BMW Region consists of counties Cavan, Donegal, Galway, Laois, Leitrim, Longford, Louth, Mayo, Monaghan, Offaly, Roscommon, Sligo, Westmeath. Its role is to: Manage the BMW Regional Operational Programme under the National Development Plan; Monitor the impact of the EU programme under the NDP/Community Support Framework; Promote the co-ordination of public services. **The BMW Assembly does not provide direct funding to individuals or organisations but funds through "Implementing Bodies".**

BORRISOKANE AREA NETWORK DEVELOPMENT

The Old Church, Borrisokane, Nenagh, Co Tipperary
T: (067) 27074 F: (067) 27517
E: bandborrisokane@eircom.net W: www.ncge.ie/service/asp?id=AP274
Contact: Ann Byrne, Manager
CATEGORIES: COMMUNITY & RURAL DEVELOPMENT

Borrisokane Area Network Development is one of the **Community Groups** funded by **Area Development Management**, as part of its Local Development programme.

BOYLAN & DODD CORPORATE SERVICES LTD

41 Percy Place, Dublin 4
T: (01) 660 7166 F: (01) 660 7193
E: mailto@businessireland.net W: www.businessireland.net
Contact: James Gormley, Donal Boylan, Chris Dodd
CATEGORIES: BUSINESS SALES/PURCHASES

Specialists in disposals of companies with turnover of £1 million+ and therefore a source of possible buy-in ventures — see the website. Linked to Boylan & Dodd Chartered Accountants.

BPLANS.org.uk

W: www.bplans.org.uk
CATEGORIES: BUSINESS PLANS; INFORMATION; WEBSITE

Bplans.org.uk contains the largest single collection of free sample business plans online. In addition, Bplans.org.uk includes practical advice on planning. See also **Palo Alto Software**.

BRAY PARTNERSHIP

4 Prince of Wales Terrace, Quinsboro Road, Bray, Co Wicklow
T: (01) 286 8266 F: (01) 286 8700
E: info@braypartnership.org
Contact: Peter Brennan, Manager
CATEGORIES: COMMUNITY & RURAL DEVELOPMENT

One of the **Area Partnerships** established by **Area Development Management,** as part of its Local Development programme.

BROOKFIELD BUSINESS CENTRE LTD
Brookfield Industrial Estate, Flax Street/Crumlin Road, Belfast BT14 7EA
T: (028) 9074 5241 F: (028) 9074 8025
W: www.flaxtrust.com/bbc.html
Contact: Bob McNeill, General Manager
CATEGORIES: INCUBATOR; WORKSPACE

The largest community regeneration project in Ireland, the Brookfield Business Centre offers 232,000 sq ft of workspace and has incubated over 330 new businesses. It is operated by the **Flax Trust**.

BROOKFIELD ENTERPRISE CENTRE
Rossfield Road, Brookfield, Dublin 24
T: (01) 462 3101 F: (01) 462 3433
Contact: Olive Whelan
CATEGORIES: WORKSPACE

The Brookfield Enterprise Centre was jointly developed by the South Dublin County Council and **Partas**, with assistance from **Enterprise Ireland**, **Tallaght Partnership**, **South County Dublin Enterprise Board**, Local Employment Service, Eastern Health Board and Roadstone. It has 15 industrial units and 10 office units.

BUSINESS EXPANSION SCHEME
Office of the Revenue Commissioners, Stamping Building, Dublin Castle, Dublin 2
T: (01) 674 8426 F: (01) 671 0012
E: b.brien@revenue.ie W: www.revenue.ie
Contact: Bert Brien
CATEGORIES: EQUITY

BES is a form of venture capital, intended to help smaller businesses and certain R&D projects. Fund-raising companies must be incorporated and resident in Ireland, must not be quoted on the Stock Exchange (other than on the Developing Companies Market), and must be engaged in a "qualifying trade". It is up to the business to find potential investors and, when it does, to obtain approval of the arrangement from the Revenue Commissioners. Subject to conditions, relief from income tax is available by way of a deduction from income to individuals who invest long-term risk capital in this way. An explanatory guide is available on the Revenue's website.

BUSINESS IN THE COMMUNITY IRELAND
32 Lower O'Connell Street, Dublin 1
T: (01) 874 7232 F: (01) 874 7637
E: admin@bitc.ie W: www.bitc.ie
CATEGORIES: COMMUNITY & RURAL DEVELOPMENT

BITC Ireland is the only business-driven network in the country specialising in corporate responsibility and community involvement.

BUSINESS INFORMATION CENTRE

Dublin City Public Libraries, Central Library, Ilac ShoppingCentre, Dublin 1
T: (01) 873 4333 / 873 3996 F: (01) 872 1451
E: businesslibrary@dublincity.ie
W: www.iol.ie/dublincitylibrary/business.htm / www.library.ie

CATEGORIES: INFORMATION

A reference service specialising in company and market research information. It stocks books, reports, directories, journals/periodicals, databases, newspapers/press cuttings (from the late 1970s) on Irish companies and organisations and a wide range of business-related subjects.

BUSINESS INNOVATION CENTRES

See individual entries for: Cork Business Innovation Centre; Dublin Business Innovation Centre ; Limerick Business Innovation Centre; NORIBIC (Business Innovation Centre, Derry); South-East Business Innovation Centre; WestBIC (Business Innovation Centre, Galway).

CATEGORIES: BUSINESS PLANS; EQUITY; INCUBATOR; INFORMATION; MARKETING; TRAINING

BICs encourage and foster innovation via services directed at the development of new ideas and their conversion into real business projects. BIC support services, which may vary between centres, include: Identification of suitable innovative projects; Programmes to develop entrepreneurs' skills; Project development assistance; Business planning/marketing planning; Financial planning/access to finance; Secretarial services/office facilities; Project incubation units.

BUSINESS INNOVATION LINK

PO Box 838, Belfast BT5 7UW
T: (028) 9041 9970 F: (028) 9041 9970
E: northsperrin58.robert@virgin.net
Contact: Robert Spence, Manager

CATEGORIES: GRANTS; R & D

Business Innovation Link is intended for the inventor or individual with a good product idea who is seeking technical advice and financial support towards product design and development. It assesses the idea, the degree of product innovation, and the likely commercial potential of the product. Financial assistance, up to stg£4,000, towards the costs of a prototype may be available.

BUSINESS PLUS

30 Morehampton Road, Dublin 4
T: (01) 660 8400 F: (01) 660 4540
E: info@businessplus.ie W: www.bizplus.ie
Contact: Nick Mulcahy, Editor

CATEGORIES: INFORMATION; PUBLICATIONS; WEBSITE

Good business magazine, with strong focus on e-business/e-commerce issues, and a useful website. The magazine is available at newsagents or on subscription.

Download Centre

Essential Business Information

Business Plus is Ireland's largest circulation business magazine. Our website bizplus.ie contains Ireland's most comprehensive online resource for business. With a few clicks you can download for free magazine articles covering entrepreneurial activity as well as expert advice from the professionals. The website's Download Centre extensive library includes:

☞ Complete listings of all recent merger and acquisition activity in Ireland, with details of legal and corporate finance advisers

☞ Handy guides to raising venture capital

☞ Economic and currency forecasts from top economists

☞ Monthly economic indicators

☞ Estate agent reviews of residential and commercial property trends

☞ Expert advice on taxation issues

☞ Daily equity briefings and share tips

Log on today – www.bizplus.ie

BUSINESS RESULTS LTD
The Business Centre, 7 Tobermore Road, Draperstown, Co Londonderry BT45 7AG
T: (028) 7962 8113 F: (028) 7962 8975
E: info@workspace.org.uk W: www.workspace.org.uk
Contact: John Clarke

CATEGORIES: COMMUNITY & RURAL DEVELOPMENT; CONSULTING

Business Results is the consultancy division of **Workspace (Draperstown) Ltd**, a community-based and community-owned development organisation. It sells economic development expertise gained by Workspace to government agencies and local groups within Ireland and abroad on a consultancy basis.

BUSINESS START
See **Northern Ireland Business Start Programme**.

BUSINESSINFORMATIONPOINT.com
16c Queen Street, Derry BT48 7EQ
T: (028) 71 37 1868
E: info@businessinformationpoint.com
W: www.businessinformationpoint.com
Contact: Dermot Harrigan, Assistant Economic Development Officer

CATEGORIES: INFORMATION; WEBSITE

This is a one-stop shop online for business information that is also available through the Derry City Information Centre (www.derrycity.gov.uk).

CAMPUS COMPANIES VENTURE CAPITAL FUND
Arancoast Ltd, Molesworth House, 8/9 Molesworth Street, Dublin 2
T: (01) 679 0818 F: (01) 679 9014
E: info@campuscapital.com W: www.campuscapital.com
Contact: Pat Ryan, Chief Executive

CATEGORIES: EQUITY

This is an €7.5 million fund set up to provide seed and early-stage development capital for businesses promoted by staff and graduates of Irish universities. It can provide from €40,000 to €600,000 for minority equity stakes in qualifying businesses in any commercial sector, including services. The main investment criteria are: Strong market orientation, commercial focus and profit motive; Clearly identifiable product of service, with sustainable growth; Sustainable competitive advantage; Investment requirement less than €600,000; Management solely focused on the business; Company based in Ireland.

CANAL COMMUNITIES PARTNERSHIP
197 Tyrconnell Road, Inchicore, Dublin 8
T: (01) 473 2196 F: (01) 453 4587
E: canalcp@iol.ie W: www.planet.ie/contact_canal.htm
Contact: Brian Kenny, Manager

CATEGORIES: COMMUNITY & RURAL DEVELOPMENT

One of the **Area Partnerships** established by **Area Development Management**, as part of its Local Development programme.

CARLOW AREA NETWORK DEVELOPMENT ORGANISATION

1 Presentation Place, Tullow Street, Carlow
T: (0503) 33457 F: (0503) 33470
E: cando@eircom.net W: www.carlow-ceb.com/cando/
Contact: David O'Flaherty, Manager

CATEGORIES: COMMUNITY & RURAL DEVELOPMENT; START-UP TRAINING

Carlow Area Network Development Organisation is one of the **Community Groups** funded by **Area Development Management**, as part of its Local Development programme. It offers programmes in enterprise creation and development and community development.

CARLOW COUNTY ENTERPRISE BOARD

98 Tullow Street, Carlow
T: (0503) 30880 F: (0503) 30717
E: info@carlow-ceb.com W: www.carlow-ceb.com
Contact: Michael P. Kelly, CEO

CATEGORIES: DEBT; E-BUSINESS; EQUITY; GRANTS; INFORMATION; MENTORING; START-UP TRAINING; TRAINING

Carlow CEB provides a support network for small business in Co Carlow and is responsible for areas not already covered by other State agencies. It provides a single point of contact at local level. Support is focused on small and micro-enterprises: typically those with the potential to employ up to 10 people. Carlow CEB also operates a Business Information Centre, which offers: A wide range of information on starting and running your own business; High-spped Internet access for business information and research; www.carlow-ceb.com, which provides a 24-hour paperless information support service; On-line research facility; Financial health-check; Business advice and mentoring.

CARLOW LEADER RURAL DEVELOPMENT COMPANY LTD

Castle Hill, Carlow
T: (0503) 34283 F: (0503) 38257
E: carlowleader@eircom.net
Contact: Assumpta O'Neill, Development Officer

CATEGORIES: COMMUNITY & RURAL DEVELOPMENT; GRANTS

Carlow LEADER administers the **LEADER+** programme in Co Carlow. It offers capital equipment grants to innovative, small enterprises in manufacturing, crafts or local services at start-up or development stage, within its operational area.

CARRÉFOURS

See individual entries for: Carréfour Cahirciveen; Carréfour Dublin;
Carréfour Galway; Carréfour Ulster; Carréfour Waterford.

CATEGORIES: COMMUNITY & RURAL DEVELOPMENT; EU INFORMATION

The Carréfours are an information network for rural areas, established by the
European Union's DG X (the Department responsible for Information,
Communication and Culture in Brussels). They provide information on all
European policies of interest to rural areas. There are more than 80 centres,
five of which are based in Ireland.

CARRÉFOUR CAHIRCIVEEN

The Old Barracks,Bridge Street, Cahirciveen, Co Kerry
T: (066) 947 2724 F: (066) 947 2725
E: info@skdp.net W: www.southkerry.ie
Contact: Janet Heeren, Carréfour Officer

CATEGORIES: COMMUNITY & RURAL DEVELOPMENT; EU INFORMATION

The Carréfour is based within the head office of the **South Kerry
Development Partnership.** It brings EU information on all aspects of rural
development to the communities of the south-west of Ireland.

CARRÉFOUR DUBLIN (EAST IRELAND CARRÉFOUR)

Enterprise House, 6 Bridge Street, Balbriggan, Co Dublin
T: (01) 841 2204 / 841 5141 F: (01) 841 5141
E: dogrady@ruraldublin.ie W: www.ruraldublin.ie/Carrefour.htm
Contact: David O'Grady, European Information Officer

CATEGORIES: COMMUNITY & RURAL DEVELOPMENT; EU INFORMATION

The Carréfour is hosted by the **Rural Dublin LEADER Company**. It brings
EU information on all aspects of rural development to the rural communities of
the Dublin area.

CARRÉFOUR GALWAY

Department of Economics, National University of Ireland, Galway
T: (091) 524411 x2501 F: (091) 524130
E: claire.noone@nuigalway.ie W: www.nuigalway.ie/ecn/carrefour

CATEGORIES: COMMUNITY & RURAL DEVELOPMENT; EU INFORMATION

The European Centre for Information and the Promotion of Rural Development
at **National University of Ireland, Galway** is part of the European-wide
Carréfour network. It serves counties Galway, Mayo, Roscommon and Clare,
informing people in these areas of European policies and programmes
relevant to rural development in the West of Ireland and encouraging
partnerships between rural groups.

CARRÉFOUR ULSTER
The Rural Centre, Creebought House, 47 Main Street, Clogher,
Co Tyrone BT76 0AA
T: (028) 8554 8872 / 8554 9438 F: (028) 8554 8203
E: info@eurolink-eu.net W: www.eurolink-eu.net
Contact: Sean P. Kelly / Heather McLaughlin

CATEGORIES: COMMUNITY & RURAL DEVELOPMENT; EU INFORMATION

Carréfour Ulster is part of the European-wide Carréfour network. It serves the counties of Northern Ireland and the border region, informing people in these areas of European policies and programmes relevant to rural development.

CARRÉFOUR WATERFORD
See **South East European Centre**.

CARRICKFERGUS ENTERPRISE AGENCY LTD
8 Meadowbank Road, Carrickfergus BT38 8YF
T: (028) 9336 9528 F: (028) 9336 9979
E: info@ceal.co.uk W: www.ceal.co.uk

CATEGORIES: DEBT; INFORMATION; START-UP TRAINING; TRAINING; WORKSPACE

CEAL is an **Enterprise Agency** and a member of **Enterprise Northern Ireland**. It offers workspace, start-up and ongoing training and loans.

CASTLECOMER DISTRICT COMMUNITY DEVELOPMENT NETWORK
11 Kilkenny Street, Castlecomer, Kilkenny
T: (056) 41966 F: (056) 41872
E: cdcdnetwork@eircom.net
Contact: Liz Hore, Manager

CATEGORIES: COMMUNITY & RURAL DEVELOPMENT

Castlecomer District Community Development Network is one of the **Community Groups** funded by **Area Development Management**, as part of its Local Development programme.

CASTLEDERG & DISTRICT ENTERPRISE COMPANY LTD
Drumquin Road, Castlederg, Co Tyrone BT81 7PX
T: (028) 8167 0414 F: (028) 8167 0731
Contact: Gerald Sproule

CATEGORIES: INFORMATION; WORKSPACE

One of the **Enterprise Agencies/Centres** in Co Tyrone.

CASTLEREAGH ENTERPRISES LTD

Dundonald Enterprise Park, Enterprise Drive, Carrowreagh Road,
Dundonald BT16 1QT
T: (028) 9055 7557 F: (028) 9055 7558
E: enterprise@castlereagh.com W: www.castlereagh.com
Contact: Jack McComiskey

CATEGORIES: DEBT; INFORMATION; START-UP TRAINING; TRAINING

Casstlereagh Enterprises is an **Enterprise Agency** and a member of **Enterprise Northern Ireland**. It aims to promote economic development and job creation in the Castlereagh Borough Council Area.

CAVAN COUNTY ENTERPRISE BOARD

Cavan Innovation & Technology Centre, Dublin Road, Cavan
T: (049) 437 7200 F: (049) 437 7250
E: info@cceb.ie W: www.cavanenterprise.ie
Contact: Vincent Reynolds, CEO

CATEGORIES: DEBT; E-BUSINESS; EQUITY; GRANTS; INFORMATION;
MENTORING; START-UP TRAINING; TRAINING

Cavan CEB provides a range of services to support micro-enterprises in its region.

CAVAN INNOVATION & TECHNOLOGY CENTRE

Dublin Road, Cavan
T: (049) 437 7200 F: (049) 437 7250
E: info@cceb.ie W: www.cavanenterprise.ie

CATEGORIES: INCUBATOR

The development of the Cavan Innovation & Technology Centre was funded by the **Cavan County Enterprise Board** and the Cavan County Enterprise Fund.

CAVAN-MONAGHAN RURAL DEVELOPMENT CO-OP SOCIETY LTD

Agricultural College, Ballyhaise, Co Cavan
T: (049) 433 8477 F: (049) 433 8189
E: info@cmrd.ie W: www.cmrd.ie
Contact: Elaine Heatherton

CATEGORIES: COMMUNITY & RURAL DEVELOPMENT; GRANTS; TOURISM
DEVELOPMENT; TRAINING

A **LEADER+** company serving Counties Cavan and Monaghan, CMRD empowers individuals and communities to work towards the sustainable economic, social, environmental, cultural and heritage development of their areas. Enterprise support and training is provided in the areas of crafts and tourism. As a LEADER+ Company, CMRD offers capital equipment grants to innovative, small enterprises in manufacturing, crafts or local services at start-up or development stage, within its operational area.

CÉIM ENTERPRISE DEVELOPMENT PROGRAMME

Letterkenny Institute of Technology, Port Road, Letterkenny, Co Donegal
T: (074) 918 6065
E: rory.mcmorrow@lyit.ie
Contact: Rory McMorrow

CATEGORIES: GRANTS; INCUBATOR; MENTORING; START-UP TRAINING

Céim is an enterprise development and training programme offered by **Letterkenny** and **Sligo IT**s, with support from **ADM**/CPA and **Enterprise Ireland**. It is targeted at graduates with innovative business ideas and offers grants, mentoring, incubation and other supports over a 12-month period.

CELTIC INVOICE DISCOUNTING PLC

71C Patrick Street, Dun Laoire, Co Dublin
T: (01) 230 0866 F: (01) 230 1121
E: pkerrigan@celtic-id.com W: www.celtic-id.com
Contact: Peter Kerrigan, MD

CATEGORIES: DEBT

Celtic Invoice Discounting provides from €2,000 to €20 million in working capital facilities via invoice discounting. This means that, as an invoice is issued to a customer, it is submitted to Celtic Invoice Discounting, which pays 75% of its value to the issuing company. When the customer pays the invoice, the balance (less fees and interest) is paid.

CENTRAL STATISTICS OFFICE

Skehard Road, Mahon, Cork
T: (021) 453 5000 F: (021) 453 5555
E: information@cso.ie W: www.cso.ie
Contact: Kevin Moriarty
Also at: Ardee Road, Rathmines, Dublin 6
T: (01) 497 7144 F: (01) 497 2360

CATEGORIES: INFORMATION; PUBLICATIONS; WEBSITE

The CSO collects, compiles, analyses and disseminates statistical information relating to the economic and social life of Ireland. It is a key source of market research information on: Industry and building; Services statistics; Labour market and Vital Statistics; Foreign trade; Agriculture; Prices; National Accounts; Balance of payments; Demography. This information is available in statistical releases, publications and associated diskettes, on the CSO's website, and via a Trade Help Desk and Information Section. Many of its publications are available from the **Government Publications** sales office.

CENTRE FOR CO-OPERATIVE STUDIES

O'Rahilly Building, University College Cork, Cork
T: (021) 490 2570 F: (021) 490 3358
E: ccs@ucc.ie W: www.ucc.ie/acad/foodecon/centre_b.html
Contact: Michael Ward

CATEGORIES: CONSULTING; CO-OPERATIVES; INFORMATION; TRAINING

CCS is a university research centre that promotes education and training and independent research and consultancy in all aspects of co-operative organisation. It publishes 12 *Co-op Guides* (€7.60), dealing with the steps in starting and running worker and community co-ops.

CENTRE FOR CROSS-BORDER STUDIES
39 Abbey Street, Armagh BT61 7EB
T: (028) 3751 1550 F: (028) 3751 1721
E: a.pollak@qub.ac.uk W: www.crossborder.ie
Contact: Andy Pollak, Director

CATEGORIES: CROSS-BORDER; INFORMATION; POLICY

The Centre is a policy research and development institute, whose purpose is to commission and publish research on issues related to opportunities for and obstacles to cross-border co-operation in all fields of society and economy. It is owned jointly by **Queen's University Belfast**, **Dublin City University** and the Workers' Education Association (Northern Ireland).

CENTRE FOR ENTREPRENEURIAL STUDIES
College of Business, University of Limerick, Limerick
T: (061) 202 183 F: (061) 213 196
E: patricia.fleming@ul.ie W: www.ul.ie
Contact: Patricia Fleming

CATEGORIES: CONSULTING; INFORMATION; START-UP TRAINING: TRAINING

The Centre for Entrepreneurial Studies at University of Limerick undertakes teaching, research and outreach activities in entrepreneurship and the small to medium-sized enterprise (SME) sector. It is also associated with the **Small Business Institute's** Business Consulting Programme, which provides confidential managerial assistance to local firms in manufacturing, tourism and agri-business sectors, the **Marketing Centre for Small Business** and the University's Campus Enterprise Programme. Its Graduate Diploma in Entrepreneurship Management is a one-year programme aimed at recent graduates, graduates with work experience or individuals with a professional qualification who wish to establish their own business.

CENTURY MANAGEMENT LTD
Century House, Newlands Business Park, Newlands Cross, Clondalkin, Dublin 22
T: (01) 459 5950 F: (01) 459 5949
E: centmgmt@century-management.ie W: www.century-management.ie
Contact: John Butler, Managing Director

CATEGORIES: CONSULTING; MARKETING; PUBLICATIONS; TRAINING

Century Management works with a wide range of Irish companies on strategic thinking and planning, organisational development, leadership issues, internal and customer audits, transforming cultures, attitude management and sales/marketing initiatives. It is now repositioning its business to embrace Internet technology and become a key player in the e-learning revolution.

It is affiliated with some of the world's leading authorities on business development - Brian Tracy International, Insights Europe, TTI International. John Butler is the author of *Successful Entrepreneurial Management*.

CERT
See **Fáilte Ireland**.

CFM CAPITAL
Block 3, Harcourt Centre, Harcourt Road, Dublin 2
T: (01) 449 6428 F: (01) 475 0032
E: mergers@cfmcapital.com W: www.cfmcapital.com
Contact: David Chapman
CATEGORIES: EQUITY

CFM Capital are corporate finance specialists, covering acquisitions, disposals, management buy-outs and buy-ins, valuations and restructurings.

CHAMBERS OF COMMERCE OF IRELAND
17 Merrion Square, Dublin 2
T: (01) 661 2888 F: (01) 661 2811
E: info@chambersireland.ie W: www.chambersireland.ie
Contact: Karen Hynes, Head of Business Development; John Dunne, Chief Executive
CATEGORIES: INFORMATION; NETWORKING

CCI is Ireland's largest business network with 53 affiliated chambers representing 11,000 member companies nationwide and over 40 corporate and affiliate members. CCI is a lobbying organisation, focused on making and keeping Ireland competitive. An official Social Partner, it represents the views of Irish business to Givernment and other decision-makers on a wide range of issues affecting competitiveness. CCI also offers value-for-money support services to Irish businesses in many areas, including training, trade and e-business. As the national "umbrella" body for its members, CCI actively promotes the growth and development of the Chamber network at a local, national and international level.

CHARITY BANK
5 Union Street, Belfast BT1 2JF
T: (028) 9024 8622
E: enquiries@charitybank.org W: www.charitybank.org
CATEGORIES: DEBT

Charity Bank is the first of its kind: a charity that can accept deposits that can earn a reward more than money alone can value; and it is a bank whose task is to make affordable loans, but only for charitable purposes.

CHARTERED INSTITUTE OF LOGISTICS & TRANSPORT
1 Fitzwilliam Place, Dublin 2
T: (01) 676 3188 F: (01) 676 4099
E: info@citi.iol.ie W: www.cilt.ie
Contact: Sheila Harris, Jim Kearney, Philip Mahony
CATEGORIES: CONSULTING; INFORMATION; TRAINING

CILT is the professional body for those engaged in logistics and all modes of transport. It also provides training and consultancy.

CHARTERED INSTITUTE OF MANAGEMENT ACCOUNTANTS
44 Upper Mount Street, Dublin 2
T: (01) 676 1721 F: (01) 676 1796
E: dublin@cimaglobal.com W: www.cimaglobal.com
CATEGORIES: ACCOUNTANTS; CONSULTING; MENTORING

Chartered Management Accountants assist small & medium-sized businesses in a wide variety of ways such as: Business Planning & Implementation; Cashflow forecasting; Weekly/Monthly Accounts preparation; Pricing/Costing; Budgeting; Credit Control; Accounting Software; Tax returns; Accounting & Business advice. CIMA members do not audit Ltd companies' accounts. If you are looking for a Chartered Management Accountant in Practice in your area, go to: www.cimaglobal.com/main/resources/services/consultants

CHARTERED INSTITUTE OF PERSONNEL & DEVELOPMENT
Stephen's House, 7-8 Upper Mount Street, Dublin 2
T: (01) 676 6655 F: (01) 676 7229
E: info@cipd.ie W: http://branchwebs.cipd.co.uk/ireland
Contact: Michael McDonnell, Director
CATEGORIES: INFORMATION; TRAINING

CIPD Ireland is the professional membership body for those involved in the management and development of people. It offers training and other suports to its members, while providing research and reports more widely.

CHOOSEENTERPRISE.com
W: www.chooseenterprise.com
CATEGORIES: INFORMATION; WEBSITE; YOUNG ENTERPRISE

A website for young people thinking about setting up their own business, set up by **Cookstown Enterprise Centre**, **Dungannon Enterprise Centre**, **Fermanagh Enterprise Centre**, **Omagh Enterprise Centre**, and **Strabane Enterprise Centre**.

CITY OF DUBLIN VOCATIONAL EDUCATIONAL COMMITTEE

Town Hall, Merrion Road, Ballsbridge, Dublin 4
T: (01) 668 0614 F: (01) 668 0710
E: jim.boland@cdvec.ie W: www.cdvec.ie
Contact: Jim Boland, Management Services; WJ Arundel, CEO

CATEGORIES: START-UP TRAINING; TRAINING

CDVEC is the local education authority for Dublin City and its inner suburbs. It offers courses for career-improvement, leisure, and self-development, including "Start Your Own Business" courses - check with your local college.

CITY OF DUBLIN YMCA

Aungier Street, Dublin 2
T: (01) 478 2607
E: stepduby@iol.ie W: www.ymca.ie

CATEGORIES: START-UP TRAINING

City of Dublin YMCA is the second-oldest YMCA in the world, founded in 1849. Its STEP (Support, Training and Enterprise Programme) is aimed at early school-leavers.

CITY/COUNTY ENTERPRISE BOARDS

See individual entries for:

- Carlow
- Cavan
- Clare
- Cork City
- Cork North County
- Donegal
- Dublin City
- Dún Laoire/ Rathdown
- Fingal (Dublin North)
- Galway County and City
- Kerry
- Kildare
- Kilkenny
- Laois
- Leitrim
- Limerick City
- Limerick County
- Longford
- Louth
- Mayo
- Meath
- Monaghan
- Offaly
- Roscommon
- Sligo
- South Cork
- South Dublin
- Tipperary North
- Tipperary South Riding
- Waterford City
- Waterford County
- West Cork
- Westmeath
- Wexford
- Wicklow

CATEGORIES: DEBT; E-BUSINESS; EQUITY; GRANTS; INFORMATION; MENTORING; START-UP TRAINING; TRAINING

The 35 City/County Enterprise Boards act as a single point of contact for small businesses in their locality to access all the information and advice they need.
Each has a Board, usually of 14 people, representing a partnership between local business, voluntary groups, social partners, State agencies and local elected representatives. The CEBs are co-funded by the **Department of Enterprise, Trade and Employment** and by the European Union (EU). Depending on the needs of the individual business, and its own allocation of resources, CEBs provide: "Start Your Own Business" courses; Business development skills training; Business information, advice and guidance; Capital grants up to €63,500 or 50% of capital investment; E-commerce implementation; Employment grants up to a maximum of €6,350 per employee

(including the promoter); Equity finance (up to €63,500); Feasibility study grants up to a maximum of €5,100 (50% grant-aid); Management development training; Mentoring support. **Enterprise Boards are putting an increased emphasis on business supports (management development programmes, mentoring and other training), rather than cash grants for jobs as before.**

CLANCY BUSINESS FINANCE LTD

Bayview House, 49 North Strand, Dublin 3
T: (01) 817 0051 F: (01) 817 0050
E: lucinda@clancybusiness.com W: www.clancybusiness.com
Contact: Lucinda Clancy, Managing Director
CATEGORIES: DEBT

Clancy Business Finance offers a range of flexible working capital finance solutions, not widely available through traditional banks. Through a commercial approach to banking, it provides funding facilities on the basis of debtors and actual transactions, rather than the client's balance sheet. This means that finance can be provided start-up and growing companies.

CLANN CREDO, THE SOCIAL INVESTMENT FUND

Irish Social Finance Centre, 10 Grattan Crescent, Inchicore, Dublin 8
T: (01) 453 1861 F: (01) 453 1862
E: info@clanncredo.ie W: www.clanncredo.ie
Contact: Paul O'Sullivan, Chief Executive
CATEGORIES: COMMUNITY & RURAL DEVELOPMENT; DEBT; SOCIAL ECONOMY

Clann Credo is a social investment fund, with €8.5m available. It funds, by way of repayable loans, projects that have a positive social impact.

CLARE COUNTY ENTERPRISE BOARD

Enterprise House, Mill Road, Ennis, Co Clare
T: (065) 684 1922 F: (065) 684 1887
E:clareceb@clareceb.ie W: www.clare-ceb.ie
Contact: Eamonn Kelly, CEO
CATEGORIES: DEBT; E-BUSINESS; EQUITY; GRANTS; INFORMATION;
MENTORING; START-UP TRAINING; TRAINING

Clare CEB provides a range of services to support micro-enterprises in its region.

CLONDALKIN PARTNERSHIP

Camac House, Unit 4, Oakfield Industrial Estate, Clondalkin, Dublin 22
T: (01) 457 6433 F: (01) 457 7145
E: mail@clondalkinpartnership.ie W: www.clondalkinpartnership.ie
Contact: Aileen O'Donoghue, Manager
CATEGORIES: COMMUNITY & RURAL DEVELOPMENT; INCUBATOR;
INFORMATION; MENTORING; NETWORKING; START-UP TRAINING; TRAINING

One of the **Area Partnerships** established by **Area Development Management,** as part of its Local Development programme. It provides supports for entrepreneurs in the Clondalkin area, including the Bawnogue Enterprise Centre, managed by **Action Clondalkin Enterprise**.

CLONMEL COMMUNITY PARTNERSHIP

Ormonde Centre, Prior Park, Clonmel, Co Tipperary
T: (052) 29616 F: (052) 29615
E: ccp@eircom.net
Contact: PJ Dooley, Co-ordinator

CATEGORIES: COMMUNITY DEVELOPMENT; TOURISM DEVELOPMENT

Clonmel Community Partnership is one of the **Community Groups** funded by **Area Development Management**, as part of its Local Development programme.

COALISLAND & DISTRICT DEVELOPMENT ASSOCIATION LTD

51 Dungannon Road, Coalisland, Co Tyrone BT71 4HP
T: (028) 8774 7215 F: (028) 8774 8695
Contact: Pat McGirr, Chief Executive

CATEGORIES: INFORMATION; WORKSPACE

One of the **Enterprise Agencies/Centres** in Co Tyrone.

COCA-COLA NATIONAL ENTERPRISE AWARDS

Regional Development Centre, Dundalk Institute of Technology,
Dublin Road, Dundalk, Co Louth
T: (042) 937 0413 F: (042) 935 1412
E: ccnea@dkit.ie W: www.rdc.ie
Contact: Anne Tinnelly, Industrial Services Officer

CATEGORIES: COMPETITIONS; MENTORING; START-UP TRAINING

The Coca-Cola National Enterprise Awards programme offers graduate entrepreneurs the opportunity to develop their ideas into meaningful commercial propositions and to compete for an award from a substantial prize fund. Managed by **Dundalk IT's Regional Development Centre**, the programme comprises intensive business training modules, individual assessment sessions and business mentoring (provided by **Enterprise Ireland**).

COFORD (NATIONAL COUNCIL FOR FOREST RESEARCH & DEVELOPMENT)

Agriculture Building, University College Dublin, Belfield, Dublin 4
T: (01) 716 7700 F: (01) 716 1180
E: info@coford.ie W: www.coford.ie
Contact: Joe O'Carroll, Operations Manager

CATEGORIES: INFORMATION

COFORD coordinates and funds appropriate and cost-effective research to secure long-term industrial viability and optimise social, environmental and cultural developments associated with forestry, and is supported under the National Development Plan 2000-2006.

COILLTE : THE IRISH FORESTRY BOARD
Leeson Lane, Dublin 2
T: (01) 661 5666 F: (01) 678 9527
E: pr@coillte.ie W: www.coillte.ie
Contact: Gerry Egan
CATEGORIES: CONSULTING; INFORMATION

Coillte manages the State-owned forests and operates nurseries, wood products, farm forestry services and consulting businesses.

COISTE CORCA DHUIBHNE
c/o Oifig An Cheoil, Sráid Dhá Gheata, An Daingean, Co Chiarraí
T: (066) 915 2222 F: (066) 915 2242
E: oac@eircom.net
Contact: Joan Maguire
CATEGORIES: COMMUNITY & RURAL DEVELOPMENT

Coiste Corca Dhuibhne is one of the **Community Groups** funded by **Area Development Management**, as part of its Local Development programme. It is a regional office of **Meitheal Forbartha na Gaeltachta Teo**.

COLERAINE ENTERPRISE AGENCY
Loughahill Industrial Estate, Coleraine, Co Londonderry BT52 2NR
T: (028) 7035 6318 F: (028) 7035 5464
E: info@coleraine-enterprise.co.uk W: www.coleraine-enterprise.com
Contact: Ray Young, Manager
CATEGORIES: DEBT; INFORMATION; START-UP TRAINING; TRAINING; WORKSPACE

Coleraine Enterprise Agency is an **Enterprise Agency** and a member of **Enterprise Northern Ireland**. It provides workshop premises and support services to small businesses. It offers Enterprise/Business Start training.

COLERAINE LOCAL ACTION GROUP FOR ENTERPRISE LTD
89 Main Street, Garvagh BT51 5AB
T: (028) 2955 8066 F: (028) 2955 8130
E: kevin@collage-ltd.com W: www.collage-ltd.com
Contact: Kevin Wilson, Rural Strategy Manager
CATEGORIES: COMMUNITY & RURAL DEVELOPMENT

One of the **LEADER+** groups in Northern Ireland. It also delivers programmes under PEACE II.

COMERFORD TECHNOLOGY MANAGEMENT LTD
Abercorn House, 57 Charleston Road, Ranelagh, Dublin 6
T: (01) 496 4446 F: (01) 496 7008
E: info@kcomerford.com W: www.kcomerford.com
Contact: Kieran Comerford
CATEGORIES: CONSULTING; R & D

Comerford Technology Management Ltd provides confidential advisory services in the management of technology as a resource and assists in the commercial exploitation of new technology.

COMHAIR CHATHAIR CHORCAÍ : CORK CITY PARTNERSHIP
Sunbeam Industrial Park, Millfield, Mallow Road, Cork
T: (021) 430 2310 F: (021) 430 2081
E: partnershipcork@eircom.net
Contact: Jim O'Flynn, Manager
CATEGORIES: COMMUNITY & RURAL DEVELOPMENT

One of the **Area Partnerships** funded by **Area Development Management**, as part of its Local Development programme.

COMHAR
17 St Andrew Street, Dublin 2
T: (01) 888 3990 F: (01) 888 3999
E: comhar@environ.ie W: www.comhar-nsdp.ie
Contact: Noel Casserly
CATEGORIES: POLICY

Comhar is a forum for national consultation and dialogue on Ireland's pursuit of sustainable development. Its membership covers the three aspects of sustainable development - environmental, economic and social interests.

COMHAR IORRAIS LEADER TEO
Sráid na tSéipéil, Béal an Mhuirthead, Co Mhuigh Eo
T: (097) 82303 F: (097) 82303
E: errisrd@iol.ie
Contact: Tim Quinn
CATEGORIES: COMMUNITY & RURAL DEVELOPMENT; GRANTS

A **LEADER+** company serving Erris Region, Comhar Ioraais LEADER Teo offers capital equipment grants to innovative, small enterprises in manufacturing, crafts or local services at start-up or development stage, in its area.

COMHDHÁIL OILEÁIN NA hÉIREANN
Rúnaíocht, Inis Oírr, Árainn, Cuan na Gaillimhe
T: (099) 75096 F: (099) 75103
E: comhdhail.oileain@indigo.ie W: www.oileain.ie
Contact: Mairéad O'Reilly
CATEGORIES: COMMUNITY & RURAL DEVELOPMENT; GRANTS

A **LEADER+** company serving the Offshore Islands, Comhdháil Oileáin na hÉireann offers capital equipment grants to innovative, small enterprises in manufacturing, crafts or local services at start-up or development stage, within its operational area.

COMMUNITY ENTERPRISE SOCIETY LTD
Terenure Enterprise Centre, 17 Rathfarnham Road, Terenure, Dublin 6W
T: (01) 490 3237 F: (01) 490 3238
E: info@terenure-enterprise.ie W: www.terenure-enterprise.ie
Contact: Pauline Doyle
CATEGORIES: BUSINESS PLANS; COMMUNITY & RURAL DEVELOPMENT;
INCUBATOR; INFORMATION

Terenure Enterprise Centre provides business incubator units, business advice and assistance with business plans, funding applications, etc. and an enterprise information library for small start-up projects unable to secure such support from other sources.

COMMUNITY EXCHANGE
Activelink, 10 Upper Grand Canal Street, Dublin 4
T: (01) 667 7326 F: (01) 667 7377
E: info@activelink.ie W: www.activelink.ie/ce/
CATEGORIES: COMMUNITY & RURAL DEVELOPMENT; NETWORKING; SOCIAL
ECONOMY

A communication channel for the community and voluntary sector in Ireland, providing a wide range of information on events, training, publications, resources, etc.

COMMUNITY GROUPS
See individual entries for:

- Action South Kildare Ltd
- Arklow Community Enterprise Ltd
- Avondhu Development Group
- Ballon - Rathoe Development Association Ltd
- Ballyhoura Community Partnership
- Bantry Integrated Development Group
- Borrisokane Area Network Development
- Carlow Area Network Development Organisation
- Castlecomer District Community Development Network
- Clonmel Community Partnership
- Coiste Corca Dhuibhne
- Community Enterprise Society Ltd
- Co-Operation Fingal (North)
- East Cork Area Development Ltd
- Eirí Corca Baiscinn
- Ennis West Partners
- IRD Duhallow Ltd
- Kerry Rural Development, Sliabh Luachra Ltd
- Kilkenny Community Action Network
- Lucan 2000
- Meitheal Forbartha na Gaeltachta Teo
- Meitheal Mhuscraí
- Mountmellick Development Association Ltd
- Navan Travellers Workshop Ltd

- Nenagh Community Network
- North Kerry Together Ltd
- North Meath Communities Development Association
- OBAIR Newmarket-on-Fergus Ltd
- Portlaoise Community Action Project

- Roscrea 2000
- Trim Initiative for Development and Enterprise (TIDE)
- Tullamore Wider Options Ltd
- West Offaly Integrated Development Partnership
- Wicklow Working Together.

CATEGORIES: COMMUNITY & RURAL DEVELOPMENT

These Community Groups are funded by **Area Development Management Ltd**), to deliver the Local Development Measure of the Social Inclusion programme. Many of the groups are also involved in other activities.

The types of activities undertaken by the groups include: Community tourism or heritage projects; Ensuring the inclusion of the most disadvantaged groups in Community Group activities and at Board level; Enterprise support programmes; Establishing and supporting networks of community and voluntary groups; Projects to improve the local environment and the visual appeal of the more disadvantaged areas; Providing childcare and other supports to ensure full participation opportunities for lone parents and unemployed people; Refurbishment of buildings for use as community resource centres; Support for community training programmes. Check with each group for details of its specific activities.

COMPANIES REGISTRATION OFFICE

Parnell House, 14 Parnell Square, Dublin 1
T: (01) 804 5200 F: (01) 804 5222
E: info@cro.ie W: www.cro.ie

CATEGORIES: INFORMATION; REGULATOR & STANDARDS

The CRO is the authority for the incorporation of new companies and the registration of business names in the Republic of Ireland. It is also responsible for the receipt and registration of post-incorporation documents, for enforcement of the filing requirements of companies and for the provision of information to the public. Almost all of the information filed with the CRO is available for public inspection, usually for a small fee. A range of forms is available for download from the CRO website.

COMPANIES REGISTRY

64 Chichester Street, Belfast BT1 4JX
T: 028 9023 4488 F: 028 9054 4888
E: info.companiesregistry@detini.gov.uk
W: www.companiesregistry-ni.gov.uk

CATEGORIES: INFORMATION; REGULATOR & STANDARDS

The Companies Registry is the authority for the incorporation of new companies in Northern Ireland. It is also responsible for the receipt and registration of post-incorporation documents, for enforcement of the filing requirements of companies and for the provision of information to the public. Almost all of the information filed with the Company's Registry is available for public inspection, usually for a small fee.

COMPANIES REGISTRATION OFFICE
AN OIFIG UM CHLÁRÚ CUIDEACHTAÍ

Important Information for New Businesses

The Companies Registration Office, (CRO) is the statutory body for the registration of all companies and business names. Companies and businesses have to file certain documents with the CRO, and these are stored electronically for later public inspection. Copies can be requested through our website **www.cro.ie**

Important things a company director should know

Every company whether trading or not, must file an annual return each year not later than 28 days from its statutory annual return date (ARD). The ARD of every company can be checked free of charge on the CRO website at **www.cro.ie/search**

An annual return (Form B1) is a document setting out certain prescribed company information. A checklist of all documents to be attached to Form B1 when filed is contained in the form. In most cases, audited accounts must be attached to the annual return. These accounts must cover a period which ends not more than nine months prior to the date to which the annual return is made up.

First Annual Return

The first ARD for a newly incorporated company is the date which is **six months** after the date of incorporation. No accounts need to be attached to this first return.

Second and subsequent ARDs will fall on the anniversary of the company's first ARD, unless the company elects to change its ARD.

Save time by completing forms online

Notify us of a change in address, change in director / secretary details or business name particulars free of charge. Register your business name and have it processed within 5 working days. Sole traders can avail of a simpler version of the Business Name Registration which has been developed specifically for one-off users.

Stay Informed

Subscribe to our free e-mail newsletter service and we'll keep you up-to-date on what's new at the CRO.

Download forms and publications

Browse through our services of information leaflets and view the latest copy of our information bulletin for company directors, "Corporate Compliance Matters".

For further information go to **www.cro.ie** or email queries to **info@cro.ie**

COMPANIES REGISTRATION OFFICE
Parnell House, 14 Parnell Square, Dublin 1

www.cro.ie

Lo Call: 1890 220 226
Tel: +353 1 804 5200   Fax: +353 1 804 5222
Email: info@cro.ie   Web: www.cro.ie

COMPANY BROKING CONSULTANTS

Horwatch House, 20 Rosemary Street, Belfast BT1 1QD, Northern Ireland
T: (028) 9024 9222 F: (028) 9024 9333
E: info@cobrco.com W: www.cobrco.com
Contact: Ursula O'Connel

CATEGORIES: BUSINESS SALES/PURCHASES

Company Broking Consultants is a specialist brokerage business dedicated to providing a range of services to buyers and sellers of private companies.

COMPANY FORMATIONS INTERNATIONAL LTD

22 Northumberland Road, Ballsbridge, Dublin 4
T: (01) 664 1111 F: (01) 664 1100
E: cfi@formations.ie W: www.formations.ie
Contact: Marc O'Connor, Chief Executive

CATEGORIES: INFORMATION; MARKETING

CFI is a specialist in company formation and secretarial and business information. CFI maintains a database of financial and marketing information on Irish companies, offering access on CD-ROM, on the Internet and on the telephone. It also operates the Irish Company Information Online (www.irion.ie) website, in association with Indigo.

COMPETITIVE BUSINESS INTELLIGENCE

Athlone Institute of Technology, Dublin Road, Athlone, Co Westmeath
T: (0906) 424567 F: (0906) 424624
E: blynch@ait.ie W: www.cbi.ait.ie
Contact: B Lynch

CATEGORIES: CONSULTING; INFORMATION; TRAINING

Based on the **Athlone IT** campus, CBI offers a wide range of training and consultancy services to enterprises and industry. It also offers a research service, supported by the library facilities of AIT and the British Library.

CONNEMARA WEST PLC

Connemara West Centre, Letterfrack, Co Galway
T: (095) 41047 F: (095) 41112
E: connwest@iol.ie W: www.furnituretechnologycentre.ie
Contact: Kieran O'Donohue, Director

CATEGORIES: COMMUNITY & RURAL DEVELOPMENT

Connemara West Plc in North West Connemara is one of the best known and successful rural community development organisations in Ireland. Connemara West has initiated a wide range of projects related to tourism, cultural affairs, the environment, youth training and education, community radio and enterprise development, including The Furniture College in Letterfrack with the **Galway Mayo Institute of Technology**.

COOKSTOWN ENTERPRISE CENTRE LTD

Derryloran Industrial Estate, Sandholes Road, Cookstown,
Co Tyrone BT80 9LU
T: (028) 8676 3660 F: (028) 8676 3160
E: cookstown.enterprise@btinternet.com W: www.cookstownenterprise.com
Contact: Ciaran Higgins, Manager

CATEGORIES: DEBT; INFORMATION; START-UP TRAINING; TRAINING; WORKSPACE

Cookstown Enterprise Centre is an **Enterprise Agency** and a member of
Enterprise Northern Ireland. The centre's main function is supporting new
businesses: Free advice, training, support, and help with obtaining financial
assistance is available to those thinking of starting a new business. It also
offers competitively-priced premises. See also **Choose Enterprise**.

CO-OPERATION FINGAL (NORTH)

The BEaT Centre, Stephenstown Industrial Estate, Unit 14, Balbriggan,
Fingal, Co Dublin
T: (01) 802 0484 F: (01) 841 3109
E: info@co-operationfingal.ie
Contact: Linda Curran, Manager; Emer Mullan, Employment Co-ordinator

CATEGORIES: COMMUNITY & RURAL DEVELOPMENT; TOURISM DEVELOPMENT

Co-operation Fingal (North) is one of the **Community Groups** funded by **Area
Development Management**, as part of its Local Development programme.

CO-OPERATION IRELAND

20 Herbert Place, Dublin 2
T: (01) 661 0588 F: (01) 661 8456
E: info@cooperationireland.org W: www.cooperationireland.org
Contact: Tony Kennedy, Chief Executive
Also at: 2nd Floor, Glendenning House, 6 Murray Street, Belfast BT1 6DN
T: (028) 9032 1462 F: (028) 9089 1000

CATEGORIES: COMMUNITY & RURAL DEVELOPMENT; GRANTS

Co-operation Ireland, formerly Co-operation North, advances mutual
understanding and respect by promoting practical co-operation between the
people of Northern Ireland and the Republic of Ireland. Co-operation Ireland
is an Intermediary Funding Body (IFB) for the EU Peace and Reconciliation
Programme for Northern Ireland and the Border Region of Ireland.

CO-OPERATIVE DEVELOPMENT SOCIETY LTD

Dominick Court, 41 Lower Dominick Street, Dublin 1
T: (01) 873 3199 F: (01) 873 3612
E: coopsoc@tinet.ie W: www.ablaze.ie/cds
Contact: Carol O'Neill

CATEGORIES: CO-OPERATIVES; INFORMATION

One of the organisations that provides Model Rules for the formation of
worker and community co-operatives.

CORK BUSINESS INNOVATION CENTRE
NSC Campus, Mahon, Cork
T: (021) 230 7005 F: (021) 230 7020
E: postmaster@corkbic.com W: www.corkbic.com
Contact: Michael O'Connor, Chief Executive

CATEGORIES: BUSINESS PLANS; EQUITY; INCUBATOR; INFORMATION;
MARKETING; TRAINING

Cork BIC assists the creation and fostering of enterprise in the Cork and Kerry regions of Ireland and provides hands-on assistance to entrepreneurs and small businesses. Its services include: Project monitoring and intervention after launch of a new business; Development of management skills; Market-led business planning and financial management; Innovation and technology assistance; Access to financing; Incubator workspace. Cork BIC is the project manager for the **National Software Campus**.

CORK CITY ENTERPRISE BOARD
1-2 Bruach na Laoi, Union Quay, Cork
T: (021) 496 1828 F: (021) 496 1869
E: corkceb@iol.ie W: www.corkceb.ie
Contact: Dave Cody, CEO

CATEGORIES: DEBT; E-BUSINESS; EQUITY; GRANTS; INFORMATION;
MENTORING; START-UP TRAINING; TRAINING

Cork City Enterprise Board offers direct grant aid to manufacturing industry, internationally traded services and, in certain circumstances, the service sector. In partnership with **South Cork Enterprise Board**, Cork Chamber of Commerce and **IBEC**, Cork CEB operates a **PLATO** training programme.

CORK INSTITUTE OF TECHNOLOGY
Rossa Avenue, Bishopstown, Cork
T: (021) 432 6100 F: (021) 454 5343
E: jsomullane@cit.ie W: www.cit.ie
Contact: Josette O'Mullane, Industrial Liaison Officer

CATEGORIES: CONSULTING; R&D

CIT provides Research & Development and services to industry and operates a number of Technology Centres. It also operates the **Genesis Enterprise Platform Programme**.

CORK NORTH COUNTY ENTERPRISE BOARD
The Enterprise Office, 26 Davis Street, Mallow, Co Cork
T: (022) 43235 F: (022) 43247
E: corknent@iol.ie
Contact: Rochie Holohan

CATEGORIES: DEBT; E-BUSINESS; EQUITY; GRANTS; INFORMATION;
MENTORING; START-UP TRAINING; TRAINING

Cork North CEB offers a full range of supports for micro-enterprises in its region.

CORPORATE FINANCE IRELAND

CFI House, Block 1, Clonskeagh Square, Dublin 14
T: (01) 283 7144 F: (01) 283 7256
E: info@cfi.ie W: www.cfi.ie
Contact: Frank Traynor

CATEGORIES: EQUITY

Corporate Finance Ireland Ltd offers financial advice and fundraising experience, spanning agri-business, transport, financial services, communications and the leisure industry. CFI also manages a fund for **Alliance Investment Capital Ltd**.

COUNTY CAVAN PARTNERSHIP

28A Bridge Street, Cavan
T: (049) 433 1029 F: (049) 433 1117
E: cavpart@iol.ie
Contact: Eilish McLaughlin, Enterprise Officer; Brendan Reilly, Manager

CATEGORIES: COMMUNITY & RURAL DEVELOPMENT

One of the **Area Partnerships** established by **Area Development Management**, as part of its Local Development programme.

COUNTY DEVELOPMENT BOARDS

W: www.cdb.ie

CATEGORIES: POLICY

County Development Boards (CDBs) have been established in all county councils and in the five major city corporations. In each CDB, local government, local development, social partners (including the community/voluntary sector) and the relevant State agencies active at local level work together for the area's economic, social and cultural development and success. For more information, contact the Director of Community and Enterprise at your local County Council or City Corporation.

COUNTY LEITRIM PARTNERSHIP

Church Street, Drumshambo, Co Leitrim
T: (078) 964 1740 F: (078) 964 1741
E: clpdr@eircom.net W: www.planet.ie
Contact: Tom Lavin, Manager

CATEGORIES: COMMUNITY & RURAL DEVELOPMENT

One of the **Area Partnerships** funded by **Area Development Management**, as part of its Local Development programme.

COUNTY LOUTH RURAL DEVELOPMENT COMPANY

See **Louth Leader**.

COUNTY WEXFORD PARTNERSHIP
Millpark Road, Enniscorthy, Co Wexford
T: (054) 37033 F: (054) 37026
E: info@wexforpartnership.ie W: www.wexfordpartnership.ie
Contact: John Nunn, CEO

CATEGORIES: COMMUNITY & RURAL DEVELOPMENT; GRANTS; INFORMATION;
START-UP TRAINING

One of the **Area Partnerships** funded by **Area Development Management**, as part of its Local Development programme, County Wexford Partnership provides services to people in the area who are starting up their own business.

CRAFTS COUNCIL OF IRELAND
Castle Yard, Kilkenny
T: (056) 61804 F: (056) 63754
E: info@ccoi.ie W: www.ccoi.ie
Contact: Emer Ferran, Business Development Manager

CATEGORIES: BUSINESS PLANS; INFORMATION; MARKETING; MENTORING;
PUBLICATIONS; TRAINING

The Crafts Council of Ireland is the national design and economic development agency for the craft industry in the Republic of Ireland, funded by **Enterprise Ireland** and the EU. The Business Development office works to provide business training and mentoring for individual craftspeople. CCOI offers a business advisory service for craftspeople setting up their own business, including grant applications and liaising with grant-aiding agencies, market research, business plans, company structure, finance and packaging (also available to people planning to set up craft-shops).

CRAIGAVON & ARMAGH RURAL DEVELOPMENT (CARD)
Craigavon Borough Council, Civic Centre, Lakeview Road,
Craigavon BT64 1AL
T: (028) 3752 9600 F: (028) 3831 2444
E: m.lavery@armagh.gov.uk W: www.craigavonarmaghrural.org
Contact: Maria Lavery

CATEGORIES: COMMUNITY & RURAL DEVELOPMENT

One of the **LEADER+** groups in Northern Ireland.

CRAIGAVON INDUSTRIAL DEVELOPMENT ORGANISATION LTD
Carn Drive, Carn Industrial Area, Portadown, Craigavon BT63 5RH
T: (028) 3833 3393 F: (028) 3835 0390
E: mail@cido.co.uk W: www.cido.co.uk
Contact: Jim Smith, Chief Executive

CATEGORIES: DEBT; INFORMATION; START-UP TRAINING; TRAINING; WORKSPACE

CIDO is an **Enterprise Agency** and a member of **Enterprise NorthernIreland**. It acts as a First Stop Shop for potential entrepreneurs, providing managed workspace, business skills training, business consultancy, a small business loans fund, business services, and information and advice. CIDO manages the **Business Start** programme across Northern Ireland and offers the **Enter Enterprise** programme for intending entrepreneurs.

CREATIVEIRELAND.com
E: editor@creativeireland.com
W: www.creativeireland.com
CATEGORIES: INFORMATION; NETWORKING; WEBSITE

Creative Ireland is the online home for the Irish creative design community. It provides news, a directory of designers, a jobsdesk, for those looking for work or designers, and a gateway to essential design resources on the Internet.

CREATIVITY SEED FUND
Department of Culture, Arts and Leisure, Interpoint, 20-24 York Street, Belfast BT15 1AQ
T: (028) 9025 8949
E: rhonda.farmer@dcaini.gov.uk W: www.dcaini.gov.uk
Contact: Rhonda Farmer
CATEGORIES: GRANTS

The fund supports creativity and innovation in individuals, businesses and organisations in Northern Ireland, with grants of up to 50% of project cost, to a maximum of stg£50,000.

CREGGAN ENTERPRISES LTD
Ráth Mór Business & Community Enterprise Centre, Bligh's Lane, Derry
E: info@rathmor.com W: www.rathmor.com/cel_intro.html
Contact: Conal McFeely, Chairperson
CATEGORIES: COMMUNITY & RURAL DEVELOPMENT; SOCIAL ECONOMY

Creggan Enterprises Ltd (CEL) works to address the social and economic needs of the local community. CEL has created the successful Ráth Mór Business and Community Enterprise Centre.

CRESCENT CAPITAL
5 Crescent Gardens, Belfast BT7 1NS
T: (028) 9023 3633 F: (028) 9032 9525
E: mail@crescentcapital.co.uk W: www.crescentcapital.co.uk
Contact: Colin Walsh
CATEGORIES: EQUITY

A Belfast-based venture capital fund, specialising in early-stage to MBO Northern Ireland investments between £250,000 and £1 million.

CROSBIE BUSINESS CENTRE
26 Ossory Road, North Strand, Dublin 3
T:(01) 836 3994 F: (01) 836 3997
E: info@crosbiebusinesscentre.com W: www.crosbiebusinesscentre.com
CATEGORIES: INCUBATOR; WORKSPACE

An incubation centre offering workspace.

CROSS ATLANTIC CAPITAL PARTNERS
3006 Lake Drive, Citywest Business Campus, Dublin 24
T: (01) 241 6100 F: (01) 241 6132
E: gmccrory@xacp.com W: www.xacp.com
Contact: Gerry McCrory
CATEGORIES: EQUITY

Cross Atlantic Capital Partners (XACP) manages a $150 million technology-focused fund. It also holds a major interest in **Crucible Corporation**. XACP is the sponsor of the **Michael Smurfit Graduate School of Business Hatchery**.

CROSSMAGLEN COMMUNITY ENTERPRISES LTD
1 Castleblaney Road, Crossmaglen, Co Armagh BT35 2JJ
T: (028) 3086 8500 / (028) 3086 1534 F: (028) 3086 8580
E: gerry.murray@btinternet.com
Contact: Gerry Murray
CATEGORIES: WORKSPACE

An **Enterprise Agency** offering workspace to SMEs.

CROWLEYS DFK
16/17 College Green, Dublin 2
T: (01) 679 0800 F: (01) 679 0805
Contact: James O'Connor
Also at: 35 Grand Parade, Cork
T: (021) 427 2900 F: (021) 427 7621
Contact: Jack Crowley
E: info@crowleysdfk.ie W: www.crowleysdfk.ie
CATEGORIES: ACCOUNTANTS; CONSULTING

A firm of chartered accountants and business advisers, experts in advising small to medium sized businesses.

CRUCIBLE CORPORATION
3006 Lake Drive, Citywest Campus, Dublin 24
T: (01) 439 2900 F: (01) 439 2930
E: info@cruciblecorp.com W: www.cruciblecorp.com
Contact: Kevin Magee
CATEGORIES: EQUITY

Crucible is an early-stage investment company concentrating on the technology sector. Its mission is to help Irish entrepreneurs develop innovative business concepts into transatlantic business operations. Crucible only invests in companies with patentable technology or which can build long-term technical barriers to entry and which are primarily targeting the US market. Typically it will invest up to $1.5 million in a seed, start-up or early-stage opportunity. Crucible will also take an active role in helping the investment secure follow-on financing as the company develops. A majority interest in Crucible is held by **Cross Atlantic Capital Partners**.

CRUICKSHANK & CO
1 Holles Street, Dublin 2
T: (01) 661 2533 F: (01) 661 2480
E: post@cruickshank.ie W: www.cruickshank.ie
Contact: Donal O'Connor
CATEGORIES: INTELLECTUAL PROPERTY

Cruickshank & Co are patent and trade mark attorneys.

CUMAS TEO (PÁIRTÍOCHT CHONAMARA & ÁRANN)
Ionad Fiontar, Rosmuc, Co na Gaillimhe
T: (091) 574353 F: (091) 574047
E: cumas@eircom.net
Contact: Gearoid O'Cosgora, Manager
CATEGORIES: COMMUNITY & RURAL DEVELOPMENT; INFORMATION; START-UP TRAINING

One of the **Area Partnerships** funded by **Area Development Management**, as part of its Local Development programme.

DAIRY PRODUCTS RESEARCH CENTRE
Moorepark, Fermoy, Co Cork
T: (025) 42222 F: (025) 42340
E: elehane@moorepark.teagasc.ie
W: www.teagasc.org/research/research_centres.htm
Contact: Dr WJ Donnelly, Head of Centre
CATEGORIES: CONSULTING; R & D

The Dairy Products Research Centre (DPC) undertakes scientific research and provides technological services to the dairy processing and food ingredients sectors. Pilot plant facilities are provided by **Moorepark Technology Ltd**.

DARLINGTON CONSULTING
Dunmore East, Co Waterford
T: (051) 383609 M: (086) 2437677 F: (051) 383055
E: info@darlington.ie W: www.darlington.ie
Contact: Mary Darlington
CATEGORIES: CONSULTING; TRAINING

Darlington Consulting are safety and HR trainers and consultants to companies nationwide on health and safety issues.

DATA PROTECTION COMMISSIONER
3rd Floor, Block 6, Irish Life Centre, Dublin 1
T: (01) 874 8544 F: (01) 874 5405
E: info@dataprivacy.ie W: www.dataprivacy.ie
CATEGORIES: REGULATOR & STANDARDS

Do you keep information about people on computer? If you do, the law says you must: Obtain it fairly; Keep it accurate and up-to-date; Use it and disclose it only in accordance with the purposes for which you obtained it; Keep it no longer than necessary; Give a copy to the individual concerned of he or she requests it. The Data Protection Commissioner's website sets out your rights as an individual and your responsibilities as a "data controller". It has a self-assessment checklist to help you comply with the law.

DELOITTE & TOUCHE
Deloitte & Touche House, Earlsfort Terrace, Dublin 2
T: (01) 417 2200 F: (01) 417 2300
W: www.deloitte.ie
CATEGORIES: ACCOUNTANTS; CONSULTING

Deloitte & Touche is a leading professional services firm, which offers assurance and advisory, tax, and consulting services through 500 people in offices in four Irish locations.

DELTA EQUITY FUND II LTD PARTNERSHIP
Delta Partners, Fujitsu Building, South County Business Park,
Leopardstown, Dublin 18
T: (01) 294 0870 F: (01) 294 0877
E: venture@delta.ie W: www.delta.ie
Contact: Frank Kenny
CATEGORIES: EQUITY

The Delta Equity Fund II Partners invests between €500k to €3 million (first round) in communications, Internet, software and life sciences businesses. If the required investment is larger, other partner venture capitalists can be introduced. The fund is managed by **Delta Partners**.

DELTA PARTNERS
Fujitsu Building, South County Business Park, Leopardstown, Dublin 18
T: (01) 294 0870 F: (01) 294 0877
E: venture@delta.ie W: www.delta.ie
Contact: Frank Kenny
CATEGORIES: EQUITY

Delta Partners is a European venture capital firm based in Ireland, focusing on early-stage technology investments. Delta invests between €500k to €3 million in communications, Internet, software and life sciences businesses. If the required investment is larger, other partner venture capitalists can be introduced. Delta manages the **Delta Equity Fund II Ltd Partnership**.

DEPARTMENT FOR EMPLOYMENT & LEARNING

Adelaide House, 39-49 Adelaide Street, Belfast BT2 8FD
T: 028 9025 7777 F: 028 9025 7778
E: del@nics.gov.uk W: www.tea-ni.org.uk

CATEGORIES: POLICY; TRAINING

The Department for Employment & Learning is responsible for third level education, training and employment measures across Northern Ireland.

DEPARTMENT OF AGRICULTURE & FOOD

Agriculture House, Kildare Street, Dublin 2
T: (01) 607 2000 (LoCall 1890 200 510) F: (01) 678 5214
E: info@agriculture.gov.ie W: www.agriculture.gov.ie

CATEGORIES: POLICY

The Department's mission is "to lead the sustainable development of a competitive, consumer-focussed agri-food sector and to contribute to a vibrant rural economy and society".

DEPARTMENT OF AGRICULTURE & RURAL DEVELOPMENT

Dundonald House, Upper Newtownards Road, Belfast BT4 3SB
T: (028) 9052 4999 (Press Office) F: (028) 9052 5003
E: library@dardni.gov.uk W: www.dardni.gov.uk

CATEGORIES: COMMUNITY & RURAL DEVELOPMENT; POLICY

DARDNI is responsible for the agricultural, forestry and fishing industries, rural development, agricultural research and education and application of EU agricultural policy in Northern Ireland. DARD's College of Agriculture, Food and Rural Enterprise has sites at **Enniskillen**, **Greenmount** and **Loughry** campuses. It also manages the EU **LEADER+** programme in Northern Ireland.

DEPARTMENT OF COMMUNITY, RURAL & GAELTACHT AFFAIRS

Dún Aimhirgin, 43-49 Mespil Road, Dublin 4
T: (01) 647 3000 F: (01) 667 0826
W: www.pobail.ie

CATEGORIES: COMMUNITY & RURAL DEVELOPMENT; POLICY

The Department has specific responsibility for: Community and local development; Programmes for Revitalising Areas by Planning, Investment and Development (RAPID); Rural development, including **LEADER+,** CLÁR, Interreg, the EU Programme for Peace and Reconciliation and the **Western Development Commission**. It also retains the responsibilities previously held by the former Department of Arts, Heritage, Gaeltacht and the Islands for both the Irish language and the Gaeltacht, and the development of the off-shore islands. Bodies reporting to the Minister for Community, Rural and Gaeltacht Affairs include: **Area Development Management Ltd; Údarás na Gaeltachta; Western Development Commission.**

DEPARTMENT OF ENTERPRISE, TRADE & INVESTMENT
Netherleigh, Massey Avenue, Belfast BT4 2JP
T: (028) 9052 9900 F: (028) 9052 9550
E: information@detini.gov.uk W: www.detini.gov.uk
CATEGORIES: POLICY

The Department of Enterprise, Trade & Investment is responsible for economic development in Northern Ireland. Organisations sponsored by the Department include: **General Consumer Council for Northern Ireland**; Geological Survey of Northern Ireland; **Health & Safety Executive for Northern Ireland**; **InterTradeIreland**; **Invest Northern Ireland**; NI-CO; **Northern Ireland Science Park**; **Northern Ireland Tourist Board**; Tourism Ireland.

DEPARTMENT OF ENTERPRISE, TRADE & EMPLOYMENT
Head Office, Kildare Street, Dublin 2
T: (01) 631 2121 F: (01) 631 2827
E: webmaster@entemp.ie W: www.entemp.ie
Contact: Information Section
CATEGORIES: POLICY

The Department's mandate is to implement Government policy in: Development of enterprise; Employment promotion; Trade development; Protection of workers; Regulation of businesses. The Offices that come under the aegis of the Department relevant to small business include: **Companies Registration Office; Director for Consumer Affairs;   Registry of Friendly Societies; Patents Office**. The Department also has policy responsibility for a number of State-sponsored bodies, including: **Enterprise Ireland; FÁS; Forfás; Health and Safety Authority; IDA Ireland; InterTradeIreland; National Standards Authority of Ireland; Shannon Development. Note that assistance to individual small businesses is not undertaken directly by the Department. Advice and financial assistance is provided by the development agencies, principally the City/County Enterprise Boards and Enterprise Ireland.** The Department also handles work permit applications from employers on behalf of non-nationals - for more information, see www.basis.ie.

DEPARTMENT OF JUSTICE, EQUALITY & LAW REFORM
72–76 St. Stephens Green, Dublin 2
T: (01) 602 8202 F: (01) 661 5461
E: info@justice.ie W: www.justice.ie
CATEGORIES: POLICY

The Department of Justice, Equality and Law Reform implements policy on the admission of persons who wish to visit, immigrate to, or seek refuge in the State in line with the best international practice and standards and in the case of persons wishing to become Irish citizens. Work permit applications by employers on behalf of non-nationals are handled by the **Department of Enterprise, Trade and Employment**.

DEPARTMENT OF JUSTICE, EQUALITY & LAW REFORM :
EQUAL OPPORTUNITIES CHILDCARE SECTION
72-76 St Stephen's Green, Dublin 2
T: 1890 20 90 30 F: (01) 602 8540
E: childcare_mail@justice.ie W: www.justice.ie

CATEGORIES: GRANTS

Capital grants are available to private sector childcare operators with more
than 20 children under their carefor building, renovating, upgrading and/or
equipping childcare facilities.

DEPARTMENT OF SOCIAL & FAMILY AFFAIRS
Aras Mhic Dhiarmada, Information Unit, 5th Floor, Store Street, Dublin 1
T: (01) 874 8444 F: (01) 704 3868
E: info@welfare.ie W: www.welfare.ie

CATEGORIES: GRANTS; INFORMATION

In addition to providing information on PRSI for employers, the Department
operates the Back to Work Allowance (Enterprise), which encourages
unemployed people, lone parents and people getting Disability Allowance or
Blind Person's Pension to become self-employed. Participants receive
support for four years along with any secondary benefits they have, subject to
certain conditions. Full details are available in the *Guide to Social Welfare
Services* (downloadable from the Department's website) and in leaflet SW93.

DEPARTMENT OF THE ENVIRONMENT & LOCAL
GOVERNMENT
Custom House, Dublin 1
T: (01) 888 2000 F: (01) 888 2888
E: press-office@environ.irlgov.ie W: www.environ.ie

CATEGORIES: POLICY

The Department services the public directly on issues such as environmental
information and awareness, anti-litter legislation, the planning system, noise
pollution, construction, local government reform and urban renewal.
Bodies that come under the aegis of the Department relevant to small
businesses include: **Comhar; Dublin Docklands Development Authority;
ENFO; Environmental Protection Agency; National Safety Council.**

DERRYLIN ENTERPRISE CENTRE
Derrylin Enterprise Ltd, 136-141 Main Street, Derrylin,
Co Fermanagh BT92 9LA
T: (028) 6632 7348

CATEGORIES: INFORMATION; START-UP TRAINING; WORKSPACE

One of several **Enterprise Centres** in Fermanagh.

DIGITAL HUB
10-13 Thomas Street, Dublin 8
T: (01) 480 6200 F: (01) 480 6201
E: info@thedigitalhub.com W: www.digitalhub.com

CATEGORIES: WORKSPACE

The Digital Hub is an Irish Government initiative to create an international digital enterprise centre in the Liberties area of Dublin City. It provides facilities for early-stage, fast-growth and established companies in: OneFiveSeven and Digital Depot. One of the Digital Hub's key tenants is **Media Lab Europe**.

DIRECTOR OF CONSUMER AFFAIRS
4–5 Harcourt Road, Dublin 2
T: (01) 402 5500 F: (01) 402 5501
E: odca@entemp.ie W: www.odca.ie
Contact: Helpline (01) 402 5555
Also at: 89/90 South Mall, Cork
T: (021) 427 4099 F: (021) 427 4109

CATEGORIES: INFORMATION; REGULATOR & STANDARDS

The principal functions of the Director of Consumer Affairs are: To inform the public of their rights as consumers; To conduct investigations under a wide range of consumer protection legislation; To prosecute offences as provided for by statute; To keep under general review practices or proposed practices by business that could impact negatively on consumers' statutory rights; To licence or authorise moneylenders, pawnbrokers, and mortgage and credit intermediaries; To monitor customer charges by credit institutions; Promotion of codes of practice. In case of difficulty, consumers should contact the Helpline on (01) 402 5555 or LoCall 1890 220229.

DOCKLANDS INNOVATION PARK
128-130 East Wall Road, Dublin 3
T: (01) 240 1300 F: (01) 240 1310
E: info@boltontrust.com W: www.boltontrust.com
Contact: Michael Drennan, Estate Manager

CATEGORIES: INCUBATOR; WORKSPACE

Established by the **Bolton Trust**, the Docklands Innovation Park is a new-style incubator that provides enterprise development programmes, incubation space and facilities, business counselling, funding and access to R&D expertise.

DOINGBUSINESSINDUNLAOGHAIRERATHDOWN.com
W: www.doingbusinessindunlaoghairerathdown.com

CATEGORIES: INFORMATION; WEBSITE

A joint project of the Southside Partnership and the Southside Local Employment Service, www.doingbusinessindunlaoghairerathdown.com contains practical information on business topics relevant to firms in the area.

DONEGAL COUNTY ENTERPRISE BOARD
Enterprise Fund Business Centre, Ballyraine, Letterkenny, Co Donegal
T: (074) 60735 F: (074) 60783
E: donegalceb@eircom.net W: www.donegalenterprise.ie
Contact: Michael Tunney, CEO

CATEGORIES: DEBT; E-BUSINESS; EQUITY; GRANTS; INFORMATION;
MENTORING; START-UP TRAINING; TRAINING

Donegal County Enterprise Board provides direct supports (capital, employment or feasibility grant aid) and indirect supports (mentoring, management development, or other capacity building programmes.)

Through its First Stop Shop, it provides access to business information, business advice and counselling. It operates a dedicated website (Virtual One-Stop-Shop — see also **BusinessInformationPoint.com**) for enterprise information and assistance. The Donegal County Enterprise Fund provides low interest finance (maximum IR£50,000 — typically IR£15,000 to IR£25,000) to qualifying projects, through a revolving loan fund, established with assistance from the **International Fund for Ireland**.

DONEGAL LOCAL DEVELOPMENT COMPANY
1 Millennium Court, Pearse Road, Letterkenny, Co Donegal
T: (074) 9127 056 F: (074) 9121 527
E: info@dldc.org W: www.dldc.org
Contact: Caoimhín Mac Aoidh, CEO

CATEGORIES: COMMUNITY & RURAL DEVELOPMENT; CROSS-BORDER;
GRANTS; INCUBATOR; INFORMATION; MENTORING; NETWORKING; START-UP
TRAINING; TRAINING

One of the **Area Partnerships** funded by **Area Development Management**, as part of its Local Development programme, and also a **LEADER+** company serving Donegal except the Gaeltacht areas & Inishowen Peninsula, DLDC currently delivers the Local Development Social Inclusion Programme. It also offers capital equipment grants to innovative, small enterprises in manufacturing, crafts or local services at start-up or development stage, within its operational area. DLDC supports the **Tyrone Donegal Partnership**.

DOONBEG COMMUNITY DEVELOPMENT LTD
Doonbeg, Co Clare
T: (065) 905 5288 F: (065) 905 5212
E: doonbegdev@eircom.net W: www.doonbeginfo.com
Contact: Patricia Dillon

CATEGORIES: COMMUNITY & RURAL DEVELOPMENT

Doonbeg Community Development Ltd encourages enterprise and community development in the region of Doonbeg and West Clare. It is sponsored by **FÁS**.

DOWN BUSINESS CENTRE
46 Belfast Road, Downpatrick, Co Down BT30 9UP
T: (028) 4461 6416 F: (028) 4461 6419
E: business@downbc.co.uk W: www.downbc.co.uk
CATEGORIES: COMMUNITY & RURAL DEVELOPMENT; DEBT; INFORMATION;
START-UP TRAINING; TRAINING; WORKSPACE

Down Business Centre is an **Enterprise Agency** and a member of **Enterprise Northern Ireland**. It mission is "To promote economic development and job creation in the Castlereagh Borough Council Area". It also offers **LEADER+** support to rural businesses. Down Business Centre is one of the enterprise agencies that offers the **Enter Enterprise** programme for intending entrepreneurs.

DROGHEDA PARTNERSHIP COMPANY
12 North Quay, Drogheda, Co Louth
T: (041) 984 2088 F: (041) 984 3358
E: drogpart@iol.ie W: www.iol.ie/~drogpart
Contact: Mary-Ann McGlynn, Manager
CATEGORIES: COMMUNITY & RURAL DEVELOPMENT; INFORMATION; START-UP
TRAINING

One of the **Area Partnerships** funded by **Area Development Management**, as part of its Local Development programme. Drogheda Partnership supports enterprise in the Drogheda area, helping to make jobs, create businesses and find jobs for the unemployed.

DUBLIN BUSINESS INNOVATION CENTRE
The Tower, TCD Enterprise Centre, Pearse Street, Dublin 2
T: (01) 671 3111 F: (01) 671 3330
E: info@dbic.ie W: www.dbic.ie
Contact: John McInerney
CATEGORIES: BUSINESS ANGELS; BUSINESS PLANS; EQUITY; INCUBATOR;
INFORMATION; MARKETING; TRAINING; WORKSPACE

Dublin BIC provides business planning advice (through its Client Assistance programme), access to incubation space (through the **Guinness Enterprise Centre**) and access to finance (through the **Dublin Seed Capital Fund** and **Irish BICs Seed Capital Fund**) to selected innovative enterprises. Dublin BIC also operates the Dublin Investor Register Service (DIRS), a "marriage bureau" linking potential investors, mainly private and corporate, with small businesses requiring equity capital in amounts below the threshold of most financial institutions — typically, €15,000 to €200,000. DIRS works on a "no foal, no fee" basis — fees are only payable when an investment has been completed. See also **Guinness Enterprise Centre**.

DUBLIN CITY ENTERPRISE BOARD
17 Eustace Street, Dublin 2
T: (01) 677 6068 F: (01) 677 6093
E: info@dceb.ie W: www.dceb.ie
Contact: Gerry Macken, CEO

CATEGORIES: DEBT; E-BUSINESS; EQUITY; GRANTS; INFORMATION;
MENTORING; START-UP TRAINING; TRAINING

Dublin City Enterprise Board supports enterprise development in Dublin city, thus strengthening the sustainability of local economies to provide employment opportunities within their own communities.

DUBLIN CITY UNIVERSITY
Office of Innovation and Business Relations, Glasnevin, Dublin 9
T: (01) 700 5175 (Direct) F: (01) 836 0830
E: anthony.glynn@dcu.ie W: www.dcu.ie
Contact: Dr Tony Glynn, Director, Office of Innovation and Business Relations

CATEGORIES: CONSULTING; INCUBATOR; INFORMATION; R & D; TRAINING

The Research Desk at **DCU**'s Office for Innovation and Business Relations facilitates the University's research interface with industry and serves as a point of contact for external organisations requiring access to DCU research expertise. The DCU Enterprise Office encourages and supports entrepreneurial activities on the campus, by raising interest in entrepreneurship among DCU students and staff and responding to specific information and skill needs. DCU is a partner in the **M50 Enterprise Platform Progamme**. It operates an on-campus Innovation and Enterprise Centre, **INVENT**, as well as DCU's Enterprise Office.

DUBLIN DOCKLANDS DEVELOPMENT AUTHORITY
Custom House Quay, Dublin 1
T: (01) 818 3300 F: (01) 818 3399
E: info@dublindocklands.ie W: www.dublindocklands.ie
Contact: Lar Bradshaw, Chairman

CATEGORIES: POLICY

The Custom House Docks Area, for which DDDA is responsible, comprises 1,300 acres between Fairview/North Strand to the Great South Wall, the junction of Ringsend/Sandymount and Butt Bridge. DDDA's Master Plan for the Area sets out its objectives for securing sustainable social and economic regeneration, improving the physical environment, developing new and existing residential communities, conserving architectural heritage, and improving the employment, training and education opportunities of those resident in the Area.

DUBLIN INNER CITY PARTNERSHIP

Equity House, 16-17 Upper Ormond Quay, Dublin 7
T: (01) 872 1321 F: (01) 872 1330
E: office@dicp.ie W: www.dicp.ie
Contact: Peter Nolan, Employment & Enterprise Co-ordinator

CATEGORIES: COMMUNITY & RURAL DEVELOPMENT; INFORMATION; START-UP TRAINING; TRAINING

One of the **Area Partnerships** established by Area Development Management, as part of its Local Development programme. Support for new businesses is provided in two locations in the inner city. Specific training is available to entrepreneurs to learn necessary skills in marketing, accounts, taxation, and workplace health and safety. See also **Inner City Enterprise**.

DUBLIN INSTITUTE OF TECHNOLOGY

Fitzwilliam House, 30 Upper Pembroke Street, Dublin 2
T: (01) 402 3442 F: (01) 402 3393
E: industry.development@dit.ie W: www.dit.ie
Contact: Margaret Whelan, Head of Industry Development

CATEGORIES: CONSULTING; INFORMATION; R & D; TRAINING

The Dublin Institute of Technology is the largest third-level college in Ireland. It comprises colleges at: Adelaide Road; Aungier Street; Bolton Street; Cathal Brugha Street; Kevin Street; Mountjoy Square; Rathmines. Each Faculty in DIT has an Innovation and Industry Services Office, which is the point of contact for DIT's Industry Programme, and which deals with any industry-related training, applied research & development queries. DIT also operates Centres of Excellence including: Food product development (see **Food Product Development Centre**) and Transport and logistics (see **National Institute for Transport and Logistics**). DIT also operates the **PDC** incubation centre.

DUBLIN SEED CAPITAL FUND

Dublin BIC, The Tower, TCD Enterprise Centre, Pearse Street, Dublin 2
T: (01) 671 3111 F: (01) 671 3330
E: dscf@dbic.ie W: www.dbic.ie
Contact: Alex Hobbs / Sinead Keogh

CATEGORIES: EQUITY

The Dublin Seed Capital fund was set up specifically to to provide early-stage seed capital to new and developing enterprises in the Dublin region. The Fund also serves as a feeder fund to other venture capital funds. It is an active investor, working with companies at board level. The Fund was established by **Dublin BIC**, supported by the private sector and **Enterprise Ireland** through the EU Seed Capital Measure of the Operational Programme for Industrial Development 1994–1999. In December 2001, an additional €5 million was committed to the Fund, increasing it to €7.5 million. It now operates under the Seed & Venture Capital Fund Scheme 2001-2006 under the National Development Plan. The fund is targeted across a broad range of technology, manufacturing and traded services sectors. An application form is available online at the Dublin BIC website.

DUN LAOIRE ENTERPRISE CENTRE

The Old Firestation, George's Place, Dun Laoire, Co Dublin
T: (01) 202 0056 F: (01) 230 1044
E: dlenterprise@clubi.ie
Contact: Harry Cullen, Manager

CATEGORIES: INCUBATOR; WORKSPACE

An incubation centre offering workspace.

DÚN LAOIRE INSTITUTE OF ART, DESIGN & TECHNOLOGY

Kill Avenue, Dun Laoire, Co Dublin
T: (01) 214 4600
E: tony.niland@iadt-dl.ie W: www.dliadt.ie
Contact: Tony Niland, External Services

CATEGORIES: INCUBATOR; MENTORING; NETWORKING; START-UP TRAINING;
TRAINING

Dun Laoire Institute of Art, Design & Technology operates the Evolve
programme with **VenturePoint** (Dun Laoire/Rathdown County Enterprise
Board) to provide micro-enterprises with a customised development plan,
personal and business skill training, mentoring and networking. It is
developing a Digital Media Incubation Centre.

DÚN LAOIRE/RATHDOWN COUNTY ENTERPRISE BOARD

Venturepoint, Nutgrove Enterprise Centre, Nutgrove Way, Rathfarnham,
Dublin 14
T: (01) 494 8400 F: (01) 494 8410
E: info@venturepoint.ie W: www.venturepoint.ie
Contact: Michael Johnson, CEO

CATEGORIES: DEBT; E-BUSINESS; EQUITY; GRANTS; INFORMATION;
MENTORING; PUBLICATIONS; START-UP TRAINING; TRAINING

Venturepoint supports the growth and development of micro enterprises in
Dun Laoire/Rathdown County, Dublin. It offers information packs on all
aspects of setting up a small business. It also operates, in co-operation with
other community agencies, three one-stop-shop information facilities.
It operates Evolve with the **Dun Laoire Institute of Art, Design &
Technology** to provide micro-enterprises with a customised development
plan, personal and business skill training, mentoring and networking. Its
website provides an online investor/promoter matching service.

DUNDALK EMPLOYMENT PARTNERSHIP LTD

Partnership Court, Park Street, Dundalk
T: (042) 933 0288 F: (042) 933 0552
E: partnership@dep.ie W: www.dep.ie
Contact: John Butler, Chief Executive

CATEGORIES: COMMUNITY & RURAL DEVELOPMENT; INFORMATION; START-UP
TRAINING; TRAINING; WOMEN; WORKSPACE

One of the Area Partnerships funded by **Area Development Management**, as part of its Local Development programme. Under its remit to encourage direct job creation, the Partnership has set up wholly-owned subsidiary companies that directly create jobs for long-term unemployed people. It also provides comprehensive services to individuals and groups planning to set up their own business, including subsidised workspace and business advice. It also offers a Women's Enterprise Development Project to suport women in Louth who want to enter, or are already in, self-employment.

DUNDALK INSTITUTE OF TECHNOLOGY
Dublin Road, Dundalk, Co Louth
T: (042) 937 0200 F: (042) 933 3505
E: webmaster@dkit.ie W: www.dkit.ie
Contact: Gerry Carroll, Head of Development
CATEGORIES: EU INFORMATION; INCUBATOR

Dundalk IT operates the **Regional Development Centre**, which provides services to industry, and hosts **Info Point Europe North East**.

DUNGANNON ENTERPRISE CENTRE LTD
2 Coalisland Road, Dungannon, Co Tyrone BT71 6JT
T: (028) 8772 3489 F: (028) 8775 2200
E: brian@dungannonenterprise.com W: www.dungannonenterprise.com
Contact: Brian MacAuley
CATEGORIES: DEBT; INCUBATOR; INFORMATION; MARKETING; START-UP TRAINING; TRAINING; WORKSPACE

Dungannon Enterprise Centre is an **Enterprise Agency** and a member of **Enterprise Northern Ireland**. Its primary aims are to: Help new business start up; Encourage existing business to expand. Dungannon Enterprise Centre provides support, such as: Industrial and office workspace units to incubate local businesses; Low interest loans for start up businesses; Professional business advice and counselling; Training on business start up and expansion planning; Support in sourcing government support and finance; Marketing planning. See also **Choose Enterprise**.

EAST BELFAST ENTERPRISE PARK LTD
308 Albertbridge Road, Belfast BT5 4GX
T: (028) 9045 5450 F: (028) 9073 2600
E: info@eastbelfast.org W: www.eastbelfast.org
Contact: Roisin Boyle, Manager
CATEGORIES: DEBT; INCUBATOR; INFORMATION; START-UP TRAINING; TRAINING; WORKSPACE

East Belfast Enterprise Park is an **Enterprise Agency** and a member of **Enterprise Northern Ireland**. Its role is to "help anyone in business or thinking of starting a business" by providing free advice and training, incubation workspace and access to finance.

EAST CORK AREA DEVELOPMENT LTD

Midleton Community Enterprise Centre, Owennacurra Business Park,
Knockgriffin, Midleton, Co Cork
T: (021) 461 3432 F: (021) 461 3808
E: info@ecad.ie W: www.eastcork.com/bintroduction.html
Contact: Ryan Howard, Chief Executive Officer

CATEGORIES: COMMUNITY DEVELOPMENT; GRANTS; TOURISM DEVELOPMENT

ECAD reflects a local partnership between various social and economic groups in response to local issues and needs. ECAD is one of the **Community Groups** funded by **ADM Ltd** and also a **LEADER+** company. It offers capital equipment grants to innovative, small enterprises in manufacturing, crafts or local services at start-up or development stage, within its operational area. ECAD now administers the Local Development Measure of the Social Inclusion Programme, the successor to the Local Development Programme and the National Rural Development Programme in East Cork. It is one of the organisations behind **FarmOptions.ie**.

EAST MAYO FORESTRY CO-OPERATIVE

Enterprise House, Aiden Street, Kiltimagh, Co Mayo
T: (094) 81494 F: (094) 81708
E: forestry@ird-kiltimagh.ie W: www.ird-kiltimagh.ie
Contact: Ms Pat Dillon

CATEGORIES: COMMUNITY & RURAL DEVELOPMENT

The East Mayo Forestry Co-operative increases farm income and productivity through converting non-agricultural areas of farms into viable woodlands. It provides information and guidance for members, including free feasibility inspections and other services.

EAST TYRONE RURAL

Gortalowry House, 94 Church Street, Cookstown BT80 8HX
T: (028) 8772 0311
E: funding@easttyronerural.co.uk W: www.easttyronerural.co.uk
Contact: Dianne Fee, Programme Manager

CATEGORIES: COMMUNITY & RURAL DEVELOPMENT

One of the **LEADER+** groups in Northern Ireland, set up to administer the Leader+ Programme throughout the Cookstown and Dungannon Districts, with the exception of Cookstown and Dungannon town centres.

EBUSINESSLEX.net

W: www.ebusinesslex.net

CATEGORIES: EBUSINESS; INFORMATION; LEGAL; WEBSITE

The Ebusinesslex.net project is co-financed by the **European Commission** - Enterprise Directorate General - to provide European SMEs with information on all legal aspects of e-business. It has been developed by the **Euro Info Centre** (EIC) Network (the Irish partner is the **EIC Waterford**) with the help of legal experts who specialise in e-business (although this portal does not constitute formal legal advice).

ECONOMIC STATISTICS NORTHERN IRELAND
W: www.economicstatistics-ni.gov.uk
CATEGORIES: INFORMATION; WEBSITE

Provided by the Statistics Research Branch of the **Department of Enterprise, Trade and Investment, Northern Ireland,** this website offers economic indicators and statistics for Northern Ireland.

EIRCOM ENTERPRISE FUND LTD
Gaiety Centre, South King Street, Dublin 2
T: (01) 701 4031 F: (01) 679 7253
E: mmoore@eircom.ie W: www.eircom-enterprise-fund.ie
Contact: Maura Moore
CATEGORIES: EQUITY

An €2.5m fund (NOW CLOSED), providing risk capital investment of between IR£30,000 and IR£300,000 in early stage businesses with growth potential, with particular emphasis on telecoms, media and technology (TMT), mainly for eircom employees. The fund also has a useful, informative website on venture capital and business planning.

EIRÍ CORCA BAISCINN
The Community Centre, Circular Road, Kilkee, Co Clare
T: (065) 905 6611 F: (065) 905 6602
E: info@eiri.org W: www.eiri.org
Contact: Sue Targett, Manager
CATEGORIES: COMMUNITY & RURAL DEVELOPMENT; SOCIAL ECONOMY

Eirí Corca Baiscinn is one of the **Community Groups** funded by **Area Development Management**, as part of its Local Development programme. Its activities include services to the unemployed, education & training, enterprise, community development, and environment and infrastructure. It is currently developing a number of social economy projects in response to local needs. It delivers the Local Development Social Inclusion Programme in West Clare.

EMERGING BUSINESS TRUST
38-42 Hill Street, Belfast BT1 2LB
T: (028) 9045 1375 F: (028) 9073 8474
E: info@emergingbusinesstrust.com W: www.emergingbusinesstrust.com
Contact: George Robinson, David Forsythe
CATEGORIES: DEBT

Emerging Business Trust is a loan fund, whose emphasis is on supporting niche businesses, either high value start-ups or expanding businesses, with new technology and/or new products, employing in the region of 10 -15 employees. EBT is an approved lender under the DTI's **Small Firms Loan**

Guarantee Scheme. It operates from three locations: Belfast, Newry and Draperstown.

EMPOWER.ie
W: www.empower.ie

CATEGORIES: E-BUSINESS; GRANTS; MENTORING; TRAINING; WEBSITE

Empower.ie is an €3.8 million e-based initiative for small businesses, delivered by City/County Enterprise Boards on behalf of the **Department of Enterprise, Trade and Employment**. Under the initiative, the Enterprise Boards provide e-business services and incentives to micro-businesses.

ENFO : ENVIRONMENTAL INFORMATION SERVICE
17 St Andrew's Street, Dublin 2
T: (01) 888 2001 F: (01) 888 3946
E: info@enfo.ie W: www.enfo.ie

CATEGORIES: INFORMATION

ENFO is an environmental information service established to promote knowledge and care of the environment. It provides a query-answering service, information leaflets, reference library with computerised database with 55,000 titles, study and research facilities, educational materials, exhibitions and lectures.

ENNIS WEST PARTNERS
Centrepoint, Orchard Lane, Hermitage, Ennis, Co Clare
T: (065) 682 3339 F: (065) 682 4442
E: ewp.ennis@eircom.net W: http://ewp.ennis.ie
Contact: Gary Rush, Co-ordinator

CATEGORIES: COMMUNITY & RURAL DEVELOPMENT; SOCIAL ECONOMY;
START-UP TRAINING

Ennis West Partners is one of the **Community Groups** funded by **Area Development Management,** as part of its Local Development programme. EWP now delivers the Local Development Social Inclusion Programme. EWP provides support for people who wish to start their own businesses. It is also involved in a number of social economy projects.

ENNISKILLEN CAMPUS, COLLEGE OF AGRICULTURE, FOOD & RURAL ENTERPRISE, DEPARTMENT OF AGRICULTURE & RURAL DEVELOPMENT
Levaghy, Enniskillen, Co Fermanagh BT74 4GF
T: (028) 6634 4853 F: (028) 6634 4888
E: enquiries@dardni.gov.uk W: www.enniskillen.ac.uk

CATEGORIES: COMMUNITY & RURAL DEVELOPMENT; INFORMATION; TRAINING

Enniskillen Campus, College of Agriculture, Food & Rural Enterprise, **DARD,** provides education, training and technology support in equine, rural development and agriculture. It offers a range of Rural Enterprise courses.

ENTER ENTERPRISE

CATEGORIES: START-UP TRAINING

A new (May 2003) programme, aimed at intending entrepreneurs, funded under the EU Building Sustainable Prosperity programme, with support from **Invest Northern Ireland** and the local District Councils. It is offered by: **Ards Business Centre Ltd; Armagh Business Centre; Banbridge District Enterprises; Craigavon Industrial Development Organisation Ltd; Down Business Centre; Newry & Mourne Enterprise Agency.**

ENTERPRISE 2000 FUND

43 Pearse Street, Dublin 2
T: (01) 677 5570 F: (01) 677 5588
E: capital@enterprise2000fund.ie W: www.enterprise2000fund.ie
Contact: Clare Shine

CATEGORIES: DEBT; EQUITY

The fund provides seed and early stage finance to qualifying businesses in various industries, ranging between €31,750 and €127,000. It supports businesses across the industry sectors with the exception of property development, retail outlets, and financial services. Equity is provided in return for a minority shareholding; loans are provided on a long-term (5-10 years) basis, without personal guarantees.

ENTERPRISE AGENCIES / CENTRES

There are many Enterprise Agencies / Centres in Northern Ireland. Those that are members of **Enterprise Northern Ireland** include:

- Acorn Business Centre
- Antrim Enterprise Agency Ltd
- Ards Business Centre Ltd
- Armagh Business Centre Ltd
- Ballymena Business Development Centre Ltd
- Banbridge District Enterprises Ltd
- Carrickfergus Enterprise Agency Ltd
- Castlereagh Enterprises Ltd
- Coleraine Enterprise Agency
- Cookstown Enterprise Centre Ltd
- Craigavon Industrial Development Organisation Ltd
- Down Business Centre
- Dungannon Enterprise Centre Ltd
- East Belfast Enterprise Park Ltd
- Enterprise North West
- Fermanagh Enterprise Ltd
- Glenwood Enterprises Ltd
- Larne Enterprise Development Company Ltd
- Lisburn Enterprise Organisation Ltd
- Moyle Enterprise Company Ltd
- Newry & Mourne Enterprise Agency
- Newtownabbey Enterprise Development Organisation
- North City Business Centre Ltd
- North Down Development Organisation Ltd
- Omagh Enterprise Company Ltd Ormeau Business Park
- ORTUS – The West Belfast Enterprise Board
- Roe Valley Enterprises Ltd
- Strabane Enterprise Agency
- Townsend Enterprise Park
- Work West Enterprise Agency (West Belfast Development Trust)
- Workspace (Draperstown) Ltd

Other Enterprise Agencies/Centres include:

- Argyle Business Centre Ltd
- Belcoo Enterprises Ltd
- Brookfield Business Centre Ltd
- Castlederg & District Enterprise Company Ltd
- Coalisland & District Development Association Ltd
- Crossmaglen Community Enterprises Ltd
- Derrylin Enterprise Centre
- Eurocentre West Ltd
- Farset Enterprise Park Ltd
- Irvinestown Trustee Enterprise Company
- Keady Business Centre Ltd
- Kesh Development Association
- Mayfair Business Centre Ltd
- Roslean Enterprises Ltd
- South West Fermanagh Development Organisation Ltd
- Westlink Enterprise Ltd

CATEGORIES: DEBT; INFORMATION; START-UP TRAINING; TRAINING; WORKSPACE

The services provided by Enterprise Agencies/Centres vary, depending on local need. Check the services offered by individual agencies.

ENTERPRISE DG

European Commission,Rue de la Science 15, B-1040 Brussels, Belgium
E: erkki.liilanen@cec.eu.int
W: www.europa.eu.int/comm/dgs/enterprise/index_en.htm
Contact: Erkki Liikanen, Commissioner

CATEGORIES: EU INFORMATION; POLICY

Under Commissioner Erkki Liikanen, the Enterprise DG's ambition is to supply the policy ideas that will foster the competitiveness of enterprises and revitalise Europe's economy, with the goal of creating a knowledge-based economy in Europe.

ENTERPRISE EQUITY (IRL) LTD

Dublin Road, Dundalk, Co Louth
T: (042) 933 3167 F: (042) 933 4857
E: info@enterpriseequity.ie W: www.enterpriseequity.ie
Contact: Conor O'Connor, Chief Executive
Also at: 78A Dublin Road, Belfast BT2 7HP
T: (028) 9024 2500 F: (028) 9024 2487
E: info@enterpriseequity.ie
Contact: Bob McGowan-Smyth
Mervue Business Park, Galway
T: (091) 764 614 F: (091) 764 615
E: rory@enterpriseequity.ie
Contact: Rory Hynes

CATEGORIES: EQUITY

Enterprise Equity provides venture capital of between €100,000 and €1 million to new and expanding businesses in the BMW regions, comprising Cavan, Donegal, Galway, Laois, Leitrim, Longford, Louth, Mayo, Monaghan, Offaly, Roscommon, Sligo and Westmeath. It was established by the **International Fund for Ireland.** It also manages the **Enterprise Equity Investment Fund** and the **Enterprise Equity Seed Capital Investment Fund.**

ENTERPRISE EQUITY INVESTMENT FUND LTD

Enterprise Equity (Irl) Ltd, Mervue Business Park, Galway
T: (091) 764 614 F: (091) 764 615
E: rory@enterpriseequity.ie W: www.enterpriseequity.ie
Contact: Rory Hynes

CATEGORIES: EQUITY

A €9 million fund, focused on the West and Border Counties, prepared to invest €500k+ first-round finance in early-stage start-ups in the nformation, communication and technology (ICT) sector. See also **Enterprise Equity (Irl) Ltd** and **Enterprise Equity Seed Capital Investment Fund.**

ENTERPRISE EQUITY SEED CAPITAL INVESTMENT FUND LTD

Enterprise Equity (Irl) Ltd, Dublin Road, Dundalk
T: (042) 933 3167 F: (042) 933 4857
E: aidan@enterpriseequity.ie W: www.enterpriseequity.ie
Contact: Aidan Devenney

CATEGORIES: EQUITY

A €7 million fund, providing seed funding (typically €150k to €500k) in the BMW (Borders, Midlands, West) areas for all sectors, except property, retail and hotels. See also **Enterprise Equity (Irl) Ltd** and the **Enterprise Equity Investment Fund**.

ENTERPRISE IRELAND

Wilton Park House, Wilton Place, Dublin 2
T: (01) 808 2000 F: (01) 808 2802
E: CSU@enterprise-ireland.com W: www.enterprise-ireland.com
Also at: Glasnevin, Dublin 9; Merrion Hall, Strand Road, Sandymount, Dublin 4; Regional Offices in Athlone, Cork, Dublin, Dundalk, Galway, Letterkenny, Killarney, Sligo, Waterford.

CATEGORIES: BUSINESS ANGELS; COMPETITIONS; DEBT; EQUITY; GRANTS; INFORMATION; MENTORING; YOUNG ENTERPRISE

Enterprise Ireland is the State body charged with assisting the development of Irish enterprise. Its clients are manufacturing and internationally-traded services companies employing more than 10 people, as well as high-potential start-ups. Five categories of support are available (for more information, see its brochure on financial support): 1. Exploring new opportunities: preliminary funding to exploit new ideas for businesses with 10 to 250 staff or high potential start-ups (HPSUs); 2. HPSUs based on technological innovation or rapidly developing niche market; 3. Existing company expansion, where more than 10 people are already employed; 4. Building international competitiveness: a new Competitiveness Fund for SMEs offers assistance to businesses with 10 to 250 staff, that have not received more than €200,000 in support over the past three years; 5. Research and development: Support under the Research technology and Innovation (RTI) Competitiveness Scheme for significant R&D projects. Key considerations in evaluating a project application include: Need for financial assistance; Value for money; Commercial considerations; Technical considerations; and Financial track record – therefore, a strong well-thought-through business plan is essential. Enterprise Ireland's services include: Access to business angels and venture capital funds; Assistance with intellectual property and technology transfer; Benchmarking; Design support; Incubation and workspaces; Linkages with EU technology support programmes; Market information and supports; Mentoring (see **Mentor Network**); Support for e-commerce/e-business. Enterprise Ireland also supports a range of other initiatives targeted at developing enterprise, including an annual Student Enterprise Awards competition.

ENTERPRISE
IRELAND

Thinking of starting a business in Ireland?

Enterprise Ireland can help complete the picture...

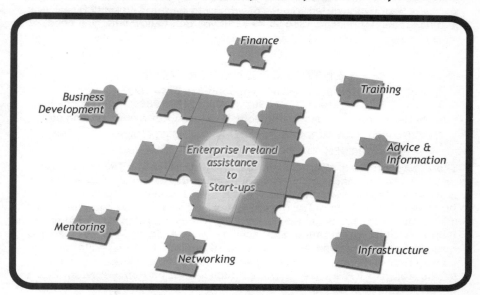

Finance

Training

Business
Development

Enterprise Ireland
assistance
to
Start-ups

Advice &
Information

Mentoring

Networking

Infrastructure

If your new business idea is:

- Based on technological innovation;

- Likely to achieve significant growth
  in 3 years (sales of €1.3m and
  employment of 10)*;

- Export oriented;

- Led by an experienced team,
  with a mixture of technical and
  commercial competencies

*Including, early stage, product led R&D companies, with equivalent sales and employment potential, following
successful completion of a defined pre-commercialisation phase.

We think your idea might be the business!

Contact us at: Startup@enterprise-ireland.com

NDP
NATIONAL DEVELOPMENT PLAN

ENTERPRISE LINK

Wilton Park House, Wilton Place, Dublin 2
Helpline: 1850 35 33 33   T: (01) 808 2000 F: (01) 808 2802
W: www.enterprise-ireland.com

CATEGORIES: INFORMATION

Enterprise Link is an initiative of the **Department of Enterprise, Trade and Employment**, operated by **Enterprise Ireland**, to direct would-be entrepreneurs to the information or assistance they need. It provides a single source of information for all sources of support to start-up and small businesses in Ireland, just by dialling **1850 35 33 33**. If you don't know what you need, or what you might be entitled to, Enterprise Link is a good starting place.

ENTERPRISE NORTH WEST

16c Queen Street, Londonderry BT48 7EQ
T: (028) 7137 1867 F: (028) 7137 1938
E: charles@north-westmarketing.com W: www.north-westmarketing.com

CATEGORIES: COMMUNITY & RURAL DEVELOPMENT; CONSULTING; DEBT;
INFORMATION; START-UP TRAINING; TRAINING

The Enterprise North West Consortium was established in 1998 to deliver a co-ordinated approach to the development of the economic outlook of the north west. The partners involved – North West Marketing; NORIBIC; RAPID; Waterside Development Trust – are geographically spread throughout the urban and rural areas of the Derry City Council region. It delivers the **Business Start** programme and acts as a First Stop Shop for existing businesses and potential entrepreneurs, providing business skills training, business consultancy, a small business loans fund, business services, information and ICT advice. It also promotes rural entrepreneurship. It is a member of **Enterprise Northern Ireland**.

ENTERPRISE NORTHERN IRELAND

See individual entries for:

- Acorn Business Centre
- Antrim Enterprise Agency Ltd
- Ards Business Centre Ltd
- Armagh Business Centre Ltd
- Ballymena Business Development Centre Ltd
- Banbridge District Enterprises Ltd
- Carrickfergus Enterprise Agency Ltd
- Castlereagh Enterprises Ltd
- Coleraine Enterprise Agency
- Cookstown Enterprise Centre Ltd
- Craigavon Industrial Development Organisation Ltd
- Down Business Centre
- Dungannon Enterprise Centre Ltd
- East Belfast Enterprise Park Ltd
- Enterprise North West
- Fermanagh Enterprise Ltd
- Glenwood Enterprises Ltd
- Larne Enterprise Development Company Ltd
- Lisburn Enterprise Organisation Ltd
- Moyle Enterprise Company Ltd
- Newry & Mourne Enterprise Agency
- Newtownabbey Enterprise Development Organisation
- North City Business Centre Ltd
- North Down Development Organisation Ltd

- Omagh Enterprise Company Ltd
- Ormeau Business Park
- ORTUS – The West Belfast Enterprise Board
- Roe Valley Enterprises Ltd
- Strabane Enterprise Agency
- Townsend Enterprise Park
- Work West Enterprise Agency (West Belfast Development Trust)
- Workspace (Draperstown) Ltd

CATEGORIES: DEBT; INFORMATION; START-UP TRAINING; TRAINING; WORKSPACE

Operating under the umbrella of Enterprise Northern Ireland, these **Local Enterprise Agencies** provide workspace accommodation, business services and administration support for small businesses just starting up. They are the local delivery points for key start-up programmes and services and provide enterprise training, loan funds, and target programmes for minority groups.

ENTERPRISE PROGRAMMES

CATEGORIES: GRANTS; INCUBATOR; MENTORING; START-UP TRAINING

The Enterprise Programmes are 12-month incubation programmes, targeted primarily at technology entrepreneurs, funded by the Department of Education and Science, the **Department of Enterprise, Trade & Employment**, and **Enterprise Ireland**. Participants receive a monthly grant of €550, training, mentoring and incubation space. Participants also may be entitled to an EU-funded CORD grant of upto half their previous salary. EPs currently operate in: Athlone - **Midlands EP**; Cork - **Genesis Enterprise Programme**; Dundalk - **North East EP**; Dublin - **M50 EP** and **HotHouse**; Galway - **Medical Device EP**; Limerick - **Fashion Knitwear EP**; Waterford - **South East EP**.

ENTREPRENEUR OF THE YEAR AWARDS

Ernst & Young, Ernst & Young Building, Harcourt Centre, Harcourt Street, Dublin 2
T: (01) 475 0575 F: (01) 475 0560
E: e-y.ireland@ie.eyi.com
W: www.ey.com/global/content.nsf/Ireland/eoy_overview
Contact: Greg Byrne

CATEGORIES: COMPETITIONS

The Entrepreneur Of The Year Awards programme celebrates entrepreneurial success and recognises the benefits of entrepreneurs and their spirit in providing Ireland with a solid foundation for future economic growth. The Awards are sponsored in Ireland by **Ernst & Young**, The Irish Times, RTE, **Enterprise Ireland** and **Shannon Development**.

ENTREWORLD.org

Kauffman Center for Entrepreneurial Leadership, Ewing Marion Kauffman Foundation, 4801 Rockhill Road, Kansas City, MO 64110, USA
E: info@entreworld.org W: www.entreworld.org

CATEGORIES: INFORMATION; WEBSITE

One of the key international online resources for entrepreneurs.

ENVIRONMENTAL PROTECTION AGENCY

P.O. Box 3000, Johnstown Castle Estate, Co Wexford
T: (053) 60600 F: (053) 60699
E: info@epa.ie W: www.epa.ie

CATEGORIES: INFORMATION; REGULATOR & STANDARDS

The EPA's responsibilities include: Promotion of environmentally sound practices through the use of environmental audits, eco-labelling, environmental quality objectives and codes of practice on matters affecting the environment; Promotion and co-ordination of environmental research; Monitoring of environmental quality; Licensing and regulation of large complex industrial and other processes (including landfills) with significant polluting potential, on the basis of integrated pollution control (IPC) and best available technologies.

ENVISION MARKETING CONSULTANTS

Envision House, Flood Street, Galway
T: (091) 568185 F: (091) 568510
E: envision@iol.ie W: www.envision-consultants.ie
Contact: Lorna Walsh

CATEGORIES: CONSULTING; MARKETING

Envision Marketing Consultants provide marketing services to companies ranging from multinationals to small indigenous businesses. Envision's consultants have experience in meeting the requirements of entrepreneurs/owners of small businesses.

EQUITYNETWORK

InterTradeIreland, The Old Gasworks Business Park, Kilmorey Street,
Newry, Co. Down BT34 2DE
T: 028 3083 4151 F: 028 3083 4155
E: equity@intertradeireland.com W: www.intertradeireland.com

CATEGORIES: BUSINESS ANGELS; EQUITY; INFORMATION

An initiative of **InterTradeIreland,** EquityNetwork provides free, value-added advisory services to businesses in Northern Ireland to assist in making them "investor-ready", as well as signposting and advice for businesses seeking equity finance.

ERNST & YOUNG

Ernst & Young Building, Harcourt Centre, Harcourt Street, Dublin 2
T: (01) 475 0555 F: (01) 475 0599
E: e-y.ireland@ie.eyi.com W: www.e-y.ie
Contact: Entrepreneurial Services Department

CATEGORIES: ACCOUNTANTS; CONSULTING

Ernst & Young provide audit, accounting, taxation, payroll and consulting services for companies of all sizes. The firm also is a sponsor of the **Entrepreneur of the Year Awards** and manages the **Excellerator** programme.

ETRADEBUSINESSIRELAND.com

W: www.etradebusinessireland.com

CATEGORIES: INFORMATION; WEBSITE

ETradeBusinessIreland.com links in to the **Empower** network to provide information on the **City/County Enterprise Boards**.

EU STRUCTURAL FUNDS

W: www.eustructuralfunds.ie

CATEGORIES: EU INFORMATION; WEBSITE

Explains how the EU Structural Funds are used to provide support in Ireland.

EURO INFO CENTRES

W: www.eic.ie

Contact: Fiona Robbins (T: 051 311138)

See individual entries for: Euro Info Centre Belfast; Euro Info Centre Cork; Euro Info Centre Galway; Euro Info Centre Sligo; Euro Info Centre Waterford.

CATEGORIES: EU INFORMATION

The Euro Info Centre Network operates as a "First Stop Shop" for enterprises as an authoritative source of information and advice on the euro, EC legislation, EU initiatives for business, public contracts, funding programmes, etc.

EURO INFO CENTRE BELFAST

Invest Northern Ireland, Upper Galwally, Belfast BT8 6TB

T: (028) 9064 6992/9049 1031 F: (028) 9064 6992

E: eic@investni.com W: www.euro-info.org.uk/centres/belfast/belfast.htm

Contact: Claire Gadd

CATEGORIES: EU INFORMATION

The Euro Info Centre for Northern Ireland. See the main **EIC** entry.

EURO INFO CENTRE CORK

Cork Chamber of Commerce, Fitzgerald House, Summerhill North, Cork

T: (021) 450 9044 F: (021) 450 8568

E: eic@corkchamber.ie W: www.corkchamber.ie

Contact: Kate Geary

CATEGORIES: EU INFORMATION

The Euro Info Centre for the South/South West. See the main **EIC** entry.

EURO INFO CENTRE GALWAY

Galway Chamber of Commerce and Industry, Commerce House, Merchants Road, Galway

T: (091) 562624 F: (091) 561963

E: elaine@galwaychamber.com W: www.galwaychamber.com/euro.htm

Contact: Elaine Wakely

CATEGORIES: EU INFORMATION

The Euro Info Centre for the West. See the main **EIC** entry.

EURO INFO CENTRE SLIGO
Sligo Chamber of Commerce, 16 Quay Street, Sligo
T: (071) 40017 F: (071) 60912
E: sligoeic@eircom.net W: www.sligoeic.com
Contact: Laura Caslin

CATEGORIES: EU INFORMATION

The Euro Info Centre for the North West. See the main **EIC** entry.

EURO INFO CENTRE WATERFORD
Waterford Chamber of Commerce, George's Quay, Waterford
T: (051) 311138 F: (051) 876002
E: eic@indigo.ie W: www.waterfordchamber.com
Contact: Fiona Robbins

CATEGORIES: EU INFORMATION

The Euro Info Centre for the South East. See the main **EIC** entry.

EUROCENTRE WEST LTD
Pennyburn Industrial Estate, Buncrana Road, Londonderry BT48 0LU
T: (028) 7136 4015 F: (028) 7126 6032
E: fdecw@aol.com
Contact: Denis Feeney

CATEGORIES: INFORMATION; WORKSPACE

One of the **Enterprise Agencies/Centres** in Derry.

EUROPA
E: europwebmaster@cec.eu.int
W: europa.eu.int

CATEGORIES: EU INFORMATION; INFORMATION; WEBSITE

The European Union's website, Europa, features information on the objectives of the EU, details on its agencies and the latest news. The URL http://europa.eu.int/comm/enterprise/index_en.htm is specific to enterprise.

EUROPEAN BIOSCIENCE FUND 1
Growcorp Ltd, 3015 Lakeside Drive, CityWest, Dublin 24
T: (01) 466 1000 F: (01) 466 1002
E: grow@growcorp.net W: www.growcorp.net
Contact: Michael Donnelly

CATEGORIES: EQUITY

A €12.7 million fund, providing seed and early-stage funding (typically €100k to €1.27 million) in the bioscience sector. It is managed by **GrowCorp Ltd**.

EUROPEAN COMMISSION

European Union House, 18 Dawson Street, Dublin 2
T: (01) 662 5113 F: (01) 662 5118
E: eu@carrcomm.iol.ie W: www.euireland.ie
Contact: Tim Kelly, Library
Also at: Windsor House, 9-15 Bedford Street, Belfast BT2 7EG
T: (028) 9024 0708 F: (028) 9024 8241
E: Jim.Dougal@cec.eu.int
W: www.europe.org.uk/info/ni
Contact: Jim Dougal

CATEGORIES: EU INFORMATION

To help SMEs, the European Commission has funded various programmes, details of which are available from: **Carréfours; Euro Info Centres; Info Points Europe; Innovation Relay Centres**. The EU Special Support Programme for Peace and Reconciliation provides funding for a range of activities, including enterprise and community development, operates in the Border counties. The Commission also supports other enterprise activities, such as the **Business Innovation Centres.**

EUROPEAN INVESTMENT BANK

100 Boulevard Konrad Adenauer, L-2950 Luxembourg
T: (00 352) 4379 3122 F: (00 352) 4379 3189
E: info@eib.org W: www.eib.org
Contact: InfoDesk / Patricia Tibbels (T: 00 35 2 4379 4317)

CATEGORIES: EU INFORMATION

The European Investment Bank is the European Union's long-term financing institution. It raises money on the international capital markets for lending to EU Member States for specific projects. It supports SMEs through "global loans" with a number of leading banks — **AIB Bank, Bank of Ireland, Bank of Scotland and Barclays Bank** — for on-lending to SMEs. **Note that the EIB does not invest directly in SMEs, only through banks**.

EUROPEAN INVESTMENT FUND

43 avenue JF Kennedy, L-2968 Luxembourg
T: (00 352) 42 66 88 1 F: (00 352) 42 66 88 200
E: info@eif.org W: www.eif.org

CATEGORIES: EU INFORMATION

The European Investment Fund invests in venture capital funds and business incubators that support SMEs, particularly those that are early stage and technology-oriented. In Ireland, the EIF has invested in: **ACT Venture Capital; Delta Equity Fund II; Guinness Ulster Bank Equity Fund; ICC Private Equity Fund; Trinity Venture Fund. Note that the EIF does not invest directly in SMEs, only through venture capital funds.**

EVP EARLY STAGE TECHNOLOGY FUND

EVP General Partner Ltd, Arena House, Arena Road,
Sandyford Industrial Estate, Dublin 18
T: (01) 213 0711 F: (01) 663 9207
E: gerry.jones@evp.ie W: www.evp.ie
Contact: Gerry Jones

CATEGORIES: EQUITY

A €5 million fund, investing in early-stage (typically €300k to €700k) high potential start-ups (HPSUs) in the information, communications and technology (ICT) sector.

EXCELLENCE IRELAND

Merrion Hall, Strand Road, Sandymount, Dublin 4
T: (01) 269 5255 F: (01) 269 8053
E: admin@excellence-ireland.ie W: www.excellence-ireland.ie
Contact: Seán Conlan, CEO

CATEGORIES: INFORMATION; REGULATOR & STANDARDS

Excellence Ireland promotes continuous improvement and business excellence among Irish companies. It organises the Quality Mark and Hygiene Mark schemes, the National Quality Hygiene Awards and the Irish Business Excellence Model. The Foundation Mark is a management development programme accredited by Excellence Ireland for established small companies.

EXCELLERATOR

Ernst & Young, Harcourt Centre, Harcourt Street, Dublin 2
T: (01) 475 0555 F: (01) 475 0556
E: info@excelleratoronline.com W: www.excelleratoronline.com
Contact: Avril McHugh

CATEGORIES: INFORMATION; TRAINING; WEBSITE

Excellerator is a community of Irish entrepreneurs, accelerating their business through knowledge exchange and the sharing of ideas, designed to speed the development of entrepreneurial companies that have the ability to become international successes. Ernst & Young is responsible for the design and content of the programme, built to address specific skills and knowledge gaps identified amongst entrepreneurs by **Enterprise Ireland** and **Shannon Development**. The website offers useful online business resources.

EXECUTIVE VENTURE PARTNERS

Arena House, Arena Road, Sandyford Industrial Estate, Dublin 18
T: (01) 213 0711 F: (01) 663 9207
E: gerry.jones@evp.ie W: www.evp.ie
Contact: Gerry Jones

CATEGORIES: EQUITY

EVP provides a comprehensive range of services that covers virtually every start-up aspect, from finance, through investor relations to sales and marketing, channel advice, **Enterprise Ireland** relations and risk reduction.

It provides direct funding of up to €750,000 and manages the **EVP Early Stage Technology Fund.**

EXPERTISEIRELAND.com

InterTradeIreland, The Old Gasworks Business Park, Kilmorey Street,
Newry, Co. Down BT34 2DE
T: 028 3083 4151 F: 028 3083 4155
E: equity@intertradeireland.com W: www.intertradeireland.com

CATEGORIES: INFORMATION; WEBSITE

expertiseireland.com is the gateway to the island's knowledge base, bringing together innovators and those at the forefront of developing the knowledge economy, be they from a business or academic background. It provides a searchable database, with up-to-date details of academic expertise and business expertise, funding information, technology transfer and collaborative opportunities. It is supported by **InterTradeIreland** and the Conference of the Heads of Irish Universities.

FÁILTE IRELAND

Baggot Street Bridge, Dublin 2 / 88-95 Amiens Street, Dublin 1
T: 1890 525 525 F: (01) 700 1000
E: info@failteireland.ie W: www.failteireland.ie

CATEGORIES: INFORMATION; MARKETING; TOURISM DEVELOPMENT; TRAINING

The Government has brought together the functions formerly carried out by CERT and Bord Fáilte and established Fáilte Ireland, the National Tourism Development Authority. It provides strategic and practical support to develop and sustain Ireland as a high quality and competitive tourist destination. Fáilte Ireland's range of supports and services provides those involved, or considering becoming involved, in Irish tourism with a "one-stop-shop" to meet their business or professional development needs. Fáilte Ireland facilitates a professional and highly efficient results-oriented working relationship with clients in the areas of Industry Development, Education and Training and Market Development.

FARMOPTIONS.ie

West Cork LEADER Co-operative Society Ltd, South Square,
Clonakilty, Co Cork
T: (023) 34035 F: (023) 34066
E: wclc@wclc.iol.ie W: www.farmoptions.ie
Contact: Ian Dempsey, Manager

CATEGORIES: COMMUNITY & RURAL DEVELOPMENT; INFORMATION; WEBSITE

FarmOptions.ie promotes and supports new enterprise development on Irish farms by implementating innovative but practical ideas to help Irish farm-families develop new income streams. It is the primary information source on alternative land-use in Ireland and in the training, funding, information and support resources available for new enterprise development in the Irish farming community. It was developed by Innovation South, a development initiative of: **East Cork Area Development**

You've bought the book, now visit the website

www.startingabusinessinireland.com
information, advice & resources for entrepreneurs

THE website for Irish start-ups, with the most comprehensive directory of sources of assistance available, North & South – over 700 entries! Plus templates for download

... and take the course ....

START-UP BOOT CAMP

An intensive one-day learning experience, designed to accelerate your progress towards start-up by providing you with the skills and information you need, plus one month's follow-up email support.

For details of **START-UP BOOT CAMP**s, visit **TheSuccessStore** at **www.oaktreepress.com** or contact **Oak Tree Press**:

- By telephone (within Ireland) 021 431 3855 or LoCall 1890 313855 or (international) + 353 21 431 3855
- By fax (within Ireland) 021 431 3496 or (international) + 353 21 431 3496
- By email at info@oaktreepress.com

FARSET ENTERPRISE PARK LTD
638 Springfield Road, Belfast BT12 7DY
T: (028) 9024 2373 F: (028) 9043 8967
E: admin@farset.com W: www.farset.com
Contact: Bill Bradley
CATEGORIES: INFORMATION; WORKSPACE

One of the **Enterprise Agencies/Centres** in Belfast.

FÁS : THE TRAINING AND EMPLOYMENT AUTHORITY
Services to Business, 27–33 Upper Baggot Street, Dublin 4
T: (01) 607 0500 F: (01) 607 0600
E: info@fas.ie W: www.fas.ie
Contact: John McGrath, Services to Industry
CATEGORIES: COMMUNITY DEVELOPMENT; GRANTS; SOCIAL ECONOMY;
START-UP TRAINING; TRAINING

FÁS provides training and employment programmes, and employment and advisory services for industry. Individuals who want to start a business can attend the Business Appraisal Training Programme, which allows them to develop business plans, enhance their skills and conduct market research. The Community Enterprise Programme provides advice, training and financial assistance to community groups involved in the creation of economically viable jobs. The Social Economy Programme supports the development of social economy enterprises that will benefit the economic and social regeneration of a community.

FASHION KNITWEAR ENTERPRISE PROGRAMME
Limerick Institute of Technology, Georges Quay, Limerick
T: (061) 319019
E: eppknit@lit.ie W: www.lit.ie
Contact: Lucy Erridge / Liz Spillane
CATEGORIES: GRANTS; INCUBATOR; MENTORING; START-UP TRAINING

The Enterprise Development Programme supports the development of entrepreneurial skills among students in the Institute. EDP projects are currently running in the LIT School of Art and Design: The School of Art and Design, Fashion Knitwear (contacts: Patricia Keilthy, Lucy Erridge); The School of Art and Design, Ceramic Giftware (contact: Kieran Whitelaw). See also **Enterprise Programmes** for EPs in other locations.

FERMANAGH ENTERPRISE LTD
Enniskillen Business Centre, Lackaghboy Industrial Estate, Tempo Road,
Enniskillen BT74 4RL
T: (028) 6632 3117 F: (028) 6632 7878
E: info@fermanaghenterprise.com W: www.fermanaghenterprise.com
Contact: John Treacy, Manager

CATEGORIES: DEBT; INCUBATOR; INFORMATION; START-UP TRAINING;
TRAINING; WORKSPACE

Fermanagh Enterprise is an **Enterprise Agency** and a member of **Enterprise Northern Ireland**. It offers support to start-ups and existing businesses, in the form of: Loans; Training (including the **Northern Ireland Business Start** and Exploring Enterprise programmes); Advisory services; and Workspace. See also **Choose Enterprise**. Other enterprise centres in Fermanagh include: **Belcoo Enterprise Centre, Derrylin Enterprise Centre, Irvinestown Enterprise Centre, Kesh Enterprise Centre, Lisnaskean Enterprise Centre, Roslean Enterprise Centre,** and **Teemore Business Complex**.

FERMANAGH LOCAL ACTION GROUP
5 The Cornsheds, Mill Street, Irvinestown, Co Fermanagh BT94 1GR
T: (028) 6862 1600 F: (028) 6862 1992
E: info@fermanaghleader.co.uk
Contact: Catherine Ryan

CATEGORIES: COMMUNITY & RURAL DEVELOPMENT

One of the **LEADER+** groups in Northern Ireland.

FGS
Molyneux House, Bride Street, Dublin 8
T: (01) 418 2000 F: (01) 418 2050
E: fgs@fgs.ie W: www.fgs.ie
Contact: Jim Mulqueen, Corporate Finance Partner

CATEGORIES: ACCOUNTANTS; CONSULTING

An independent firm of business advisers and consultants, FGS is one of Ireland's top 10 accountancy practices, delivering added value through experience, expertise and innovation. It provides a range of accountancy services, including audit, due diligence and corporate compliance, and an advisory service, specialising in corporate restructuring, technology consulting, corporate finance, tax, property and consulting. Associated with Moores Rowland International, FGS has offices in Dublin and Belfast.

FINGAL COUNTY ENTERPRISE BOARD
Mainscourt, 23 Main Street, Swords, Co Dublin
T: (01) 890 0800 F: (01) 813 9991
E: info@fingalceb.ie W: www.fingalceb.ie
Contact: Oisin Geoghegan, CEO

CATEGORIES: DEBT; E-BUSINESS; EQUITY; GRANTS; INFORMATION;
MENTORING; START-UP TRAINING; TRAINING

Fingal CEB is part of a network of 35 City and County Enterprise Boards nationwide. It provides assistance to existing and potential small business promoters located in Fingal County (north County Dublin). Fingal CEB's support includes: Business advice and mentoring for start-up and micro businesses; Training and information services, Start Your Own Business courses, computer training and management development workshops; Enterprise awareness; Business networks, including **PLATO** and a Women in Business network; and financial assistance, depending on the type of business activity.

FINGAL EMPLOYEES YOUTH BUSINESS FUND
c/o Fingal County Hall, Main Street, Swords, Co Dublin
T: (01) 840 0149/890 5000 F: (01) 840 5175
W: www.fingalcoco.ie
Contact: Sean Ring
CATEGORIES: GRANTS

The Fund was set up by Fingal County Council staff to meet the needs of those who fall through the loopholes left by other schemes. Applicants must be aged between 18 and 30, either be from Fingal (North County Dublin) or want to start a business in Fingal, have a sound business idea, and be prepared to work to make it a success. The Fund will assist R&D, feasibility studies, start-up finance and equipment.

FINGLAS BUSINESS INITIATIVE
Rosehill House, Finglas Road, Dublin 11
T: (01) 836 1666 F: (01) 864 0211
E: info@fcp.ie W: www.fcp.ie
Contact: David Orford

CATEGORIES: BUSINESS PLANS; GRANTS; INFORMATION; MENTORING

The Finglas Business Initiative is operated by the **Finglas/Cabra Partnership** and offers mentoring, business information and advice, assistance with business planning and funding applications and loan finance to businesses in the Finglas area of Dublin.

FINGLAS/CABRA PARTNERSHIP
Rosehill House, Finglas Road, Dublin 11
T: (01) 836 1666 F: (01) 864 0211
E: info@fcp.ie W: www.fcp.ie
Contact: Michael P Bowe

CATEGORIES: COMMUNITY & RURAL DEVELOPMENT; INFORMATION

One of the **Area Partnerships** funded by **Area Development Management**, as part of its Local Development programme. It operates the **Finglas Business Initiative**.

FIRST POINT BUSINESS DEVELOPMENT CONSULTANCY LTD

Ardee Business Park, Hale Street, Ardee, Co Louth
T: (041) 685 7680 F: (041) 685 7681
E: ardbuspark@eircom.net W: www.ardeebusinesspark.ie

CATEGORIES: CONSULTING; START-UP TRAINING; TRAINING

First Point offers training and consultancy for SMEs, often in conjunction with **FÁS** and **Louth County Enterprise Board**.

FIRST STEP

Jefferson House, Eglinton Road, Donnybrook, Dublin 4
T: (01) 260 0988 F: (01) 260 0989
E: firststep@eircom.net
Contact: Mary Saunders

CATEGORIES: DEBT; EQUITY

First Step provides micro-finance (loans less than €25,000) to individuals who cannot access funds through normal channels. Up to mid-2003, First Step has supported 1,200 small businesses through its revolving loan funds. Its partners in these funds include **Bank of Ireland**, **Enterprise Ireland** and the **Department of Social and Family Affairs**. **AIB Bank** supports First Step's mentor programme.

FIRST TRUST BANK

92 Ann Street, Belfast BT1 3AY
T: 028 9032 5599 F: 028 9032 1754
W: www.firsttrustbank.co.uk

CATEGORIES: DEBT

First Trust Bank is **Allied Irish Bank's** Northern Ireland business banking service.

FIRST TUESDAY

Investnet Ltd, Invent, Dublin City University, Dublin
T: 01 700 8508 F: 01 700 5505
W: www.firsttuesday.ie

CATEGORIES: BUSINESS ANGELS; EBUSINESS; NETWORKING

First Tuesday is a forum (held, as the name suggests, on the first Tuesday each month) and open marketplace for entrepreneurs, start-ups, investors and service providers in the new economy. Every month, top-tier Internet entrepreneurs address the community, sharing lessons learned and how they implemented their personal visions. First Tuesday is operated by **Investnet**.

FIRSTHAND PUBLISHING LTD
24 Terenure Road East, Rathgar, Dublin 6
T: (01) 490 2244 F: (01) 492 0578
E: info@ryb.ie
Contact: Donal McAuliffe, Editor
CATEGORIES: INFORMATION; PUBLICATIONS

Firsthand is the publisher of the Small Firms Association magazine, *Running Your Business*, also on general sale at newsagents.

FLAX TRUST
Brookfield Business Centre, 333 Crumlin Road, Belfast BT14 7EA
T: (028) 9074 5241 F: (028) 9074 8025
E: info@flaxtrust.com W: www.flaxtrust.com
CATEGORIES: COMMUNITY & RURAL DEVELOPMENT; INCUBATOR; WORKSPACE

The Flax Trust is the largest community regeneration project in the whole of Ireland and is committed to the "reconciliation of a divided community through economic and social development, bringing peace to both communities, one person and one job at a time". Using abandoned linen mills located within the Ardoyne/Shankill interface, a Belfast "no man's land", it developed the **Brookfield Business Centre**, where over 330 new businesses have been incubated in 232,000 sq ft of workspace.

FOOD INNOVATION CENTRE
Ardbuckle Row, Ballina, Co Mayo
T: (096) 72557/8 F: (096) 72559
E: foodinn@iol.ie W: www.mayo-ireland.ie/sites/fic/fic.htm
Contact: Pauline Beecher
CATEGORIES: INCUBATOR

The Food Innovation Centre is part-funded by the European Union under the **LEADER+** programme, the **Mayo County Enterprise Board** and **Enterprise Ireland**. It provides support to tenants at the centre and to established companies and potential entrepreneurs throughout the region. It is a joint venture between **Moy Valley Resources**, a community-owned enterprise development company and a sub-office of **Meitheal Mhaigh Eo**, and the North Connacht Farmers Co-operative (NCF).

FOOD PRODUCT DEVELOPMENT CENTRE
31 Marlborough Street, Dublin 1
T: (01) 814 6080 F: (01) 874 8572
E: fpdc@dit.ie W: www.fpdc.dit.ie
Contact: Mary Dineen
CATEGORIES: CONSULTING; R & D; TRAINING

The Food Product Development Centre at the **Dublin Institute of Technology** develops innovative food concepts through investigating value-added opportunities in Irish and European markets. It provides a confidential service to clients. Its development work includes: Idea generation; Concept and prototype development; Ingredient sourcing and testing; Shelf life studies; Sensory assessment and market research; Nutritional declaration; Labelling. The Centre also offers training workshops.

FOOD SAFETY AUTHORITY OF IRELAND
Abbey Court, Lower Abbey Street, Dublin 1
T: (01) 817 1300 F: (01) 817 1301
E: info@fsai.ie W: www.fsai.ie
CATEGORIES: INFORMATION; REGULATOR & STANDARDS

The Food Safety Authority of Ireland's mission is to protect consumers' health by ensuring that food consumed, distributed, marketed or produced in Ireland meets the highest standards of food safety and hygiene. It offers information to industry on all aspects of food safety, including the safe handling and preparation of food, food safety and training, Hazard Analysis Critical Control Point (HACCP), labelling and food safety legislation. FSAI has also produced a fact sheet outling the steps to be taken when starting a food business in Ireland. An Advice operates on **1890 33 66 77**.

FORFÁS
Wilton Park House, Wilton Place, Dublin 2
T: (01) 607 3000 F: (01) 607 3030
E: info@forfas.ie or aideen.fitzgerald@forfas.ie W: www.forfas.ie
Contact: Aideen Fitzgerald, Communications Manager
CATEGORIES: POLICY

Forfás is the national policy and advisory board for enterprise, trade, science, technology and innovation and the body through which powers are delegated to Enterprise Ireland for promotion of indigenous industry and to IDA Ireland for promotion of inward investment. IN July 2003, Science foundation Ireland was established as a third agency of Forfás. Bodies associated with Forfás include: Irish Council for Science, Technology and Innovation; National Competitiveness Council and the Expert Group on Future Skills Needs. Forfás publishes a range of reports that are available for download from its website.

FOUNDATION FOR INVESTING IN COMMUNITIES
32 Lower O'Connell Street, Dublin 1
T: (01) 874 7354 F: (01) 874 7637
E: admin@foundation.ie W: www.foundation.ie
Contact: Tina Roche, CEO
CATEGORIES: COMMUNITY & RURAL DEVELOPMENT

The Foundation for Investing in Communities comprises three divisions, each a separate Ltd company bearing charitable status: Communities Foundation for Ireland; National Children's Trust; Business in the Community. organisations. **Business in the Community** aims to develop corporate social responsibility strategies and involvement in the community. The former Enterprise Trust is incorporated into the Foundation.

FR KELLY & CO

27 Clyde Road, Ballsbridge, Dublin 4
T: (01) 231 4848   F: (01) 614 4756
E: info@frkelly.com   W: www.frkelly.com
Contact: Patents: Philip Coyle, Trade Marks: Shane Smyth

CATEGORIES: INTELLECTUAL PROPERTY

FR Kelly & Co offers expertise and experience in all aspects of intellectual property law, trade marks and brand name protection.

FRANCHISEDIRECT.com

Unit 27, Guinness Enterprise Centre, Taylor's Lane, Dublin 8
T: (01) 410 0667   F: (01) 410 0733
E: akay@franchisedirect.com
W: www.franchisedirect.com; www.franchisedirect.ie
Contact: Mary Lyons

CATEGORIES: BUSINESS SALES/PURCHASES; FRANCHISES; INFORMATION; WEBSITE

FranchiseDirect.com is a leading international franchising resource, owned and operated by McGarry Internet. The website provides views, news and advice to entrepreneurs and franchisers, including: A directory of franchisers seeking franchisee partners; A "Franchise Seeker" facility through which visitors to the site can provide information about themselves and have it relayed quickly to the franchisers in whom they are interested; A "Master Licence Locator" for companies or individuals who want to acquire a master licence for a country or territory; Advice and guidance on franchising as a business concept. See also **ManagementDirect.com**.

GAHAN & CO

14 South Lotts Road, Dublin 4
T: (01) 668 4411   F: (01) 668 4428
E: pgahan@gahan.ie   W: www.gahan.ie
Contact: Patrick Gahan

CATEGORIES: ACCOUNTANTS; TRAINING

A firm of chartered accountants. In addition to the usual accountancy/auditing services, Gahan also provides workshops in effective financial management and strategic planning.

GALWAY CITY PARTNERSHIP

3 The Plaza, Headford Road, Galway
T: (091) 773466   F: (091) 773468
E: info@gcp.ie   W: www.gcp.ie
Contact: Declan Brassil, Manager

CATEGORIES: COMMUNITY & RURAL DEVELOPMENT; GRANTS; INFORMATION; SOCIAL ECONOMY; START-UP TRAINING

One of the **Area Partnerships** funded by **Area Development Management**, as part of its Local Development programme. It supports local people on the Back to Work Enterprise Area Allowance Scheme, a **Department of Social**

and Family Affairs initiative that offers support to individuals who wish to start their own businesses. It allows participants to retain benefits, over a four-year period, and also offers further support such as training programmes, mentoring and small grants. Set-up support, capital grants and loan financing are available to support community enterprises that create real jobs while meeting a social need within the community.

GALWAY COUNTY AND CITY ENTERPRISE BOARD
Woodquay Court, Woodquay, Galway
T: (091) 565269 F: (091) 565384
E: charles@galwayenterprise.ie W: www.galwayenterprise.ie
Contact: Charles Lynch, CEO

CATEGORIES: DEBT; E-BUSINESS; EQUITY; GRANTS; INFORMATION; MENTORING; START-UP TRAINING; TRAINING; WEBSITE

Galway CEB provides a full range of supports for micro-enterprises in its region. Its website also offers online tools for entrepreneurs, as well as reference articles and other information.

GALWAY RURAL DEVELOPMENT COMPANY
Old Church Street, Athenry, Co Galway
T: (091) 844335 F: (091) 845465
E: grdc@grd.ie W: www.grd.ie
Contact: Eamonn Kealy, Manager

CATEGORIES: COMMUNITY & RURAL DEVELOPMENT; GRANTS; INFORMATION; START-UP TRAINING

One of the **Area Partnerships** funded by **Area Development Management**, as part of its Local Development programme. It now administers the Social Inclusion Programme and the National Rural Development Programme (**LEADER+**). Galway Rural Development provides enterprise supports, from facilitating small private and community enterprises to expand and improve their businesses, working with farm families to explore their options, and facilitating long-term unemployed people to become self-employed through the Back to Work Enterprise Allowance Scheme. It offers capital equipment grants to innovative, small enterprises in manufacturing, crafts or local services at start-up or development stage, within its operational area.

GALWAY TECHNOLOGY CENTRE
Mervue Business Park, Galway
T: (091) 770 007 F: (091) 755 635
E: gtc@iol.ie W: www.gtc.ie
Contact: Louise Leonard; John Brennan, Manager

CATEGORIES: INCUBATOR

The Galway Technology Centre provides a self-sustaining centre for market-driven IT companies. It is also home to **WestBIC**, the Galway Business Innovation Centre.

GALWAY–MAYO INSTITUTE OF TECHNOLOGY
Dublin Road, Galway
T: (091) 753161 F: (091) 751107
E: andrew.darcy@gmit.ie W: www.gmit.ie
Contact: Andrew D'Arcy, Head of Development
Also at: Castlebar, Letterfrack and Cluain Mhuire

CATEGORIES: CONSULTING; R & D; START-UP TRAINING; TRAINING

GMIT's Development office makes available the expertise and facilities of GMIT on a commercial basis. Technical consultancy is provided on virtually all aspects of business and industry. GMIT also offers research, training, consultancy and enterprise development services to existing and new businesses.

GE CAPITAL WOODCHESTER
Woodchester House, Golden Lane, Dublin 8
T: (01) 478 0000 F: (01) 402 1295
E: infoireland@gecapital.com W: www.gecapital.com

CATEGORIES: DEBT

GE Capital Woodchester specialises in leasing and hire purchase for cars and equipment, through a nation-wide network of branches.

GENERAL CONSUMER COUNCIL FOR NORTHERN IRELAND
Elizabeth House, 116 Holywood Road, Belfast BT4 1NY
T: (028) 9067 2488 F: (028) 9065 7701
E: info@gccni.org.uk W: www.gccni.org.uk

CATEGORIES: INFORMATION; REGULATOR & STANDARDS

The General Consumer Council for Northern Ireland is a statutory body whose aims are to promote and safeguard the interests of all consumers in Northern Ireland. It campaigns on behalf of consumers for the best possible standards of service and protection; undertakes research and data collection; gives advice, information and issues publications. The Council is funded by the **Department of Enterprise, Trade and Investment**.

GENESIS ENTERPRISE PROGRAMME
Unit 10, Melbourne Business Park, Model Farm Road, Cork
T: (021) 486 7535 F: (021) 486 7530
E: dosullivan@gep.ie W: www.gep.ie
Contact: Drew O'Sullivan, Programme Manager

CATEGORIES: GRANTS; INCUBATOR; MENTORING; START-UP TRAINING

The Genesis Enterprise Programme is a 12-month rapid incubation programme to support and accelerate graduate entrepreneurs in developing a business. The GEP allows participants to focus on developing the business concept into a viable business, while still receiving an income. It aims to accelerate the learning process for participants through formal training, a mentor and the shared knowledge of other participants. Partners in the

Programme are the **Cork Institute of Technology, the Institute of Technology Tralee, the Cork Business Innovation Centre, University College Cork** and **Enterprise Ireland**. See also **Enterprise Programmes** for EPs in other locations.

GET TALLAGHT WORKING
See **Partas**.

GLENWOOD ENTERPRISES LTD
Glenwood Business Centre, Springbank Industrial Estate, Poleglass,
Belfast BT17 0QL
T: (028) 9061 0311 F: (028) 9060 0929
E: office@glenwoodbc.com W: www.glenwoodbc.com
Contact: Martina Walsh

CATEGORIES: COMMUNITY & RURAL DEVELOPMENT; DEBT; INFORMATION;
SOCIAL ECONOMY; START-UP TRAINING; TRAINING; WOMEN; WORKSPACE

Glenwood Enterprises is an **Enterprise Agency** and a member of **Enterprise Northern Ireland**. Belfast's first enterprise agency, Glenwood provides workspace, secretarial services, financial assistance, business advice and counselling and business skills training. It promotes job creation and economic development through practical support for small businesses. It offers "Women into Enterprise" and "Community Business Support" training programmes.

GLOBAL TECHNOLOGY, ENTREPRENEURSHIP AND COMMERCIALISATION BUSINESS PLAN COMPETITION
DuPree College of Management, Georgia Institute of Technology, 800 West
Peachtree Street NW, Atlanta, Georgia 30328, USA
T: (00 1) 404 385 4504 F: (00 1) 404 894 1552
E: nick.voigt@mgt.gatech.edu W: www.globaltechbiz.gatech.edu
Contact: Nick Voigt

CATEGORIES: COMPETITION

GTEC is the first global business plan competition to focus exclusively on commercialisation of technology. Teams from all around the world will be invited to Atlanta in April 2004 to compete for more than US$100,000 in prizes.

GOLDEN PAGES
St Martin's House, Waterloo Road, Dublin 4
T: (01) 618 8000 F: (01) 618 8001
E: info@goldenpages.ie W: www.goldenpages.ie

CATEGORIES: INFORMATION; PUBLICATIONS

The *Golden Pages* classified telephone directories are an excellent research resource for identifying your competition.

GORANN LTD
68 Harcourt Street, Dublin 2
T: (01) 418 8112 F: (01) 633 5781
E: dublin@gorann.com W: www.gorann.com
CATEGORIES: CONSULTING; EQUITY; INCUBATOR

Gorann is a project management services firm, with offices in New York and Dublin. Its venture consulting practice works with client companies to maximise their growth potential, tailoring services to meet client needs.

GOVERNMENT DIRECT FOR BUSINESS
W: www.nics.gov.uk/ni-direct/
CATEGORIES: INFORMATION; WEBSITE

The website provides information on government regulations applicable to Northern Ireland, as well as forms commonly used by businesses.

GOVERNMENT PUBLICATIONS
51 St Stephen's Green, Dublin 2
Locall: 1890 213414 T: (01) 647 6000 F: (01) 661 0747
E: patricia.ward@opw.ie W: www.opw.ie
Contact: Sean Benton, Chairman
Also at: Sales Office: Sun Alliance House, Molesworth Street, Dublin 2
CATEGORIES: INFORMATION; PUBLICATIONS

All Government publications are available from the sales office, including **Central Statistics Office** reports.

GREENENTREPRENEURS.net
W: www.greenentrepreneurs.net
CATEGORIES: INFORMATION; WEBSITE

Green Entrepreneurs is an interactive training tool aimed at guiding people in the creation of small businesses offering environmental products and services. The tool is also of use to small businesses considering diversifying their product/service range to include environmental alternatives. Green Entrepreneurs was created by a range of European small business support and environmental organisations, under the EU-funded Leonardo da Vinci programme. **Banbridge District Enterprises** is the Irish partner.

GREENMOUNT CAMPUS, COLLEGE OF AGRICULTURE, FOOD & RURAL ENTERPRISE, DEPARTMENT OF AGRICULTURE & RURAL DEVELOPMENT
22 Greenmount Road, Antrim BT41 4PU
T: (0800) 0284291 F: (028) 9442 6606
E: enquiries@dardni.gov.uk W: www.greenmount.ac.uk
CATEGORIES: COMMUNITY & RURAL DEVELOPMENT; INFORMATION; TRAINING

Greenmount Campus, College of Agriculture, Food & Rural Enterprise, **DARD**, provides education, training and technology support in agriculture, horticulture, rural and countryside management and veterinary nursing. It also offers a range of Rural Enterprise and Business Management courses.

GROWCORP GROUP LTD
3015 Lake Drive, Citywest Business Campus Park, Dublin 24
T: (01) 466 1000 F: (01) 466 1002
E: grow@growcorp.net W: www.growcorp.net
CATEGORIES: EQUITY; INCUBATOR

Growcorp develops businesses with leading-edge platform technologies in bioscience, through an incubation process that delivers the resources to ensure success in the global marketplace. Growcorp has a 16,000 square feet state-of-the-art incubation facility in the National Digital Park at Citywest, Dublin.

GUARANTEED IRISH LTD
1 Fitzwilliam Place, Dublin 2
T: (01) 661 2607 F: (01) 661 2633
E: info@guaranteed-irish.ie W: www.guaranteed-irish.ie
CATEGORIES: MARKETING; REGULATOR & STANDARDS

Guaranteed Irish Ltd aims to increase awareness of and demand for Irish products and services, thereby maximising employment and prosperity in Ireland. The Guaranteed Irish symbol has become the definitive mark of excellence for Irish products and services.

GUINNESS ENTERPRISE CENTRE
Taylor's Lane, Dublin 8
T: (01) 410 0600 F: (01) 410 0602
E: info@guinness-enterprisectr.com W: www.guinness-enterprisectr.com
Contact: Dolores Dempsey, Administration Manager
CATEGORIES: INCUBATOR; WORKSPACE

A 77-unit, 6,000 square metre enterprise/incubation centre managed by **Dublin BIC**.

GUINNESS IRELAND ULSTER BANK EQUITY FUND
NCB Ventures Ltd, 3 George's Dock, IFSC, Dublin 1
T: (01) 611 5942 F: (01) 611 5987
E: info@ncb.ie W: www.ncbdirect.com
Contact: Michael Murphy, michael.murphy@ncb.ie; Mark Mulqueen, mark.mulqueen@ncb.ie
CATEGORIES: EQUITY

Managed by **NCB Ventures**, this is a €19 million fund that invsted across all sectors, with an investment between €95k and €1 miilion. The fund was established with assistance from **Enterprise Ireland**, under the Seed & Venture Capital Measure of the Operational Programme 2001-2006.

GUINNESS WORKERS' EMPLOYMENT FUND LTD
St James's Gate, Dublin 8
T: (01) 453 6700 F: (01) 408 4967
E: thornbur@guinness2.team400.ie
Contact: Rowena Thornburgh; Andy Shirran (Part-time)
CATEGORIES: DEBT

Funded by Guinness workers and pensioners, the Fund provides start-up businesses with financial assistance, and supports expansion of existing businesses, usually by way of a term loan, at interest rates below those charged by the commercial banks. Entrepreneurs must submit applications on the fund's official application form. GWEF also helped to fund the development of the **Guinness Enterprise Centre**.

HEALTH & SAFETY AUTHORITY
10 Hogan Place, Dublin 2
T: (01) 614 7000 F: (01) 614 7020
E: infotel@hsa.ie W: www.hsa.ie
CATEGORIES: INFORMATION; PUBLICATIONS; REGULATOR & STANDARDS; TRAINING

The HSA has overall responsibility for the administration and enforcement of health and safety at work in Ireland, and: Monitors compliance with legislation at the workplace and can take enforcement action (including prosecutions); Is an expert centre for information and advice to employers, employees and self-employed; Promotes education, training and research. The Safety, Health and Welfare at Work Act, 1989 covers all who work, all workplaces, visitors and passers-by and also places responsibilities on manufacturers and suppliers (including designers, installers and erectors).

HEALTH & SAFETY EXECUTIVE FOR NORTHERN IRELAND
83 Ladas Drive, Belfast BT6 9FR
T: (028) 9024 3249 F: (028) 9023 5383
E: hseni@detini.gov.uk W: www.hseni.gov.uk
CATEGORIES: INFORMATION; PUBLICATIONS; REGULATOR & STANDARDS; TRAINING

HSENI's mission is to see that the risks to people's health and safety arising from work activities are effectively controlled, thereby contributing to the overall economic and social well-being of the community. It has published a *Guide to Workplace Health & Safety*, illustrating the general scope of the laws covering health and safety at work. The guide is useful to anyone starting up a new firm, managing a small work unit, preparing a safety policy for a company or looking for general health and safety information.

HIBERNIA CAPITAL PARTNERS LTD
Ground Floor, Beech House, Beech Hill Office Campus, Clonskeagh, Dublin 6
T: (01) 205 7770 F: (01) 205 7771
E: equity@hcp.ie W: www.hcp.ie
Contact: John Bolger, CEO / Luke Crosbie
CATEGORIES: EQUITY

Hibernia provides equity and equity-related finance for development capital, management buy-outs and buy-ins, and start-ups with significant scale and demonstrable market potential. Unusually, each of the Hibernia team invests personally in every transaction the fund completes. Hibernia can invest up to €16 million from its own resources in any one transaction, and further funds through co-invest arrangements with partners worldwide. Equity-related funding under €2.5 million is normally referred to a sister fund, **Trinity Venture Capital.**

HM CUSTOMS & EXCISE

Custom House, Queen's Square, Belfast BT1 3ET
T: (028) 9056 2600 F: (028) 9056 2970
E: enquiries.ni@hmne.gsi.gov.uk W: www.hmce.gov.uk
VAT Registration Unit
PO Box 40, Carnbane Way, Damolly, Newry, Co Down BT35 6PJ
T: (028) 3026 1114 F: (028) 3026 4165

CATEGORIES: REGULATOR & STANDARDS

For advice on VAT, contact your nearest VAT Business Advice Centre. HM Customs & Excise's website provides a list of centres.

HOTHOUSE

PDC, Docklands Innovation Park, 128-130 East Wall Road, Dublin 3
T: (01) 240 1300 F: (01) 240 1310
E: info@pdc.ie W: www.pdc.ie
Contact: Bernadette O'Reilly

CATEGORIES: GRANTS; INCUBATOR; MENTORING; START-UP TRAINING

HotHouse is a year-long programme that helps entrepreneurs of knowledge-intensive businesses to start-up and build firms with global potential. It comprises: Practical workshops; Strategic business counselling; 'Buddy counselling' from experienced entrepreneurs; Office space and facilities; Access to funding. See also **Enterprise Programmes**.

HOTORIGIN

64 Lower Mount Street, Dublin 2
T: (01) 678 8480 F: (01) 678 8477
E: ventures@hotorigin.com W: www.hotorigin.com
Contact: David Dalton

CATEGORIES: CONSULTING; EQUITY; INCUBATOR

HotOrigin is an e-commerce and software accelerator focused on fast-tracking new e-companies. It also makes seed-stage investments of up to €300,000 in software ventures, corporate-backed e-commerce ventures or non-European ventures looking to expand into Europe. HotOrigin operates the **HotOrigin Fund 1**.

HOTORIGIN FUND 1

Tennal Investments Ltd, 64 Lower Mount Street, Dublin 2
T: (01) 678 8480 F: (01) 678 8477
E: ventures@hotorigin.com W: www.hotorigin.com
Contact: David Dalton

CATEGORIES: EQUITY

This €2.3 million fund targets seed and early-stage software, hardware and bio-informatics companies, investing in the €100k to €300k range. The **HotOrigin** team hands-on expertise to its portfolio companies. The fund was established with assistance from **Enterprise Ireland**, under the Seed & Venture Capital Measure of the Operational Programme 2001-2006.

IBEC

Confederation House, 84–86 Lower Baggot Street, Dublin 2
T: (01) 605 1500 F: (01) 638 1500
E: info@ibec.ie W: www.ibec.ie

CATEGORIES: INFORMATION

IBEC (The Irish Business and Employers Confederation) represents and provides economic, commercial, employee relations and social affairs services to some 7,000 companies and organisations from all sectors of economic and commercial activity. It works to shape policies and influence decision-making in a way that develops and protects members' interests and contributes to the development and maintenance of an economy that promotes enterprise and productive employment.

ICC REGIONAL VENTURE CAPITAL FUND

72-74 Harcourt Street, Dublin 2
T: (01) 415 5555 F: (01) 475 0437
E: jconcannon@icc.ie W: www.iccvc.ie
Contact: Joe Concannon

CATEGORIES: EQUITY

Managed by **ICC Venture Capital**, this fund targets seed, early-stage and developing companies throughout Ireland with high growth potential. Typical investments are in the €500k to €1 million range. The fund was established with assistance from **Enterprise Ireland**, under the Seed & Venture Capital Measure of the Operational Programme 2001-2006.

ICC VENTURE CAPITAL

72-74 Harcourt Street, Dublin 2
T: (01) 415 5555 F: (01) 475 0437
E: jconcannon@icc.ie W: www.iccvc.ie
Contact: Joe Concannon

CATEGORIES: EQUITY

Owned by **Bank of Scotland (Ireland) Ltd**, ICC Venture Capital provides expansion and MBO/MBI finance to established businesses, though sometimes to early-stage businesses. The main sectors of investment are software and technology. It manages the **ICC Regional Venture Capital Fund**.

IDA IRELAND

Wilton Park House, Wilton Place, Dublin 2
T: (01) 603 4000 F: (01) 603 4040
E: idaireland@ida.ie W: www.idaireland.com

CATEGORIES: INWARDS INVESTMENT

IDA Ireland has national responsibility for securing new investment from overseas in manufacturing and international services sectors and for encouraging existing foreign enterprises in Ireland to expand their businesses. It markets Ireland as an attractive location through its offices abroad and reports to the Minister for Enterprise, Trade and Employment.

IE DOMAIN REGISTRY LTD

Windsor House, 14 Windsor Terrace, Sandycove, Co Dublin
T: (01) 230 0797 F: (01) 230 0365
E: info@iedr.ie W: www.iedr.ie

CATEGORIES: E-BUSINESS; REGULATOR & STANDARDS

IEDR manages the **.ie** namespace in the interest of the Irish and global e-business communities. It is the Irish national Internet registry.

INFO POINT EUROPE

See individual entries for: Info Point Europe Athlone; Info Point Europe; Mullingar; Info Point Europe North East.

CATEGORIES: EU INFORMATION

The Info Point Europe network provides a wide range of information on EU activity to the local business community.

INFO POINT EUROPE ATHLONE

Athlone Chamber of Commerce & Industry, Jolly Mariner Marina, Coosan Road, Athlone, Co Westmeath
T: (0902) 73173 F: (0902) 74386
E: athcci@iol.ie W: www.athlonechamber.ie/europe/
Contact: Siobhan Bigley

CATEGORIES: EU INFORMATION

See the main **Info Point Europe** entry for more information.

INFO POINT EUROPE MULLINGAR

Mullingar Chamber of Commerce, Market House, Mullingar, Co Westmeath
T: (044) 44044 F: (044) 44045
E: info@mullingar-chamber.ie W: www.mullingar-chamber.ie

CATEGORIES: EU INFORMATION

See the main **Info Point Europe** entry for more information.

INFO POINT EUROPE NORTH EAST

Dundalk Institute of Technology, Dublin Road, Dundalk, Co Louth
T: (042) 937 0492 F: (042) 933 8313
E: eu-info@dkit.ie W: www.dkit.ie/eu-info
Contact: Fergus Ashe

CATEGORIES: EU INFORMATION

See the main **Info Point Europe** entry for more information.

INFRASTRUCTURE.ie

W: www.infrastructure.ie

CATEGORIES: INFORMATION; WEBSITE

Established by **Forfás**, the site contains information on physical infrastructure, social infrastructure, and the companies supported by the industrial development agencies in all towns with a population of 1,500 and over (1996 Census), and the four Dublin county council areas.

INISHOWEN PARTNERSHIP BOARD

2 Victoria Villas, St Mary's Road, Buncrana, Co Donegal
T: (077) 62218 F: (077) 62990
E: inishpar@indigo.ie W: www.inishpar.ie
Contact: Shauna McClenaghan, Manager

CATEGORIES: COMMUNITY & RURAL DEVELOPMENT; DEBT; INFORMATION;
START-UP TRAINING; TRAINING

One of the **Area Partnerships** funded by **Area Development Management**, as part of its Local Development programme. Inishowen Partnership Board can help SMEs to access seed capital funding through the Donegal Enterprise Assistance Loan Scheme, managed by the **Donegal County Enterprise Board**. It also provides training and other forms of assistance.

INISHOWEN RURAL DEVELOPMENT LTD

Pound Street, Carndonagh, Co Donegal
T: (077) 73083 F: (077) 73084
E: irdl@iol.ie W: www.inishowen.ie
Contact: Andrew Ward

CATEGORIES: COMMUNITY & RURAL DEVELOPMENT; GRANTS

As a **LEADER+** company serving the Inishowen peninsula, IRDL offers capital equipment grants to innovative, small enterprises in manufacturing, crafts or local services at start-up or development stage, within its operational area. It also operates as a "one-stop shop" for local development issues.

INITIATIVE

Whitespace Ltd, 2051 CityWest Business Campus, Co Dublin
T: (01) 403 8150 F: (01) 466 0524
E: initiative@whitespace.ie W: www.whitespace.ie
Contact: John Costello, Editor

CATEGORIES: INFORMATION; PUBLICATIONS

A magazine, published on the first Thursday of each month free with the *Irish Independent*, with useful business articles and a regular start-up section.

INLAND REVENUE

Beaufort House, 31 Wellington Place, Belfast BT1 6BH
T: (028) 9053 2300 F: (028) 9053 2310
W: www.inlandrevenue.gov.uk

CATEGORIES: PUBLICATIONS; REGULATOR & STANDARDS

The Inland Revenue is responsible, under the overall direction of Treasury Ministers, for the efficient administration of income tax, tax credits, corporation tax, capital gains tax, petroleum revenue tax, inheritance tax, national insurance contributions and stamp duties. Its job is to provide an effective and fair tax service to the country and Government.

A guide on the taxation and other implications of starting a business is available at www.inlandrevenue.gov.uk/startingup. The website also provides a list of Inland Revenue offices throughout Northern Ireland.

INNER CITY ENTERPRISE

56–57 Lower Gardiner Street, Dublin 1
T: (01) 836 4073 F: (01) 836 3742
E: ice@iol.ie
Contact: Eamon Brady, Development Manager

CATEGORIES: INFORMATION; START-UP TRAINING

Inner City Enterprise is a private charity that pre-dates the **Area Partnerships**. It works closely with other enterprise support organisations in the inner city, including the **Dublin Inner City Partnership**. It provides information, advice and financial support for unemployed people in the inner city who want to start a business, as well as a commercial starter enterprise support service in the inner city on behalf of DICP.

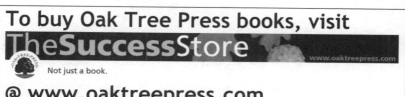

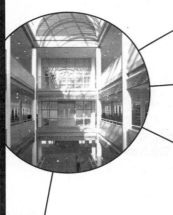

INNOVATION PARTNERS
1 Fry Place, Athlone, Co Westmeath
T: (0902) 21596 F: (0902) 94925
E: danny@innovation-partners.com W: www.innovation-partners.com
Contact: Danny Gleeson , Managing director

CATEGORIES: BUSINESS PLANNING; CONSULTING; R & D; TRAINING

An innovation management consulting, Innovation Partners offers consulting and training in innovation and technology transfer.

INNOVATION RELAY CENTRE FOR IRELAND
Enterprise Ireland, Glasnevin, Dublin 9
T: (01) 808 2305 F: (01) 808 2376
E: irc@enterprise-ireland.com W: www.enterprise-ireland.com
Contact: Patricia Seery

CATEGORIES: R & D

A network of Innovation Relay Centres (IRC) has been set up under the European Commission's Framework Programme for Research and Technological Development. Enterprise Ireland hosts the Innovation Relay Centre for Ireland. The main role of the IRC is to promote transnational technology transfer.

INNOVATION RELAY CENTRE FOR NORTHERN IRELAND
Invest Northern Ireland, 17 Antrim Road, Lisburn BT28 3AL
T: (028) 9262 3181 F: (028) 9049 0490
E: info@investni.com W: www.investni.com/irc
Contact: Marshall Addidle

CATEGORIES: R & D

A network of Innovation Relay Centres has been set up throughout Europe under the Fifth Framework Programme for Research and Technological Developments. The IRC in Northern Ireland is hosted by **Invest Northern Ireland** and works closely with the local **European Information Centre**. The main role of the IRC is to promote transnational technology transfer.

INNOVATIONWORKS
Shannon Development, National Technological Park, Limerick
T: (061) 338177 F: (061) 338065
E: corcoranj@shannon-dev.ie W: www.shannon-dev.ie/innovation/
Contact: J Corcoran

CATEGORIES: INCUBATOR; MENTORING; R & D; START-UP TRAINING; TRAINING; WORKSPACE

InnovationWorks, formerly the Innovation Centre, at the **National Technological Park,** Limerick, is a digitally-networked business incubation centre and is part of the **Shannon Development Knowledge Network**. It offers a wide range of services to high potential, technology and knowledge-intensive companies. It also hosts **Limerick Business Innovation Centre**.

There are also InnovationWorks at **Kerry Technology Park**, Tipperary Technology Park, Birr Technology Centre and Information Age Park Ennis.

INNOVATOR

Dolmen Associates, 18 Dame Street, Dublin 2
E: info@innovator.ie W: www.innovator.ie

CATEGORIES: R & D; TRAINING

Innovator runs courses/workshops for new and existing R+D performers to give them the skill tools required to manage the process.

INSTITUTE OF BUSINESS ADVISERS

Irish Branch: Chairman: Willie Maxwell
T: (01) 883 4806 E: info@acumenprogramme.com
Northern Ireland Branch: Chairman: Gordon Gough
T: (028) 3834 7020 E: gordongough@cido.co.uk
E: enquiries@iba.org.uk W: www.iba.org.uk

CATEGORIES: CONSULTING; MENTORING; TRAINING

IBA's membership comprises business advisers, counsellors, mentors and trainers who specialise in helping small firms.

INSTITUTE OF CERTIFIED PUBLIC ACCOUNTANTS IN IRELAND

9 Ely Place, Dublin 2
T: (01) 676 7353 F: (01) 661 2367
E: cpa@cpaireland.ie W: www.cpaireland.ie
Contact: Eamonn Siggins, Chief Executive

CATEGORIES: ACCOUNTANTS

ICPAI is one of the accountancy bodies whose members are permitted to audit company accounts. It has 1,000+ members throughout the island of Ireland. If you're looking for an accountant, ICPAI can direct you to one of its members.

INSTITUTE OF CHARTERED ACCOUNTANTS IN IRELAND

CA House, 87–89 Pembroke Road, Ballsbridge, Dublin 4
T: (01) 637 7200 F: (01) 668 0842
E: ca@icai.ie W: www.icai.ie
Contact: John McCarthy
Also at: 11 Donegall Square South, Belfast BT1 5JE
T: (028) 9032 1600 F: (028) 9023 0071
Contact: Katie Doran

CATEGORIES: ACCOUNTANTS

ICAI is one of the accountancy bodies whose members are permitted to audit company accounts. It has 10,000+ members throughout the island of Ireland. If you're looking for an accountant, ICAI can direct you to one of its members.

INSTITUTE OF DIRECTORS IN IRELAND

89 James's Street, Dublin 8
T: (01) 408 4548 F: (01) 408 4550
E: info@iodireland.ie W: www.iodireland.ie
Contact: Susan Thornber, Chief Executive

CATEGORIES: INFORMATION; NETWORKING; TRAINING

IOD Ireland is an independent body affiliated to the Institute of Directors worldwide. It offers members access to a wide range of networking, database, and reciprocal service opportunities, provides a forum for the exchange of ideas and information, encourages members to improve their standards and performance as directors and principals, and represents the views of business leaders to government and other organisations.
IOD Ireland operates the **Boardroom Centre**, a resource for companies looking for non-executive directors to strengthen their board.

INSTITUTE OF INDUSTRIAL ENGINEERS

P.O. Box 790, Sandyford, Dublin 18
T: (01) 294 3156 F: (01) 294 3131
E: enquiries@iie.ie W: www.iie.ie
Contact: Timothy Byrne

CATEGORIES: INFORMATION; NETWORKING

IIE is dedicated to serving the professional needs of industrial engineers and all individuals involved with improving quality and productivity.

INSTITUTE OF LEISURE & AMENITY MANAGEMENT LTD

5 College Way, Clane, Co Kildare
T: (045) 861201 F: (045) 893195
E: info@ilamireland.ie W: www.ilamireland.ie
Contact: Kilian Fisher, Chief Executive

CATEGORIES: INFORMATION; NETWORKING; TRAINING

ILAM is the professional body for the leisure industry in Ireland. It exists as an independent national organisation operating on a "non-profit" basis to meet the needs of a growing industry.

INSTITUTE OF MANAGEMENT CONSULTANTS IN IRELAND

84/86 Lower Baggot Street, Dublin 2
T: (01) 660 1011 F: (01) 660 1717
E: info@imci.ie W: www.imci.ie

CATEGORIES: INFORMATION

A management consultant is an independent and qualified person who provides a professional service identifying and investigating problems concerned with strategy, policy, markets, organisation, procedures, systems, practices and methods, and formulating recommendations for appropriate action. IMCI's website gives guidelines on how to choose and use consultants, as well as a listing of registered practices.

INSTITUTE OF PROJECT MANAGEMENT
25 Upper Mount Street, Dublin 2
T: (01) 661 4677 F: (01) 661 3588
E: instpmgm@iol.ie W: www.projectmanagement.ie
Contact: Ed Naughton
CATEGORIES: INFORMATION; TRAINING

IPM offers training programmes in project management.

INSTITUTE OF PUBLIC ADMINISTRATION
57-61 Lansdowne Road, Dublin 4
T: (01) 668 6233 F: (01) 668 9135
E: information@ipa.ie; sales@ipa.ie W: www.ipa.ie
Publications available from:
Vergemount Hall, Clonskeagh, Dublin 6
T: (01) 269 7011 F: (01) 269 8644
CATEGORIES: INFORMATION; PUBLICATIONS

Publisher of the *Administration Yearbook & Diary*, a reference database of 6,000+ entries about Ireland, a useful research resource for any business.

INSTITUTES OF TECHNOLOGY
See individual entries for: Athlone Institute of Technology; Cork Institute of Technology; Dundalk Institute of Technology; Galway–Mayo Institute of Technology; Institute of Technology Blanchardstown; Institute of Technology Carlow; Institute of Technology Sligo; Institute of Technology Tallaght; Institute of Technology Tralee; Letterkenny Institute of Technology; Limerick Institute of Technology; Waterford Institute of Technology.

INSTITUTE OF TECHNOLOGY BLANCHARDSTOWN
Blanchardstown Road North, Blanchardstown, Dublin 15
T: (01) 885 1000 F: (01) 885 1001
E: info@itb.ie W: www.itb.ie
Contact: Tom Doyle, Head of Development
CATEGORIES: CONSULTING; INCUBATOR; R & D; START-UP TRAINING; TRAINING

IT Blanchardstown's Learning and Innovation centre provides on-campus Research and Development, as well as incubation facilities and business training development services. The Institute of Technology Blanchardstown is a partner in the **M50 Enterprise Programme**.

INSTITUTE OF TECHNOLOGY CARLOW
Kilkenny Road, Carlow
T: (0503) 70400 F: (0503) 70500
E: info@itcarlow.ie W: www.itcarlow.ie
Contact: James McEntee, Head of External Services
CATEGORIES: CONSULTING; INCUBATOR; R&D; TRAINING

IT Carlow's Business & Technology Centre provides services to local industry, including research, training and consultancy in computing, applied sciences, civil, electronic and mechanical engineering and business services. The Campus Innovation Centre provides industrial and commercial space in incubator units, allowing local enterprise access to the Institute's facilities and services.

INSTITUTE OF TECHNOLOGY SLIGO
Ballinode, Sligo
T: (071) 55222 F: (071) 44096
E: info@itsligo.ie W: www.itsligo.ie
Contact: Des McConville, Head of Development
CATEGORIES: CONSULTING; INCUBATOR

A new Business Innovation Centre acts as an incubation centre for joint academic/industry projects and new business start-ups. See also the **Céim Enterprise Development Programme.**

INSTITUTE OF TECHNOLOGY TALLAGHT
Tallaght, Dublin 24
T: (01) 404 2000 F: (01) 404 2700
E: eamon.tuffy@it-tallaght.ie W: www.it-tallaght.ie
Contact: Eamon Tuffy, Head of Development and External Services
CATEGORIES: CONSULTING; R&D; START-UP TRAINING; TRAINING

The Development and External Services Department provides advanced business and technical training and R&D consultancy. The E-learning Centre offers Information & Communication Technology in the chemical, pharmaceutical and healthcare industries. IT Tallaght is a partner in the **M50 Enterprise Platform Programme.**

INSTITUTE OF TECHNOLOGY TRALEE
Clash, Tralee, Co Kerry
T: (066) 714 5600 F: (066) 712 5711
E: henry.lyons@ittralee.ie W: www.ittralee.ie
Contact: Henry Lyons, Head of Development
CATEGORIES: CONSULTING; R&D; TRAINING

IT Tralee is a recognised Centre of Excellence in: Information technology and software development; Multi-media; Natural resources; Manufacturing technology; Tourism; Environmental technology; Product and process development in chemicals and pharmaceuticals and in food, microbiology and healthcare. The research & development facilities and staff at the Institute are available to, and used by, firms wishing to develop both existing and new products and services. Access to the IT's facilities and services can be arranged through the Development Office.

INSTITUTION OF ENGINEERS OF IRELAND
22 Clyde Road, Dublin 4
T: (01) 668 4341 F: (01) 668 5508
E: info@iei.ie W: www.iei.ie
Contact: Paddy Purcell, Director General

CATEGORIES: INFORMATION; NETWORKING

The largest professional body in Ireland, representing almost 17,000 engineering professionals of every discipline, the Institution of Engineers of Ireland (IEI) promotes the art & science of engineering in Ireland.

INTERNATIONAL FUND FOR IRELAND
PO Box 2000, Belfast BT4 2QY
T: (028) 9076 8832 F: (028) 9076 3313
PO Box 2000, Dublin 2
T: (01) 478 0655 F: (01) 475 1351
W: www.internationalfundforireland.com
Contact: Paddy Purcell, Director General

CATEGORIES: COMMUNITY & RURAL DEVELOPMENT; DEBT; EQUITY

The International Fund for Ireland (IFI) was established by the Irish and British Governments in 1986 to promote economic and social advancement throughout Ireland. It runs six programmes relevant to small business: Disadvantaged Areas Initiative; Business Enterprise and Technology; Tourism; Urban Development; Rural Development; and Wider Horizons. The Fund also assists local community groups in providing workspace accommodation and business-loan funds to help small businesses. Its investment company — **Enterprise Equity (Ireland) Ltd** — provides seed capital on normal commercial criteria to existing and start-up businesses.

INTERTRADEIRELAND
The Old Gasworks Business Park, Kilmorey Street, Newry,
Co. Down BT34 2DE
T: 028 3083 4151 F: 028 3083 4155
E: info@intertradeireland.com W: www.intertradeireland.com

CATEGORIES: INFORMATION; POLICY

InterTradeIreland's remit is to accelerate trade and business development across the whole island of Ireland. See also **EquityNetwork.**

INTERTRADEIRELAND ACUMEN
Linncomm House, Balbriggan Industrial Estate, Balbriggan, Co Dublin
T: (01) 883 4806
E: info@acumenprogramme.com
Contact: Willie Maxwell, Director
Also at: Omagh Business Complex, Gortrush Industrial Estate, Omagh BT78 5LU
T: (028) 8225 0404 F: (028) 8225 0416
Contact: Michael McElroy, Regional Development Manager

CATEGORIES: CROSS-BORDER; GRANTS

The InterTradeIreland Acumen programme is a business development programme designed to stimulate cross-border trade between SMEs on both sides of the Border. It provides tailored consultancy and salary support for market-builders.

INVENT

The Innovation and Enterprise Centre, Dublin City University, Dublin 9
T: (01) 700 7777
E: leah.lynch@invent.dcu.ie W: www.invent.dcu.ie
Contact: Leah McKenna, Marketing Executive
CATEGORIES: INCUBATOR; START-UP TRAINING

Invent is a state-of-the-art innovation centre, located in the heart of **Dublin City University** campus. Invent aims to facilitate the creation and development of innovation-led businesses. Invent also manages the **Mallinn/Invent Start-up Awards**.

INVENTORS ASSOCIATION OF IRELAND

1 Manor Avenue, Thornbury Heights, Rochestown, Cork
T: (021) 489 0577 F: (021) 434 3587 (mark for attn of IAI)
E: nichyfield@eircom.net
Contact: Nicola Field
CATEGORIES: INFORMATION; NETWORKING; R & D

A membership organisation that supports Irish inventors.

INVENTORS GARAGE

1 Manor Avenue, Thornbury Heights, Rochestown, Cork
T: (021) 489 0577 F: (021) 489 3587
E: info@inventors-garage.com W: www.inventors-garage.com
Contact: Nicola Field
CATEGORIES: INTELLECTUAL PROPERTY; R & D

Inventors Garage helps inventors commercialise their ideas. The process starts with a feasibility review, incuding a patent search.

INVEST NORTHERN IRELAND

64 Chichester Street, Belfast BT1 4JX
T: 028 9023 9090 F: 028 9049 0490
E: info@investni.com W: www.investni.com
CATEGORIES: GRANTS; INFORMATION; INWARDS INVESTMENT

A key source of assistance and information on business start-up in Northern Ireland, InvestNI was formed by bringing together the Industrial Development Board, LEDU, IRTU and parts of other agencies. Its objective is to encourage international competitiveness in Northern Ireland and to attract new inwards investment. Although it aims to reduce grant-dependency, InvestNI offers capital and revenue grants for business development - full details are on its website. InvestNI has Regional Information Centres in: Ballymena; Londonderry; Newry; and Omagh.

INVESTNET LTD
Invent, Dublin City University, Glasnevin, Dublin 9
T: (01) 700 8508 F: (01) 700 5505
W: www.firsttuesday.ie
CATEGORIES: BUSINESS ANGELS; eBUSINESS; NETWORKING

Investnet operates First Tuesday in Ireland. Investnet's objectives are to promote, accelerate and assist the entrepreneurial process through knowledge sharing events and industry platforms. Investnet also provides discreet matchmaking services for financiers and entrepreneurs as well as managed events for member companies and sponsors.

INVESTORS IN PEOPLE
Northern Ireland Quality Centre, Department for Employment and Learning,
2nd Floor, Fountain Street, Belfast BT1 5EX
T: (028) 9044 1792 F: (028) 9044 1811
E: paul.bryans@delni.gov.uk W: www.investorsinpeople.co.uk
CATEGORIES: REGULATOR & STANDARDS

Investors in People UK is responsible for the promotion, quality assurance and development of the Investors in People National Standard. See also **Your People Manager**.

INVEST-TECH
27 Ardmeen Park, Blackrock, Co Dublin
T: (01) 283 4083 F: (01) 278 2391
E: info@planware.org W: www.planware.org
Contact: Brian Flanagan
CATEGORIES: BUSINESS PLANS; CONSULTING; INFORMATION

Invest-Tech provides advice and assistance to startups and SMEs in business planning, strategy development and financial plans. Its PlanWare website contains white papers and free "on-line" tools. It also offers an extensive range of freeware, shareware and software for writing a business plan, making financial forecasts and strategic planning.

ION EQUITY LTD
Fitzwilton House, Wilton Place, Dublin 2
T: (01) 611 0500 F: (01) 611 0510
E: info@ionequity.com W: www.ionequity.com
Contact: Neil O'Leary, Chief Executive
CATEGORIES: EQUITY

Ion Equity is a leading Irish corporate finance firm and private equity investor.

IRD DUHALLOW LTD

James O'Keeffe Institute, Newmarket, Co Cork
T: (029) 60633 F: (029) 60694
E: duhallow@eircom.net
Contact: Maura Walsh, Manager

CATEGORIES: COMMUNITY & RURAL DEVELOPMENT; GRANTS; INCUBATOR; TRAINING

IRD Duhallow is a community-based rural development company, established in 1989 to promote rural development in its catchment area of NorthWest County Cork and parts of East Kerry. One of its main objectives is to establish and support initiatives directed towards the generation of enterprise in the area. It employs a full-time Enterprise Officer to assist and advise micro-business start-ups. Under the **LEADER+** programme, IRD Duhallow provides a range of supports, including: Grant aid, including feasibility study grants; Training and mentoring support; Advice and assistance in the preparation of business plans.

IRD KILTIMAGH

Enterprise House, Aiden Street, Kiltimagh, Co Mayo
T: (094) 81494 F: (094) 81884
E: manager@ird-kiltimagh.ie W: www.ird-kiltimagh.ie
Contact: Joe Kelly

CATEGORIES: COMMUNITY & RURAL DEVELOPMENT; INCUBATOR

IRD Kiltimagh's mission is "the development of the economic potenital of Kiltimagh and its hinterland to the fullest and in a way which will benefit the whole community". It operates two Enterprise Centres, and has undertaken the successful implementation of a re-development programme for the Kiltimagh area in conjunction with the state and private sectors. IRD Kiltimagh administers the East Mayo Local Development Programme under the auspices of **Meitheal Mhaigh Eo** and the **LEADER+** Programme for East Mayo as part of the **Western Rural Development Company**.

IRISH BICS SEED CAPITAL FUND

Dublin BIC, The Tower, TCD Enterprise Centre, Pearse Street, Dublin 2
T: (01) 671 3111 F: (01) 671 3330
E: info@dbic.ie W: www.dbic.ie
Contact: Alex Hobbs

CATEGORIES: EQUITY

The €1.9 million Irish BICs Seed Capital Fund (managed by **Dublin BIC**) provides early-stage seed capital from €12,700 to €127,000 to new and developing enterprises in the Republic of Ireland. It was established by **Dublin Business Innovation Centre, Cork Business Innovation Centre, Limerick Business Innovation Centre, South East Business Innovation Centre, WestBIC** and **Enterprise Ireland** through the EU Seed and Venture Capital Measure of the Operational Programme for Industrial Development 1994-1999 (and now operates under the Seed & Venture Capital Measure 2001-2006 of the National Development Plan). An online application form is available on the Dublin BIC website.

IRISH BIOSCIENCE VENTURE CAPITAL FUND
Unit 1C, TCD Enterprise Centre, Pearse Street, Dublin 2
T: (01) 675 0026 F: (01) 675 0026
E: info@seroba.ie W: www.seroba.ie
Contact: Peter Sandys
CATEGORIES: EQUITY

This €15 million fund targets seed and early-stage companies in the biotechnology, pharmaceutical and medical sectors. Typical investments are in the €300k to €1 million range. The fund was established with assistance from **Enterprise Ireland**, under the Seed & Venture Capital Measure of the Operational Programme 2001-2006.

IRISH BUSINESS SALES
Harcourt Centre, Block 3, Harcourt Road, Dublin 2
T: (01) 418 2287 F: (01) 418 2223
E: info@irishbusinesssales.com W: www.irishbusinesssales.com
Contact: Eamonn Gaffney, Gerry Walsh
CATEGORIES: BUSINESS SALES/PURCHASES

Irish Business Sales is a facilitator in: The buying and selling of businesses; Effecting management buy-outs/buy-ins; Sourcing partners/investors; Raising project finance. Its website provides a range of businesses for sale and acquisitions sought, as well as investors seeking businesses/projects and businesses seeking investment.

IRISH COMPUTER SOCIETY
Crescent Hall, Mount Street Crescent, Dublin 2
T: (01) 644 7840 F: (01) 662 0244
E: info@ics.ie W: www.ics.ie
CATEGORIES: INFORMATION; NETWORKING

The Irish Computer Society's mission is to advance, promote and represent the interests of information technology professionals in Ireland.

IRISH CO-OPERATIVE ORGANISATION SOCIETY LTD
The Plunkett House, 84 Merrion Square, Dublin 2
T: (01) 676 4783 F: (01) 662 4502
E: info@icos.ie W: www.icos.ie
CATEGORIES: CO-OPERATIVES; INFORMATION

As the co-ordinating organisation for co-operatives in Ireland, ICOS provides a rnage of services to its member co-operatives and represents them on national and international organisations. It can also advise on, and provide Model Rules for, the setting-up of a co-operative.

IRISH COUNCIL FOR SCIENCE, TECHNOLOGY & INNOVATION
Forfás, Wilton Park House, Wilton Place, Dublin 2
T: (01) 607 3000 F: (01) 607 3030
E: info@forfas.ie W: www.forfas.ie/icsti/
Contact: Josephine Lynch, Secretary
CATEGORIES: POLICY

The Council advises the Minister for Science & Technology on the strategic direction of science, technology and innovation policy.

IRISH COUNTRY HOLIDAYS
Discovery Centre, Rearcross, Co Tipperary
T: (062) 79330 F: (062) 79331
E: info@country-holidays.ie W: www.country-holidays.ie
CATEGORIES: COMMUNITY & RURAL DEVELOPMENT; GRANTS; TOURISM DEVELOPMENT

A **LEADER+** company, Irish Country Holidays offers capital equipment grants to innovative, small enterprises in manufacturing, crafts or local services at start-up or development stage, within its operational area.

IRISH COUNTRYWOMEN'S ASSOCIATION
58 Merrion Road, Ballbridge, Dublin 4
T: (01) 668 0453 F: (01) 660 9423
E: office@icwa.ie W: www.ica.ie
Contact: Maureen Holden, General Secretary
CATEGORIES: INFORMATION; NETWORKING; TRAINING; WOMEN

Aimed at improving rural and urban life, the ICA has about 1,000 guilds nationwide where local women meet to exchange ideas, for instruction in home and farm management, and handcrafts. Facilities for initiating home and small business, both individual and co-operative, with emphasis on high standard of craftsmanship, is an important aspect of ICA activity.

IRISH DIRECT MARKETING ASSOCIATION
93A Lagan Road, Dublin Industrial Estate, Glasnevin, Dublin 11
T: (01) 830 4752 F: (01) 830 8914
E: info@idma.ie W: www.idma.ie
Contact: Mark Cassin, Chairman
CATEGORIES: INFORMATION; MARKETING; NETWORKING; TRAINING

The IDMA is the trade association for companies that practise in or supply the direct marketing industry in Ireland. IDMA offers training in direct marketing techniques.

IRISH ENERGY CENTRE
See **Sustainable Energy Ireland**.

IRISH ENTREPRENEUR

Morrissey Media Ltd, Clondaw House, Clondaw Lower, Ferns, Co Wexford
T: (053) 36884 F: (053) 36849
E: irishentrepreneur@eircom.net W: www.irishentrepreneur.com
Contact: Maree Morrissey, Publisher

CATEGORIES: INFORMATION; PUBLICATIONS

Much-needed enterprise-focused magazine, with great design. Available from newsagents and on subscription.

IRISH EXPORTERS ASSOCIATION

28 Merrion Square, Dublin 2
T: (01) 661 2182 F: (01) 661 2315
E: iea@irishexporters.ie W: www.irishexporters.ie
Contact: John Whelan, Chief Executive

CATEGORIES: INFORMATION; NETWORKING; TRAINING

The Irish Exporters Association represents and promotes exporters' interests. The Association has regional branches in Cork, Dublin, Dundalk, Galway and Limerick. The Association offers a Diploma in International Trade and Marketing, as well as a series of short courses on aspects of international trade practice.

IRISH FARMERS' ASSOCIATION

Irish Farm Centre, Bluebell, Dublin 12
T: (01) 450 0266 F: (01) 455 1043
E: postmaster@ifa.ie W: www.ifa.ie

CATEGORIES: INFORMATION; NETWORKING

The IFA is a lobby organisation for Irish farmers.

IRISH FARMHOUSE HOLIDAYS

2 Michael Street, Limerick
T: (061) 400700 F: (061) 400771
E: info@irishfarmholidays.com W: www.irishfarmholidays.com
Contact: Kathryn Delany

CATEGORIES: COMMUNITY & RURAL DEVELOPMENT; GRANTS: TOURISM DEVELOPMENT

A **LEADER+** company.

For updates to this Directory, go to
www.startingabusinessinireland.com
information, advice & resources for entrepreneurs

SUBSCRIBE NOW!

AND YOU COULD WIN...

- **A HAMPER WORTH €200, COURTESY OF ALL HAMPERS, WWW.ALLHAMPERS.COM**
- **APPLE IPOD, COURTESY OF COMPUSTORE**
- **HOLIDAY VOUCHER WORTH €200**

Apple Ipod €300

Hamper worth €200

Please send me issues of The Irish Entrepreneur for 1 year, from the date of received subscription. Complete the following & return, with payment by cheque or Visa, for €75 to Morrissey Media Ltd, Clondaw House, Clondaw Lower, Ferns, Co. Wexford.

Full Name:

Job Title:

Company Name:

Company Address/personnel address:

Telephone :

Fax:

E-mail:

Date

Signature

Pay by Cheque/Postal Order

I enclose my cheque/postal order (payable to Morrissey Media Ltd) for €_____

Pay by credit card

Please charge my card account

☐ Master Card   ☐ Visa

Card Expiry Date ☐☐ / ☐☐

Please ensure the cardholder's address is shown on this order form

Signature

IRISH FILM BOARD : BORD SCANNAN NA HEIREANN
Rockfort House, St Augustine Street, Galway
T: (091) 561398 F: (091) 561405
E: info@filmboard.ie W: www.filmboard.ie
CATEGORIES: DEBT; EQUITY

The Irish Film Board provides loans and equity investment to independent Irish film-makers to assist in the development and production of Irish films.

IRISH FRANCHISE ASSOCIATION
Unit 27, Guinness Enterprise Centre, Taylor's Lane, Dublin 8
T: (01) 410 0667 F: (01) 410 0733
CATEGORIES: FRANCHISES; INFORMATION

A membership organisation for the franchise industry in Ireland.

IRISH HOTELS FEDERATION
13 Northbrook Road, Dublin 6
T: (01) 497 6459 F: (01) 497 4613
E: info@ihf.ie W: www.ihf.ie
Contact: John Power, Chief Executive
CATEGORIES: INFORMATION; TOURISM DEVELOPMENT

The Irish Hotels Federation is the national organisation of the hotel and guesthouse industry in Ireland. It assists members on economic, legal and technical matters including grading, copyright, safety legislation, fire precautions, liability insurance, labour relations, licensing and taxation and IT.

IRISH INSTITUTE FOR TRAINING & DEVELOPMENT
Leinster Mills, Millennium Business Park, Osberstown, Naas, Co Kildare
T: (045) 881166 F: (045) 881192
E: info@iitd.com W: www.iitd.ie
CATEGORIES: INFORMATION; NETWORKING; TRAINING

IITD is the professional body for human resource development professionals in Ireland. It conducts courses nationwide in training & development, leading to Certificate or Diploma level qualifications, and supports continuing professional development through a programme of events around the country. IITD keeps members updated on national training and development issues.

IRISH INSTITUTE OF CREDIT MANAGEMENT
128 Lower Baggot Street, Dublin 2
T: (01) 676 7822 F: (01) 639 1102
E: iicm@indigo.ie W: www.iicm.ie
Contact: Declan Flood, Chief Executive
CATEGORIES: INFORMATION; TRAINING

The goals of the Institute are to increase awareness among Irish companies of sound credit management and to provide continuing educational opportunities to enhance members' effectiveness and position within the management structure.

IRISH INSTITUTE OF PURCHASING & MATERIALS MANAGEMENT

5 Belvedere Place, Dublin 1
T: (01) 855 9257 F: (01) 855 9259
E: iipmm@iipmm.ie W: www.iipmm.ie

CATEGORIES: INFORMATION; NETWORKING; TRAINING

The Irish Institute of Purchasing and Materials Management is the professional body and main point of reference for purchasing and supply management professionals in Ireland. Its website provides a "Sourcing Database".

IRISH INTERNET ASSOCIATION

43/44 Temple Bar, Dublin 2
T: (01) 670 7621 / 2 F: (01) 670 7623
E: info@iia.ie W: www.iia.ie
Contact: Sinead Murnane, Operations Manager

CATEGORIES: E-BUSINESS; INFORMATION; NETWORKING; WEBSITE

The IIA is the professional body for those conducting business via the Internet in Ireland. IIA provides information to and runs seminars for members on e-business, education & training, security, employer/employee rights, raising capital, marketing, design & development and languages/ platforms.
The IIA website offers "iia internet resources", with catalogued links and articles within each topic.

IRISH LEAGUE OF CREDIT UNIONS

33-41 Lower Mount Street, Dublin 2
T: (01)614 6700 F: (01) 614 6701
E: info@creditunion.ie W: www.creditunion.ie

CATEGORIES: CO-OPERATIVES; DEBT; INFORMATION

Members of credit unions or businesses structured as co-operatives may qualify for a credit union loan. Each application is treated in the utmost confidence and will be considered on its own merits. In deciding whether to grant the loan, the member's record of saving and repayments, as well as ability to repay, and need will be taken into account. ILCU's website offers a database of credit unions in Ireland.

IRISH MANAGEMENT INSTITUTE

Sandyford Road, Dublin 16
T: (01) 207 8400 F: (01) 295 5150
E: reception@imi.ie W: www.imi.ie
Contact: Hilda Collins

CATEGORIES: INFORMATION; NETWORKING; TRAINING

Ireland's centre for management development, the IMI is a member organisation providing a forum for practising managers to exchange leading-edge experience, and facilitating access to Irish and international management experts. It offers full- and part-time courses, on-line support services and research resources.

IRISH MANAGEMENT INSTITUTE (NORTHERN IRELAND) LTD
Interpoint Building, 20-24 York Street, Belfast BT15 1AQ
T: (028) 9053 0093 F: (028) 9053 0094
E: brian.hunter@imi.ie W: www.imi.ie
Contact: Brian Hunter, Regional Manager
CATEGORIES: INFORMATION; NETWORKING; TRAINING

IMI (Northern Ireland) Ltd is a subsidiary of the Irish Management Institute. It offers full- and part-time courses, on-line support services and research resources.

IRISH ORGANIC FARMERS & GROWERS ASSOCIATION
Harbour Building, Harbour Road, Kilbeggan, Co Westmeath
T: (0506) 32563 F: (0506) 32063
E: info@irishorganic.ie W: www.irishorganic.ie
CATEGORIES: INFORMATION

IOFGA offers a range of services, including: Promoting the production and consumption of organic products; Maintaining a rigorous set of production standards; Operating an inspection and certification scheme; Publishing practical information for farmers and gardeners. It has regional groups throughout Ireland, North and South.

IRISH PRODUCTIVITY CENTRE
Block 4B-5, Blanchardstown Corporate Park, Blanchardstown, Dublin 15
T: (01) 822 7125 F: (01) 822 7116
E: ipc@ipc.ie W: www.ipc.ie
Contact: Tom McGuinness, Chief Executive
CATEGORIES: CONSULTING

The IPC offers advice and practical assistance to businesses in solving commercial, organisational, financial and management problems and in the development of change through partnership.

IRISH RESEARCH SCIENTISTS' ASSOCIATION
Department of Chemistry, NUI Galway, Galway
T: (091) 512149
E: Donal.Leech@nuigalway.ie W: www.irsa.ie
Contact: Donal Leech
CATEGORIES: INFORMATION; NETWORKING

The Irish Research Scientists' Association promotes excellence in scientific research in Ireland, a greater awareness of the role of research in our lives and Ireland's scientific heritage. It is a voluntary association of individuals and organisations interested in this aim.

IRISH RETAIL NEWSAGENTS ASSOCIATION

2 Priory Hall, Stillorgan, Co Dublin
T: (01) 288 3284 / 288 F: (01) 288 7224
E: info@irna.ie W: www.irna.ie
Contact: Mr. Pat McKeown, CEO

CATEGORIES: INFORMATION; NETWORKING

IRNA represents news retailers in Ireland and acts as a legislative and industrial relations watchdog, informing members of any changes that are of relevance to them. It also provides other services including group central billing and a shop insurance scheme.

IRISH ROAD HAULAGE ASSOCIATION

CGI Building, Unit 12, Blanchardstown Corporate Park, Dublin 15
T: (01) 822 4888 F: (01) 822 4898
E: info@irha.ie W: www.irha.ie
Contact: Jim Toner, Chairman

CATEGORIES: INFORMATION; NETWORKING

IRHA represents the interests of the licensed transport industry at home and abroad and provides members with assistance and membership benefits.

ISME
IRISH SMALL AND MEDIUM
ENTERPRISES ASSOCIATION LTD

SMALL BUSINESS ASSISTANCE

ISME – the independent Association, established to assist small businesses.

What *ISME* can do for you:

- *Save you Money through Group Purchasing Schemes, Subsidised Training and give you the low down on Government Grants*

- *Give Expert Professional Advice and support on Relevant Legislation, Industry Practices and the best ways to work within the system*

- *Connect you to a nationwide Network of Owner Managers*

- *Ensure your voice is heard through Independent Representation at the Highest Level*

ISME – Increasing the Profitability of your business through your Improved Performance

Membership of ISME gives you:

- ➪ Access to our 24 hour Specialised Advisory Service
- ➪ Monthly Newsletters
- ➪ A series of Guides and Sample Policies, invaluable to the day-to-day running of your business
- ➪ Regionalised Business Briefing Sessions

17 Kildare Street
Dublin 2
www.isme.ie

To join ISME contact us on 01 662 2755, fax 01 661 2157 or email info@isme.ie

IRISH SMALL & MEDIUM ENTERPRISES ASSOCIATION
17 Kildare Street, Dublin 2
T: (01) 662 2755 F: (01) 661 2157
E: info@isme.ie W: www.isme.ie
Contact: Mark Fielding, Chief Executive

CATEGORIES: INFORMATION; NETWORKING; PUBLICATIONS; TRAINING

ISME's membership is composed exclusively of entrepreneurs who own and manage competitive businesses. It offers a range of services to members, including publications on wages and conditions, employers' obligations, Government-sponsored grant schemes and a member-to-member sourcing directory.

IRISH SOFTWARE ASSOCIATION
Confederation House, 84-86 Lower Baggot Street, Dublin 2
T: (01) 605 1582 F: (01) 638 1569
E: isa@ibec.ie W: www.software.ie
Contact: Kathryn Raleigh, Director

CATEGORIES: INFORMATION; NETWORKING

The Irish Software Association represents Irish and multi-national software and computing services companies.

IRISH TRAVEL AGENTS ASSOCIATION
32 South William Street, Dublin 2
T: (01) 679 4089 F: (01) 671 9897
E: info@itaa.ie W: www.itaa.ie
Contact: Brendan Moran, Chief Executive

CATEGORIES: INFORMATION; TOURISM DEVELOPMENT

ITAA consists of 366 retail travel agents (more than 80% of all Irish travel agents) and 25 tour operators nationwide. All ITAA travel agents and tour operators are licensed and bonded with the Department of Public Enterprise in accordance with the provisions of the Transport (Tour Operators and Travel Agents) Act 1982 and the Package Holidays and Travel Trade Act 1995.

IRISH VENTURE CAPITAL ASSOCIATION
T: (01) 230 1725 F: (01) 280 9396
E: secretary@ivca.ie W: www.ivca.ie
Contact: Ciara Burrowes, Administrator

CATEGORIES: EQUITY

The IVCA represents the venture capital industry in Ireland. Its website has a list of members and associates.

IRISH WIND ENERGY ASSOCIATION
Arigna, Carrick-on-Shannon, Co Roscommon
T: (071) 964 6072 F: (071) 964 6080
E: office@iwea.com W: www.iwea.com
Contact: Ann Curneen

CATEGORIES: INFORMATION; NETWORKING

The IWEA promotes the use of wind energy in Ireland. Its members are business people, environmentalists, academics and farmers who recognise that wind energy will soon become one of Ireland's most significant sources of energy.

IRISHBUSINESSESFORSALE.COM
T: (021) 481 2397 F: (021) 481 3311
E: info@irishbusinessesforsale.com
W: www.irishbusinessesforsale.com; www.buyabiz.ie
Contact: Bill Mahony

CATEGORIES: BUSINESS SALES/PURCHASES

The website provides a point of reference for both investors and sellers, and covers commercial property, manufacturing, retail, services and leisure businesses and franchises.

IRLGOV.ie : IRISH GOVERNMENT WEBSITE
W: www.irlgov.ie

CATEGORIES: INFORMATION; WEBSITE

This website provides detailed information on the operation of the State, with links to Government departments and local authorities. See also **BASIS**.

IRVINESTOWN ENTERPRISE CENTRE
Irvinestown Enterprise Trustee Company Ltd (ITEC), Irvinestown Business Park, The Market Yard, Irvinestown, Co Fermanagh BT94 1GR
T: (028) 6862 1977 F: (028) 6862 8414
E: r.williams@can-online.org.uk
Contact: Ryan Williams

CATEGORIES: INFORMATION; START-UP TRAINING; WORKSPACE

One of several **Enterprise Centres** in Fermanagh.

JPA BRENSON LAWLOR
Brenson Lawlor House, Argyle Square, Morehampton Road, Dublin 4
T: (01) 668 9760 F: (01) 668 9778
E: info@brenson-lawlor.ie W: www.brenson-lawlor.ie

CATEGORIES: ACCOUNTANTS

JPA Brenson Lawlor offers corporate and personal taxation, corporate finance solutions, financial management, IT, marketing and audit services. Its website offers guidance on business formation options and the elements of a business plan.

JUNIOR ACHIEVEMENT / YOUNG ENTERPRISE IRELAND
89 Upper Leeson Street, Dublin 2
T: (01) 660 3000 F: (01) 660 3038
E: info@juniorachievement.ie W: www.juniorachievement.ie
Contact: Della Clancy, Executive Director
CATEGORIES: YOUNG ENTERPRISE

Junior Achievement / Young Enterprise Ireland is a non-profit making organisation dedicated to building a bridge between the classroom and the workplace. It provides an opportunity for young people to participate in a range of educational programmes designed to help them understand the world of work, as well as the risks and rewards of entrepreneurship through a unique business and education partnership.

KEADY BUSINESS CENTRE LTD
10 Annvale Road, St Patrick's Street, Keady, Co Armagh BT60 2RP
T: (028) 6632 7348 F: (028) 6632 7878
CATEGORIES: WORKSPACE

Keady Business Centre is an Enterprise Centre managed by **Armagh Business Centre**.

KERNEL CAPITAL PARTNERS PRIVATE EQUITY FUND
See **Bank of Ireland Kernel Capital Partners Private Equity Fund.**

KERRY COUNTY ENTERPRISE BOARD
Manor West Complex, Ratass, Tralee, Co Kerry
T: (066) 718 3522 F: (066) 712 6712
E: kerryceb@kerrycoco.ie W: www.kerryceb.ie
Contact: Martin Collins, CEO
Also at: The Courthouse,Cahersiveen, Co Kerry
T: (066) 947 2053 F: (066) 947 3082
E: dcournane@kerrycoco.ie
Contact: Denis Cournane, Assistant CEO

CATEGORIES: DEBT; E-BUSINESS; EQUITY; GRANTS; INFORMATION; MENTORING; PUBLICATIONS; START-UP TRAINING; TRAINING

Kerry County Enterprise Board provides a wide range of supports for local SMEs and intending entrepreneurs. It has an outreach programme of monthly clinics to assist in referrals of clients and complement the work of the Local Development Groups. People with new ideas are encouraged to make an appointment for an in-depth discussion in complete confidence, or to just drop in with a general enquiry.

KERRY RURAL DEVELOPMENT : SLIABH LUACHRA LTD
The Island Centre, Main Street, Castleisland, Co Kerry
T: (066) 714 2576 F: (066) 714 2676
E: eamonnoreilly@eircom.net ; sliabhluachra@eircom.net
Contact: Eamonn O'Reilly, Manager

CATEGORIES: COMMUNITY & RURAL DEVELOPMENT

Kerry Rural Development is one of the **Community Groups** funded by **Area Development Management**, as part of its Local Development programme.

KERRY TECHNOLOGY PARK
Dromtacker, Tralee, Co Kerry
T: (066) 719 0000 F: (066) 719 0070
E: lynchm@shannondev.ie W: www.shannon-dev.ie/ktp/
Contact: Marie Lynch, Development Manager

CATEGORIES: INCUBATOR

Kerry Technology Park is an initiative of **Shannon Development** in co-operation with the **Institute of Technology Tralee** and in partnership with **IDA Ireland**, Tralee Urban District Council, Kerry County Council and the private sector. The Park includes: A new 63-acre campus for the Institute of Technology Tralee; 50 acres of enterprise space including fully-serviced industrial sites; A Business Incubation Centre (Enterprise House); A range of quality manufacturing and office accommodation.

KESH ENTERPRISE CENTRE
Kesh Development Association, Mantlin Road, Kesh, Co Fermanagh BT93 1TT
T: (028) 6863 2158 F: (028) 6863 2158
E: ruth@kesh.org.uk W: www.kesh.org.uk
Contact: Ruth McKane

CATEGORIES: INFORMATION; START-UP TRAINING; WORKSPACE

One of several **Enterprise Centres** in Fermanagh.

KILDARE COUNTY ENTERPRISE BOARD
The Woods, Clane, Co Kildare
T: (045) 861707 F: (045) 861712
E: info@kildareceb.ie W: www.kildareceb.ie
Contact: Donal Dalton, CEO

CATEGORIES: DEBT; E-BUSINESS; EQUITY; GRANTS; INFORMATION; MENTORING; PUBLICATIONS; START-UP TRAINING; TRAINING; WOMEN

Kildare CEB offers a wide range of supports to SMEs and intending entrepreneurs. Business Advice clinics are held on an ongoing basis, aimed at anyone who wishes to talk on a one-to-one basis with a staff member from the CEB. It operates a "Women in Business" programme to foster and encourage entrepreneurship, self employment and enterprise.

KILDARE EUROPEAN LEADER II TEO
The Woods, Clane, Co Kildare
T: (045) 861 973 F: (045) 861 975
E: kelt@indigo.ie
Contact: Pat Dowling
CATEGORIES: COMMUNITY & RURAL DEVELOPMENT; GRANTS; TOURISM
DEVELOPMENT

A **LEADER+** company serving County Kildare. It helps individuals and communities to access funding and supports in order to develop innovative projects in tourism, agriculture, crafts, local services, and the environment.

KILKENNY COMMUNITY ACTION NETWORK
1 - 2 Colliers Court, Colliers Lane, Kilkenny
T: (056) 52811 F: (056) 52812
E: kcan@iolfree.ie
Contact: Fergus Keane
CATEGORIES: COMMUNITY & RURAL DEVELOPMENT

Kilkenny Community Action Network is one of the **Community Groups** funded by **Area Development Management,** as part of its Local Development programme.

KILKENNY COUNTY ENTERPRISE BOARD
42 Parliament Street, Kilkenny
T: (056) 775 2662 F: (056) 775 1649
E: enquiries@kceb.ie W: www.kceb.ie
Contact: Sean McKeown, CEO
CATEGORIES: DEBT; E-BUSINESS; EQUITY; GRANTS; INFORMATION;
MENTORING; START-UP TRAINING; TRAINING

The objective of the Kilkenny County Enterprise Board over the period 2001 - 2006 is based upon two strategic aims: Micro-Enterprise Development: To develop the entrepreneurial capability and job creation potential of micro-enterprises in County Kilkenny and to maximise their contribution to the local economy; General Indigenous Development: To develop Kilkenny's profile as a competitive, innovative centre of excellence through utilisation of existing core strengths. The CEB offers: Business information, advice and counselling; Selective financial assistance; Training and management development support.

KILKENNY INDUSTRIAL DEVELOPMENT COMPANY
c/o Bowen Water Technology Ltd, Purcellsinch, Co Kilkenny
T: (056) 63950
Contact: Fergus Cronin
CATEGORIES: INCUBATOR

Kilkenny Industrial Development Company (KIDCo) was established in 1996, to facilitate development and the promotion of industrial development within Kilkenny. It represents the business community in Kilkenny plus Kilkenny

County Council and Kilkenny Borough Council. It recently constructed a 25,000 sq. ft. advance enterprise centre on the Purcellsinch Industrial Park on the Kilkenny Ring Road.

KILLARNEY TECHNOLOGY INNOVATION LTD

KTI Centre, Killarney, Co Kerry
T: (064) 37034 F: (066) 37030
E: kticentre@eircom.net W: www.killarney-innovation.com
Contact: George Nash, Development Manager

CATEGORIES: INCUBATOR

The KTI Centre is a purpose built, technology-rich enterprise incubation, innovation and training complex. It offers both full office units and mini-incubator/desk-space.

KIMMAGE/WALKINSTOWN/CRUMLIN/DRIMNAGH PARTNERSHIP

Unit 9, Ashleaf Centre, Crumlin Cross, Dublin 12
T: (01) 405 9300 F: (01) 405 9359
E: info@kwcd.ie W: www.kwcd.ie
Contact: Brian Nugent, Manager

CATEGORIES: COMMUNITY & RURAL DEVELOPMENT; INFORMATION

One of the **Area Partnerships** funded by **Area Development Management**, as part of its Local Development programme.

KOMPASS IRELAND

Parnell Court, 1 Granby Row, Dublin 1
T: (01) 872 8800 F: (01) 873 3711
E: info@kompass.ie W: www.kompass.ie
Contact: Michael McGowan

CATEGORIES: INFORMATION; MARKETING; PUBLICATIONS

Kompass is a marketplace for business: sellers present their products and services; buyers find what they need. It uses a unique classification system to accurately link each buyer to the product or service that will satisfy his or her requirement and offers each seller unique methods to target qualified clients. Originally published on paper as *Kompass Registers of Industry*, the information is now published on CD-ROMs and the Internet.

KPMG

1 Stokes Place, St Stephen's Green, Dublin 2
T: (01) 410 1000 F: (01) 412 1122
E: feedback@kpmg.ie W: www.kpmg.ie

CATEGORIES: ACCOUNTANTS; CONSULTING

KPMG is a major firm of chartered accountants and business advisers, providing services to clients in all sectors of Irish business. It is the Irish national practice of the accountancy organisation, KPMG International.

MY *FAMILY* DOESN'T **UNDERSTAND** ME!

COPING STRATEGIES for ENTREPRENEURS

YANKY FACHLER

Available from good bookshops
or direct from OAK TREE PRESS,
LoCall 1890 313855.

www.oaktreepress.com

LAOIS COUNTY ENTERPRISE BOARD

"We have time for you"

Empowering Business through:

ASSISTING SMALL BUSINESS

Grant-aid for eligible projects in the form of:

- Capital grants
- Employment grants
- Feasibility study
- E-commerce supports

PROMOTING SMALL BUSINESSES

- Raising enterprise awareness
- Creating an enterprise culture
- Information – one-stop-shop
- Schools programme
- Workshops
- Local radio/press
- Information clinics
- Community group meetings
- Enterprise evenings

SUPPORTING SMALL BUSINESSES

- Advisory service
- Mentoring service
- Management development
- Business development

TRAINING PROGRAMMES

- Write Your Own Business Plan
- Customer Care
- Personal Development
- Tax for Self-Employed
- Making a Presentation
- Website Design
- Retail Development
- Management & Business Skills for Women
- Time Management
- Employment Law
- Meeting your Bank

Laois County Enterprise Board
IBS House, Dublin Road, Portlaoise, Co Laois
Tel: 0502 61800 Fax: 0502 61797
Email: admin@laoisenterprise.com
Web: www.laoisenterprise.com

LAOIS COUNTY ENTERPRISE BOARD

LAOIS COUNTY ENTERPRISE BOARD
IBS House, Dublin Road, Portlaoise, Co Laois
T: (0502) 61800 F: (0502) 61797
E: admin@laoisenterprise.com W: www.laoisenterprise.com
Contact: Maria Callinan, CEO

CATEGORIES: DEBT; E-BUSINESS; EQUITY; GRANTS; INFORMATION;
MENTORING; START-UP TRAINING; TRAINING

The Laois County Enterprise Board empowers local enterprise through:
Advice, counselling, and mentoring for those wishing to start or expand their
business; Informative publications for businesses, such as "Starting your own
business", "Writing your own Business Plan", "Health & Safety Guide", etc; A
wide range of SME-related training courses designed to prepare owner
managers and their staff to compete in the current business climate; Providing
a range of financial assistance under the EU BMW Operational Programme.

LAOIS LEADER RURAL DEVELOPMENT COMPANY
Pepper's Court, Portlaoise, Co Laois
T: (0502) 61900 F: (0502) 61902
E: info@laois-leader-rdc.ie W: www.laois-leader-rdc.ie
Contact: Anne Goodwin, Programme Manager

CATEGORIES: COMMUNITY & RURAL DEVELOPMENT; GRANTS

A **LEADER+** company, Laois LEADER offers grant aid to small enterprises that
will create employment, are innovative and do not create displacement. Its
website explains the programmes, grants and other supports available.

LARNE ENTERPRISE DEVELOPMENT COMPANY LTD
Industrial Estate, Bank Road, Larne, Co Antrim BT40 3AW
T: (028) 2827 0742 F: (028) 2827 5653
E: info@ledcom.org W: www.ledcom.org
Contact: David Gillespie

CATEGORIES: DEBT; INFORMATION; START-UP TRAINING; TRAINING; WORKSPACE

LEDCOM is an **Enterprise Agency** and a member of **Enterprise Northern
Ireland**. It provides an effective local focus for business suport, acting as a
catalyst for economic development. LEDCOM also manages over stg£200,000
of capital within its own loan funds.

LAW SOCIETY OF IRELAND
Blackhall Place, Dublin 7
T: (01) 672 4800 F: (01) 672 4801
E: general@lawsociety.ie W: www.lawsociety.ie
Contact: Ken Murphy, Director General

CATEGORIES: LEGAL

The Law Society exercises statutory functions under the Solicitors Acts 1954-
1994 in relation to the education, admission, enrolment, discipline and
regulation of over 6,000 solicitors in Ireland. If you're looking for a lawyer, the
Law Society can direct you to one of its members.

LAW SOCIETY OF NORTHERN IRELAND

Law Society House, 98 Victoria Street, Belfast BT1 3JZ
T: (028) 9023 1614 F: (028) 9023 2606
E: info@lawsoc-ni.org W: www.lawsoc-ni.org

CATEGORIES: LEGAL

The Law Society regulates the solicitors' profession in Northern Ireland with the aim of protecting the public. If you're looking for a lawyer, it can direct you to one of its members.

LEADER+

W: www.irishleadernetwork.org

CATEGORIES: COMMUNITY & RURAL DEVELOPMENT

LEADER+ is a European Community initiative for assisting rural communities in improving the quality of life and economic prosperity in their local area. LEADER+ is aimed at encouraging and supporting high quality and ambitious integrated strategies for local rural development, putting a strong emphasis on co-operation and networking between rural areas. See individual entries for:

- Arigna Catchment Area Community Company
- Ballyhoura Development Ltd
- Barrow-Nore-Suir Rural Development Ltd
- Blackwater Resource Development
- CARLOW LEADER RURAL DEVELOPMENT COMPANY LTD
- Cavan-Monaghan Rural Development Co-op Society Ltd
- Comhar Iorrais LEADER Teo
- Comhdháil Oileáin na hÉireann
- Donegal Local Development Company
- East Cork Area Development Ltd
- Galway Rural Development Company
- Inishowen Rural Development Ltd
- IRD Duhallow Ltd
- Irish Country Holidays
- Irish Farmhouse Holidays
- Kildare European LEADER II Teo
- Laois LEADER Rural Development Company
- Longford Community Resources Ltd
- Louth LEADER
- Meath LEADER
- Meitheal Forbartha na Gaeltachta Teo
- Mid-South Roscommon Rural Development Company
- Muintir na Tíre
- Offaly LEADER II Company Ltd
- Rural Dublin LEADER Co Ltd
- Rural Resource Development Ltd
- Sligo LEADER Partnership Co Ltd
- South Kerry Development Partnership
- South West Mayo Development Company (South Mayo LEADER)
- Tipperary LEADER Group
- Tuatha Chiarraí Teo
- Waterford LEADER Partnership Ltd
- West Cork LEADER Co-operative Society Ltd
- West Limerick Resources Ltd
- Western Rural Development Company
- Westmeath Community Development Ltd
- Wexford Organisation for Rural Development
- Wicklow Rural Partnership Ltd.

LEADER+ NORTHERN IRELAND

W: www.ukleader.org.uk

CATEGORIES: COMMUNITY & RURAL DEVELOPMENT

LEADER+ is a European Community initiative for assisting rural communities in improving the quality of life and economic prosperity in their local area. LEADER+ is aimed at encouraging and supporting high quality and ambitious integrated strategies for local rural development, putting a strong emphasis on co-operation and networking between rural areas. See individual entries for LEADER groups in Northern Ireland:

- Coleraine Local Action Group for Enterprise Ltd
- Craigavon & Armagh Rural Development (CARD)
- East Tyrone Rural
- Fermanagh Local Action Group
- Magherafelt Area Partnership Ltd
- Newry & Mourne Local Action Group
- North Antrim LEADER
- RAPID (Rural Area Partnership in Derry)
- REAP South Antrim
- Roe Valley Rural Development Ltd
- Rural Down Partnership
- West Tyrone Rural Ltd

LEGAL-ISLAND

Rathcoole Business Centre, Main Street, Rathcoole, Co Dublin
T: (01) 401 3874
PO Box 46, Limavady, Northern Ireland BT49 0SQ T: (028) 7775 0590
F: (070) 9233 8943
E: legal@legal-island.com W: www.legal-island.com

CATEGORIES: INFORMATION; LEGAL

The leading web site for information and advice relevant to the legal jurisdictions in Northern Ireland and the Republic of Ireland.

LEITRIM ENTERPRISE BOARD

Carrick-on-Shannon Business Park, Dublin Road, Carrick-on-Shannon, Co Leitrim
T: (078) 20450 F: (078) 21491
E: info@leitrimenterprise.ie W: www.leitrimenterprise.ie
Contact: Joe Lowe, CEO

CATEGORIES: DEBT; E-BUSINESS; EQUITY; GRANTS; INFORMATION; MENTORING; START-UP TRAINING; TRAINING

Leitrim County Enterprise Board seeks to stimulate and support the indigenous business development potential in Co. Leitrim with the creation of new, sustainable employment opportunities. This involves the provision of appropriate supports to the micro enterprise sector, the promotion of an enterprise culture, provision of information, advice and counselling. It was instrumental in the establishment of the Carrick-on-Shannon Business Park.

LETTERKENNY BUSINESS DEVELOPMENT CENTRE
Letterkenny Institute of Technology Campus, Port Road, Letterkenny,
Co. Donegal
T: (074) 67402 F: (074) 64111
E: bdc@lyit.ie W: www.lyit.ie/research_industry/bdc.htm
Contact: Noeleen Lafferty, Centre Manager
CATEGORIES: INCUBATOR

The Centre provides campus-based incubation facilities for start-up business companies, as well as facilities for industrial research and commercial services to local industry, on the campus of Letterkenny IT. The Centre has been designed to provide a supportive, learning, innovative and entrepreneurial environment to start-up businesses with managerial and administrative support at a competitive cost.

LETTERKENNY INSTITUTE OF TECHNOLOGY
Port Road, Letterkenny, Co Donegal
T: (074) 64100 F: (074) 64111
E: jack.oherlihy@lyit.ie W: www.lyit.ie
Contact: Jack O'Herlihy, Head of Development
CATEGORIES: CONSULTING; INCUBATOR; R & D; TRAINING; WORKSPACE

Through its Development Office, Letterkenny IT provides training programmes, consultancy and research expertise to meet the education and development needs of the industrial and commercial sector and wider community. The **Business Development Centre** provides campus-based incubation facilities to start-up companies, facilities for industrial research and commercial services to local industry, and managerial and administrative support at a competitive cost. See also the **Céim Enterprise Development Programme.**

LIFFEY TRUST
117–126 Upper Sheriff Street, Dublin 1
T: (01) 836 4645 F: (01) 855 6798
E: liffey-trust@clubi.ie W: www.liffey-trust.com
Contact: Séamus McDermott, Director
CATEGORIES: BUSINESS PLANS; CONSULTING; INCUBATOR; MARKETING;
START-UP TRAINING

The Liffey Trust Ltd is financed entirely by its own efforts and without Government assistance. The Trust: Helps to prepare business plans, feasibility studies and grant applications, free of charge; Advises on raising finance; Provides guidance on how to set up accountancy and control systems; Provides free management and marketing consultancy; Takes care of bureaucratic procedures; Rents incubator units at reduced rents until enterprises are established. The Trust runs "Start Your Own Business" courses in the Institute of Adult Education, Dublin Libraries and in Wheatfield and Mountjoy Prisons and gives regular lectures on enterprise in schools in the Dublin area.

LIMAVADY SMALL BUSINESS AGENCY
See **Roe Valley Enterprises Ltd.**

LIMERICK BUSINESS INNOVATION CENTRE
InnovationWorks, National Technological Park, Limerick
T: (061) 338177, 338118 F: (061) 338065
E: dillonj@shannon-dev.ie W: www.shannon-dev.ie/innovation
Contact: John Dillon, Manager

CATEGORIES: BUSINESS PLANS; EQUITY; INCUBATOR; INFORMATION;
MARKETING; TRAINING

Limerick BIC acts as a specialist venture consultancy to improve the survival rate and growth potential of new and existing businesses by providing hands-on assistance. It is part of **Shannon Development's Knowledge Network**.

LIMERICK CITY ENTERPRISE BOARD
The Granary, Michael Street, Limerick
T: (061) 312611 F: (061) 311889
E: info@limceb.ie W: www.limceb.ie
Contact: Eamon Ryan, CEO

CATEGORIES: DEBT; E-BUSINESS; EQUITY; GRANTS; INFORMATION;
MENTORING; START-UP TRAINING; TRAINING

Limerick City CEB's mission is to facilitate the creation of sustainable jobs through the development of an Enterprise Culture and the provision of support to enterprise in Limerick City. It offers financial assistance and advice, business guidance and training support.

LIMERICK COUNTY ENTERPRISE BOARD
County Buildings, 79–84 O'Connell Street, Limerick
T: (061) 319319 F: (061) 319 318
E: info@lcoeb.ie W: www.lcoeb.ie
Contact: Ned Toomey, CEO

CATEGORIES: DEBT; E-BUSINESS; EQUITY; GRANTS; INFORMATION;
MENTORING; START-UP TRAINING; TRAINING

Limerick County Enterprise Board assists entrepreneurs in developing a business from the initial idea to start-up and at all stages of its development.

LIMERICK ENTERPRISE DEVELOPMENT PARTNERSHIP
Limerick Enterprise Development Park, Roxboro Road, Limerick
T: (061) 316833 / 316083 F: (061) 319318
E: lmcelligott@ledp.ie W: www.ledp.ie
Contact: Liam McElligott, CEO

CATEGORIES: INCUBATOR

LEDP operates an Enterprise Centre on the site of the former Krups factory. See also **Limerick Enterprise Network**.

LIMERICK ENTERPRISE NETWORK
Limerick Enterprise Development Park, Roxboro Road, Limerick
T: (061) 316833 / 316083 F: (061) 319318
E: lmcelligott@ledp.ie W: www.ledp.ie
Contact: Liam McElligott, CEO
CATEGORIES: COMMUNITY & RURAL DEVELOPMENT; DEBT

Limerick Enterprise Network empowers those experiencing disadvantage and marginalisation at an individual and collective level, to create a sustainable economic environment that substantially improves equality of participation in society while having a positive impact on overall quality of life. Through its "start to finish" guidance and direction, LEN provides support to ensure a successful transition from long -erm unemployment to operating a business. It also operates a loan fund which is backed by Limerick Territorial Employment Pact, **PAUL Partnership** and **First Step**. LEN is a founding member of the **Limerick Enterprise Development Partnership**.

LIMERICK FOOD CENTRE
Raheen Industrial Park, Limerick
T: (061) 302033 F: (061) 301172
E: odriscollc@shannondev.ie W: www.shannon-dev.ie/foodcentre
Contact: Colman O'Driscoll
CATEGORIES: CONSULTING; INFORMATION; MARKETING; R & D; TRAINING

The Limerick Food Centre provides food manufacturing and processing units, access to equipment, a full research, information and advice service, and a specialist Agribusiness and Natural Resources Support Unit. It also provides a range of professional, entrepreneurial support and marketing programmes for existing and potential business, linked to the wider supports, financial and investment services of **Shannon Development.**

LIMERICK INSTITUTE OF TECHNOLOGY
Moylish Park, Limerick
T: (061) 208803 F: (061) 208209
E: information@lit.ie W: www.lit.ie
Contact: Dr Fergal Barry, Industrial Services Manager
CATEGORIES: CONSULTING; R & D; TRAINING

Limerick Institute of Technology is a centre for research and development in the Mid-West region. Its Enterprise Development Programme is one of the **Enterprise Platform Programmes** and supports the development of entrepreneurial skills among students in the LIT School of Art and Design.

LISBURN ENTERPRISE ORGANISATION LTD
Enterprise Crescent, Ballinderry Road, Lisburn, Co Antrim BT28 2BP
T: (028) 9266 1160 F: (028) 9260 3084
E: centre@lisburn-enterprise.co.uk W: www.lisburn-enterprise.co.uk
CATEGORIES: CONSULTING; DEBT; INFORMATION; START-UP TRAINING; TRAINING; WORKSPACE

Lisburn Enterprise Organisation is an **Enterprise Agency** and a member of **Enterprise Northern Ireland**. It offers office and workshop units, for start-up and small growth businesses, a Small Business library, and market research services. In addition, it manages the Synergy Fund and the Seed Corn Fund Loan Scheme. It also operates the **Synergy 2000** business angel network.

LISNASKEAN ENTERPRISE CENTRE

Lisnaskea Community Enterprise Ltd, Drumbrughas North, Lisnaskea, Co Fermanagh BT92 0PE
T: (028) 6772 1081

CATEGORIES: INFORMATION; START-UP TRAINING; WORKSPACE

One of several **Enterprise Centres** in Fermanagh.

LIVEANDLEARN.ie

W: www.liveandlearn.ie

CATEGORIES: TRAINING; WEBSITE

Life-long learning via online courses from the **National College of Ireland**.

LOMBARD & ULSTER BANKING LTD

Ulster Bank Group Centre, Georges Quay, Dublin 2
T: (01) 608 5499 / 1850 215 000 F: (01) 608 5001
W: www.lombard.ie

CATEGORIES: DEBT

Lombard & Ulster Banking Ltd offers a range of flexible and innovative financing products and packages to meet specific requirements.

LONGFORD COMMUNITY RESOURCES LTD

6 Earl Street, Longford
T: (043) 48555 F: (043) 48675
E: enquiries@lcrl.ie
Contact: Monica O'Malley, Manager

CATEGORIES: COMMUNITY & RURAL DEVELOPMENT; GRANTS

One of the Area Partnerships funded by **Area Development Management**, as part of its Local Development programme, and also a **LEADER+** company serving County Longford.

LONGFORD COUNTY ENTERPRISE BOARD

38 Ballymahon Street, Longford
T: (043) 42757 F: (043) 40968
E: info@longfordceb.ie W: www.longfordceb.ie
Contact: Michael Nevin, CEO

CATEGORIES: DEBT; E-BUSINESS; EQUITY; GRANTS; INFORMATION; MENTORING; START-UP TRAINING; TRAINING

Longford CEB provides a full range of supports for micro-enterprises in its area. Its website includes news section, a business directory and details of available funding, including capital, employment and feasability study grants.

LOUGHRY CAMPUS, COLLEGE OF AGRICULTURE, FOOD & RURAL ENTERPRISE, DEPARTMENT OF AGRICULTURE & RURAL DEVELOPMENT

Cookstown, Co Tyrone BT80 9AA
T: (0800) 216139 (Freephone) F: (028) 8676 1043
E: loughry.admissions@dardni.gov.uk W: www.loughry.ac.uk

CATEGORIES: INCUBATOR; INFORMATION; R & D; START-UP TRAINING; TRAINING

Loughry Campus, College of Agriculture, Food and Rural Enterprise, DARD, provides education, training and technology support for the food industry. Its Innovation Team is dedicated to the development, demonstration and adoption of new products, processes and systems. It operates a **Food Business Incubation Centre** and a Food Technology Centre – the facilities of both centres are available to entrepreneurs.

LOUGHRY COLLEGE FOOD BUSINESS INCUBATION CENTRE, LOUGHRY CAMPUS, COLLEGE OF AGRICULTURE, FOOD & RURAL ENTERPRISE

Cookstown, Co Tyrone BT80 9AA
T: (0800) 216139 (Freephone) F: (028) 8676 1043
E: peter.simpson@dardni.gov.uk W: www.loughry.ac.uk
Contact: Peter Simpson, Centre Manager

CATEGORIES: INCUBATOR

The Food Business Incubation Centre at **Loughry Campus, College of Agriculture, Food & Rural Enterprise** provides 8 food-processing factory units, available to food business entrepreneurs wishing to establish food manufacturing operations.

LOUTH COUNTY ENTERPRISE BOARD

Enterprise House, The Ramparts, Dundalk, Co Louth
T: (042) 932 7099 F: (042) 932 7101
E: info@lceb.ie W: www.lceb.ie
Contact: Ronan Dennedy, CEO

CATEGORIES: CROSS-BORDER; DEBT; E-BUSINESS; EQUITY; GRANTS; INFORMATION; MENTORING; START-UP TRAINING; TRAINING; WOMEN

Louth CEB provides business support and services to micro-enterprises in the county, including business information, training and mentoring, management development programmes and international product transfer and franchising opportunities. It provides financial support to start-up and developing companies through employment and capital grants, refundable aid and equity investment. It offers a "Women in Business" programme, funded in part by the **Dept. of Justice, Equality & Law Reform, Drogheda Partnership, Dundalk Employment Partnership** and supported by **Louth LEADER**. It also supports

LouthCraftMark.com and **PLATO**. Louth CEB is involved in cross-border enterprise support with **Newry & Mourne Enterprise Agency**, including the *Tradefinder* programme.

LOUTH COUNTY ENTERPRISE FUND

Rock Road, Blackrock, Dundalk, Co Louth
T: (042) 932 2987 F: (042) 932 2987
E: louth.enterprise.fund@oceanfree.net
Contact: Dominic Smyth, Secretary

CATEGORIES: DEBT

The Louth County Enterprise Fund was formed as part of the **International Fund for Ireland's** Border Counties initiative in 1988. Its aim is to lend money for business purposes to promoters who cannot get a hearing elsewhere. Funding is from the EU Special Support Programme for Peace & Reconciliation, **Louth County Enterprise Board, the Department of Social and Family Affairs, Drogheda Partnership, Dundalk Partnership and Louth LEADER**.

LOUTH LEADER

Market Street, Ardee, Co Louth
T: (041) 685 7375 F: (041) 685 6787
E: info@louthleader.com W: www.louthleader.com
Contact: Maureen Ward, Manager

CATEGORIES: COMMUNITY & RURAL DEVELOPMENT; GRANTS; TOURISM DEVELOPMENT; TRAINING

Louth LEADER adminsiters the **LEADER+** and National Rural Development programmes in Co Louth. It offers capital equipment grants to innovative, small enterprises in manufacturing, crafts or local services at start-up or development stage, within its operational area.

LOUTHCRAFTMARK.com

T: (042) 932 7099
E: karenferguson@louthcraftmark.com W: www.louthcraftmark.com
Contact: Karen Ferguson, Crafts Development Officer

CATEGORIES: INFORMATION; TRAINING; WEBSITE

LouthCraftmark.com showcases the work of local artists and craftspeople. It is funded by the EU programme for Peace and Reconciliation, **Dundalk Employment Partnership, Drogheda Partnership and Louth County Enterprise Board**. It also offers training and a downloadable Handbook of business support, craft resources and education.

The M50 Enterprise Programme aims to provide practical support to knowledge intensive start-up enterprises.

The programme provides incubation facilities, training, business coaching and mentoring, networking and peer learning opportunities, and financial support to entrepreneurs over a 12 month period.

The **M50 Enterprise Programme** in conjunction with **Oak Tree Press,** have developed a unique clinic-based approach which offers individualised support in the business planning, skills and knowledge acquisition processes.

The ideal target participant on the programme is mature, with a third-level qualification, relevant work experience and, most importantly, a feasible business idea that involves technology innovation or has a knowledge-based dimension. The dedication, full-time commitment, motivation, and business acumen of applicants are also considered, as is the job creation and export potential of their business ideas.

enterprise
programme

For further information:

M50 Enterprise Programme,
Institute of Technology Tallaght,
Dublin 24

Tel: (01) 404 2376
Fax: (01) 404 2174
Web: www.m50-enterprise.ie

Contact: Patricia O'Sullivan
email: m50@it-tallaght.ie

The M50 Enterprise Programme is jointly run by:

- Institute of Technology Tallaght
- Dublin City University/Invent
- University College Dublin/NovaUCD
- Institute of Technology Blanchardstown

LUCAN 2000

1 Church View, Lower Main Street, Lucan, Co Dublin
T: (01) 621 3205 F: (01) 621 3204
E: info@lucan2000.com W: www.lucan2000.com
Contact: Fionnuala McCarthy, Manager

CATEGORIES: COMMUNITY & RURAL DEVELOPMENT; INFORMATION

Lucan 2000 is one of the **Community Groups** funded by **Area Development Management,** as part of its Local Development programme. Lucan 2000 provides an enterprise advice service to individuals in Maynooth, Celbridge, Leixlip and Palmerstown who are in business or wish to become self-employed, linking them with the supports available.

M50 ENTERPRISE PROGRAMME

Synergy Centre, Institute of Technology Tallaght, Tallaght, Dublin 24
T: (01) 404 2000/404 2376 F: (01) 404 2174
E: m50@it-tallaght.ie W: www.m50-enterprise.ie
Contact: Patricia O'Sullivan, Programme Manager

CATEGORIES: GRANTS; INCUBATOR; MENTORING; START-UP TRAINING

IT Tallaght and **IT Blanchardstown**, with **Dublin City University/Invent** and **University College Dublin/NovaUCD**, run an Enterprise Programme in the M50 corridor. The one-year full-time programme provides: Funding; Mentoring; Incubation space; Training. It aims to provide the participants with the skills to develop a business idea to launch-stage or, in the case of businesses already trading, to strengthen their market and trading position. Participants must have an innovative business idea and a third level qualification in any discipline. See also **Enterprise Programmes** for details of EPPs in other locations.

MACLACHLAN & DONALDSON

47 Merrion Square, Dublin 2
T: (01) 676 3465 F: (01) 661 2083
E: mail@maclachlan.ie W: www.maclachlan.ie

CATEGORIES: INTELLECTUAL PROPERTY

MacLachlan & Donaldson are European Patent and Community Trade Mark attorneys.

MACRA NA FEIRME

National Headquarters, Irish Farm Centre, Bluebell, Dublin 12
T: (01) 450 8000 F: (01) 451 4908
E: macra@macra.ie W: www.macra.ie

CATEGORIES: COMMUNITY & RURAL DEVELOPMENT; NETWORKING

Macra members come from a variety of backgrounds, are aged between 17 and 35 and are affiliated to one of Macra's 300 nation-wide clubs.

MADDEN CONSULTANTS LTD
4 Maxwell Road, Rathgar, Dublin 6
T: (01) 497 9262 / 491 1593
E: james@maddenconsultants.com W: www.maddenconsultants.com
Contact: James Madden

CATEGORIES: BUSINESS PLANS; CONSULTING; MARKETING; TRAINING

Madden Consultants provides a wide range of services to start-up and developing businesses including: Arranging grant assistance, feasibility studies, market research, finding sales leads, advising on strategy, facilitating the development of business plans, as well strategic development, marketing and export plans. It also provides training.

MAGHERAFELT AREA PARTNERSHIP LTD
50 Ballyronan Road, Magaherafelt, Co Londonderry BT45 6EN
T: (028) 7939 7979 F: (028) 79397980
E: info@magherafelt.org W: www.magherafelt.com
Contact: Charlie Monaghan, Programme Manager

CATEGORIES: COMMUNITY & RURAL DEVELOPMENT

One of the **LEADER+** groups in Northern Ireland.

MALLINN / INVENT START-UP AWARDS
Invent, The Innovation and Enterprise Centre, Dublin City University, Dublin 9
T: (01) 700 7777
E: leah.lynch@invent.dcu.ie W: www.invent.dcu.ie
Contact: Leah McKenna, Marketing Executive

CATEGORIES: COMPETITIONS

The Mallinn / Invent Start-up Awards, managed by Invent, aim to encourage undergraduates, final year students, postgraduates, recent graduates, alumni and **DCU** staff and researchers to set up a new business and give them the support necessary to translate their idea into a viable business. It's now too late to apply for the 2003 awards but check the website for the 2004 competition.

MANAGEMENT TRAINING AND FINANCE GROUP
38-42 Hill Street, Belfast BT1 2LB
T: (028) 9031 1660 F: (028) 9031 1880
E: admin@mtf.com W: www.mtf.com

CATEGORIES: ACCOUNTANTS; MARKETING; TRAINING

MTF was established in 1985 and consists of three core businesses: Finance and accountancy services; Telemarketing and market research; Training. It manages the **Emerging Business Trust**.

MANAGEMENTDIRECT.com

Unit 27, Guinness Centre, Taylor's Lane, Dublin 8
T: (01) 4100 667 F: (01) 4100 733
E: info@managementdirect.com W: www.managementdirect.com
Contact: Sean McGarry

CATEGORIES: INFORMATION; MENTORING; WEBSITE

ManagementDirect.com is an interactive business advice and online mentoring website for Irish SMEs. The Management Direct service covers a broad spectrum of of management topics, all delivered with the small business owner-manager in mind. The online mentoring service is used by some of the **City/County Enterprise Boards** for their clients. See also **FranchiseDirect.com**.

MANUFACTURING TECHNOLOGY PARTNERSHIP

Springvale Business Park, 1b Millennium Way, Belfast BT12 7AL
T: (028) 9027 9860 F: (028) 9027 9869
E: info@mtpltd.com W: www.mtpltd.com
Contact: Mike Heath, Chief Executive

CATEGORIES: CONSULTING; R & D

MTP improves the competitiveness of client companies by helping them to identify and adopt appropriate and affordable technologies. In association with **Loughry College, Queen's University Belfast, Invest Northern Ireland and University of Ulster**, it offers practical hands-on help.

MARINE INSTITUTE

80 Harcourt Street, Dublin 2
T: (01) 476 6500 F: (01) 478 4988
W: www.marine.ie

CATEGORIES: INFORMATION; R & D

The Marine Institute is the national agency responsible for undertaking, co-ordinating, promoting and assisting in marine research and development, and providing such services related to marine research and development that, in the opinion of the Institute, will promote economic development, create employment and protect the environment.

MARKETING CENTRE FOR SMALL BUSINESS

University of Limerick, Limerick
T: (061) 202 986 F: (061) 202 588
E: mark.oconnell@ul.ie W: www.mcsb.ul.ie
Contact: Mark O'Connell, Manager

CATEGORIES: CONSULTING; MARKETING

The Marketing Centre for Small Business (MCSB) is a marketing and market research consultancy, that offers marketing assistance to start-up companies operating in the Shannon Region. The MCSB is a campus company of the **University of Limerick**, operated with the assistance of the Department of Management & Marketing.

MARKETING INSTITUTE OF IRELAND

Marketing House, South County Business Park, Leopardstown, Dublin 18
T: (01) 295 2355 F: (01) 295 2453
E: info@mii.ie W: www.mii.ie
Contact: Ed McDonald, Chief Executive

CATEGORIES: INFORMATION; MARKETING; TRAINING

The Marketing Institute is the professional representative body for marketing people in Ireland. Its aim is to set, promote and develop high standards of marketing practice in Irish business. It operates a free online marketplace at www.marketingservicesireland.com.

MAYFAIR BUSINESS CENTRE LTD

193-205 Garvaghy Road, Portadown, Co Armagh BT62 1HA
T: (028) 3839 1666 F: (028) 3839 1586
E: office@m-b-c.demon.co.uk W: www.m-b-c.demon.co.uk
Contact: Michael McCooe, Chief Executive

CATEGORIES: INFORMATION; WORKSPACE

One of the **Enterprise Agencies/Centres** in Co Armagh. Its primary goal is to enhance the opportunity for start-up businesses and business growth in the community. It provides workspace and business services.

MAYO COUNTY ENTERPRISE BOARD

McHale Retail Park, McHale Road, Castlebar, Co Mayo
T: (094) 24444 F: (094) 24416
E: info@mayoceb.com W: www.mayoceb.com
Contact: Frank Fullard, CEO

CATEGORIES: DEBT; E-BUSINESS; EQUITY; GRANTS; INCUBATOR;
INFORMATION; MENTORING; START-UP TRAINING; TRAINING

The Mayo County Enterprise Board offers a range of financial supports, business advice, counselling and management development training to SMEs based in County Mayo.

MAZARS

Harcourt Centre, Block 3, Harcourt Road, Dublin 2
T: (01) 449 4400 F: (01) 475 0030
E: mdivilly@mazars.ie W: www.mazars.ie
Contact: Mairéad Divilly, Partner

CATEGORIES: ACCOUNTANTS; CONSULTING; EQUITY

Mazars is a leading firm of chartered accountants and business advisors, providing services in accounting audit, tax, consulting and corporate finance. It provides services to companies in all sectors of Irish business, with a specific market focus and team dedicated to the SME sector. Mazars is a full member of the Mazars international partnership, Europe's largest indigenous firm.

MEATH COMMUNITY PARTNERSHIP COMPANY (MEATH LEADER)
Tom Blake House, Bective Street, Kells, Co Meath
T: (046) 49333 F: (046) 49338
E: mleader2@iol.ie
Contact: Christine O'Shea

CATEGORIES: COMMUNITY & RURAL DEVELOPMENT; GRANTS

A **LEADER+** company serving Co Meath, Meath LEADER offers capital equipment grants to innovative, small enterprises in manufacturing, crafts or local services at start-up or development stage, within its operational area.

MEATH COUNTY ENTERPRISE BOARD
Navan Enterprise Centre, Trim Road, Navan, Co Meath
T: (046) 78400 F: (046) 27356
E: mhceb@meath.com W: www.meath.com
Contact: Pauline Baker

CATEGORIES: DEBT; E-BUSINESS; EQUITY; GRANTS; INFORMATION; MENTORING; START-UP TRAINING; TRAINING

Meath CEB assists enterprise development in the county through the creation of an enterprise culture, the provision of advice and support and the granting of financial aid. It provides: Advice and guidance; Business information, including information packs specific to the needs of new and expanding small businesses; Mentoring support; and Management development programmes.

MEDIA LAB EUROPE
Sugar House Lane, Bellevue, Dublin 8
T: (01) 474 2800 F: (01) 474 2809
E: info@medialabeurope.org W: www.medialabeurope.org
Contact: Lia O'Sullivan

CATEGORIES: R & D

Media Lab Europe is a not-for-profit research institute that works in partnership with industry and Governmental organisations to leverage the innovative and entrepreneurial operating model of the world-renowned MIT Media Lab to discover big and original ideas that transform the way we live and work. Media Lab Europe invents by bringing together scientists, engineers and artists from different disciplines to aid the creation of technologies and possibilities that have barely been dreamt of before.

MEDICAL DEVICE ENTERPRISE PROGRAMME
Development Office, Galway-Mayo Institute of Technology, Dublin Road, Galway
T: (091) 730850
E: gorourke@westbic.ie W: www.gmit.ie
Contact: Gert O'Rourke, Programme Manager

CATEGORIES: GRANTS; INCUBATOR; MENTORING; START-UP TRAINING

The programme assists graduates to establish a new enterprise in the medical device sector, through a one-year rapid incubation process involving a balance of formal education, training, personal development, counselling, business mentoring and business guidance. **Udaras na Gaeltachta** is a partner in the programme, and **WestBIC** manages day-to-day activities. See also **Enterprise Programmes** for EPs in other locations.

MEITHEAL FORBARTHA NA GAELTACHTA TEO
Baile an Fheirtéaraigh, Trá Lí, Co Chiarraí
T: (066) 915 6400 F: (066) 915 6199
E: mfgciarrai@eircom.net W: www.mfg.ie
Contact: Antaine M Ó Sé
CATEGORIES: COMMUNITY & RURAL DEVELOPMENT; GRANTS

Meitheal Forbatha na Gaeltachta implements the National Rural Development programme in Gaeltacht areas. It has regional offices in Baile an Fhéirtearaigh, Co Chiarraí; Indreabhán, Co na Gaillimhe; and Na Doirí Beaga, Co Dhún na nGall. Sub-groups of MFG implement the **ADM**-funded Social Inclusion Programme: **Páirtíocht Gaeltacht Thír Chonaill,** Dhún na nGall; Comhlucht Forbatha Acla, Co Mhuigheo; **Comhar Dhuibhne**, Co Chiarraí and **Meitheal Mhuscraí**, Co Chorcaí.

MEITHEAL MHAIGH EO (NORTH MAYO PARTNERSHIP)
Lower Main Street, Foxford, Co Mayo
T: (094) 56745 F: (094) 56749
E: info@meithealm.com W: www.meithealm.com
Contact: Justin Sammon, Manager
CATEGORIES: COMMUNITY & RURAL DEVELOPMENT; GRANTS; INCUBATOR; INFORMATION; MENTORING; NETWORKING; START-UP TRAINING; TRAINING

One of the **Area Partnerships** established by **Area Development Management**, currently delivering the Local Development Social Inclusion Programme as part of the Government's National Development Plan. It has sub-offices in: Achill (Achill LDP); Ballina **(Moy Valley Resources);** Newport **(South West Mayo Development Company)**; Belmullet (Erris LDP); East Mayo (East Mayo LDP, managed by **IRD Kiltimagh**). It is implementing a Rural Regeneration Programme that seeks to address the problems associated with rural depopulation experienced by many communities throughout the county, by encouraging and assisting new families to relocate to Co Mayo.

MEITHEAL MHUSCRAÍ
MFG Teo, Réidh na nDoirí, Maigh Chromtha, Co Chorcaí
T: (026) 45661 F: (026) 45661
E: muscrai@eircom.net
Contact: Áine La Brosse
CATEGORIES: COMMUNITY & RURAL DEVELOPMENT

Meitheal Muscraí is one of the **Community Groups** funded by **Area Development Management**, as part of its Local Development programme. It is a regional office of **Meitheal Forbartha na Gaeltachta Teo.**

MENTOR CAPITAL PARTNERS LTD PARTNERSHIP
Mentor Capital Ltd, Mentec House, Pottery Road, Dun Laoire, Co Dublin
T: (01) 205 9716 F: (01) 205 9889
E: info@mentorcapital.ie W: www.mentorcapital.ie
Contact: Mark Horgan
CATEGORIES: EQUITY; MENTORING

This €7.5 million fund targets companies with core enabling technology in the information, communciations and technology sectors. Typical investments are in the €500k to €1.5 million range. Mentor Capital provides mentoring to its portfolio companies.

MENTOR NETWORK
Enterprise Ireland, Glasnevin, Dublin 9
T: (01) 206 6366 F: (01) 206 6225
E: mentor@enterprise-ireland.com W: www.enterprise-ireland.com
Contact: Charlie Kelly, Mentor Manager
CATEGORIES: BUSINESS ANGELS; MENTORING

Managed by **Enterprise Ireland**, the Mentor Network matches high-calibre experienced executives, all volunteers, with SMEs in need of business advice. It also links companies seeking finance with business angels. Access to the Mentor Network is available through: **City / County Enterprise Boards; Enterprise Ireland; Shannon Development; Udaras na Gaeltachta.**

MICHAEL SMURFIT GRADUATE SCHOOL OF BUSINESS HATCHERY
University College Dublin, Blackrock, Co Dublin
T: (01) 716 8895 F: (01) 283 2429
E: tony.condon@ucd.ie W: ucdbusiness.ucd.ie
Contact: Tony Condon, Director of Development
CATEGORIES: GRANTS; INCUBATOR; START-UP TRAINING

The Smurfit School Hatchery at UCD is aimed at early stage development projects and the commercialisation of research. The Hatchery provides graduates of the Smurfit School with the time, funding, technology, know-how and network to leverage entrepreneurial skills and to test and prepare business. Typically, grants of between €20,000 and €60,000 are available to graduates in their first year of a new start-up venture.

MIDLANDS ENTERPRISE PROGRAMME
Athlone Institute of Technology, Innovation Centre, Dublin Road, Athlone, Co Westmeath
T: (0902) 24400
E: amkearns@ait.ie W: www.ait.ie
Contact: Ann-Marie Kearns, Programme Manager
CATEGORIES: GRANTS; INCUBATOR; MENTORING; START-UP TRAINING

A newly-established Enterprise Programme, because of its location, the Midlands programme has an emphasis on pharmaceutical businesses. See also **Enterprise Programmes** for EPs in other locations.

MID-SOUTH ROSCOMMON LEADER

Curraghboy, Athlone, Co Roscommon
T: (0902) 648 8292 F: (0902) 648 8046
E: info@southrosleader.ie
Contact: Pat Daly

CATEGORIES: COMMUNITY & RURAL DEVELOPMENT; GRANTS; TOURISM DEVELOPMENT; TRAINING

Mid-South Roscommon LEADER administers the **LEADER+** and National Rural Development programmes in South Roscommon.

MILLENNIUM ENTREPRENEUR FUND

4 Charleville, Lower Churchtown Road, Dublin 14
T: (01) 295 1959
E: tshiels@iol.ie
Contact: Tony Shiels

CATEGORIES: EQUITY

The Millennium Entrepreneur Fund is a €1.5 million fund (NOW CLOSED) established by **Bank of Ireland**, **Enterprise Ireland** and other investors.

MOMENTUM, THE NORTHERN IRELAND ICT FEDERATION

Phillip House, 123–137 York Street, Belfast BT15 1AB
T: (028) 9033 3939 F: (028) 9033 3454
E: info@momentumNI.org W: www.sif.co.uk

CATEGORIES: INFORMATION; NETWORKING

Momentum represents Northern Ireland companies with a common interest in the growth and development of the software industry. Membership includes software developers, in-house computing departments, hardware suppliers, computer services companies, universities and colleges, and consultants.

MONAGHAN COUNTY ENTERPRISE BOARD

Unit 9, M:TEK Building, Knockaconny, Monaghan
T: (047) 71818 F: (047) 84786
E: info@mceb.ie W: www.mceb.ie
Contact: John McEntegart, CEO

CATEGORIES: DEBT; E-BUSINESS; EQUITY; GRANTS; INFORMATION; MENTORING; START-UP TRAINING; TRAINING

The role of the Monaghan County Enterprise Board is to develop indigenous potential and stimulate economic activity at local level, primarily through the provision of financial and technical assistance, as well as ongoing non-financial enterprise supports. The Monaghan CEB Company Directory is a free listing of all the companies that work with the CEB.

MONAGHAN PARTNERSHIP BOARD
Monaghan Road, Castleblaney, Co Monaghan
T: (042) 974 9500 F: (042) 974 9504
E: info@monaghanpartnership.com
Contact: Lorraine McKenna, Manager

CATEGORIES: COMMUNITY & RURAL DEVELOPMENT

One of the **Area Partnerships** funded by **Area Development Management**, as part of its Local Development programme, Monaghan Partnership Board seeks to to devise and implement practical solutions that break down barriers preventing those who live with lack of opportunity from accessing training, education and employment options.

MOOREPARK TECHNOLOGY LTD
Moorepark, Fermoy, Co Cork
T: (025) 42222 F: (025) 42340
E: stuohy@moorepark.teagasc.ie
W: www.teagasc.org/research/research_centres.htm
Contact: Dr Sean Tuohy, General Manager

CATEGORIES: CONSULTING; R & D

Moorepark Technology Ltd is a joint venture between **Teagasc** and commercial food companies. It provides pilot plant and research services to the food processing industry, including: Contract R & D; Small-scale manufacturing; Technical consultancy

MORAN & ASSOCIATES
36 Rushbrook Park, Templeogue, Dublin 6W
T: (01) 450 0084 F: (01) 450 0084
E: brendanmoran@iol.ie
Contact: Brendan Moran

CATEGORIES: START-UP TRAINING; TRAINING

Moran & Associates provide training for start-ups and existing small businesses.

MOUNTMELLICK DEVELOPMENT ASSOCIATION SOCIAL INCLUSION LTD
Irishtown, Mountmellick, Co Laois
T: (0502) 24525 F: (0502) 44343
E: mdaltd@indigo.ie W: www.mda-mdasi.com
Contact: Mary Dolan, Programme Manager

CATEGORIES: COMMUNITY & RURAL DEVELOPMENT

Mountmellick Development Association is one of the **Community Groups** funded by **Area Development Management**, as part of its Local Development programme. it now delivers the Local Development Social Inclusion Programme. MDA has been instrumental in the development of the Mountmellick Business Park, providing greater opportunities for enterprise.

MOVETOIRELAND.com

Ambit Ireland Internet Services Ltd, Currabaha, Dungarvan, Co Waterford
T: (058) 45066
E: info@irishireland.com W: www.movetoireland.com
Contact: Scott Simons

CATEGORIES: INFORMATION; INWARDS INVESTMENT; WEBSITE

MoveToIreland.com provides useful information (from an American now resident in Ireland) on preparing, making and surviving the move. Part of the site is free, part available on subscription (US$30 pa).

MOYLE ENTERPRISE COMPANY LTD

61 Leyland Road, Ballycastle, Co Antrim BT54 6EZ
T: (028) 2076 3737 F: (028) 2076 9690
E: moyle.enterprise@dnet.co.uk
Contact: Colette McMullen, Manager

CATEGORIES: INFORMATION; START-UP TRAINING; TRAINING; WORKSPACE

Moyle Enterprise is an **Enterprise Agency** and a member of **Enterprise Northern Ireland.**

MUINTIR NA TÍRE

Canon Hayes House, Tipperary
T: (062) 51163 F: (062) 51200
E: headoffice@muintir.ie W: www.muintirnatire.com
Contact: Tom Fitzgerald, Chief Administrative Officer

CATEGORIES: COMMUNITY & RURAL DEVELOPMENT; GRANTS

A sector group within **LEADER+.**

NATIONAL ASSOCIATION OF BUILDING CO-OPERATIVES LTD

50 Merrion Square East, Dublin 2
T: (01) 661 2877 F: (01) 661 4462
E: admin@nabco.ie : www.nabco.ie

CATEGORIES: CO-OPERATIVES; INFORMATION

One of the organisations that provides Model Rules for the formation of worker and community co-operatives.

NATIONAL COLLEGE OF IRELAND

Mayor Street, IFSC, Dublin 1
T: (01) 406 0500 F: (01) 497 2200
E: info@ncirl.ie W: www.ncirl.ie

CATEGORIES: INFORMATION; TRAINING

Through its new campus in the IFSC, its network of 40 off-campus centres, on-site educational hubs within industry, and online programme, NCI provides leading edge programmes in Business, Management, Financial Services, Informatics, Humanities, and related fields. NCI encourages life-long learning through its website, **liveandlearn.ie.**

NATIONAL FEDERATION OF BUSINESS & PROFESSIONAL WOMEN'S CLUBS, IRELAND

E: national.president@bpw.ie
W: www.bpw.ie
Contact: Anne Reynolds Bowen, National President
CATEGORIES: NETWORKING; WOMEN

BPW Ireland organises the **02 Business and Professional Woman 2003 awards**.

NATIONAL FOOD CENTRE

Dunsinea, Castleknock, Dublin 15
T: (01) 805 9500 F: (01) 805 9550
E: vtarrant@nfc.teagasc.ie
W: www.teagasc.org/research/research_centres.htm
Contact: Dr Vivion Tarrant, Head of Centre
CATEGORIES: CONSULTING; R & D; TRAINING

The National Food Centre is a division of **Teagasc**. Its mission is to provide leadership and excellence in research, consultancy and training to the food sector, thereby encouraging product innovation and enhanced food safety and quality. It serves the meat, fish and poultry sectors, as well as vegetable, fruit and cereal processors. (The **Dairy Products Research Centre** provides support for the dairy sector.) The Centre supports food companies and start-up businesses with product and business development, including product formulation and pilot-scale manufacture. Its ISO-accredited laboratories provide back-up analysis and testing. The Centre conducts basic and strategic research on key aspects of food safety, quality and innovation.

NATIONAL GUILD OF MASTER CRAFTSMEN

3 Greenmount Lane, Harolds Cross, Dublin 12
T: (01) 473 2543 F: (01) 473 2018
E: info@nationalguild.ie W: www.nationalguild.ie
CATEGORIES: INFORMATION; REGULATOR & STANDARDS

An organisation dedicated to achieving the highest standards of quality and workmanship in all trades and disciplines. It operates a referral system for members.

NATIONAL INSTITUTE FOR TRANSPORT AND LOGISTICS

Dublin Institute of Technology, 17 Herbert Street, Dublin 2
T: (01) 669 0806 F: (01) 661 1943
E: nitl@dit.ie W: www.nitl.ie
Contact: Randal Faulkner, Director of Consulting
CATEGORIES: CONSULTING; TRAINING

NITL operates within the **Dublin Institute of Technology**. It works with Irish and international companies on projects involving logistics and supply chain management, and provides training in these areas.

NATIONAL IRISH BANK LTD
7-8 Wilton Terrace, Dublin 2
T: (01) 638 5000 F: (01) 638 5198
W: www.nib.ie
Contact: Brian Leydon, Sales
CATEGORIES: DEBT

NIB offers a range of banking facilities to assist in the creation and development of small and medium-sized businesses. Access is through any of NIB's branches or the specialist regional offices.

NATIONAL MICROELECTRONICS APPLICATION CENTRE
UL Building, National Technological Park, Limerick
T: (061) 334699 F: (061) 338500
E: j.oflaherty@mac.ie W: www.mac.ie
Contact: Dr John J. O'Flaherty, Technical Director
CATEGORIES: CONSULTING; E-BUSINESS; R & D

MAC is Ireland's primary electronics/software concept-to-product development company. It develops and web-enables products/services for entrepreneurs and industry, and provides complete end-to-end solutions that integrate embedded electronics, wireless communications and intelligent transactional web services.

NATIONAL MICROELECTRONICS RESEARCH CENTRE
University College Cork, Lee Maltings, Prospect Row, Cork
T: (021) 490 4177 F: (021) 427 0271
E: admin@nmrc.ie W: www.nmrc.ie
Contact: Professor Gabriel Crean, Director
CATEGORIES: CONSULTING; R & D; TRAINING

NMRC, operating within **University College Cork**, is a Centre of Excellence in selected Information and Communication Technologies fields. An advanced research division, with groups in the areas of computational modelling, nanotechnology, photonics and transducers, has been established to broaden NMRC's longer-term basic technological research base. NMRC provides Irish and European industry and higher education with access to an extensive range of technology from advanced research to new product development and the provision of technical support services. An Industry division provides a single entry point to industry R&D, services and training at NMRC.

NATIONAL SAFETY COUNCIL
4 Northbrook Road, Ranelagh, Dublin 6
T: (01) 496 3422 F: (01) 496 3306
E: info@nsc.ie W: www.nsc.ie
Contact: Gavin Freeman, Information Officer
CATEGORIES: INFORMATION; TRAINING

The National Safety Council promotes Road Safety and Fire Safety through education programmes, media campaigns and public relations activities.

NATIONAL SOFTWARE CENTRE
NSC Campus, Mahon, Cork
T: (021) 230 7005 F: (021) 230 7020
E: postmaster@corkbic.com W: www.corkbic.com
Contact: Michael O'Connor, Cork BIC

CATEGORIES: INCUBATOR

The Centre has been funded on a public-private partnership basis, with backing from Cork Corporation, **Enterprise Ireland**, ICC Bank, the **National Software Directorate**, and private investors. It is managed by **Cork Business Innovation Centre** as a software development hub in the southern region.

NATIONAL SOFTWARE DIRECTORATE
Enterprise Ireland, Merrion Hall, Strand Road, Sandymount, Dublin 4
T: (01) 206 6310 F: (01) 206 6278
E: info@nsd.ie W: www.nsd.ie
Contact: Jennifer Condon, Director

CATEGORIES: INFORMATION; NETWORKING

The NSD's website provides useful news on software developments, a directory of venture capital funding in Ireland, and useful publications.

NATIONAL STANDARDS AUTHORITY OF IRELAND
Glasnevin, Dublin 9
T: (01) 807 3800 F: (01) 807 3838
E: nsai@nsai.ie
Also at: The Granary, Michael Street, Limerick
T: (061) 411 872 F: (061) 411 874
E: delaneyv@nsai.ie W: www.nsai.ie
Contact: Vincent Delaney, Business Development Manager

CATEGORIES: INFORMATION; REGULATOR & STANDARDS

NSAI formulates, publishes and sells Irish Standards, part of the harmonised European and worldwide system of standards in which NSAI is a designated "National Standards Body". It also assists industry to understand and meet the technical, quality and safety requirements of harmonised European and international standards in the domestic and overseas markets and provides a comprehensive quality auditing and product certification service for industry and commerce in accordance with current European and international practice.

NATIONAL TECHNOLOGY PARK LIMERICK
Plassey Ltd, Park House, Limerick
T: (061) 336555 F: (061) 336545
E: parkhouse@shannon-dev.ie W: www.shannon-dev.ie/ntp/
Contact: Orla Kelly, Marketing Executive

CATEGORIES: INCUBATOR

The National Technological Park is home to over 90 high-technology and knowledge-based companies, employing close to 5,000 skilled people and consists of 30+ buildings with a total floor area of circa 1.5 million sq.ft. It includes Shannon Development's **InnovationWorks**, part of **Shannon Development's Knowledge Network**, which also houses **Limerick BIC**.

NATIONAL UNIVERSITY OF IRELAND GALWAY
University Road, Galway
T: (091) 524411 F: (091) 525700
E: joe.watson@mis.nuigalway.ie W: www.nuigalway.ie
Contact: Dr Joe Watson, Industrial Liaison Officer
CATEGORIES: COMMUNITY & RURAL DEVELOPMENT; EU INFORMATION;
START-UP TRAINING; TRAINING

NUIG offers part-time Programmes in Rural Development, aimed at community leaders and development agents, in conjunction with **FÁS**. Its European Centre for Information and the Promotion of Rural Development hosts **Carréfour Galway**. NUI Galway also runs a one-year Technology Enterprise Programme, part-funded by **Enterprise Ireland**.

NAVAN TRAVELLERS WORKSHOP LTD
P.O. Box 28, Fairgreen, Navan, Co Meath
T: (046) 27801 F: (046) 73298
E: infontw@eircom.net
Contact: David Murray
CATEGORIES: COMMUNITY & RURAL DEVELOPMENT

Navan Travellers Workshop is one of the **Community Groups** funded by **Area Development Management**, as part of its Local Development programme.

NCB VENTURES
3 George's Dock, IFSC, Dublin 1
T: (01) 611 5611 F: (01) 611 5999
E: info@ncb.ie W: www.ncb.ie
Contact: Tommy Conway (tommy.conway@ncb.ie)
CATEGORIES: EQUITY

NCB Ventures is the venture capital arm of **Ulster Bank**, dealing with investments ranging from €75,000 to €900,000 — the average investment is €250,000. It manages investment funds directed at small to medium-sized enterprises with significant growth potential. It manages the **Guinness Ulster Bank Equity Fund** and has €13 million in **BES** funds under management.

NDP.ie
W: www.ndp.ie
CATEGORIES: INFORMATION; WEBSITE

NDP.ie is the website for the National Development Plan, the source of much of the current round of development funding in Ireland.

NENAGH COMMUNITY NETWORK
84 Connolly Street, Nenagh, Co Tipperary
T: (067) 34900 F: (067) 34088
E: ncn@eircom.net
Contact: Pat Power, Manager
CATEGORIES: COMMUNITY & RURAL DEVELOPMENT

Nenagh Community Network is one of the **Community Groups** funded by **Area Development Management**, as part of its Local Development programme.

NETWORK IRELAND
P.O. Box 306, Naas, co Kildare
T: (01) 499 1086
E: jacquieh@eircom.net W: www.networkireland.ie
Contact: Jacquie Hennessey, National President
CATEGORIES: INFORMATION; NETWORKING; TRAINING; WOMEN

Network is a national organisation for women in business, management, the professions and the arts. It facilitates women in the promotion and development of their careers through regular meetings and educational seminars.

NEWRY & MOURNE ENTERPRISE AGENCY
Enterprise House, WIN Business Park, Canal Quay, Newry,
Co Down BT35 6PH
T: (028) 3026 7011 F: (028) 3026 1316
E: info@nmea.net W: www.nmea.net
Contact: Conor Patterson, Chief Executive
CATEGORIES: CROSS-BORDER; DEBT; INCUBATOR; INFORMATION; INWARDS INVESTMENT; START-UP TRAINING; TRAINING

Newry & Mourne Enterprise Agency is an **Enterprise Agency** and a member of *Enterprise Northern Ireland*. It manages the WIN Business Park in Newry, a Regional Development Centre (RDC) also at WIN, an Enterprise Centre in Warrenpoint and centres at Flurrybridge and Crossmaglen in South Armagh. It is planning to develop an Enterprise Centre in Kilkeel in 2004. NMEA offers cross-border support to start-ups and existing businesses. "Do Business in Ireland", for example, is operated with **Louth County Enterprise Board**, as a cross-border programme aimed at attracting inwards investment. NMEA is one of the enterprise agencies that offers the **Enter Enterprise** programme for intending entrepreneurs.

NEWRY & MOURNE LOCAL ACTION GROUP
Bank Parade, Newry, Co Down BT35 6HP
T: (028) 3026 3177 F: (028) 3026 3395
E: info@newryandmourneleader.com W: www.newryandmourneleader.com
Contact: Miceal McCoy
CATEGORIES: COMMUNITY & RURAL DEVELOPMENT

A local rural development company contracted to deliver the **LEADER +** Programme in the Newry & Mourne District.

NEWTOWNABBEY ENTERPRISE DEVELOPMENT ORGANISATION LTD

Mallusk Enterprise Park, Mallusk Drive, Newtownabbey, Co Antrim BT36 4GN
T: (028) 9083 8860 F: (028) 9084 1525
E: info@mallusk.org W: www.mallusk.org
Contact: Deborah Johnston, General Manager

CATEGORIES: DEBT; INFORMATION; START-UP TRAINING; TRAINING; WORKSPACE

Newtownabbey Enterprise Development Organisation is an **Enterprise Agency** and a member of **Enterprise Northern Ireland**. It offers workspace, start-up and ongoing training and loans.

NORIBIC (BUSINESS INNOVATION CENTRE, DERRY)

Northland Building, NWIFHE, Strand Road, Derry, Northern Ireland BT48 7AY
T: (028) 7126 4242 F: (028) 7126 9025
E: noribic@nwifhe.ac.uk W: www.noribic.com
Contact: Dr Bernard R Toal, Chief Executive

CATEGORIES: BUSINESS PLANS; EQUITY; GRANTS; INCUBATOR; INFORMATION; MARKETING; START-UP TRAINING; TRAINING

NORIBIC provides support services for those seeking to start their own businesses or to develop existing businesses into sustainable, well-managed innovative businesses. It offers: Business planning; Acquisition of business start and development capital; Market planning and development; Development of innovative management techniques; Creativity and innovation audits; "Start Your Own Business" courses; and Finance.

NORTH ANTRIM LEADER

Old Schoolhouse, 25 Mill Street, Cushendall, Ballymena BT44 0RR
T: (028) 2177 2138 F: (028) 2177 2137
E: north-antrim-leader@antrim.net W: www.northantrimleader.org
Contact: Andrew McAlister

CATEGORIES: COMMUNITY & RURAL DEVELOPMENT

One of the **LEADER+** groups in Northern Ireland. It aims to promote and assist small rural business in North Antrim, which covers the Ballymena, Ballymoney, Larne and Moyle district council areas.

NORTH CITY BUSINESS CENTRE LTD

2 Duncairn Gardens, Belfast BT15 2GG
T: (028) 9074 7470 F: (028) 9074 6565
E: info@north-city.co.uk W: www.north-city.co.uk
Contact: Michael McCorry, Manager

CATEGORIES: DEBT; INFORMATION; START-UP TRAINING; TRAINING; WORKSPACE

North City Business Centre is an **Enterprise Agency** and a member of **Enterprise Northern Ireland**. It offers workspace, start-up and ongoing training and loans. North City Business Centre is a purpose built business park located in the north inner city area of Belfast. It encourages the development of small and medium-sized businesses in the surrounding community, thereby creating employment and providing a focus for the social and economic regeneration of the district.

NORTH DOWN DEVELOPMENT ORGANISATION LTD

Enterprise House, 2-4 Balloo Avenue, Balloo Industrial Estate, Bangor,
Co Down BT19 7QT
T: (028) 9127 1525 F: (028) 9127 0080
E: mail@nddo.u-net.com W: www.nddo.u-net.com
Contact: Lynne Vance, Chief Executive

CATEGORIES: INFORMATION; START-UP TRAINING; TRAINING; WORKSPACE

North Down Development Organisation is an **Enterprise Agency** and a member of **Enterprise Northern Ireland**.

NORTH EAST ENTERPRISE PROGRAMME

Regional Development Centre, Dundalk Institute of Technology, Dublin Road,
Dundalk, Co Louth
T: (042) 937 0511 / 937 0413 F: (042) 935 1412
E: fiona.odonnell@dkit.ie W: www.rdc.ie
Contact: Fiona O'Donnell, Programme Manager

CATEGORIES: CROSS-BORDER; INCUBATOR; START-UP TRAINING

The North East Enterprise Programme is a cross-border enterprise support programme, operated by the **Regional Development Centre**, and designed to assist entrepreneurs and existing small companies with technology-based product or service ideas. Entrepreneurs selected to participate in the programme are offered support services to help them through the early stages of business development. See also **Enterprise Programmes** for EPs in other locations.

NORTH KERRY TOGETHER LTD

58 Church Street, Listowel, Co Kerry
T: (068) 23429 F: (068) 22930
E: nktlocaldevelopment@eircom.net W: www.northkerry.ie
Contact: Robert Carey, Manager

CATEGORIES: COMMUNITY & RURAL DEVELOPMENT

North Kerry Together is one of the **Community Groups** funded by **Area Development Management**, as part of its Local Development programme.

NORTH MEATH COMMUNITIES DEVELOPMENT ASSOCIATION

Catherine McAuley Centre, Kenlis Place, Kells, Co Meath
T: (046) 49300 F: (046) 49022
E: nmcda@eircom.net
Contact: John Burns

CATEGORIES: COMMUNITY & RURAL DEVELOPMENT

North Meath Communities Development Association is one of the **Community Groups** funded by **Area Development Management**, as part of its Local Development programme.

NORTHERN BANK LTD

Business Services Department, Donegall Square West, Belfast BT1 6JS
T: (028) 9024 5277 F: (028) 9023 1349
E: colm.dundas@eu.nabgroup.com W: www.nbonline.co.uk
Contact: Colm Dundas, Head of Business Services

CATEGORIES: DEBT

As well as traditional banking services, Northern Bank offers specialist services in foreign exchange, leasing and hire purchase, debtor finance, corporate banking and agriculture.

NORTHERN IRELAND BUSINESS START PROGRAMME

W: www.nibsp.com

CATEGORIES: START-UP TRAINING

The Northern Ireland Business Start Programme provides a package of support to anyone interested in setting up a business. It offers: A business advisory service; A training cours; Financial planning service. The programme is delivered free of charge by the local enterprise agencies that are members of **Enterprise Northern Ireland**, the **Belfast First Stop Shop** and **Enterprise North West**. It is funded by **Invest Northern Ireland**, the 26 District Councils and the European Regional Development Fund.

NORTHERN IRELAND CENTRE IN EUROPE

33 Clarendon Dock, Laganside, Belfast BT1 3BT
T: (028) 9043 5800 F: (028) 9043 5801
E: focus@ni-centre-in-europe.com

CATEGORIES: EU INFORMATION

NICE provides its members summaries of key EU developments focused on the needs of Northern Ireland.

NORTHERN IRELAND CENTRE FOR ENTREPRENEURSHIP

Room 2B22, University of Ulster, Shore Road, Newtownabbey, BT37 0QB
T: (028) 9036 6018 F: (028) 9036 6015
E: nicent@ulster.ac.uk W: www.ulster.ac.uk/nicent/
Contact: Peter Corrigan, Centre Manager

CATEGORIES: INFORMATION; START-UP TRAINING; TRAINING

NICENT is led by the **University of Ulster** in partnership with **Queens University Belfast** and **Loughry College**. Its primary aim is to promote and support entrepreneurship in science and technology subjects. It also aims to embed a culture of entrepreneurship within the university community.

NORTHERN IRELAND CHAMBER OF COMMERCE & INDUSTRY

22 Great Victoria Street, Belfast BT2 7BJ
T: (028) 9024 4113 F: (028) 9024 7024
E: mail@northernirelandchamber.com W: www.nicci.co.uk

CATEGORIES: INFORMATION; NETWORKING

NICCI represents 4,000 member businesses across Northern Ireland. It provides members with a broad range of services and events.

NORTHERN IRELAND FOOD & DRINK ASSOCIATION

Quay Gate House, 15 Scrabo Street, Belfast BT5 4BD
T: (028) 9045 2424 F: (028) 9045 3373
E: mbell@nifda.co.uk W: www.nifda.co.uk
Contact: Michael Bell, Executive Director

CATEGORIES: INFORMATION; MARKETING; NETWORKING; TRAINING

NIFDA is a voluntary organisation committed to helping Northern Ireland food and beverage companies compete successfully and to represent and promote their interests. It was established to provide services to enhance, promote, inform, educate and develop member businesses.

NORTHERN IRELAND SCIENCE PARK

Queen's Road, Queen's Island, Belfast, BT3 9DT
T: (028) 9053 4560 F: (028) 9053 4561
E: www.nisp.co.uk W: www.nisp.co.uk
Contact: Michael Graham

CATEGORIES: INCUBATOR

The Northern Ireland Science Park aims to be a hub for knowledge-based businesses on the island. Its first building, a 56,000 sq ft Innovation Centre, has been completed and work on the **Queen's University Belfast** Electronics, Communications and Information Technology Research Institute is well underway. Both the Queen's University and **University of Ulster** are partners in the park.

NORTHERN IRELAND STATISTICS & RESEARCH AGENCY

McAuley House, 2-14 Castle Street, Belfast BT1 1SA
T: (028) 9034 8100 F: (028) 9034 8106
E: norman.caven@dfpni.gov.uk W: www.nisra.gov.uk
Contact: Dr. Norman Caven, Acting Chief Executive (T: (028) 9034 8102)

CATEGORIES: INFORMATION

NISRA is an Executive Agency within the Department of Finance and Personnel. It provides statistics, social research and registration services, and is responsible for the census of population.

NORTHERN IRELAND TOURIST BOARD
St Anne's Court, 59 North Street, Belfast BT1 1NB
T: (028) 9023 1221 F: (028) 9024 0960
E: info@nitb.com W: www.discovernorthernireland.com
CATEGORIES: GRANTS; INFORMATION; MARKETING; TOURISM DEVELOPMENT
NITB provides funding for marketing tourism projects in Northern Ireland.

NORTH MAYO PARTNERSHIP
See **Meitheal Mhaigh Eo.**

NORTH WEST KILDARE/NORTH OFFALY PARTNERSHIP
See **OAK Partnership.**

NORTHSIDE PARTNERSHIP
Coolock Development Centre, Bunratty Drive, Coolock, Dublin 17
T: (01) 848 5630 F: (01) 848 5661
E: denise.brennan@northsidepartnership.ie
W: www.northsidepartnership.ie
Contact: Denise Brennan, Enterprise Projects Co-ordinator
CATEGORIES: COMMUNITY & RURAL DEVELOPMENT; INCUBATOR;
INFORMATION; MENTORING; START-UP TRAINING

One of the **Area Partnerships** established by **Area Development Management**, as part of its Local Development programme. Since 1993, the Northside Partnership has been providing an enterprise support service to unemployed local people. The cornerstone of this service is delivered on a one-to-one basis by the enterprise officers who provide advice, support and information to clients.

NovaUCD
University College Dublin, Belfield, Dublin 4
T: (01) 716 3707 F: (01) 716 3707
E: nova@ucd.ie W: www.novaucd.ie
Contact: Peter Finnegan, Project Manager - Enterprise Development
CATEGORIES: INCUBATOR; INTELLECTUAL PROPRTY

NovaUCD is an innovation and technology transfer centre on the **UCD** campus. It provides support for entrepreneurs and campus companies, including: Advice and support on project development - Technology and Marketing; Building the entrepreneurial team; Developing the business model; Financial planning and management; Preparation of business plans; Company formation; Access to finance; Business growth. NovaUCD is also responible for the management of intellectual property arising from UCD research programmes.

O'CONNOR, LEDDY & HOLMES

Century House, Harold's Cross Road, Dublin 6W
T: (01) 496 1444 F: (01) 496 1637
E: oclh@iol.ie W: www.oclh.ie
Contact: JD Leddy

CATEGORIES: ACCOUNTANTS; BUSINESS PLANS

O'Connor, Leddy & Holmes is a firm of chartered accountants and business consultants, which offers accountancy, taxation, business planning and funding application services to Irish companies.

O2 BUSINESS & PROFESSIONAL WOMAN 2003

National Federation of Business and Professional Women's Clubs, Ireland,
Ballymanagh, Craughwell, Co Galway
W: www.bpw.ie
Contact: Ann M Torres

CATEGORIES: COMPETITIONS; WOMEN

This competition aims to identify, reward and promote outstanding women in business in the Republic of Ireland and is managed by **National Federation of Business and Professional Women's Clubs, Ireland**.

OAK PARTNERSHIP

Edenderry Business Park, Edenderry, Co Offaly
T: (0405) 32688 F: (0405) 32690
E: oakpart@iol.ie W: www.offaly.ie/developmentorganisations/oak.asp
Contact: Pat Leogue, Manager

CATEGORIES: COMMUNITY & RURAL DEVELOPMENT; GRANTS; INCUBATOR;
INFORMATION; SOCIAL ECONOMY; START-UP TRAINING; TRAINING

The North West Kildare/North Offaly Partnership is better known as the OAK (Offaly and Kildare) Partnership. It is one of the **Area Partnerships** funded by **Area Development Management**, as part of its Local Development programme. OAK provides financial support — grant assistance, interest subsidy and loan guarantees — for the unemployed to develop enterprise projects. Advice on business planning, finance and insurance and other issues is also available. For community groups, facilitation and training is supported and encouraged as a prerequisite to project funding.

OAK TREE PRESS

19 Rutland Street, Cork
T: (021) 431 3855 F: (021) 431 3496
E: info@oaktreepress.com W: www.oaktreepress.com
Contact: Brian O'Kane

CATEGORIES: INFORMATION; PUBLICATIONS; START-UP TRAINING; TRAINING;
WEBSITE

Ireland's leading business book publisher, focussed on titles relevant to Irish SMEs, many of them standards in their field. Oak Tree Press is now an international developer and publisher of enterprise training and support materials. It also offers training for entrepreneurs – see website.

OBAIR NEWMARKET-ON-FERGUS LTD
Main Street, Newmarket-on-Fergus, Co Clare
T: (061) 368030 F: (061) 368717
E: obairnewmarket@tinet.ie W: www.shannonheartland.ie
Contact: Aine Mellet, Manager

CATEGORIES: COMMUNITY & RURAL DEVELOPMENT

OBAIR Newmarket-on-Fergus is one of the **Community Groups** funded by **Area Development Management**, as part of its Local Development programme.

OFFALY COUNTY ENTERPRISE BOARD
Cormac Street, Tullamore, Co Offaly
T: (0506) 52971/2 F: (0506) 52973
E: info@offalyceb.ie W: www.offaly.ie/businessnet.asp
Contact: Seán Ryan, CEO

CATEGORIES: DEBT; E-BUSINESS; EQUITY; GRANTS; INFORMATION; MENTORING; START-UP TRAINING; TRAINING

The Offaly County Enterprise Board develops and supports local entrepreneurship and enterprise within the framework of a coherent, integrated county action plan so as to build a local economy of real strength and permanence. It manages the County Enterprise Fund, which assists through grant-aid in the establishment of small-scale economic projects. It also operates a "walk-in" Enterprise Information Centre.

OFFALY LEADER + COMPANY LTD
Rural and Community Development Centre, Harbour Street, Tullamore, Co Offaly
T: (0506) 22850 F: (0506) 22851
E: admin@offalyleader.ie W: www.offalyleader.ie
Contact: Perpetua McDonagh Programme Manager

CATEGORIES: COMMUNITY & RURAL DEVELOPMENT; GRANTS

A **LEADER+** company serving Co Offaly, Offaly LEADER offers capital equipment grants to innovative, small enterprises in manufacturing, crafts or local services at start-up or development stage, within its operational area.

OMAGH ENTERPRISE COMPANY LTD
Omagh Business Complex, Gortrush Industrial Estate, Great Northern Road, Omagh, Co Tyrone BT78 5LU
T: (028) 8224 9494 F: (028) 8224 9451
E: info@oecl.co.uk W: www.oecl.co.uk

CATEGORIES: DEBT; INFORMATION; START-UP TRAINING; TRAINING; WORKSPACE

Omagh Enterprise Company is an **Enterprise Agency** and a member of **Enterprise Northern Ireland**. See also **Choose Enterprise**.

OPTIMUM RESULTS LTD

Carroll House, Carroll Village, Dundalk, Co. Louth
T: (042) 933 3033 F: (042) 933 3233
E: info@optimumresults.ie W: www.optimumresults.ie
Contact: Aidan Harte, Managing director
Also at: Zion Court, Zion Road, Rathgar, Dublin 6
T: (01) 497 0082

CATEGORIES: START-UP TRAINING; TRAINING

Optimum Results provides training for SMEs, including a "Dynamic Business Start-up" in association with **Fingal County Enterprise Board**.

ORGANIC COLLEGE

Dromcollogher, Co Limerick
T: (063) 83604 F: (063) 83604
E: ionadglas.ias@eircom.net W: www.organiccollege.com
Contact: Dr Sinéad Neiland, Jim McNamara

CATEGORIES: TRAINING

The Organic College offers a Diploma in Organic Enterprise, including six months' work placement and mentoring by organic producers.

ORMEAU BUSINESS PARK

8 Cromac Avenue, Belfast BT7 2AJ
T: (028) 9033 9906 F: (028) 9033 9937
E: info@ormeaubusinesspark.com W: www.ormeaubusinesspark.com
Contact: Patricia McNeill, Business Development Manager

CATEGORIES: BUSINESS PLANS; MARKETING; MENTORING; START-UP
TRAINING; WORKSPACE

Ormeau Business Park is an **Enterprise Agency** and a member of **Enterprise NorthernIreland**. Its aims are to: Promote enterprise awareness; Assist in the development of new business start-ups and the further expansion of existing businesses; Encourage entrepreneurs to fulfil their potential; Respond to local needs by supporting economic development in the area. It offers 33,000 sq ft of workspace, as well as free business advice and support.

ORTUS, THE WEST BELFAST ENTERPRISE BOARD

Twin Spires Centre, Curran House, 155 Northumberland Street, Belfast BT1 3 2JF
T: (028) 9031 1002 F: (028) 9031 1005
E: hq@ortus.org W: www.ortus.org

CATEGORIES: CONSULTING; DEBT; INFORMATION; START-UP TRAINING;
TRAINING; WOMEN; WORKSPACE

ORTUS is an **Enterprise Agency** and a member of **Enterprise Northern Ireland**. As well as managing three enterprise centres in West Belfast, it administers its own ORTUS Business Loan Fund. It also provides consultancy and training, including a "Women into Business" programme.

YOUR NEXT STEP

...

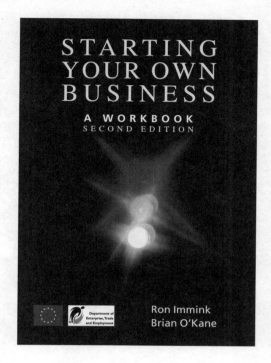

STARTING YOUR OWN BUSINESS: A WORKBOOK,
THE standard for business planning for start-ups in
Ireland. Packed full of advice and information in a
logical, easy-to-follow sequence, **STARTING YOUR OWN
BUSINESS** has helped over 25,000 Irish entrepreneurs.
Complete with Business Plan templates.

Available from good bookshops
or direct from **OAK TREE PRESS**,
LoCall 1890 313855.

www.oaktreepress.com

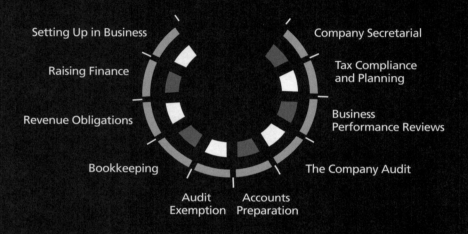

OSK ACCOUNTANTS & BUSINESS CONSULTANTS

East Point Plaza, East Point, Dublin 3
T: (01) 439 4200 F: (01) 439 4299
E: advice@osk.ie W: www.osk.ie

CATEGORIES: ACCOUNTANTS; CONSULTING

OSK Small Business Support is the leading supplier of audit and taxation services in the SME market and provides a full-service package that assists and supports clients in all aspects of their business from start-up to development and expansion. OSK also provides advice on all areas of starting your own business including company set-up, business plans, raising finance, audit, and taxation services.

PÁIRTÍOCHT CHONAMARA & ÁRANN

See **Cumas Teo**.

PÁIRTÍOCHT GAELTACHT THÍR CHONAILL

MFG Teo, Aonad Earagail 1, An t-Eastát Tionsclaíoch, Na Doirí Beaga,
Leitir Ceanainn, Co Dún na nGall
T: (075) 32017 F: (075) 32428
E: mfgtc@eircom.net
Contact: Eithne Nic Lochlainn, Manager

CATEGORIES: COMMUNITY & RURAL DEVELOPMENT; INFORMATION; START-UP
TRAINING

One of the **Area Partnerships** funded by **Area Development Management**, as part of its Local Development programme. Páirtíocht Ghaeltacht Thír Chonaill is a regional office of **Meitheal Forbartha na Gaeltachta Teo**.

PALO ALTO SOFTWARE UK
72 Hammersmith Road, London W14 8TH
T: 0207 559 3500 F: 0207 900 2773
E: info@paloalto.co.uk W: www.paloalto.ie / www.paloalto.co.uk
Contact: Alan Gleeson, Managing director
CATEGORIES: BUSINESS PLANS

Palo Alto Software Ltd is the developer of the UK editions of Business Plan Pro and Business Plan Premier, the award winning business planning software developed by Palo Alto Software, Inc. Business Plan Pro/Premier are endorsed by SFEDI, the Small Firms Enterprise Development Initiative, a UK government-appointed organisation that works with practitioners in small business training, education and advice to make sure that there are good quality, accessible websites, training products, programmes and qualifications in the market to help entrepreneurs and endorses suitable products with its logo. See also **www.bplans.org.uk** and **www.bplans.ie**.

PARTAS
Bolbrook Enterprise Centre, Avonmore Road, Tallaght, Dublin 24
T: (01) 414 5700 F: (01) 414 5799
E: mcollins@partas.ie W: www.partas.ie
Contact: Miriam Collins
CATEGORIES: COMMUNITY & RURAL DEVELOPMENT; CONSULTING; INCUBATOR; MENTORING; START-UP TRAINING; TRAINING; WORKSPACE

Partas is one of Ireland's leading providers of enterprise support for start-up, micro and small firms. It provides a one-to-one enterprise development and business support service in Tallaght for the Tallaght Partnership, targeted at the long-term unemployed who wish to enter into self-employment. Partas offers the New Enterprise Support Thrust (NEST) programme, which provides a structured framework of support for start-ups. It also offers affordable office and workshop space in four centres in Tallaght: Bolbrook, Brookfield Enterprise Centre, Killinarden and Main Road, Tallaght. Partas also provides consulting and training for community and enterprise groups on a national basis.

PARTNERSHIP TRÁ LÍ
37 Ashe Street, Tralee, Co Kerry
T: (066) 718 0190 F: (066) 712 9562
E: mail@partnershiptrali.com W: www.partnershiptrali.com
Contact: Seamus O'Hara, Manager; Anne Hennessy, Micro Enterprise Officer (E: ahennessy@partnershiptrali.com); Tom O'Leary, Community Enterprise Officer (E: toleary@partnershiptrali.com)
CATEGORIES: COMMUNITY & RURAL DEVELOPMENT; GRANTS; INFORMATION; MENTORING; START-UP TRAINING; TRAINING

Partnership Tra Lí is one of the **Area Partnerships** funded by **Area Development Management**, as part of its Local Development programme.
Its Enterprise Unit offers clients access to a loan fund in association with **First Step**, as well as a Mentoring programme.

PATENTS OFFICE

Government Buildings, Hebron Road, Kilkenny
T: (056) 772 0111; LoCall 1890 220 223 F: (056) 772 0100
E: patlib@entemp.ie W: www.patentsoffice.ie
Contact: Declan Finlay
Also at: Patents Information Office, Earlsfort Centre, Lower Hatch Street, Dublin 2
T: (01) 631 2603; LoCall 1890 220 222 F: (01) 631 2551
CATEGORIES: INFORMATION; INTELLECTUAL PROPERTY

The principal statutory functions of the Office are: The granting of patents; The registration of industrial designs and trade marks; Providing information in relation to patents, designs and trade marks; Certain Ltd functions under the Copyright Act in relation to copyright disputes.

PAUL PARTNERSHIP LIMERICK

Unit 25, The Tait Centre, Dominic Street, Limerick
T: (061) 419388 F: (061) 418098
E: info@paulpartnership.ie W: www.planet.ie
Contact: Ann Kavanagh, Manager
CATEGORIES: BUSINESS PLANS; COMMUNITY & RURAL DEVELOPMENT;
INFORMATION; MENTORING; START-UP TRAINING

One of the **Area Partnerships** funded by **Area Development Management**, as part of its Local Development programme. It supported the establishment of the **Limerick Enterprise Development Partnership**. It provides entrepreneurs and start-up businesses with advice on business planning and the Back-to-Work Allowance. It also offers mentoring.

PDC

Docklands Innovation Park, 128-130 East Wall Road, Dublin 3
T: (01) 240 1300 F: (01) 240 1310
E: info@pdc.ie W: www.pdc.ie
Contact: Bernadette O'Reilly
CATEGORIES: BUSINESS PLANS; EQUITY; INCUBATOR; INFORMATION;
MENTORING; NETWORKING; START-UP TRAINING; TRAINING

The Project Development Centre (PDC), an intiative of the **Dublin Institute of Technology,** is an incubator that provides enterprise development programmes, incubation space and facilities, business counselling, funding and access to R&D expertise as a package that allows entrepreneurs to start up and grow global businesses. Through its network, PDC helps innovative companies to access markets, strategic partners and venture capital. Programmes at PDC include: PROSPECT, HotHouse and Fast Growth. The PDC, in conjunction with the **Bolton Trust**, is a promoter of the **Small Enterprise Seed Fund**.

PREMIER BUSINESS CENTRES
128 Lower Baggot Street, Dublin 2
T: (01) 639 1100
E: tmullane@premgroup.com
W: www.premierbusinesscentres.com
Contact: Therese Mullane, Business Development Manager
CATEGORIES: WORKSPACE

Premier Business Centres provide both serviced and unserviced office accommodation, offering traditional Georgian buildings in the heart of Dublin city centre and modern purpose-built facilities in suburban Dublin and Belfast city centre. It offers companies a complete move-in package on flexible lease terms that includes office furniture, telephone systems, full computer networking with a number of connectivity options ranging from ISDN to ADSL, secretarial and reception staff, along with boardroom and equipment hire. It also offers a virtual office service, "Premier Connection", which provides companies with a mailing address, dedicated phone number and line answering the company name, from €130 monthly. This service was designed for companies or individuals wishing to establish a presence and test the market, without committing to an office.

PRICEWATERHOUSECOOPERS
Wilton Place, Dublin 2
T: (01) 678 9999 F: (01) 662 6200
E: mark.b.lynch@ie.pwc.com W: www.pwc.com/ie/eds
Contact: Mark Lynch, Enterprise Development Services
CATEGORIES: ACCOUNTANTS; BUSINESS PLANS; CONSULTING; PUBLICATIONS

PricewaterhouseCoopers' Enterprise Development Services practice works with start-up entrepreneurs to develop business plans, prepare financial projections, raise finance, identify opportunities to avail of grant aid, and establish businesses in as tax-efficient a manner as possible.

PRINCE'S TRUST NORTHERN IRELAND
Block 5, Jennymount Court, North Derby Street, Belfast BT15 3HN
T: (028) 9074 5454 F: (028) 9074 8416
E: ptnire@princes-trust.org.uk W: www.princes-trust.org.uk
Contact: Tommy Fegan, Director
CATEGORIES: DEBT; GRANTS; INCUBATOR; MENTORING; TRAINING

The Prince's Trust Northern Ireland is the largest cross-community charity investing in young people. Through its Business Programme, the Trust offers: Low interest loans of up to stg£5,000; Test marketing grants of up to stg£250; Bursaries of up to stg£1,500; Up to three years' mentor support; Incubation workspace. Applicants should be: Aged 18–30; Unemployed, under-employed or of Ltd means; Unable to raise all the necessary finance from banks, families or other sources; Have completed an appropriate business training course, and have a viable business plan.

PREMIER BUSINESS CENTRES
128 Lower Baggot Street, Dublin 2
T: (01) 639 1100
E: tmullane@premgroup.com
W: www.premierbusinesscentre.com
Contact: Therese Mullane, Business Development Manager

CATEGORIES: WORKSPACE

Premier Business Centres provide both serviced and unserviced office accommodation, offering traditional Georgian buildings in the heart of Dublin city centre and modern purpose-built facilities in suburban Dublin and Belfast city centre. It offers companies a complete move-in package on flexible lease terms that includes office furniture, telephone systems, full computer networking with a number of connectivity options ranging from ISDN to ADSL, secretarial and reception staff, along with boardroom and equipment hire. It also offers a virtual office service, "Premier Connection", which provides companies with a mailing address, dedicated phone number and line answering the company name, from €130 monthly. This service was designed for companies or individuals wishing to establish a presence and test the market, without committing to an office.

PRICEWATERHOUSECOOPERS
Wilton Place, Dublin 2
T: (01) 678 9999 F: (01) 662 6200
E: mark.b.lynch@ie.pwc.com W: www.pwc.com/ie/eds
Contact: Mark Lynch, Enterprise Development Services

CATEGORIES: ACCOUNTANTS; BUSINESS PLANS; CONSULTING; PUBLICATIONS

PricewaterhouseCoopers' Enterprise Development Services practice works with start-up entrepreneurs to develop business plans, prepare financial projections, raise finance, identify opportunities to avail of grant aid, and establish businesses in as tax-efficient a manner as possible.

PRINCE'S TRUST NORTHERN IRELAND
Block 5, Jennymount Court, North Derby Street, Belfast BT15 3HN
T: (028) 9074 5454 F: (028) 9074 8416
E: ptnire@princes-trust.org.uk W: www.princes-trust.org.uk
Contact: Tommy Fegan, Director

CATEGORIES: DEBT; GRANTS; INCUBATOR; MENTORING; TRAINING

The Prince's Trust Northern Ireland is the largest cross-community charity investing in young people. Through its Business Programme, the Trust offers: Low interest loans of up to stg£5,000; Test marketing grants of up to stg£250; Bursaries of up to stg£1,500; Up to three years' mentor support; Incubation workspace. Applicants should be: Aged 18–30; Unemployed, under-employed or of Ltd means; Unable to raise all the necessary finance from banks, families or other sources; Have completed an appropriate business training course, and have a viable business plan.

Welcome to...

PREMIER CONNECTION

- **Are you** starting up your own business?
- **Are you** working from home?
- **Are you** operating in Ireland and looking to test the Dublin market?
- **Are you** renting office space that you don't really need?
- **Are you** an overseas company looking at the possibility of setting up an office in Dublin?

Premier Connection is a **cost effective** and **efficient** way to run your business allowing you to have the benefits of operating from a fully serviced office, **without actually being in an office**.

With a Virtual Office you have a prestigious mailing address and dedicated phone answering in your company name **from as little as €130** per month.

PREMIER BUSINESS
C E N T R E S

Contact us at
Premier Business Centre
128 Lower Baggot Street, Dublin 2
Tel: +353 1 639 1248   Fax: +353 1 639 1102
E-mail: pbc@premgroup.com

www.premierbusinesscentre.com

Benefits and features

A prestigious business address in Dublin or Belfast

Dedicated call answering in your company name

Dedicated digital voicemail box

Daily, weekly office lets

Daily, weekly meeting room hire

Sign up for a month or a year

Progress to an office when business takes off

Standard Package includes*

Dedicated line answering in your company name

Dedicated digital voicemail box

Prime postal address

Mail handling

Fax number

*Can be tailored to suit individual needs

Price

Dublin City Centre   €200 per month
(Baggot, Pembroke, Fitzwilliam and Merrion Street)

Suburban Dublin   €130 per month
(Citywest, Sandyford and Tallaght)

Belfast   stg£85 per month

Additional services available

Day office lets

Dublin – €100 per day, subject to availability

Meeting room hire

Competitive pricing on hourly/daily basis

Capacity 2–80

PROFILES IRELAND

Harbour Business Centre, New Road, Kilcock, Co. Kildare
T: (01) 628 7037 F: (01) 628 7019
E: info@profilesireland.com W: www.profilesireland.com
Contact: Deiric McCann

CATEGORIES: CONSULTING

Profiles Ireland offers a number of online assessment tools for employers that help them to make better hiring, training, managing, and promoting decisions. The Profile answers four critical questions about a candidate for employment: Can the person do the job? Will the person do the job? Does the person have the personality to enjoy the job? Does the individual fit the job?

PUBLIC RELATIONS CONSULTANTS ASSOCIATION

78 Merrion Square, Dublin 2
T: (01) 661 8004 F: (01) 676 4562
E: info@prca.ie W: www.prca.ie

CATEGORIES: INFORMATION

The Public Relations Consultant Association Ireland represents most of the PR consultancy businesses in Ireland. It can help with selection of a consultancy. The PRCA is for consultancies, while the PRII is for individual PR practitioners.

PUBLIC RELATIONS INSTITUTE OF IRELAND

78 Merrion Square, Dublin 2
T: (01) 661 8004 F: (01) 676 4562
E: info@prii.ie W: www.prii.ie

CATEGORIES: INFORMATION

The Public Relations Institute of Ireland is the professional body for public relations practitioners (individuals) in Ireland. Note that the PRII is for individual PR practitioners, while the PRCA is for consultancies.

QUBIS LTD

Lanyon North, The Queen's University of Belfast, University Road, Belfast BT7 1NN
T: (028) 9068 2321 F: (028) 9027 3899
E: info@qubis.co.uk W: www.qubis.co.uk
Contact: Edward Cartin, Chief Executive

CATEGORIES: EQUITY

Qubis provides equity investment for technology-based businesses originating from the **Queen's University of Belfast**.

QUEEN'S UNIVERSITY BELFAST

Research & Regional Services, Lanyon North, Queen's University, Belfast BT7 1NN
T: (028) 9027 2568 F: (028) 9027 2570
E: rrs@qub.ac.uk W: www.qub.ac.uk/rrs/
Contact: Trevor Newsom, Director

CATEGORIES: INCUBATOR; START-UP TRAINING

Queen's University has a long-established reputation for research. The Research & Regional Services department handles all consultancy enquiries from business. Recent developments include: A new Centre for Creative Industries; The first Chair of Innovation in Northern Ireland; A new Institute for Electronics, Communications and Information Technologies (ECIT) located as a flagship development in the **Northern Ireland Science Park**. The Northern Ireland Technology Centre, built on the QUB campus, operates as a self-financing practical experience centre dedicated to technology transfer. QUB also operates an Enterprise Unit. QUB established **Qubis Ltd** to manage equity investments in campus companies.

RAPID (RURAL AREA PARTNERSHIP IN DERRY)

The Old School, 2 Foreglen Road, Killaloo, Co Londonderry BT47 3TP
T: (028) 7133 7149 F: (028) 7133 7146
E: leaderplus@globalnet.co.uk ; info@rapidni.com
W: www.rapidni.com Contact: Susan Mullan

CATEGORIES: COMMUNITY & RURAL DEVELOPMENT

One of the **LEADER+** groups in Northern Ireland.

RATHMINES INFORMATION CENTRE

11 Wynnefield Road, Rathmines, Dublin 6
T: (01) 496 5558 F: (01) 496 5590
E: info@rathminesinformationcentre.com
Contact: Tara Smith

CATGEORIES: COMMUNITY & RURAL DEVELOPMENT; INFORMATION; TRAINING

The Rathmines Information and Community Services Centre is an **ADM**-funded group under the Local Development Social Inclusion Programme that offers Enterprise Services in Rathmines, alongside services to the unemployed, community development, community-based youth services, information services and education and training opportunities.

REAP SOUTH ANTRIM LTD

c/o Antrim Borough Council, The Steeple, Antrim BT41 1BJ
T: (028) 9446 1311 F: (028) 9442 8059
E: admin@reapsouthantrim.com W: www.reapsouthantrim.com
Contact: Paul Kelly

CATEGORIES: COMMUNITY & RURAL DEVELOPMENT

The Rural Economic Action Partnership South Antrim is a new rural development company, established to disperse **LEADER+** funding in the rural wards of Antrim, Carrickfergus and Newtownabbey Boroughs.

REGIONAL DEVELOPMENT CENTRE

Dundalk Institute of Technology, Dublin Road, Dundalk, Co Louth
T: (042) 933 1161 F: (042) 935 1412
E: dencen@dkit.ie W: www.rdc.ie
Contact: Gerard Carroll, Head of Development

CATEGORIES: CONSULTING; INCUBATOR; INFORMATION; R & D; START-UP
TRAINING; TRAINING

The Regional Development Centre was established by **Dundalk Institute of Technology** to act as a commercially-oriented interface between the IT and the industrial, commercial and business life of the region, making available the Institute's expertise, facilities and resources for the wider benefit of the regional economy. The Industrial Services Office (ISO) liaises with local industry and offers: Entrepreneurial development programmes; Incubation facilities for knowledge and technology-based enterprises; Industrial applied research, consultancy and information services. RDC's entrepreneurial development programes include: **Coca-Cola National Enterprise Awards**; **North East Enterprise Platform Programme**.

REGISTER OF ELECTRICAL CONTRACTORS OF IRELAND

Unit 9, KCR Industrial Estate, Ravensdale Park, Kimmage, Dublin 12
T: (01) 492 9966 F: (01) 492 9983
E: info@reci.ie W: www.reci.ie
Contact: Denise McAuley, Customer Service Executive

CATEGORIES: INFORMATION; REGULATOR & STANDARDS

RECI is the regulatory body for electrical contracting, and provides assistance to the industry in meeting national standards. With a countrywide list of over 2,000 Registered Contractors, it can help you to find a contractor.

REGISTRY OF BUSINESS NAMES

Companies Registration Office, Parnell House, 14 Parnell Square, Dublin 2
T: (01) 804 5200 F: (01) 804 5222
E: info@cro.ie W: www.cro.ie

CATEGORIES: INFORMATION; REGULATOR & STANDARDS

By law, entrepreneurs are obliged by law to register their business with the Registry of Business Names, or the relevant body in the case of co-operatives, if it carries on a business under a name other than its own. The CRO's website explains the procedures involved.

REGISTRY OF FRIENDLY SOCIETIES

Parnell House, 14 Parnell Square, Dublin 1
T: (01) 804 5499 F: (01) 804 5498

CATEGORIES: CO-OPERATIVES; REGULATOR & STANDARDS

A co-operative society can be formed by any group of seven or more people over the age of 18, and can be registered with the Registry of Friendly Societies. The advantage of registration is Ltd liability. **The Co-operative Development Society Ltd, Irish Co-operative Society Ltd, and National**

Association of Building Co-operatives Ltd have Model Rules for co-operatives that have been approved by the Registry of Friendly Societies for use by those wishing to form a co-operative.

RESTAURANTS ASSOCIATION OF IRELAND
11 Bridge Court, City Gate, St Augustine Street, Dublin 8
T: (01) 677 9901 F: (01) 671 8414
E: info@rai.ie W: www.rai.ie
CATEGORIES: INFORMATION; NETWORKING

The RAI is the representative voice of the Restaurant Industry in Ireland. It provides opportunities for restauranteurs to have their voice heard, network with colleagues locally and nationally, seek staff or in-house training, access information and keep up-to-date in this fast-moving industry.

REVENUE COMMISSIONERS
Dublin Castle, Dublin 2
Central Telephone Information Office: (01) 414 9700 / 9777
Forms and leaflets: 1890 30 67 06(24 hours a day, 7 days a week)
W: www.revenue.ie
Personal Callers: Central Revenue Information Office, Cathedral Street, off O'Connell Street, Dublin 1.
CATEGORIES: INFORMATION; PUBLICATIONS; REGULATOR & STANDARDS; WEBSITE

Revenue's Mission is to serve the community by fairly and efficiently collecting taxes and duties and implementing import and export controls. You can now submit returns online to the Revenue Commissioners using the Revenue On-line Service (ROS) - see the Revenue website.

RICHMOND BUSINESS CAMPUS
North Brunswick Street, Dublin 7
T: (01) 809 0400 F: (01) 872 6252
E: richmond@iol.ie W: www.richmondbusinesscampus.com
Contact: Rory O'Meara
CATEGORIES: INCUBATOR; WORKSPACE

The Business Incubation Centre offers multi-purpose premises and in-house supports - ISDN telephone system, fax, photocopying, boardroom, kitchen facilities, security, car parking - with other services being provided by external consultants. It offers "start-up" facilities from €7 per day.

ROE VALLEY ENTERPRISES LTD
Aghanloo Industrial Estate, Aghanloo Road, Limavady, Co Londonderry BT49 0HE
T: (028) 7776 2323 F: (028) 7776 5707
E: info@roevalleyenterprises.co.uk W: www.lysba.com
Contact: Martin Devlin, Manager
CATEGORIES: INCUBATOR; INFORMATION; MARKETING; START-UP TRAINING; TRAINING; WORKSPACE

Roe Valley Enterprises (Limavady Small Business Agency) is an Enterprise **Agency** and a member of **Enterprise Northern Ireland**. Its aim is to develop enterprise within the Limavady Borough Council area by encouraging new business start-up and growth within the SME sector. Roe Valley Enterprises provides: Industrial and office workspace units to incubate local businesses; Low interest loans for start-ups; Professional business advice and counselling; Training on start-up and expansion planning; Support in sourcing government support and finance; Marketing planning. Roe Valley Enterprises delivers: **NI Business Start-up Programme**; Community Business Start Up Programme; New Deal Self Employment Option; New Beginnings.

ROE VALLEY RURAL DEVELOPMENT LTD
The Council Offices, 7 Connell Street, Limavady BT49 0HA
T: (028) 7776 0306 F: (028) 7772 2010
E: paul.beattie@limavady.gov.uk W: www.roevalleyleaderplus.co.uk
Contact: Paul Beattie, Project Officer
CATEGORIES: COMMUNITY & RURAL DEVELOPMENT

One of the **LEADER+** groups in Northern Ireland. RVRD Ltd aims to "improve the quality of life for the rural inhabitants of the Limavady Borough" through: Support for the establishment of small businesses; The creation of new jobs; The provision of infra-structural business support; The opportunity to facilitate peoples' reintegration into the labour market; General development of the rural economic base.

ROLEX AWARDS FOR ENTERPRISE
Secretariat, P.O. Box 131, 1211 Geneva 26, Switzerland
T: (00 41) 22 302 2200 F: (00 41) 22 302 2585
E: secretariat@rolexawards.com W: www.rolexawards.com
CATEGORIES: COMPETITIONS

The awards cover five categories: Science and medicine; Technology and innovation; Exploration and discovery; The environment; and Cultural heritage. The five most outstanding applicants in 2004 will each receive US$100,000 as a financial contribution to implement their projects, a Rolex chronometer and world-wide recognition. Any one of any age or from any country may apply. See website for application details and closing dates.

ROSCOMMON COUNTY ENTERPRISE BOARD LTD
Library Buildings, Abbey Street, Roscommon
T: (0903) 26263 F: (0903) 25474
E: ceb@roscommon.ie W: www.roscommon.ie
Contact: Ann Flynn, CEO
CATEGORIES: DEBT; E-BUSINESS; EQUITY; GRANTS; INFORMATION;
MENTORING; START-UP TRAINING; TRAINING

Roscommon County Enterprise Board is committed to the economic development of the county and, since its establishment, has provided an integrated service where business ideas have been translated into commercial reality with its assistance and guidance. As well as financial support, the CEB provides training, mentoring and other supports.

ROSCOMMON PARTNERSHIP COMPANY
The Square, Castlerea, Co Roscommon
T: (0907) 21337/8/9 F: (0907) 21340
E: roscommonptnship@eircom.net W: www.planet.ie
Contact: Patricia Murphy-Byrne, Manager
Also at: Castle Street, Roscommon
T: (0903) 27424 F: (0903) 27478
E: roscommonptnshipros@eircom.net
Contact: Noel Connolly
CATEGORIES: COMMUNITY & RURAL DEVELOPMENT; INFORMATION; START-UP
TRAINING

One of the **Area Partnerships** funded by **Area Development Management**, as part of its Local Development programme.

ROSCREA 2000
Community Resource Centre, Newline, Roscrea, Co Tipperary
T: (0505) 23379 F: (0505) 23386
E: ros2000@eircom.net W: homepage.eircom.net/~ros2000
Contact: Michael Murray, Manager
CATEGORIES: COMMUNITY & RURAL DEVELOPMENT

Roscrea 2000 is one of the **Community Groups** funded by **Area Development Management,** as part of its Local Development programme.

ROSLEAN ENTERPRISE CENTRE
Roslean Enterprise Ltd, Liskilly, Roslea, Co Fermanagh BT92 7FH
T: (028) 6775 1851 F: (028) 6775 1851
CATEGORIES: INFORMATION; START-UP TRAINING; WORKSPACE

One of several **Enterprise Centres** in Fermanagh.

RUNNING YOUR BUSINESS
See **Firsthand Publishing**.

RURAL AREA PARTNERSHIP IN DERRY
See **RAPID**.

RURAL COMMUNITY NETWORK
38A Oldtown Street, Cookstown, Co Tyrone BT80 8EF
T: (028) 8676 6670 F: (028) 8676 6006
E: rcn@ruralcommunitynetwork.org W: www.ruralcommunitynetwork.org
CATEGORIES: COMMUNITY & RURAL DEVELOPMENT; INFORMATION;
NETWORKING

A voluntary organisation with over 500 members that identifies and provides a voice on issues of concern to rural communities in relation to poverty, disadvantage and community development.

RURAL DEVELOPMENT COUNCIL
17 Loy Street, Cookstown, Co Tyrone BT80 8PZ
T: (028) 8676 6980 F: (028) 8676 6922
E: info@rdc.org.uk W: www.rdc.org.uk
Contact: Albert Hunter
CATEGORIES: COMMUNITY & RURAL DEVELOPMENT

The Rural Development Council (RDC) exists to address the needs of deprived rural areas in Northern Ireland. The RDC's principal activity is the delivery of support services to organisations that are involving people locally in planning and regeneration projects which meet real needs in disadvantaged rural communities. It provides a specialist service focusing on enterprise in the rural economy and building on the work of other local development groups.

RURAL DOWN PARTNERSHIP
Banbridge District Council, Downshire Road, Banbridge, Co Down BT32 3JY
T: (028) 4066 0609 F: (028) 4066 0601
E: ruraldown@banbridgedc.gov.uk W: www.banbridgedc.gov.uk
Contact: Therese Rafferty
CATEGORIES: COMMUNITY & RURAL DEVELOPMENT

One of the **LEADER+** groups in Northern Ireland, the Rural Down Partnership is a partnership established by Down, Ards and Banbridge District Councils with statutory and social partners with the objective to support the rural economy in those Council areas.

RURAL DUBLIN LEADER CO LTD
11 Parnell Square, Dublin 1
T: (01) 878 0564 F: (01) 878 0572
E: info@ruraldublin.ie W: www.ruraldublin.ie
Contact: Jeanna Deegan, Manager
Also at: Enterprise House, 6 Bridge Street, Balbriggan, Co Dublin
T: (01) 841 2204 / 841 5141 F: (01) 841 5141
E: dogrady@ruraldublin.ie
Contact: David O'Grady, European Information Officer
CATEGORIES: COMMUNITY & RURAL DEVELOPMENT; GRANTS; START-UP
TRAINING

A **LEADER+** company serving County Dublin. Its NEST (New Enterprise Support and Training) programme is targeted at unemployed people and potential entrepeneurs with a business idea. It provides both group and one-to-one sessions with participants to assess viability, research and prepare business plans for projects. It also offers a Rural Enterprise Development Programme. It offers capital equipment grants to innovative, small enterprises in manufacturing, crafts or local services at start-up or development stage, within its operational area.

RURAL ECONOMY RESEARCH CENTRE
Teagasc, 19 Sandymount Avenue, Dublin 4
T: (01) 637 6097 F: (01) 668 8443
E: epitts@hq.teagasc.ie
W: www.teagasc.org/research/research_centres.htm
Contact: Eamonn Pitts, Head of Centre

CATEGORIES: COMMUNITY & RURAL DEVELOPMENT; INFORMATION

The Centre conducts research in the areas of agri-policy and market analysis, agri-production economics and analysis of international competitiveness.

RURAL RESOURCE DEVELOPMENT LTD
Town Hall, Shannon, Co Clare
T: (061) 361 144 F: (061) 361 954
E: rrd@eircom.net

CATEGORIES: COMMUNITY & RURAL DEVELOPMENT; GRANTS

A **LEADER+** company serving Co Clare, Rural Resource Development actively encourages and supports people in local communities to reclaim responsibility for their own future, underpinned by a self-help approach. It offers capital equipment grants to innovative, small enterprises in manufacturing, crafts or local services at start-up or development stage, within its operational area.

RURAL SUPPORT.org.uk
Armagh and Dungannon Health Action Zone, Unit T9, Dungannon Enterprise Centre, 2 Coalisland Road, Dungannon BT71 6JT
T: (0845) 606 7607 (helpline)
E: eskelton@adhaz.org.uk
W: www.ruralsupport.org.uk

CATEGORIES: COMMUNITY & RURAL DEVELOPMENT; INFORMATION; WEBSITE

The aim of the Rural Support website is to provide support and assistance to farmers, their families and those living in rural areas. The Finance section of the website provides advice and information on the financial and business support available to farmers, and provides information for those wishing to develop their agricultural business units in non-traditional ways through farm diversification. The website was developed by the Armagh and Dungannon Health Action Zone partnership, and funded by the **Department of Agriculture and Rural Development** Rural Stress Fund.

RURALDEV-LEARNINGONLINE.ie
W: www.ruraldev-learningonline.ie

CATEGORIES: COMMUNITY & RURAL DEVELOPMENT; INFORMATION; TRAINING; WEBSITE

RuralDev-LearningOnline.ie provides an e-learning degree programme in Rural Development, offered by the colleges of the National University of Ireland (University College Cork, University College Dublin, National University of Ireland, Galway and National University of Ireland, Maynooth).

SAGE IRELAND
3096 Lake Drive, CityWest Business Park, Dublin 24
T: (01) 642 0863 F: (01) 642 0867
E: customercare@sage.ie W: www.sage.ie
CATEGORIES: ACCOUNTANTS

A leading supplier of accounting, payroll, CRM and business management software and services for small and medium-sized businesses.

SALES INSTITUTE OF IRELAND
Nelson House, 50–52 Pembroke Road, Dublin 4
T: (01) 667 2166 F: (01) 667 2167
E: info@salesinstitute.ie W: www.salesinstitute.ie
CATEGORIES: INFORMATION; MARKETING; NETWORKING; TRAINING

The Sales Institute promotes professionalism and standards of excellence in the sales profession in Ireland. It has over 1,300 members. It provides events, education and training for its members.

SCIENCE FOUNDATION IRELAND (NATIONAL FOUNDATION FOR EXCELLENCE IN SCIENTIFIC RESEARCH)
Wilton Park House, Wilton Place, Dublin 2
T: (01) 607 3200 F: (01) 607 3201
E: info@sfi.ie W: www.sfi.ie
CATEGORIES: GRANTS

Science Foundation Ireland (SFI) is investing €646 million between 2000-2006 in academic researchers and research teams who are most likely to generate new knowledge, leading edge technologies and competitive enterprises in the fileds underpinning two broad areas: biotechnology and information and communications technology. SFI makes grants based on the merit review of distinguished scientists. SFI also advances co-operative efforts among education, government and industry that support its fields of emphasis and promotes Ireland's ensuing achievements around the world.

SEED CAPITAL SCHEME
Office of the Revenue Commissioners, Dublin Castle, Dublin 2
T: (01) 702 4107 F: (01) 671 0012
E: mgalvin@revenue.ie W: www.revenue.ie
Contact: John Cheasty; Marie Galvin
CATEGORIES: EQUITY

The Seed Capital Scheme repays income tax to people leaving employment to start their own businesses (only companies qualify). Qualifying individuals may claim back the tax paid in respect of up to €31,744 of income in each of the previous five tax years, to a maximum of €158,718. An explanatory guide is available on the **Revenue Commissioners'** website.

SEROBA BIOVENTURES
Unit 1c, Trinity Enterprise Centre, Pearse Street, Dublin 2
T: (01) 675 0026
E: info@seroba.ie W: www.seroba.ie
CATEGORIES: EQUITY

Seroba provides support to promising start-up and early-stage lifescience and medical technology companies arising from leading Irish research institutes, universities, research hospitals and existing companies. It manages the **Irish BioSciences Venture Capital Fund**, Ireland's first venture capital fund exclusively dedicated to life science and medical technologies.

SHANNON DEVELOPMENT
Shannon, Co Clare
T: (061) 361 555 F: (061) 361 903
E: info@shannondev.ie W: www.shannondev.ie
Contact: Kevin Thompstone, Chief Executive
Also offices in Birr, Ennis, Limerick, Nenagh, Thurles and Tralee.
CATEGORIES: BUSINESS ANGELS; DEBT; EQUITY; GRANTS; INCUBATOR; INFORMATION; MENTORING; START-UP TRAINING; TRAINING; WORKSPACE

Shannon Development is the Regional Development Agency responsible for development in the Shannon Region, comprising Counties Limerick, Clare, North Tipperary, South-west Offaly and North Kerry. It offers grants and other assistance to businesses in the Shannon region, broadly in line with the assistance available nationally from **Enterprise Ireland**, although these are tailored to the specific needs of individual high-potential technology and knowledge-based start-ups, as well manufacturing and internationally-traded services companies. The **Shannon Development Knowledge Network** brings business, education and innovation together to create world-class locations for living and working in the knowledge age. **InnovationWorks** is a digitally-networked business incubation centre, supporting knowledge-based businesses. Shannon Development also offers VentureStart and AlumniStart programmes, as well as a campus industry programme, and access to a "Business Angel" network.

SHANNON DEVELOPMENT KNOWLEDGE NETWORK
Shannon, Co Clare
T: (061) 361 555 F: (061) 361 903
E: info@shannon-dev.ie W: www.shannon-dev.ie
Contact: Kevin Thompstone, Chief Executive
CATEGORIES: INCUBATOR; WORKSPACE

The Shannon Development Knowledge Network brings business, education and innovation together to create world-class locations for living and working in the knowledge age. The Network comprises: **National Technology Park Limerick;**

Kerry Technology Park, Tralee; Tipperary Technology Park, Thurles; Birr Technology Centre, Birr, Co Offaly; Information Age Park, Ennis, Co Clare.

SHELL LIVEWIRE
Irish Shell, Beech Hill, Clonskeagh, Dublin 4
T: (01) 207 8712 F: (01) 283 8312
E: livewire@shellireland.com W: www.shell-livewire.org
Contact: Angela Brady
CATEGORIES: COMPETITIONS; YOUNG ENTERPRISE

Shell LiveWire helps 16-30 year-olds to start and develop their own business and hosts an annual competition for business start-ups. Shell LiveWIRE is jointly sponsored by Shell Ireland, **Bank of Ireland** and the **City / County Enterprise Boards.**

SLIABH LUACRA LTD
See **Kerry Rural Development**.

SLIGO COUNTY ENTERPRISE BOARD
Sligo Development Centre, Cleveragh Road, Sligo
T: (071) 914 4779 F: (071) 914 6793
E: info@sligoenterprise.ie W: www.sligoenterprise.ie
Contact: John Reilly, CEO
CATEGORIES: DEBT; E-BUSINESS; EQUITY; GRANTS; INFORMATION;
MENTORING; START-UP TRAINING; TRAINING

Sligo County Enterprise Board aims to generate sustainable employment in the county, through development of an enterprise culture, forging of multi-sectoral partnerships, fostering of economic development and provision of direct financial supports. It operates in the micro-enterprise sector, supporting start-up businesses and the expansion of existing enterprises whose employment potential does not exceed 10 employees. It also operates the **Sligo County Enterprise Fund**, which offers loans to small enterprise.

SLIGO COUNTY ENTERPRISE FUND COMPANY
Sligo Enterprise & Technology Centre, Sligo Airport Business Park,
Strandhill, Co Sligo
T: (071) 916 8477 F: (071) 914 4863
E: info@sligoenterprise.com W: www.www.enterprise-sligo.com
Contact: Christie Leonard
CATEGORIES: DEBT

The Sligo County Enterprise Fund was established in 1988 as part of The **International Fund for Ireland**'s border counties initiative. The primary role of the Enterprise Fund is providing low-interest loans to individuals and community group starting up or expanding viable economic projects. It has built the Enterprise & Technology Centre to stimulate local enterprise development.

SLIGO LEADER PARTNERSHIP COMPANY LTD

Sligo Development Centre, Cleveragh Road, Sligo
T: (071) 41138 / 55 F: (071) 41162
E: slpc@iol.ie W: www.slpc.ie
Contact: Michael Quigley, CEO

CATEGORIES: COMMUNITY & RURAL DEVELOPMENT; GRANTS

One of the **Area Partnerships** established by **Area Development Management**, as part of its Local Development programme, and also a LEADER+ company serving part of Co Sligo. It offers capital equipment grants to innovative, small enterprises in manufacturing, crafts or local services at start-up or development stage, within its operational area.

SMALL BUSINESS INSTITUTE

University of Limerick, Limerick
T: (061) 202183 F: (061) 338171
E: patricia.fleming@ul.ie W: www.ul.ie
Contact: Patricia Fleming

CATEGORIES: CONSULTING

The **University of Limerick's** Small Business Institute offers a Business Consulting programme to entrepreneurs. This offers entrepreneurs access to the resources of an undergraduate team of multidisciplinary students for one academic term to undertake research in accordance with an agreed research brief.

SMALL ENTERPRISE SEED FUND

The Bolton Trust, Docklands Innovation Park, 128-130 East Wall Road, Dublin 3
T: (01) 240 1300 F: (01) 240 1310
E: info@boltontrust.com W: www.boltontrust.com

CATEGORIES: EQUITY

The Small Enterprise Seed Fund, an initiative of the **Bolton Trust,** is a designated **Business Expansion Scheme** (BES) Fund. The Fund raises monies from private investors to provide seed funding to a portfolio of young growth-oriented businesses.

SMALL FIRMS ASSOCIATION

Confederation House, 84–86 Lower Baggot Street, Dublin 2
T: (01) 605 1500 F: (01) 661 2861
E: info@sfa.ie W: www.sfa.ie
Contact: Pat Delaney, Director

CATEGORIES: INFORMATION; NETWORKING; PUBLICATIONS; TRAINING

The Small Firms Association is the national organisation exclusively representing the needs of small enterprises in Ireland. It represents and provides economic, commercial, employee relations and social affairs advice and assistance to over 8,000 member companies, and holds a range of seminar programmes and member networking evenings annually. In addition, the association conducts regular surveys of business trends in the sector and publishes a monthly magazine "Running Your Business" along with many reports on the needs of small Irish business. The SFA has also put in place a range of cost-effective group services, exclusive to member companies. These Group schemes include Insurance, ISO 9001: 2000, VHI, debt collection, pensions, crime management, and AA membership. In addition, its website, www.sfa.ie has been designed and developed to provide all information and services on-line to members and to allow members to advertise their products and network with each other.

SMALL FIRMS LOAN GUARANTEE SCHEME
W: www.sbs.gov.uk
CATEGORIES: DEBT

In Northern Ireland, the SFLGS: Offers a single guarantee rate of 75% for all new loans; Includes Retailing, Catering, Coal, Hairdressing and Beauty Parlours, House and Estate Agents, Libraries, Museums and Cultural Activities, Motor Vehicle Repair and Servicing, Steel and Travel Agents; Increases the maximum turnover level for non-manufacturing businesses to £3m; Charges a premium of 2% per year on the outstanding balance for all new loans. Apply direct to the lenders, including: **Bank of Ireland Northern Ireland**; Barclays Bank; **Emerging Business Trust Ltd; First Trust Bank; Ulster Bank**.

SOCIAL ECONOMY AGENCY
45-47 Donegall Street, Belfast BT1 2FG
T: (028) 9096 1115 F: (028) 9096 1116
E: info@socialeconomyagency.org W: www.socialeconomyagency.org
Contact: Elaine Morrison
Also at: 2 Bay Road, Derry BT48 7SH
T: (028) 7137 1733 F: (028) 7137 0114
CATEGORIES: BUSINESS PLANS; COMMUNITY & RURAL DEVELOPMENT; CO-OPERATIVES; DEBT; INFORMATION; SOCIAL ECONOMY; TRAINING

The Social Economy Agency provides support to the co-operative movement. It offers services including business plans and feasibility studies, local area profiles, legal structures and customised training packages, as well as training and a loan fund.

SOCIETY OF SAINT VINCENT DE PAUL
8 New Cabra Road, Dublin 7
T: (01) 838 4164 F: (01) 838 7355
E: info@svp.ie W: www.svp.ie
Also at: 196-200 Antrim Road, Belfast BT15 2AJ
T: (028) 9035 1561
E: info@svpni.co.uk W: www.svp-ni.org

CATEGORIES: COMMUNITY & RURAL DEVELOPMENT; DEBT; INFORMATION

The Society of Saint Vincent de Paul is active in the area of community enterprise. One of its programmes is the Enterprise Support scheme, which provides seed capital loans on an interest-free basis (to a maximum of IR£4,000) and business advice. SVP targets exclusively people living in poverty with no other access to seed funding. It supports **Action Tallaght's** Enterprise programme.

SOUTH CORK ENTERPRISE BOARD
Unit 6A, South Ring Business Park, Kinsale Road, Cork
T: (021) 497 5281 F: (021) 497 5287
E: enterprise@sceb.ie W: www.sceb.ie
Contact: Jim Brennan, CEO

CATEGORIES: DEBT; E-BUSINESS; EQUITY; GRANTS; INFORMATION;
MENTORING; START-UP TRAINING; TRAINING

South Cork CEB supports the creation of economically-sustainable niche micro-enterprise opportunities in the manufacturing, internationally traded services and highly innovative local traded services sectors through the provision of information, advice, mentoring, management development and business counselling. It also offers grants and financial supports.

SOUTH DUBLIN COUNTY ENTERPRISE BOARD
3 Village Square, Old Bawn Road, Tallaght, Dublin 24
T: (01) 405 7073/4 F: (01) 451 7477
E: webmaster@sdenterprise.com W: www.sdenterprise.com
Contact: Loman O'Byrne, CEO

CATEGORIES: DEBT; E-BUSINESS; EQUITY; GRANTS; INFORMATION;
MENTORING; START-UP TRAINING; TRAINING; WEBSITE

The South Dublin CEB develops and supports local entrepreneurship and enterprise in the county of South Dublin. It offers an Open Learning Centre, with interactive computer-based training programmes available for use. Its website is a "First Stop Shop", with a series of *Management Guidelines* available for download and also offers an *Enterprise Information Portal*, providing links to useful sources of information for small businesses.

SOUTH EAST ENTERPRISE PROGRAMME
Research & Innovation Centre, Waterford Institute of Technology,
Waterford Business Park, Cork Road, Waterford
T: (051) 302953 F: (051) 302901
E: atkelly@wit.ie W: www.seepp.ie
Contact: Alan Kelly, Programme Manager

CATEGORIES: GRANTS; INCUBATOR; MENTORING; START-UP TRAINING

SEEP is a 12-month incubation programme fo technology start-ups, offering training, mentoring, grants and other support. See also **Enterprise Programmes** for EPs in other locations.

SOUTH EAST EUROPEAN CENTRE (CARRÉFOUR WATERFORD)
Waterford LEADER Partnership Ltd, 21 Church Street, Dungarvan, Co Waterford
T: (058) 54646 / 44077 F: (058) 54126
E: seec@iol.ie W: www.eurospeak.org
Also at: Main Street West, Lismore, Co Waterford
T: (058) 54646 F: (058) 54126
E: abradley@iol.ie
Contact: Julie O'Donnell

CATEGORIES: EU INFORMATION

The South East European Centre is a member of the network of Rural Information and Promotion Carréfours of the European Commission. It is hosted by the **Waterford LEADER Partnership** in its Dungarvan office and serves counties Carlow, Kilkenny, Tipperary, Waterford and Wexford.

SOUTH KERRY DEVELOPMENT PARTNERSHIP
The Old Barracks, Valentia Road, Caherciveen, Co Kerry
T: (066) 947 2724 F: (066) 947 2725
E: mlyne@skdp.net W: www.southkerry.net
Contact: Mary Lyne

CATEGORIES: COMMUNITY & RURAL DEVELOPMENT; EU INFORMATION; GRANTS; INFORMATION; START-UP TRAINING; TRAINING

Originally, one of the **Area Partnerships** established by **Area Development Management,** as part of its Local Development programme, SKDP is also a **LEADER+** group and hosts **Carréfour Cahirciveen**. It delivers the Social Inclusion Programme under the National Development Plan 2001-2006. It offers capital equipment grants to innovative, small enterprises in manufacturing, crafts or local services at start-up or development stage, within its operational area.

SOUTH MAYO LEADER
See **South West Mayo Development Company.**

SOUTH WEST MAYO DEVELOPMENT COMPANY
(SOUTH MAYO LEADER)
Carey Walsh Building, Georges Street, Newport, Co Mayo
T: (098) 41950 F: (098) 41952
E: leader@smayo.iol.ie
W: www.mayo-ireland.ie/Mayo/SMayoLC/SMayoLC.htm
Contact: Paul Kirkpatrick

CATEGORIES: COMMUNITY & RURAL DEVELOPMENT; GRANTS; INFORMATION; MENTORING; TRAINING

A **LEADER+** company serving South-West Mayo, and a sub-office of **Meitheal Mhaigh Eo**. It is a company Ltd by guarantee, owned by community organisations and self-help groups in South Mayo. It helps small enterprises through the provision of business advice, capital grants, training, mentoring, interest and rent subsidies, and marketing assistance. It offers capital equipment grants to innovative, small enterprises in manufacturing, crafts or local services at start-up or development stage, within its operational area.

SOUTH WEST FERMANAGH DEVELOPMENT ORGANISATION LTD
See **Teemore Business Complex**.

SOUTH-EAST BUSINESS INNOVATION CENTRE
Unit 1 B, Industrial Park, Cork Road, Waterford
T: (051) 356300 F: (051) 354415
E: info@sebic.ie W: www.sebic.ie
Contact: Maire Gallagher, Administration Manager

CATEGORIES: BUSINESS PLANS; EQUITY; INCUBATOR; INFORMATION; MARKETING; TRAINING

SEBIC was established in 1995 with the support of the European Commission, local public organisations and the private sector to stimulate the creation and development of innovative SMEs in the South East Region. Its services include advice and assistance in business and strategic planning, management, marketing, technology, financial management and accessing capital in counties Carlow, Kilkenny, South Tipperary, Waterford and Wexford. Its Incubation Centre provides office space, as well as business development support.

SOUTHSIDE PARTNERSHIP
24 Adelaide Street, Dun Laoire, Co Dublin
T: (01) 230 1011 F: (01) 202 0630
E: info@sspship.ie W: www.southsidepartnership.ie
Contact: Maire Carroll, Manager

CATEGORIES: COMMUNITY & RURAL DEVELOPMENT; INFORMATION; SOCIAL ECONOMY; START-UP TRAINING; TRAINING

Southside Partnership is the independent local development organisation for Dun Laoghaire Rathdown and Whitechurch, directly funded under the Social Inclusion Programme in the National Development Plan 2000 - 2006 by the Irish

Government through **Area Development Management. FAS**, the **Department of Social and Family Affairs,** the East Coast Area Health Board, the European Union, private companies and charities also provide funding. SouthSide Partnership's Economic Development Programme supports the target groups to start their own businesses and develop community and social economy enterprises. See also **DoingBusinessinDunLaoghaireRathdown.com**.

SPADE ENTERPRISE CENTRE
St Paul's, North King Street, Dublin 7
T: (01) 677 1026 F: (01) 677 1558
E: spade@tinet.ie
Contact: Ken Price
CATEGORIES: INCUBATOR; WORKSPACE

SPADE opened in 1990 in the former St Paul's Church, offering incubator workspace for small businesses.

STARTUP.ie
Shannon Development, InnovationWorks, Kerry Technology Park, Tralee,
Co Kerry
T: (066) 719 0000 F: (066) 712 4267
E: info@startup.ie W: www.startup.ie
CATEGORIES: INFORMATION; WEBSITE

Established by **Shannon Development**, Startup.ie provides an information and referral service for start-ups and established SMEs within the Shannon Region.

STRABANE ENTERPRISE AGENCY
Unit 4, Ballycolman Industrial Estate, Strabane, Co Tyrone BT82 9PH
T: (028) 7138 2518 F: (028) 7188 4531
E: seagency@aol.com W: www.strabaneenterprise.com
Contact: Christina Mullan
CATEGORIES: DEBT; INFORMATION; START-UP TRAINING; TRAINING; WORKSPACE

Strabane Enterprise Agency is an **Enterprise Agency** and a member of **Enterprise Northern Ireland**. It offers workspace, start-up and ongoing training and loans.

SUNDAY BUSINESS POST
80 Harcourt Street, Dublin 2
T: (01) 602 6000 F: (01) 679 6498
E: sbpost@iol.ie F: www.sbpost.ie
CATEGORIES: PUBLICATIONS

Ireland's only dedicated business newspaper.

It's been a

VINTAGE
YEAR

CRISTALINO

Awarded Value Brand
Wine&Spirits
2003
of the Year

THE SUNDAY BUSINESS POST

52,115

Sales are bubbling over

Up by 1%   (502 copies)

ABC Jan - June 2004
For advertising information contact 01 6023000

THE SUNDAY BUSINESS POST
IRELAND'S FINANCIAL, POLITICAL AND ECONOMIC NEWSPAPER

SUSTAINABLE ENERGY IRELAND
Glasnevin, Dublin 9
T: (01) 836 9080 F: (01) 837 2848
E: info@sei.ie W: www.sei.ie
Contact: Tom Halpin, Consumer Awareness
Also at: Renewable Energy Information Office, Shinagh House, Bandon, Co Cork
T: (023) 29145 F: (023) 41304
Contact: Paul Kellett

CATEGORIES: INFORMATION; TRAINING

Formerly the Irish Energy Centre, Sustainable Energy Ireland is Ireland's national agency for energy efficiency and renewable energy information, advice and support. EU-funded, it provides guidance on the potential for more efficient use of energy in home, office, industry and municipal activities and on the development of renewable energy resources, from commercial projects to domestic applications. In addition, the Centre offers advice on potential sources of funding for sustainable energy initiatives.

SYNERGY 2000
Lisburn Enterprise Organisation, Enterprise Crescent, Ballinderry Road, Lisburn BT28 2BP
T: (028) 9266 1160
E: aisling@lisburn-enterprise.co.uk W: www.lisburn-enterprise.co.uk
Contact: Aisling Owens

CATEGORIES: BUSINESS ANGELS; EQUITY

Synergy 2000 is a business angel network, operating across Northern Ireland and the Border counties, matching businesses seeking funding with private investors seeking investment opportunities. It is managed by **Lisburn Enterprise Organisation**.

SYNERGY eBUSINESS INCUBATOR
1 Millennium Way, Belfast BT12 7AL
T: (028) 9028 8830 F: (028) 9028 8850
E: opportunity@synergy-ebi.com W: www.synergy-ebi.com
Contact: Ken Magee, General Manager

CATEGORIES: EBUSINESS; INCUBATOR

A joint venture between the **University of Ulster** and ICL, based on the **UUSRP** Belfast Science Park.

TALLAGHT PARTNERSHIP
Killinarden Enterprise Park, Killinarden, Tallaght, Dublin 24
T: (01) 466 4280 F: (01) 466 4288
E: info@tallpart.com
Contact: Anna Lee

CATEGORIES: COMMUNITY & RURAL DEVELOPMENT; INFORMATION; START-UP TRAINING

One of the **Area Partnerships** funded by **Area Development Management**, as part of its Local Development programme. It has contracted its enterprise support activities to **Partas**, which provides a one-to-one enterprise development and business support service in Tallaght on its behalf targeted at the long-term unemployed.

TALLAGHT TRUST FUND

Partas, Bolbrook Enterprise Centre, Avonmore Road, Tallaght, Dublin 24
T: (01) 414 5700
E: jkearns@partas.ie

CATEGORIES: CO-OPERATIVES; DEBT

Working with **First Step**, the Fund provides loans ranging between €125 and €6,350 to small businesses locally. It also provides revolving loan fund for co-operatives nationally, with loans ranging from €650 to €63,500. The Fund is managed by **Partas**.

TCD ENTERPRISE CENTRE

Pearse Street, Dublin 2
T: (01) 677 5655 F: (01) 677 5487
E: bnoone@tcd.ie W: www.tcd.ie
Contact: Bridget Noone, Enterprise Executive

CATEGORIES: INCUBATOR

Originally established by **IDA Ireland**, the centre is now owned by **University of Dublin, Trinity College**. It is home to 30 businesses, including the **Dublin Business Innovation Centre**.

TEAGASC : THE AGRICULTURE, FOOD & DEVELOPMENT AUTHORITY

19 Sandymount Avenue, Ballsbridge, Dublin 4
T: (01) 637 6000 F: (01) 668 8023
E: mmiley@hq.teagasc.ie W: www.teagasc.ie
Contact: Public Relations & Information: Michael Miley; Advisory Services: Tom Kirley

CATEGORIES: CONSULTING; TRAINING

Teagasc offers a Certificate in Rural Business for farmers exploring opportunities for starting new businesses linked to the rural environment. It also offers training courses at its **National Food Centre and Dairy Products Research Centre**, to strengthen in-company capabilities in quality systems, food safety and hygiene, food technology and product development and marketing. Through its Rural Enterprise Service, Teagasc provides foundation and advanced training courses for food entrepreneurs in rural areas. Teagasc research centres provide technical services on a cost-recovery basis.

TECHNOLOGY TRANSFER INITIATIVE
E: info@technologytransfer.ie
W: www.technologytransfer.ie
CATEGORIES: INFORMATION; MENTORING; R & D

The TTI is co- funded by **University College Cork, National University of Ireland, Galway, University of Limerick,** and **Enterprise Ireland** under the National Development Plan 2000-2006 and the European Union ERSF. It offers SMEs in the West, Mid-West and South-West: Collaborative Research and Development Service; Technology Brokering; Specialist Training Activities; Mentoring; Innovation Clubs; Outreach Programmes.

TECHNOLOGY WEST
Galway Technology Centre, Mervue Business Park, Galway
T: (091) 770007 F: (091) 755635
E: gtc@iol.ie W: www.gtc.ie
Contact: Louise Leonard; John Brennan, Manager
CATEGORIES: INCUBATOR; NETWORKING

Technology West is a Galway-based forum for the west of Ireland, generating opportunities for networking and business development in the western region's technology-based industry. It is organised and managed by the **Galway Technology Centre,** which incubates technology-based companies.

TECNET - THE TECHNOLOGY NETWORK
Crestfield Centre, Glanmire, Co Cork
T: (021) 485 8060 F: (021) 482 3725
E: info@tecnet.ie W: www.tecnet.ie
Contact: Eugene O'Leary, Chief Executive officer
CATEGORIES: CONSULTING; INFORMATION; R & D

TecNet, the Technology Network, was established in 1999 by the Council of Directors of the **Institutes of Technology** and is jointly funded by **Enterprise Ireland.** Its mission is to enhance the research and development capacities of the Institutes of Technology through strategic networks in support of regional economic development. It provides industry with research & development, consulting services and technology transfers by using the skills and facilities available within the ITs. Examples of services provided include: Technical prototyping; Commercial feasibility studies; Technical feasibility reports; Product scoping; Market analysis; Product testing; Competitive analysis.

TEEMORE BUSINESS COMPLEX
South West Fermanagh Development Organisation Ltd, Teemore, Derrylin, Co Fermanagh BT92 9BL
T: (028) 6774 8893 F: (028) 6774 8493
E: teemorecomplex@hotmail.com
Contact: James McBarron, General Manager
CATEGORIES: INFORMATION; START-UP TRAINING; WORKSPACE

One of several **Enterprise Centres** in Fermanagh.

TELEWORK IRELAND
Ballaghana, Mountnugent, Co Cavan
T: 1800 421 426
E: info@telework.ie
W: www.telework.ie
Contact: Siobhán Duffy; Riona Carroll

CATEGORIES: EBUSINESS; INFORMATION; NETWORKING; PUBLICATIONS

Telework Ireland represents the interests of Irish teleworkers (of whom there are estimated to be 15,000) and provides a teleworking information and advice service for members. It publishes a *Manual for Employees and Business Start-Ups*, as a book and on CD. Its website has a FAQ section on teleworking issues.

TIPPERARY INSTITUTE
Nenagh Road, Thurles, Co Tipperary
T: (0504) 28000 F: (0504) 28001
Also at: Cashel Court, Clonmel, Co Tipperary
T: (0504) 28000 F: (0504) 28001
E: info@tippinst.ie W: www.tippinst.ie

CATEGORIES: COMMUNITY & RURAL DEVELOPMENT; MENTORING; TRAINING

TI provides locally responsive and interactive educational, training, communication, mentoring and support services to rural communities. It is piloting a distance learning competency training programme for owner/managers of SMEs.

TIPPERARY LEADER GROUP
Canon Hayes House, Tipperary
T: (062) 33360 F: (062) 33787
E: tlg@iol.ie
Contact: John Devane

CATEGORIES: COMMUNITY & RURAL DEVELOPMENT; GRANTS

A **LEADER+** company serving parts of County Tipperary and North-East Limerick, Tipperary LEADER offers capital equipment grants to innovative, small enterprises in manufacturing, crafts or local services at start-up or development stage, within its operational area.

TIPPERARY NORTH COUNTY ENTERPRISE BOARD
Connolly Street, Nenagh, Co Tipperary
T: (067) 33086 F: (067) 33605
E: info@tnceb.ie W: www.tnceb.ie
Contact: Rita Guinan, Chief Executive

CATEGORIES: DEBT; E-BUSINESS; EQUITY; GRANTS; INFORMATION;
MENTORING; START-UP TRAINING; TRAINING

Tipperary North CEB stimulates a spirit of enterprise and facilitates the creation of employment and the development of sustainable micro-enterprises in North Tipperary through support, assistance and promotional activities whether financial, training or otherwise.

TIPPERARY SOUTH RIDING COUNTY ENTERPRISE BOARD

1 Gladstone Street, Clonmel, Co Tipperary
T: (052) 29466 F: (052) 26512
E: ceb@southtippcoco.ie W: www.southtippceb.ie
Contact: Toss Hayes, CEO

CATEGORIES: DEBT; E-BUSINESS; EQUITY; GRANTS; INFORMATION; MENTORING; START-UP TRAINING; TRAINING

Tipperary South CEB helps to create jobs by facilitating the establishment, development and expansion of small enterprises in the county. It provides financial assistance, mentoring and training programmes.

TIU TECHNOLOGY INVESTMENT & UNDERWRITING

Guinness Enterprise Centre, Taylor's Lane, Dublin 8
T: (01) 410 0939 F: (01) 410 0985
E: tiu@tiu.ie W: www.tiu.ie
Contact: Garret Hickey, Chief Executive

CATEGORIES: CONSULTING; INFORMATION

TIU enables high growth technology companies to exploit and capitalise on success. It integrates corporate finance and business consulting — underpinned by research and publications — to develop and expand private and public technology companies in Ireland and worldwide.

TOMKINS

5 Dartmouth Road, Dublin 6
T: (01) 660 5033 F: (01) 660 6920
E: post@tomkins.com W: www.tomkins.ie
Contact: Niall Rooney

CATEGORIES: INTELLECTUAL PROPERTY

Tomkins are European intellectual property experts. Established in 1930 by Arthur Bellamy Tomkins (who celebrated his 103rd birthday in July 2003!), Tomkins is one of Europe's longest established intellectual property law specialists.

TOWNSEND BUSINESS PARK

28 Townsend Street, Belfast BT3 2ES
T: (028) 9089 4500 F: (028) 9089 4502
E: admin@townsend.co.uk W: www.townsend.co.uk
Contact: George Briggs, Manager

CATEGORIES: DEBT; INFORMATION; START-UP TRAINING; TRAINING; WORKSPACE

Townsend Enterprise Park is an **Enterprise Agency** and a member of **Enterprise Northern Ireland**. The Park offers a wide range of services to small and medium sized businesses in their pre-start, start up and growth stages, which include offering support, training and advice on marketing, finance, business plans and business development as well as the provision of serviced workspace.

TRADENETIRELAND LTD

E: info@tradenetireland.com W: www.tradenetireland.com
Contact: Anne McCann, Internet Marketing Executive

CATEGORIES: CROSS-BORDER; E-BUSINESS; INFORMATION; MARKETING; WEBSITE

TradeNetIreland Ltd is an Internet-based business tool designed to deliver targeted information and trading opportunities to companies and to encourage SMEs to access electronic information and participate in electronic commerce. It is supported by the EU Special Support Programme for Peace and Reconciliation, with matching funding support from 15 local enterprise development organisations along the Belfast/Dublin corridor.

TRADING STANDARDS SERVICE NORTHERN IRELAND

176 Newtownbreda Road, Belfast BT8 6QS
T: (028) 9025 3900 F: (028) 9025 3988
E: tss@detini.gov.uk W: www.tssni.gov.uk

CATEGORIES: INFORMATION; REGULATOR & STANDARDS

TSSNI provides information on, and enforces, a wide range of consumer legislation, including: Weights and measures; False or misleading descriptions of goods; Misleading price indications; Credit transactions; Counterfeit goods.

TRIM INITIATIVE FOR DEVELOPMENT AND ENTERPRISE

Enterprise Centre, Riverbank, Trim, Co Meath
T: (046) 37245 F: (046) 37336
E: admin@tide.ie W: www.tide.ie
Contact: Paddy O'Reilly, Manager

CATEGORIES: COMMUNITY & RURAL DEVELOPMENT

Trim Initiative for Development and Enterprise (TIDE) is one of the **Community Groups** funded by **Area Development Management**.

TRINITY VENTURE CAPITAL LTD

Beech House, Beech Hill Office Campus, Clonskeagh, Dublin 6
T: (01) 205 7700 F: (01) 205 7701
E: info@tvc.com W: www.tvc.com
Contact: John Tracey, CEO

CATEGORIES: EQUITY

Trinity Venture Capital manages the **Trinity Venture Fund II**. Additional capital can be sourced through **Hibernia Capital Partners**, a sister company.

TRINITY VENTURE FUND II

Trinity Venture Capital Ltd, Beech House, Beech Hill Office Campus, Clonskeagh, Dublin 6
T: (01) 205 7700 F: (01) 205 7701
E: info@tvc.com W: www.tvc.com
Contact: John Tracey, CEO

CATEGORIES: EQUITY

This €138.7 million fund, managed by **Trinity Venture Capital**, targets primarily early-stage and expanding software companies, investing €1+ million in its initial investment. The fund was established with assistance from **Enterprise Ireland**, under the Seed & Venture Capital Measure of the Operational Programme 2001-2006.

TRIODOS BANK

Brunel House, 11 The Promenade, Clifton, Bristol BS8 3NN
T: (0117) 973 9339 F: (0117) 973 9303
E: mail@triodos.co.uk W: www.triodos.co.uk
Contact: Kieran Brennan, Irish representative
CATEGORIES: COMMUNITY & RURAL DEVELOPMENT; DEBT

Triodos Bank has been lending in Ireland for some time, building on over 20 years' experience supporting social, environmental and cultural projects in Europe. It supports organic and renewable energy projects to social and child development initiatives, as well as charities, community ventures, cultural and educational projects and childcare programmes.

TSA CONSULTANCY

Irish Social Finance Centre, 10 Grattan Crescent, Inchicore, Dublin 8
T: (01) 457 7420 F: (01) 457 7415
E: tomdaly@tsa.ie
Contact: Tom Daly, Managing Director
CATEGORIES: CONSULTING; SOCIAL ECONOMY; TRAINING

TSA Consultancy (Third System Approaches) are consultants and trainers in the area of the social economy.

TUATHA CHIARRAÍ TEO

Church Lane, Church Street, Tralee, Co Kerry
T: (066) 712 0390 F: (066) 712 0804
E: tuhakiri@iol.ie
Contact: Tom O'Donnell
CATEGORIES: COMMUNITY & RURAL DEVELOPMENT; GRANTS

A **LEADER+** company serving parts of Kerry outside the Gaeltacht and South Kerry, Tuatha Chiarrai offers capital equipment grants to innovative, small enterprises in manufacturing, crafts or local services at start-up or development stage, within its operational area.

TULLAMORE WIDER OPTIONS LTD

Church Road, Tullamore, Co Offaly
T: (0506) 52467 F: (0506) 52574
E: two@eircom.net
W: www.offaly.ie/developmentorganisations/tullamorewideroptions.asp
Contact: Eamonn Henry, Co-ordinator
CATEGORIES: COMMUNITY & RURAL DEVELOPMENT

Tullamore Wider Options is one of the **Community Groups** funded by **Area Development Management**, as part of its Local Development programme.

TYRONE DONEGAL PARTNERSHIP

Donegal Local Development Company, 1 Millennium Court, Pearse Road,
Letterkenny, Co Donegal
T: (074) 912 7056 F: (074) 912 1527
E: info@dldc.org W: www.dldc.org
Contact: Caoimhín Mac Aoidh, CEO
Omagh Enterprise Company Ltd, Omagh Business Complex, Gortrush
Industrial Estate, Great Northern Road, Omagh, Co Tyrone BT78 5LU
T: (028) 8224 9494 F: (028) 8224 9451
E: info@oecl.co.uk W: www.oecl.co.uk
Contact: Hugo Sweeney, Cross-Border Projects Manager
CATEGORIES: COMMUNITY & RURAL DEVELOPMENT; CROSS-BORDER

The Tyrone Donegal Partnership is a cross-border development company that identifies, develops and supports innovative initiatives in its rural communities. Its vision is to improve the social and economic conditions for all in the area. It delivers a Rural Enterprise Programme that provides unemployed young people with a combination of entrepreneurial training and work experience.

ÚDARÁS NA GAELTACHTA

Na Forbacha, Gaillimh
T: (091) 503100 F: (091) 503101
E: eolas@udaras.ie W: www.udaras.ie
Contact: Ruan O Bric, Chief Executive
Also offices in Cork, Dingle, Donegal and Mayo.
CATEGORIES: GRANTS; INCUBATOR; INFORMATION; MENTORING; START-UP
TRAINING; TRAINING

Údarás na Gaeltachta combines an economic development role (that of creating sustainable jobs and attracting investment to the Gaeltacht regions) with community, cultural and language-development activities, working in partnership with local communities and organisations. Projects in manufacturing, internationally-traded services and natural resources such as mariculture are the priority for assistance. It offers grant schemes and incentives to help small and medium-sized enterprises in the Gaeltacht areas, broadly in line with those available nationally from **Enterprise Ireland**.

ULSTER BANK

Small Business Office, 33 College Green, Dublin 2
T: (01) 702 5225 F: (01) 702 5350
E: mary.kelly@ulsterbank.com W: www.ulsterbank.com
Contact: Mary Kelly, Manager, Small Business
Group Head Office, 11-16 Donegall Square East, Belfast BT1 5UB
T: (028) 9027 6017 F: (028) 9027 6033
Contact: Deirdre Gallagher, Regional Small Business Adviser
CATEGORIES: DEBT; FRANCHISES; PUBLICATIONS

Ulster Bank, a member of the RBS-NatWest Group, has a Small Business Adviser in every branch to guide and advise entrepreneurs through the start-up process and explain, help and direct them through every aspect of business banking. Start-up businesses with a turnover below £100,000 (€127,000) qualify for 12 months free banking. Ulster Bank has various lending schemes available including overdrafts, loans, leasing and invoice discounting, and offers Internet banking and e-commerce facilities.

ULSTER COMMUNITY INVESTMENT TRUST
13 - 19 Linenhall Street, Belfast BT2 8AA
T: (028) 9031 5003 F: (028) 9031 5008
E: info@ucitltd.com W: www.ucitltd.com
CATEGORIES: COMMUNITY & RURAL DEVELOPMENT; DEBT; SOCIAL ECONOMY

Ulster Community Investment Trust Ltd is a provider of loan finance and support to the community economic sector in Northern Ireland and the Border Counties of the Republic of Ireland. Its aims are to: Create jobs, income and wealth essential to long term stability in Northern Ireland and the Border Counties of the Republic of Ireland; Contribute to increase the self-suffiency of the Northern Ireland and Border Counties' Community Economic Development Organisations (CEDOs); Attract investment funds from Domestic and International Bodies that would not have previously been available.

ULSTER FACTORS
60 Lower Baggot Street, Dublin 2
T: (01) 676 2240 F: (01) 602 4777
E: enquiries@ulsterfactors.com W: www.ulsterfactors.com
7 North Street, Belfast BT1 1NH
T: (028) 9032 4522 F: (028) 9023 0336
E: wjm@ulsterfactors.com
Contact: Bill Murray
CATEGORIES: DEBT

Ulster Factors offers an invoice factoring service to facilitate cash flow for small and medium-sized businesses.

UNIQUE PERSPECTIVES LTD
14 Upper Fitzwilliam Street, Dublin 2
T: (01) 662 8585 F: (01) 662 8484
E: info@uniqueperspectives.ie W: www.uniqueperspectives.ie
CATEGORIES: CONSULTING; MARKETING

A marketing consultancy that offers SMEs a fixed-fee marketing review and strategic action plan to help to improve business performance. It also offers an interactive online consultation on its website.

UNIVERSITIES
See individual entries for: Dublin City University; National University of Ireland Galway; Queen's University Belfast; University College Cork;

University College Dublin; University of Dublin, Trinity College; University of Limerick; University of Ulster.

UNIVERSITY COLLEGE CORK
Cork
T: (021) 490 3000 F: (021) 490 3612
E: tony.weaver@ucc.ie W: www.ucc.ie
Contact: Tony Weaver, Industrial Liaison Officer
CATEGORIES: CONSULTING; R & D; TRAINING

UCC operates a number of Centres of Excellence, including: **Aquaculture Development Centre**; Biosciences Research Institute; Executive Systems Research Centre; Food Industry Training Unit; Institute for Nonlinear Science; National Food Biotechnology Centre; **National Microelectronics Research Centre**.

UNIVERSITY COLLEGE DUBLIN
University Industry Programme, Industry Centre, Belfield, Dublin 4
T: (01) 716 3710 F: (01) 716 3709
E: pat.frain@ucd.ie W: www.ucd.ie/uip
Contact: Dr Pat Frain, Director, University Industry Programme
CATEGORIES: CONSULTING; INCUBATOR; R & D; TRAINING

The University Industry Programme is a point of contact for industry and academic staff seeking to do business on campus. The Programme is responsible for facilitating innovation, technology transfer, enterprise development, continuing professional development and all other forms of university/industry co-operation. Incubation facilities for campus companies and support services for continuing professional education are located in the Campus Innovation Centre and a new and larger Innovation Centre, NovaUCD, has just come onstream. Specialist centres have been established at UCD in areas of technology and business that are of strategic importance to Irish Industry.

UNIVERSITY OF DUBLIN, TRINITY COLLEGE
College Green, Dublin 2
T: (01) 608 1427 F: (01) 671 0037
E: eponeill@tcd.ie W: www.tcd.ie
Contact: Eoin O'Neill, Director
CATEGORIES: CONSULTING; INCUBATOR; R & D; TRAINING

Trinity's Research and Innovation Service promotes links between Trinity College researchers and business and industry. Its focus is to develop knowledge-based companies, which are spun off from the College's research and teaching expertise. The Innovation Centre is linked to many international networks that promote entrepeneurship, innovation and commercialisation of research. The Centre provides access to expertise in biotechnology and medical science, materials science, advanced computer science and telecomms, as well as national economics and business studies and serves as an incubator for campus companies that evolve from academic research. Trinity also owns the **TCD Enterprise Centre** in Dublin.

UNIVERSITY OF LIMERICK
Limerick
T: (061) 202700 F: (061) 330316
E: john.mcginn@ul.ie W: www.ul.ie
Contact: Dr John McGinn, Industrial Liaison Officer
CATEGORIES: CONSULTING; MARKETING; R & D; TRAINING

UL has a long-established reputation in the area of enterprise. It operates: Centre for Entrepreneurial Studies; Small Business Institute; Technology and Enterprise Development Unit ; Marketing Centre for Small Business.

UNIVERSITY OF LIMERICK ALUMNI ASSOCIATION ENTREPRENEURSHIP PROGRAMME
Alumni Association, University of Limerick, Limerick
T: (061) 202475 F: (061) 202228
E: ulaa@ul.ie W: www.ul.ie/~alumni
Contact: Deirdre Killelia
CATEGORIES: EQUITY; INCUBATOR; START-UP TRAINING

The University of Limerick Alumni Association with **Shannon Development** have combined — through the Innovation Centre and the National Technological Park — to offer an entrepreneurship programme to support alumni interested in creating a new business.

UNIVERSITY OF ULSTER
Campuses at Belfast, Jordanstown, Magee, Coleraine
E: online@ulster.ac.uk
W: www.ulster.ac.uk
CATEGORIES: COMMUNITY & RURAL DEVELOPMENT; CONSULTING;
INCUBATOR; R & D; START-UP TRAINING; TRAINING

The University of Ulster is the largest university on the island of Ireland. The Regional Development Office co-ordinates direct linkages, partnerships and interaction with business, community, economic and regeneration organisations. The Office of Innovation & Enterprise is responsible for identifying and exploiting the commercial opportunities arising from the University's intellectual property, business support services, and research park activities. The University takes a stake in spin-out companies through **UUTech Ltd**. UU established **UUSRP Ltd**, a wholly-owned company, to develop and manage its campus-based science research parks. UU operates a number of applied research centres.

UNIVERSITY OF ULSTER, OFFICE OF INNOVATION & ENTERPRISE

University of Ulster, Coleraine BT52 1SA
T: (028) 7032 4343 F: (028) 7032 4922
E: innovations@ulster.ac.uk
W: www.innovations.ulster.ac.uk/technologytransfer.jsp
Contact: Professor John Hughes

CATEGORIES: CONSULTING; R & D; TRAINING

The University's Office of Innovation and Enterprise is responsible for identifying and exploiting the commercial opportunities arising from our intellectual property, business support services, and research park activities. University of Ulster takes a stake in all university spin-out companies through its subsidiary, **UUTech Ltd**. These companies receive full incubation support on the University's science parks, through another subsidiary, **UUSRP Ltd**.

UNIVERSITY OF ULSTER, REGIONAL DEVELOPMENT SERVICES

Room MF226B, University of Ulster, Magee Campus, Londonderry BT48 7JL
T: (028) 7137 5564 F: (028) 7137 5368
E: rds@ulster.ac.uk W: www.ulster.ac.uk/rdo/
Contact: Noel Sweeney

CATEGORIES: COMMUNITY & RURAL DEVELOPMENT; INFORMATION

The Regional Development Office co-ordinates direct linkages, partnerships and interaction with business, community, economic and regeneration organisations and creates strategic alliances with partner organisations such as district councils, partnership boards, and government agencies involved in regional economic and community development. RDO services include: Business support; Access to knowledge; Embedding entrepreneurship, through the **Northern Ireland Centre for Entrepreneurship**; Community and voluntary sector support.

UUSRP LTD

University of Ulster at Jordanstown, Shore Road, Newtownabbey,
Co. Antrim BT37 0QB
T: (028) 7028 0000 F: (028) 7029 0010
E: scienceparks@ulst.ac.uk
W: innovations.ulster.ac.uk/technologytransfer.jsp
Contact: Dr CR Barnett, CEO

CATEGORIES: INCUBATOR

UUSRP Ltd manages a number of science parks for the **University of Ulster** in: Coleraine - Science Innovation Centre; Derry - Technology and Software Innovation Centre; Jordanstown - Technology and Engineering Innovation Centre; Belfast - Applied Research Centre. The science parks aim to create clusters of knowledge-based companies in close proximity to the centres of research excellence in Northern Ireland, in order to maximise the opportunity for continued innovation and commercial acquisition of new technologies arising from the University research base.

UUTECH LTD

University of Ulster, Cromore Road, Coleraine, Co Londonderry BT52 1ST
T: (028) 7028 0000 F: (028) 7028 0010
E: innovations@ulster.ac.uk W: www.ulst.ac.uk/uusrp
Contact: Dr Chris Barnett, Technology Transfer Manager

CATEGORIES: CONSULTING; INCUBATOR; R & D; TRAINING

The **University of Ulster** established UUTech Ltd to implement and develop its technology and knowledge transfer policy. UUTech has a remit to take a venture stake-holding in a start-up company, to lease out university incubator units and to manage university consultancy activities. It manages and negotiates all matters related to intellectual property rights (IPR), such as patenting and licensing, to maximise the benefit to the University, its staff and students.

VIRIDIAN GROWTH FUND

Clarendon Fund Managers Ltd, 12 Cromac Place, Belfast BT7 2JB
T: (028) 9032 6465 F: (028) 9032 6473
E: info@clarendon-fm.co.uk W: www.clarendon-fm.co.uk
Contact: Paul Leonard, Alan Mawson

CATEGORIES: DEBT; EQUITY

The Viridian Growth Fund is a stg£10 million fund, financed by private sector investors, the **Department of Enterprise, Trade and Investment**, and the **European Investment Bank**, with support under the EU Programme for Peace and Reconciliation, to provide investment to SMEs in Northern Ireland. The Fund provides finance by way of equity investment and loan, usally in amounts between stg£50k and stg£250k. Normally a non-executive Director will be appointed on behalf of the Fund to assist in the development of the business.

WANBO.org

W: www.wanbo.org

CATEGORIES: INFORMATION; WEBSITE; WOMEN

The Women and New Business Opportunities website has been designed and developed for women, who are interested in running their own business, and either do not have a business idea at this stage or are considering starting up a business in one of the identified sectoral areas of growth: Tourism; Environment; ICT; Services. It was funded by the **European Commission** under the Leonardo II Programme.

WATERFORD AREA PARTNERSHIP

Unit 4, Westgate Business Centre, Tramore Road, Waterford
T: (051) 841740 F: (051) 843153
E: areapart@iol.ie W: www.planet.ie
Contact: Joe Stokes, Manager

CATEGORIES: COMMUNITY & RURAL DEVELOPMENT; INFORMATION; START-UP TRAINING

Waterford Area Partnership is one of the **Area Partnerships** funded by **Area Development Management**, as part of its Local Development programme.

WATERFORD CITY ENTERPRISE BOARD
Enterprise House, New Street Court, Waterford
T: (051) 852883 F: (051) 877494
E: info@waterfordceb.com W: www.waterfordceb.com
Contact: Bill Rafter, CEO
CATEGORIES: DEBT; E-BUSINESS; EQUITY; GRANTS; INFORMATION; MENTORING; START-UP TRAINING; TRAINING

Waterford City Enterprise Board provides a full range of supports for micro-enterprises in its region. It provides information and advice on all aspects of establishing and developing a small business, including advice on a range of financial supports available to business.

WATERFORD COUNTY ENTERPRISE BOARD
Court House, Dungarvan, Co Waterford
T: (058) 44811 F: (058) 44817
E: waterfordceb@cablesurf.com
Contact: Gerard Enright, CEO
CATEGORIES: DEBT; E-BUSINESS; EQUITY; GRANTS; INFORMATION; MENTORING; START-UP TRAINING; TRAINING

Waterford County Enterprise Board provides a full range of supports for micro-enterprises in its region.

WATERFORD INSTITUTE OF TECHNOLOGY
Development Office, Cork Road, Waterford
T: (051) 302039 F: (051) 378292
E: enquiries@wit.ie; development@wit.ie W: www.wit.ie
Contact: Kathryn Kiely, External Services Manager
CATEGORIES: CONSULTING; R & D; TRAINING

WIT operates research groups in applied optics, Advanced Manufacturing Technology (AMT) and electronics. WIT also operates the **South East Enterprise Programme**.

WATERFORD LEADER PARTNERSHIP LTD
Teagasc Centre, Lismore, Co Waterford
T: (058) 54646 F: (058) 54126
E: wdp@eircom.net; seec@iol.ie
Contact: Julie O'Donnell; Jimmy Taafe, General Manager
CATEGORIES: COMMUNITY & RURAL DEVELOPMENT; EU INFORMATION; GRANTS; INFORMATION; START-UP TRAINING; WOMEN

Waterford LEADER Partnership is one of the **Area Partnerships** funded by **Area Development Management**, as part of its Local Development programme, and also a **LEADER+** company serving Co Waterford. It provides: Enterprise development; Rural tourism; Education & training; Community development & services for the unemployed. It hosts the **Carréfour** for the South-East region in its Dungarvan office, is one of the organisations behind **FarmOptions.ie**, and offers a Start-up Business Programme for Women.

WEST BELFAST DEVELOPMENT TRUST
See **WorkWest Enterprise Agency**.

WEST CORK ENTERPRISE BOARD
8 Kent Street, Clonakilty, Co Cork
T: (023) 34700 F: (023) 34702
E: enterprise@wceb.ie W: www.wceb.ie
Contact: Michael Hanley, CEO
CATEGORIES: DEBT; E-BUSINESS; EQUITY; GRANTS; INFORMATION;
MENTORING; START-UP TRAINING; TRAINING

The West Cork Enterprise Board is a state agency responsible for enterprise development in the West Cork area. It provides advice, training and mentoring services for business development, as well as financial assistance in the form of refundable aid and capital grants, employment grants and assistance towards innovative feasibility studies.

WEST CORK LEADER CO-OPERATIVE SOCIETY LTD
South Square, Clonakilty, Co Cork
T: (023) 34035 F: (023) 34066
E: wclc@wclc.iol.ie W: www.westcorkleader.ie
Contact: Ian Dempsey, Manager
CATEGORIES: COMMUNITY & RURAL DEVELOPMENT; GRANTS

A LEADER+ company serving the area from West Cork to Kinsale, the Lee Valley and the Owenabue Valley, it operates an integrated approach at local level in identifying, harnessing, and optimising the development potential of local resources by: Provision of technical assistance supports; Provision of training assistance to address skills deficiencies; Support for capital investment, and marketing assistance, within eligible measures; Development of strategic partnerships; Support for local community initiatives in developing viable projects. It is one of the organisations behind **FarmOptions.ie**. It also operates the very successful Fuschia Brands, the West Cork regional branding initiative.

WEST LIMERICK RESOURCES LTD
The Weigh House, Market Yard, Newcastlewest, Co Limerick
T: (069) 62222 F: (069) 61870
E: wlr@eircom.net
W: www.westlimerickresourcesltd.com
Contact: Brenda Cahill, Manager
CATEGORIES: COMMUNITY & RURAL DEVELOPMENT; GRANTS; INFORMATION;
MENTORING; NETWORKING; START-UP TRAINING; TRAINING

West Limerick Resources is one of the **Area Partnerships** funded by **Area Development Management**, as part of its Local Development programme, and also a **LEADER+** company serving West Limerick. It has offices in Abbeyfeale and Askeaton. It gives assistance financially and in the form of training and business advice to would be enterpreneurs. It also provides mentoring. It offers capital equipment grants to innovative, small enterprises in manufacturing, crafts or local services at start-up or development stage, within its operational area.

WEST OFFALY INTEGRATED DEVELOPMENT PARTNERSHIP

Crank House, Banagher, Co Offaly
T: (0509) 51622 F: (0509) 51798
E: wop@eircom.net
W: www.offaly.ie/developmentorganisations/westoffalypartnership.asp
Contact: Brendan O'Loughlin, Programme Manager

CATEGORIES: COMMUNITY & RURAL DEVELOPMENT; INCUBATOR

West Offaly Integrated Development Partnership is one of the **Community Groups** funded by **Area Development Management**, as part of its Local Development programme. The Partnership acts as a catalyst for local development, particularly in Enterprise where it complements the pre-application work with a business support service for the first six to 12 months of operation.

WEST TYRONE RURAL LTD

Omagh Business Complex, Great Northern Road, Omagh,
Co Tyrone BT78 5LU
T: (028) 8225 2647 F: (028) 8225 2672
E: info@westtyronerural
Contact: Anita McConnell

CATEGORIES: COMMUNITY & RURAL DEVELOPMENT

A **LEADER+** company, serving the Strabane & Omagh district council area. West Tyrone Rural 2000 also supports the Donegal/Tyrone Partnership Rural Enterprise programme (T: (028) 8225 0962, Contact: Hugo Sweeney), managed by **WestBIC**.

WESTBIC (BUSINESS INNOVATION CENTRE, GALWAY)

Galway Technology Centre, Mervue Business Park, Galway
T: (091) 730 850 F: (091) 730 853
E: mryan@westbic.ie W: www.westbic.ie
Contact: Mary Ryan

CATEGORIES: BUSINESS PLANS; CROSS-BORDER; EQUITY; INCUBATOR;
INFORMATION; MARKETING; TRAINING

WestBIC's mission is to "hand-hold" high potential entrepreneurs in the West and North-West region, by offering them business planning, information, marketing advice, and seed funding. It has access to the **Irish BICs Seed**

Capital Fund, which provides early stage seed capital to SMEs. It manages the **Donegal/Tyrone Partnership Rural Enterprise Programme**, which provides entrepreneurial skills training, exposure to sites of excellence at home and overseas, group workshops and hands-on business planning assistance to entrepreneurs. The programme is funded by the **International Fund for Ireland**, with support from **Donegal Local Development Company** and **West Tyrone Rural.**

WESTERN DEVELOPMENT COMMISSION
Dillon House, Ballaghaderreen, Co Roscommon
T: (0907) 61441
E: info@wdc.ie W: www.wdc.ie
CATEGORIES: COMMUNITY & RURAL DEVELOPMENT; DEBT; EQUITY; POLICY

The Western Development Commission is a statutory body promoting economic and social development in counties Donegal, Leitrim, Sligo, Mayo, Roscommon, Galway and Clare. Its activities include: Review and development of strategic regional policies for a range of sectors; Securing the implementation of major regional development initiatives; Management of the **Western Investment Fund.**

WESTERN INVESTMENT FUND
Dillon House, Ballaghaderreen, Co Roscommon
T: (0907) 61441
E: info@wdc.ie W: www.wdc.ie
CATEGORIES: DEBT; EQUITY

The Western Investment Fund provides risk capital by way of equity and loans on a commercial basis to projects and businesses within counties Donegal, Leitrim, Sligo, Mayo, Roscommon, Galway and Sligo. It is managed by the **Western Development Commission.**

WESTERN MANAGEMENT CENTRE
IDA Business Park, Newcastle, Galway
T: (091) 528777 F: (091) 528649
E: wmc@iol.ie W: www.western-management.com
Contact: Berni Ferris
CATEGORIES: TRAINING

The Western Management Centre offers training and development programmes geared towards the needs of business owners/entrepreneurs.

WESTERN RURAL DEVELOPMENT COMPANY
Ballina Road, Tubbercurry, Co Sligo
T: (078) 20079 F: (078) 20079
E: leader3@eircom.net
Contact: Ursula Crossen
CATEGORIES: COMMUNITY & RURAL DEVELOPMENT; GRANTS

A **LEADER+** company serving parts of Co Mayo and Sligo, Western Rural Development Company offers capital equipment grants to innovative, small enterprises in manufacturing, crafts or local services at start-up or development stage, within its operational area.

WESTLINK ENTERPRISE CENTRE
Grosvenor Road, Belfast BT12 5BJ
T: (028) 9033 1549 F: (028) 9033 0803
E: mcopeland@ortus.org W: www.ortus.org
CATEGORIES: INFORMATION; WORKSPACE

One of the **Enterprise Agencies/Centres** in Belfast, Westlink Enterprise Centres is managed by **ORTUS**, which provides financial supports, business training and advice.

WESTMEATH COMMUNITY DEVELOPMENT LTD
Presentation House, Harbour Street, Mullingar, Co Westmeath
T: (044) 48571 F: (044) 48441
E: westcd@iol.ie W: www.planet.ie
Contact: Joe Potter
CATEGORIES: COMMUNITY & RURAL DEVELOPMENT; GRANTS; INFORMATION; START-UP TRAINING

Westmeath Community Development is one of the **Area Partnerships** funded by **Area Development Management**, as part of its Local Development programme, and also a **LEADER+** company serving Co Westmeath. It offers capital equipment grants to innovative, small enterprises in manufacturing, crafts or local services at start-up or development stage, within its operational area.

WESTMEATH COUNTY ENTERPRISE BOARD LTD
Business Information Centre, Church Avenue, Mullingar, Co Westmeath
T: (044) 49222 F: (044) 49009
E: info@westmeath-enterprise.ie W: www.westmeath-enterprise.ie
Contact: Christine Charlton, CEO
CATEGORIES: DEBT; E-BUSINESS; EQUITY; GRANTS; INFORMATION; MENTORING; START-UP TRAINING; TRAINING

Westmeath CEB offers a full range of supports for micro-enterprises in its region. It is a one-stop-shop for business advice and information in Westmeath County.

WEXFORD AREA PARTNERSHIP
Cornmarket, Mallin Street, Wexford
T: (053) 23994 F: (053) 21024
E: paulaw@wap.iol.ie
Contact: Bernard O'Brien, General Manager
CATEGORIES: COMMUNITY & RURAL DEVELOPMENT; GRANTS; INFORMATION; START-UP TRAINING

One of the **Area Partnerships** established by **Area Development Management**, as part of its Local Development programme.

WEXFORD COUNTY ENTERPRISE BOARD
16–17 Mallin Street, Cornmarket, Wexford
T: (053) 22965 F: (053) 24944
E: info@wexfordceb.ie W: www.wexfordceb.ie
Contact: Sean Mythen, CEO

CATEGORIES: DEBT; E-BUSINESS; EQUITY; GRANTS; INFORMATION;
MENTORING; START-UP TRAINING; TRAINING

Wexford County Enterprise Board offers financial and technical assistance to both start-up and existing businesses. It also offers a 10-week "Start Your Own Business" programme.

WEXFORD ENTERPRISE CENTRE
Kerlogue Industrial Park, Rosslare Road, Wexford
T: (053) 41711 F: (053) 43648
E: info@wec.ie W: www.wec.ie
Contact: Brendan Ennis, Chief Executive

CATEGORIES: INCUBATOR

A 40,000 sq.ft. Enterprise Centre comprising Industrial, Food Processing, Laboratory and Office incubation workspace. Established in 1989, the Wexford Enterprise Centre is one of the largest of its kind in Ireland. The Centre is currently developing a new ICT Business Hall which, when developed, will support organic growth during the initial stages of both start-up and low-size companies within ICT-related sectors. Wexford Enterprise Centre is a Wexford Community Development Association (WCDA) Innovation Project.

WEXFORD ORGANISATION FOR RURAL DEVELOPMENT
Johnstown Castle, Redmondstown, Johnstown, Co Wexford
T: (053) 46453 F: (053) 46456
E: info@wexfordleader.ie W: www.wexfordleader.ie
Contact: Bill Walsh

CATEGORIES: COMMUNITY & RURAL DEVELOPMENT; GRANTS

A **LEADER+** company serving Co Wexford, WORD has developed a strategy of integrated rural development, delivered through: Community development; Training and capacity building; Environment, heritage and culture; Small firms, crafts enterprises and local services; Agriculture, food, forestry and fishery products.

WICKLOW COUNTY ENTERPRISE BOARD
1 Main Street, Wicklow
T: (0404) 67100 F: (0404) 67601
E: wicklowceb@eircom.net
W: www.wicklow.ie/countyagencies/ceb/
Contact: Tom Broderick, CEO

CATEGORIES: DEBT; E-BUSINESS; EQUITY; GRANTS; INFORMATION;
MENTORING; START-UP TRAINING; TRAINING

Wicklow CEB's services include information and advice, training and
mentoring, and financial assistance. It also offers a "Start Your Own Business"
course and an information pack containing details of the supports available.

WICKLOW RURAL PARTNERSHIP LTD
Ann Devlin Annex, Fairgreen, Rathdrum, Co Wicklow
T: (0404) 46977 F: (0404) 46978
E: wrp@wicklow.ie W: www.wicklow.ie/wrp
Contact: Jim Healy, Programme Manager

CATEGORIES: COMMUNITY & RURAL DEVELOPMENT; GRANTS

A **LEADER+** company serving Co Wicklow, WRP is a community
organisation, whose main aim is to establish a self-sustaining system for
promoting employment through: Providing finance through LEADER funding;
Promoting new enterprises; Conserving a high quality natural environment;
Developing a cultural environment.

WICKLOW WORKING TOGETHER
7 Convent Road, Wicklow, Co Wicklow
T: (0404) 61841 F: (0404) 66843
E: info@wicklowworkingtogether.org
Contact: Jo Conroy

CATEGORIES: COMMUNITY & RURAL DEVELOPMENT

Wicklow Working Together is one of the **Community Groups** funded by
Area Development Management, as part of its Local Development
programme.

WOMEN IN TECHNOLOGY & SCIENCE
P.O. Box 3783, Dublin 4
T: (01) 668 8524
E: wits@iol.ie
W: www.witsireland.com

CATEGORIES: NETWORKING; WOMEN

Women in Technology and Science (WITS) actively promotes women in
science in Ireland. The association has members from a broad range of
scientific, engineering and technological backgrounds including teachers,
computer experts, technicians and journalists. They range in age and
experience from third level students to some of the country's most senior
scientists and academics. Individual membership is open to women

throughout Ireland who work, have worked or who are studying in any area of science, engineering or technology.

WORK WEST ENTERPRISE AGENCY (WEST BELFAST DEVELOPMENT TRUST)
301 Glen Road, Belfast BT11 8BU
T: (028) 9061 0826 F: (028) 9062 2001
E: info@workwest.co.uk W: www.workwest.co.uk
Contact: Claire Ferris, Manager

CATEGORIES: DEBT; INFORMATION; START-UP TRAINING; TRAINING; WORKSPACE

WorkWest is an **Enterprise Agency** and a member of **Enterprise Northern Ireland**. It offers workspace, start-up and ongoing training and loans.

WORKSPACE (DRAPERSTOWN) LTD
The Business Centre, 7 Tobermore Road, Draperstown,
Co Londonderry BT45 7AG
T: (028) 7962 8113 F: (028) 7962 8975
E: info@workspace.org.uk W: www.workspace.org.uk
Contact: John Clarke

CATEGORIES: DEBT; INFORMATION; MARKETING; MENTORING; START-UP TRAINING; TRAINING; WORKSPACE

Workspace is an **Enterprise Agency** and a member of **Enterprise Northern Ireland**. It provides a full range of services to start-ups and SMEs: information, advice and support or pre-start training, innovation, design, product development, marketing, finance, management development, IT or software training skills, e-commerce or business mentors. A consultancy division, **Business Results Ltd**, offers community development services.

WORLD CLASS RURAL CLUSTER
Biúro Oifige Teo, An Daingain, Co Chiarraí
T: (066) 915 0100 F: (066) 915 1784
E: biuro@iol.ie
Contact: Dónal Ó Liatháin

CATEGORIES: TRAINING

WCRC is a consortium made up of **Údaras na Gaeltachta, Enterprise Ireland** and local business representatives. The project was conceived in the face of a need among micro-enterprises to adopt best practice models across the full range of their operations, in order to compete more effectively and develop their maximum potential. It developed a tailored system for the extension of Advanced Manufacturing and Management Techniques (AMMT) to micro-industries.

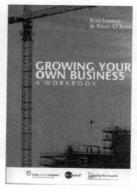
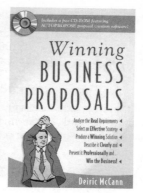
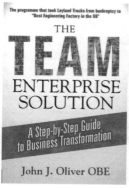

XANTHAL LTD

Suite 101, 71 George's Street Lower, Dun Laoire, Co Dublin
T: (086) 271 8485 F: (01) 633 5528
E: info@xanthal.com W: www.xanthal.com
Contact: Anthony Quigley
CATEGORIES: CONSULTING; MARKETING

Xanthal provides marketing, sales development and business growth services to start-up and expanding companies. It helps companies formulate and execute their "go-to-market" plans.

YOUNG ENTREPRENEURS SCHEME

YES National Committee, 29 Arnold Grove, Glenageary, Co Dublin
T: (01) 282 3909 F: (01) 282 3909
E: info@yes.ie W: www.yes.ie
Contact: Catherine McCarthy, National Co-ordinator
CATEGORIES: COMPETITIONS; YOUNG ENTERPRISE

In association with **City/County Enterprise Boards**, the Young Entrepreneurs Scheme (YES) stimulates enterprise among second-level students aged 12-18. Students create and operate their own mini-businesses, selling products or services to students or to consumers outside the school, and participate in enterprise competitions. School winners advance to county-level and regional competitions and regional winners participate in the YES National Final. Over 40,000 students to date have participated in YES.

YOUNG ENTERPRISE IRELAND

See **Junior Achievement / Young Enterprise Ireland.**

YOUNG ENTERPRISE NORTHERN IRELAND

Unit 11, Curran House, 155 Northumberland Street, Belfast BT13 2JF
T: 028 9032 7003 F: 028 9032 6995
W: www.yeni.co.uk
CATEGORIES: YOUNG ENTERPRISE

Young Enterprise delivers vocational training programmes in entrepreneurship and economic literacy to the 15-25 plus age group. See also **Junior Achievement / Young Enterprise Ireland**.

YOUR PEOPLE MANAGER

3 Waterhouse Square, 142 Holborn, London EC1N 2NX
T: 0207 961 0300
E: feedback@yourpeoplemanager.com W: www.yourpeoplemanager.com
CATEGORIES: TRAINING

YPM is a new service from Investors in People UK, aimed at helping the managers of small businesses deal with the everyday questions, issues and problems of managing staff.

Get your new business up and running with an OAK TREE PRESS

START-UP BOOT CAMP

An intensive one-day learning experience, designed to accelerate your progress towards start-up by providing you with the skills and information you need, plus one month's follow-up email support. Includes **STARTING YOUR OWN BUSINESS** workbook – retail price €20.

"I found your first hand knowledge and experience invaluable. Your course is also excellent value for money."
Eoin Sherlock, Cartridge World, Drogheda

For details of **START-UP BOOT CAMP**s, visit **TheSuccessStore** at **www.oaktreepress.com** or contact **Oak Tree Press**:
- By telephone (within Ireland) 021 431 3855 or LoCall 1890 313855 or (international) + 353 21 431 3855
- By fax (within Ireland) 021 431 3496 or (international) + 353 21 431 3496
- By email at info@oaktreepress.com

OAK TREE PRESS

Ireland's leading business book publisher,
Oak Tree Press is increasingly an international
developer and publisher of enterprise training and
support solutions.

Oak Tree Press has developed "platforms" of
Pre-start-up, Start-up, Growth and Support content,
which include publications, websites, software,
assessment models, training, consultancy and
certification.

Oak Tree Press' enterprise training and support
solutions are in use in Ireland, the UK, USA,
Scandinavia and Eastern Europe and are available
for customisation to local situations and needs.

For further information, contact:
Ron Immink or Brian O'Kane

OAK TREE PRESS

19 Rutland Street, Cork, Ireland
T: + 353 21 431 3855 F: + 353 21 431 3496
E: info@oaktreepress.com
W: www.oaktreepress.com

www.oaktreepress.com

* HSE.IE Health & safety
* Registry of friendly societies
* SKPOST.IE (Ireland's only dedicated
* SEI.IE (Sustainable business newspaper
      sustainable energy , Ireland)

pg 77 ; 98-99 ↑
         (R&D)

saches Breathing room?

PS-100 ↑
(theming)

Furnishing

to check   logistics & transport !

Selling pictures in restaurants   For ex. in
Dalkey   beautiful   art
shop!!!!